Microsoft® Visual C#® .NET

Joyce Farrell
University of Wisconsin – Stevens Point

THOMSON

COURSE TECHNOLOGY

Australia • Canada • Mexico • Singapore • Spain • United Kingdom • United States

Microsoft® Visual C#® .NET

by Joyce Farrell

Product Manager:
Tricia Boyle

Associate Product Manager:
Janet Aras

Compositor:
GEX Publishing Services

Senior Editor:
Jennifer Muroff

Production Editor:
Aimee Poirier

Manufacturing Coordinator:
Denise Sandler

Development Editor:
Lisa Ruffolo

Cover Designer:
Steve Deschene

Disclaimer
Course Technology reserves the right to revise this publication and make changes from time to time in its content without notice.

ISBN 0-619-06273-8

TABLE OF
Contents

CHAPTER SEVEN
Introduction to Inheritance   231

CHAPTER EIGHT
Exception Handling   279

CHAPTER NINE
Using GUI Objects and the Visual Studio IDE   313

Preface

Microsoft Visual C# .NET provides the beginning programmer with a guide to developing programs in C#, a new language developed by the Microsoft Corporation as part of their newly released Visual Studio .NET platform. The .NET framework contains a wealth of libraries for developing applications for the Windows family of operating systems. You can write programs for .NET in many languages, but C# is the only language designed specifically for .NET. With C#, you can build small, reusable components that are well-suited to twenty-first century Web-based programming applications. Although similar to Java and C++, many features of C# make it easier to learn and ideal for the beginning programmer. You can program in C# using a simple text editor and the command prompt, or you can manipulate program components using Visual Studio's sophisticated Integrated Development Environment. This book provides you with the tools to use both techniques.

This textbook assumes that you have little or no programming experience. The writing is non-technical and emphasizes good programming practices. The examples are business examples; they do not assume mathematical background beyond high school business math. Additionally, the examples illustrate one or two major points; they do not contain so many features that you become lost following irrelevant and extraneous details. This book provides you with a solid background in good object-oriented programming techniques and introduces you to object-oriented terminology using clear, familiar language.

ORGANIZATION AND COVERAGE

Microsoft Visual C# .NET presents C# programming concepts, enforcing good style, logical thinking, and the object-oriented paradigm. Chapter 1 introduces you to the language by letting you create working C# programs using both the simple command line and the Visual Studio environment. In Chapter 2 you learn about data and how to input, store, and output data in C#. Chapter 3 is a thorough study of methods, including passing parameters into and out of methods and overloading them. Chapter 4 provides a thorough study of the object-oriented concepts of classes, objects, data hiding, constructors, and destructors. In Chapters 5 and 6 you learn about the classic programming structures and how to implement them in C#: making selections, looping, and manipulating arrays.

After completing Chapters 7 and 8 you will be thoroughly grounded in the object-oriented concepts of inheritance and exception handling, and will be able to take advantage of both features in your C# programs. Chapters 9 and 10 introduce you to GUI objects. You will learn about controls, how to set their properties, and how to make attractive, useful, graphical, and interactive programs. Chapter 11 takes you further into the intricacies of handling events in your interactive GUI programs.

FEATURES

Microsoft Visual C# .NET is a superior textbook because it also includes the following features:

- Objectives: Each chapter begins with a list of objectives so you know the topics that will be presented in the chapter. In addition to providing a quick reference to topics covered, this feature provides a useful study aid.

- Tips: These notes provide additional information—for example, an alternative method of performing a procedure, another term for a concept, background information on a technique, or a common error to avoid.

- Summaries: Following each section is a summary that recaps the programming concepts and techniques covered in the section. This feature provides a concise means for you to recap and check your understanding of the main points in each chapter.

- Exercises: Each chapter concludes with meaningful programming exercises that provide additional practice of the skills and concepts you learned in the chapter. These exercises increase in difficulty and are designed to allow you to explore logical programming concepts.

TEACHING TOOLS

The following supplemental materials are available when this book is used in a classroom setting. All of the teaching tools available with this book are provided to the instructor on a single CD-ROM.

Electronic Instructor's Manual. The Instructor's Manual that accompanies this textbook includes:

- Additional instructional material to assist in class preparation, including suggestions for lecture topics.

- Solutions to Review Questions and end-of-chapter exercises.

ExamView®. This textbook is accompanied by ExamView, a powerful testing software package that allows instructors to create and administer printed, computer (LAN-based), and Internet exams. ExamView includes hundreds of questions that correspond to the topics covered in this text, enabling students to generate detailed study guides that include page references for further review. The computer-based and Internet testing components allow students to take exams at their computers, and also save the instructor time by grading each exam automatically.

PowerPoint Presentations. This book comes with Microsoft PowerPoint slides for each chapter. These are included as a teaching aid for classroom presentation, to make available to students on the network for chapter review, or to be printed for classroom distribution. Instructors can add their own slides for additional topics they introduce to the class.

Solution Files. Solutions to steps within a chapter and end-of-chapter exercises are provided on the Teaching Tools CD-ROM and may also be found on the Course Technology Web site at **www.course.com**. The solutions are password protected.

Distance Learning. Course Technology is proud to present online courses in WebCT and Blackboard, as well as MyCourse 2.0, Course Technology's own course enhancement tool, to provide the most complete and dynamic learning experience possible. When you add online content to one of your courses, you're adding a lot: self tests, lecture notes, a gradebook, and, most of all, a gateway to the twenty-first century's most important information resource. Instructors are encouraged to make the most of your course, both online and offline. For more information on how to bring distance learning to your course, contact your local Course Technology sales representative.

ACKNOWLEDGMENTS

I would like to thank all of the people who helped to make this book a reality, especially Lisa Ruffolo, Development Editor, who worked tirelessly to produce this book. Her suggestions were always improvements, and her improvements have made this a quality instructional tool. Thanks also to Tricia Boyle, Product Manager, who kept all the balls in the air and always provided good cheer. Thanks to Kristen Duerr, Publisher; Jennifer Muroff, Senior Editor; Aimee Poirier, Production Editor; Janet Aras, Associate Product Manager; and Alex White and Serge Palladino, Quality Assurance Testers, who provided thorough examination of the manuscript and consistently valuable suggestions. I am grateful to be able to work with so many fine people who are dedicated to producing quality instructional materials.

I am also grateful to the many reviewers who provided helpful comments and encouragement during this book's development, including Dr. Barbara Doyle, Jacksonville University; Jean Evans, Brevard Community College; Valerie Frear, Daytona Beach Community College; Matthew McCaskill, Brevard Community College; John Morack, Waukesha County Technical College; Von Plessner, Northwest State Community College; John Stryker, Oakton Community College; Paul Turnage, Schoolcraft College; and Matt Weisfeld, Cuyahoga Community College.

Thanks, too, to my husband, Geoff, without whom I never would have written my first book and who makes the work worth all the trouble. Finally, this book is dedicated to my friend Ginny Kroening.

Joyce Farrell

Read This Before You Begin

TO THE USER

To complete the exercises in this book, you will need data files that have been created specifically for this book. Your instructor will provide the data files to you. You also can obtain the files electronically from the Course Technology Web site by connecting to *www.course.com* and then searching for this book title. Note that you can use a computer in your school lab or your own computer to complete the exercises in this book.

The data files for this book are organized such that the examples and exercises are divided into folders named Chapter.*xx*, where *xx* is the chapter number. You can save these files in the same folder unless specifically indicated otherwise in the chapter.

Using Your Own Computer

To use your own computer to complete the steps and exercises, you will need the following:

- **Software**. Microsoft Visual C# .NET Professional Edition including the Microsoft .NET Framework.
- **Hardware**. A Pentium II-class processor, 450 MHz or higher, personal computer, and Windows NT, Windows 2000, or Windows XP.
- **Data Files**. You will not be able to complete the exercises in this book using your own computer unless you have the data files. You can get the data files from your instructor, or you can obtain the data files electronically from the Course Technology Web site by connecting to *www.course.com* and then searching for this book title.

TO THE INSTRUCTOR

To complete all the exercises and chapters in this book, your users must work with a set of user files, called a Data disk. These files are included in the Instructor's Resource Kit. They may also be obtained electronically through the Course Technology Web site at *www.course.com*. Follow the instructions in the Help file to copy the user files to your server or standalone computer. You can view the Help file using a text editor, such as WordPad or Notepad.

Once the files are copied, you can make Data disks for the users yourself, or tell them where to find the files so they can make their own Data disks. Make sure the files are copied correctly onto the Data disks by following the instructions in the Data disks section, which will ensure that users have enough disk space to complete all the chapters and exercises in this book.

Course Technology Data Files

You are granted a license to copy the Data files to any computer or computer network used by individuals who have purchased this book.

1

A FIRST PROGRAM USING C#

In this chapter you will learn:

♦ About programming tasks

♦ Object-oriented programming concepts

♦ About the C# programming language

♦ How to write a C# program that produces output

♦ How to select identifiers to use within your programs

♦ How to compile and execute a C# program from the command line

♦ How to add comments to a C# program

♦ How to compile and execute a program using the Visual Studio IDE

♦ How to eliminate the reference to Out by using the System namespace

Programming a computer is an interesting, challenging, fun, and some-times frustrating task. As a programmer, you must be precise and careful as well as creative. First learning to program is fascinating; learning a new programming language expands your horizons.

As new programming languages are developed and introduced, your job becomes easier and more difficult at the same time. Programming becomes easier because built-in capabilities are added to every new language that is developed, and tasks that might have taken you weeks or months to develop a decade ago are now included in the language so you can add them to a program with a few keystrokes. Programming becomes more difficult for the same reason—new languages have so many features that you must devote a significant amount of time to learning them.

C# is a new language that provides you with a wide range of options and features. As you work through this book, you will master many of them, one step at a time. If this is your first programming experience, you are in for a mind-expanding treat. If you know how to program but are new to C#, you will be impressed by its capabilities.

In this chapter you will learn about the background of programming that led to the development of C#, and you will write and execute your first C# programs.

PROGRAMMING

A computer **program** is a set of instructions that you write to tell a computer what to do. Internally, computers are constructed from circuitry that consists of small on/off switches; the language that computers use to control the operation of those switches is called **machine language**, which is the most basic circuitry-level language. Machine language is expressed as a series of 1s and 0s—1s represent switches that are on, and 0s represent switches that are off. If programmers had to write computer programs using machine language, they would have to keep track of the hundreds of thousands of 1s and 0s involved in programming any worthwhile task. Not only would writing a program be a time-consuming and difficult task, but modifying programs, understanding others' programs, and locating errors within programs would also be cumbersome. Additionally, the number and location of switches vary from computer to computer, which means you would need to customize a machine-language program for every type of machine on which the program had to run.

Fortunately, programming has evolved into an easier task because of the development of high-level programming languages. A **high-level programming language** allows you to use a vocabulary of reasonable terms such as "read," "write," or "add" instead of the sequence of on/off switches that perform these tasks. High-level languages also allow you to assign reasonable names to areas of computer memory; you can use names such as "HoursWorked" or "PayRate," rather than having to remember the memory locations (switch numbers) of those values.

Each high-level language has its own **syntax**, or rules of the language. For example, depending on the specific high-level language, you might use the verb "print" or "write" to produce output. All languages have a specific, limited vocabulary, and a set of rules for using that vocabulary. Programmers use a computer program called a **compiler** to translate their high-level language statements into machine code. The compiler issues an error message each time a programmer uses the language incorrectly; subsequently, the programmer can correct the error and attempt another translation by compiling the program again. When you learn a computer programming language such as C#, C++, Visual Basic, Java, or COBOL, you really are learning the vocabulary and syntax rules for that language.

 In some languages, such as BASIC, the language translator is called an interpreter. In others, such as assembly language, it is called an assembler. These translators operate in different fashions, but the ultimate goal of each is to translate the higher-level language into machine language.

In addition to learning the correct syntax for a particular language, a programmer must understand computer programming logic. The **logic** behind any program involves executing the various statements and procedures in the correct order to produce the desired results. For example, you might be able to execute perfect individual notes on a musical instrument, but if you do not execute them in the proper order (or execute a B flat when an F sharp was expected), no one will enjoy your performance. Similarly, you might be able to use a computer language's syntax correctly, but be unable to execute a logically constructed, workable program. Examples of logical errors include multiplying two values when you meant to divide them, or attempting to calculate a paycheck before obtaining the appropriate payroll data.

Object-Oriented Programming

There are two popular approaches to writing computer programs: procedural programming and object-oriented programming.

When you write a **procedural program**, you use your knowledge of a programming language to create and name computer memory locations that can hold values, and you write a series of steps or operations to manipulate those values. The named computer memory locations are called **variables** because they hold values that might vary. In programming languages, a variable is referenced by using a one-word name with no embedded spaces. For example, a company's payroll program might contain a variable named `PayRate`. The memory location referenced by the name `PayRate` might contain different values at different times. For instance, an organization's payroll program might contain a different value for `PayRate` for each of 100 employees. Additionally, a single employee's `PayRate` variable might contain different values before or after a raise, or before or after surpassing 40 work hours in one week. During the execution of the payroll program, each value stored under the name `PayRate` might have many **operations** performed on it—for example, reading it from an input device, multiplying it by another variable representing hours worked, and printing it on paper.

 When programmers do not capitalize the first letter of a variable name but do capitalize each new word, as in `payRate`, they call the style *camel casing*, because the variable name appears to have a hump in the middle. When programmers adopt the style of capitalizing the first letter of all new words in a variable name, even the first one, as in `PayRate`, they call the style *Pascal casing*. Most C# programmers use Pascal casing when creating variable names, but this convention is not required to produce a workable program.

For convenience, the individual operations used in a computer program often are grouped into logical units called **procedures**, **methods**, or **functions**. For example, a series of four or five comparisons and calculations that together determine an employee's federal tax withholding value might be grouped as a procedure named `CalculateFederalWithholding()`. A procedural program defines the variable memory locations, then **calls** or **invokes** a series of procedures to input, manipulate, and output the values stored in those locations. A single procedural program often contains hundreds of variables and thousands of procedure calls.

In C#, all procedure names are followed by a set of parentheses. When you pronounce a procedure name, you ignore the parentheses. When this book refers to a procedure, the name will be followed with parentheses. This practice helps distinguish procedure names from variable and class names.

Object-oriented programming is an extension of procedural programming. Object-oriented programs contain variables, procedures, and six other features:

- Objects
- Classes
- Encapsulation
- Interfaces
- Polymorphism
- Inheritance

Although procedural and object-oriented programming techniques are somewhat similar, they raise different concerns in the systems design and development phase that occurs before programs are written.

The object-oriented components called **objects** are similar to concrete objects in the real world. You create objects that contain their own variables and procedures, and then you manipulate those objects to achieve a desired result. Writing object-oriented programs involves both creating objects and creating applications that use those objects.

If you've ever used a computer that has a command-line operating system (such as DOS), and if you've used a GUI (a graphical user interface, such as Windows), then you already have an idea of the difference between procedural and object-oriented programs. If you want to move several files from a floppy disk to a hard disk, you can use either a typed command at a prompt or command line, or a mouse in a graphical environment, to accomplish the task. The difference lies in whether you issue a series of sequential commands to move the three files or drag icons representing the files from one screen location to another, much as you would physically move paper files from one file cabinet to another. You can move the same three files using either operating system, but the GUI system allows you to manipulate the files in the same way as their real-world paper counterparts. In other words, the GUI system allows you to treat files as objects.

Objects in both the real world and in object-oriented programming are made up of attributes and methods. The **attributes** of an object represent its characteristics. For example, some of your Automobile's attributes are its make, model, year, and purchase price. Other attributes describe whether the Automobile is currently running, its gear, its speed, and whether it is dirty. All Automobiles possess the same attributes, but not the same values, or **states**, for those attributes. For example, some Automobiles currently are running, but some are not. The value of an attribute can change over time; for example, some Automobiles are running now, but will not be running in the future. Therefore, the states of an Automobile are variable. Similarly, your Dog has attributes that include its breed, name, age, and shot status (that is, whether its shots are current); the states for a particular dog might be Labrador retriever, Murphy, 7, and yes.

A **class** is a category of objects or a type of object. A class describes the attributes and methods of every object that is an **instance**, or example, of that class. For example, Automobile is a class whose objects have a year, make, model, color, and current running status. Your 1997 red Chevrolet is an instance of the class that is made up of all Automobiles; so is my supervisor's 2002 black Porsche. Your Collie named Bosco is an instance of the class that is made up of all Dogs; so is my Labrador named Murphy. Thinking of items as instances of a class allows you to apply your general knowledge of the class to its individual members. The particular instances of these objects contain all of the attributes that their general category contains; only the states of those attributes vary. If your friend purchases an Automobile, you know it has some model name; if your friend gets a Dog, you know it has some breed. You probably don't know the exact contents or current state of the Automobile's speed or the Dog's shots, but you do know that those attributes exist for the Automobile and Dog classes. Similarly, in a GUI operating environment, you expect each Window you open to have specific, consistent attributes, such as a menu bar and a title bar, because each Window includes these attributes as a member of the general class of GUI Windows.

 By convention, programmers using C# begin their class names with an upper-case letter. Thus the class that defines the attributes and methods of an automobile would probably be named Automobile, and the class that contains dogs would probably be named Dog. However, following this convention is not required to produce a workable program.

Besides attributes, objects possess **methods** or procedures that they use to accomplish tasks, including changing attributes and discovering the values of attributes. Automobiles, for example, have methods for moving forward and backward. They also can be filled with gasoline or be washed; both are methods that change some of an Automobile's attributes. Methods also exist for ascertaining the status of certain attributes, such as the current speed of an Automobile and the status of its gas tank. Similarly, a Dog can walk or run, eat, and get a bath, and there are methods for determining whether it needs food, a walk, or a bath. GUI operating system components can be maximized, minimized, and dragged and, depending on the component, can have their color or font style altered.

Like procedural programs, object-oriented programs have variables (attributes) and procedures (methods), but the attributes and methods are encapsulated into objects that are then used much like real-world objects. **Encapsulation** is the technique of packaging an object's attributes and methods into a cohesive unit that can be used as an undivided entity. Programmers sometimes refer to encapsulation as using a "black box," a device you use without regard for the internal mechanisms. If an object's methods are well written, the user is unaware of the low-level details of how the methods are executed; in such a case, the user must understand only the **interface** or interaction between the method and object. For example, if you can fill your Automobile with gasoline, it is because you understand the interface between the gas pump nozzle and the vehicle's gas tank opening. You don't need to understand how the pump works or where the gas tank is located inside your vehicle. If you can read your speedometer, it does not matter how the display figure is calculated. In fact, if someone produces a superior, more accurate speedometer and inserts it into your Automobile, you don't have to know or care how it operates, as long as your interface remains the same. The same principles apply to well-constructed objects used in object-oriented programs.

Object-oriented programming languages support two other distinguishing features in addition to organizing objects as members of classes. One feature, **polymorphism**, describes the ability to create methods that act appropriately depending on the context. For example, you are able to "fill" both a Dog and an Automobile, but you do so by very different means. A friend would have no trouble understanding your meaning if you said "I need to fill my Automobile" and distinguishing the process from filling your Dog, your BankAccount, or your AppointmentCalendar. Older, non-object-oriented languages could not make similar distinctions, but object-oriented languages can.

Object-oriented languages also support inheritance. **Inheritance** provides the ability to extend a class so as to create a more specific class. The more specific class contains all the attributes and methods of the more general class and usually contains new attributes or methods as well. For example, if you have created a Dog class, you might then create a more specific class named ShowDog. Each instance of the ShowDog class would contain all the attributes and methods of a Dog, plus an attribute to hold the number of ribbons won and a method for entering a dog show. The advantage of inheritance is that when you need a class such as ShowDog, you often can extend an existing class, thereby saving a lot of time and work.

THE C# PROGRAMMING LANGUAGE

The **C#** (pronounced "C Sharp") **programming language** was developed as an object-oriented and component-oriented language. It exists as part of Visual Studio .NET, a package that contains a platform for developing applications for the Windows family of operating systems. Unlike other programming languages, C# allows every piece of data to be treated as an object and to employ the principles of object-oriented programming. C# provides constructs for creating components with properties, methods, and events, making it an ideal language for twenty-first-century programming, where building small, reusable components is more important than building huge, stand-alone applications.

C# contains a GUI interface that makes it similar to Visual Basic. Visual Basic, however, is not fully object-oriented. C# is truly object-oriented, yet it is simpler to use than many other object-oriented languages. It is modeled after the C++ programming language, but some of the most difficult features to understand in C++ have been eliminated in C#. For example, pointers are not used in C#, object destructors and forward declarations are not needed, and using #include files is not necessary. Multiple inheritance, which causes many C++ programming errors, is not allowed in C#.

 Technically, you can use pointers in C#, but only in a mode called unsafe, which is rarely used.

C# is very similar to Java, because Java was also based on C++. In Java, simple data types are not objects; therefore, they do not work with built-in methods. In C#, every piece of data is an object, providing all data with the functionality of true objects. Additionally, in Java, parameters must be passed by value, which means a copy must be made of any data that is sent to a method for alteration, and the copy must be sent back to the original object. C# provides the convenience of passing by reference, which means the actual object can be altered by a method without a copy being passed back. If you have not programmed before, the difference between C# and other languages means little to you. However, experienced programmers will appreciate the thought that the developers of C# put into its features.

WRITING A C# PROGRAM THAT PRODUCES OUTPUT

At first glance, even the simplest C# program involves a fair amount of confusing syntax. Consider the simple program in Figure 1-1. This program is written on seven lines, and its only task is to print "This is my first C# program" on the screen.

```
public class FirstClass
{
      public static void Main()
      {
            System.Console.Out.WriteLine("This is my first C# program");
      }
}
```

Figure 1-1   First console application

The statement that does the actual work in this program is in the middle of the figure: `System.Console.Out.WriteLine("This is my first C# program");`. The statement ends with a semicolon because all C# statements do.

The text "This is my first C# program" is a **literal string** of characters—that is, a series of characters that will appear exactly as entered. Any literal string in C# appears between double quotation marks.

The string "This is my first C# program" appears within parentheses because the string is a **parameter** or an **argument** to a method, and parameters to methods always appear within parentheses. Parameters represent information that a method needs to perform its task. For example, if making an appointment with a dentist's office was a C# method, you would write `MakeAppointment("September 10", "2 p.m.")`. Accepting and processing a dental appointment is a method that consists of a set of standard procedures. However, each appointment requires different information—the date and time—and this information can be considered the `MakeAppointment()` method's parameters. If you make an appointment for September 10 at 2 p.m., you expect different results than if you make one for September 11 at 8 a.m. or December 25 at midnight. Likewise, if you pass the parameter "Happy Holidays" to a method, you will expect different results than if you pass the parameter "This is my first C# program."

Within the statement `System.Console.Out.WriteLine("This is my first C# program");`, the method to which you are passing the string "This is my first C# program" is named `WriteLine()`. The **WriteLine()** method prints a line of output on the screen, positions the cursor on the next line, and stands ready for additional output.

In C#, you usually refer to method names by including their parentheses, as in `WriteLine()`. This practice makes it easy for you to distinguish method names from variable names.

The `Write()` method is very similar to the `WriteLine()` method. With `WriteLine()`, the cursor appears on the following line after the message is displayed. With `Write()`, the cursor does not advance to a new line; it remains on the same line as the output.

Within the statement `System.Console.Out.WriteLine("This is my first C# program");`, `Out` is an object. The `Out` object represents the screen on the terminal or computer where you are working. Of course, not all objects have a `WriteLine()` method (for instance, you can't write a line to a computer's mouse, your Automobile, or your Dog), but the creators of C# assumed that you frequently would want to display output on the screen at your terminal. For this reason, the `Out` object was created and endowed with the method named `WriteLine()`. Soon, you will create your own C# objects and endow them with your own methods.

The C# programming language is case sensitive. Thus the object named Out is a completely different object than one named out, OUT, or oUt.

Within the statement `System.Console.Out.WriteLine("This is my first C# program");`, `Console` is a class. It defines the attributes of a collection of similar "Console" objects just as the Dog class defines the attributes of a collection of similar Dog objects. One of the Console objects is `Out`. (You might guess that another Console object is `In`; which represents the keyboard.)

Within the statement `System.Console.Out.WriteLine("This is my first C# program");`, `System` is a namespace. A **namespace** is a scheme that provides a way to group similar classes. To organize your classes, you can (and will) create your own namespaces. The System namespace, which is built into your C# compiler, holds commonly used classes.

You will create your own namespaces in Chapter 3.

An advantage to using Visual Studio .NET is that all of its languages use the same namespaces. In other words, everything you learn about any namespace in C# is knowledge you can transfer to Visual C++ and Visual Basic.

The dots (periods) in the statement `System.Console.Out.WriteLine("This is my first C# program");` are used to separate the names of the namespace, class, object, and method. You will use this same namespace-dot-class-dot-object-dot-method format repeatedly in your C# programs.

The statement `System.Console.Out.WriteLine("This is my first C# program");` appears within a method named `Main()`. Every method in C# contains a header and a body. The body of every method is contained within a pair of curly braces. In the program in Figure 1-1, there is only one statement between the curly braces of the `Main()` method. Soon, you will write methods with many more statements. For every opening curly brace ({) in a C# program, there must be a corresponding closing curly brace (}). The precise position of the opening and closing curly braces is not important to the compiler. For example, the method in Figure 1-2 is executed exactly the same way as the one shown in Figure 1-1. The only difference is in the amount of whitespace used in the method. In general, whitespace is optional in C#. **Whitespace** is any combination of spaces, tabs, and carriage returns (blank lines). You use whitespace to organize your program code and make it easier to read. Usually, code in which you vertically align each pair of opening and closing curly braces is easier to read.

```
public static void Main(){System.Console.Out.WriteLine
("This is my first C# program");}
```

Figure 1-2   A `Main()` method with little whitespace

The **method header** for the `Main()` method contains four words. In the method header `public static void Main()`, the word `public` is an access modifier. As opposed to the case in which a method is **private**, the access modifier **public** indicates that other classes may use this method.

If you do not use an access modifier within a method header, then by default the method is private.

In the English language, the word *static* means "showing little change" or "stationary." In C#, the reserved keyword **static** has the same meaning. It indicates that you do not need to create an object of type **FirstClass** to use the **Main()** method defined within **FirstClass**. In C#, **static** also implies uniqueness. Only one **Main()** method for **FirstClass** will ever be stored in the memory of the computer. Of course, other classes eventually might have their own, different **Main()** methods.

In English, the word *void* means empty. When the keyword **void** is used in the **Main()** method header, it does not indicate that the **Main()** method is empty, but rather that the method does not return any value when called. This doesn't mean that **Main()** doesn't produce output—it does. The **Main()** method does not send any value back to any other method that might call it. You will learn more about return values when you study methods in greater detail.

In the method header, the name of the method is **Main()**. All C# applications must include a method named **Main()**, and most C# applications will have additional methods with other names. When you execute a C# application, the compiler always executes the **Main()** method first.

You will write many C# *classes* that do not contain a **Main()** method. However, all executable *applications* must contain a **Main()** method.

You also can write the **Main()** method header as public static int Main(), public static void Main(string[] args), or public static int Main(string[] args). You will learn more about these alternative forms of **Main()** as you continue to study C#.

SELECTING IDENTIFIERS

Every method that you use within a C# program must be part of a **class**. To create a class, you use a class header and curly braces in much the same way you use a header and braces for a method within a class. When you write **public class FirstClass**, you are defining a class named **FirstClass**. A class name does not have to contain the word "Class" as **FirstClass** does. You can define a C# class using any name or **identifier** you need, as long as it meets the following requirements:

- An identifier must begin with an underscore or a letter. (Letters include foreign-alphabet letters such as π and Σ, which are contained in the set of characters known as Unicode.)

- An identifier can contain only letters or digits, not special characters such as #, $, or &.

- An identifier cannot be a C# reserved keyword, such as public or class. Table 1-1 provides a complete list of reserved keywords. (Actually, you can use a keyword as an identifier if you precede it with an "at" sign, as in @class. This feature allows you to use code written in other languages that do not have the same set of reserved keywords. However, when you write original C# programs, you should not use the keywords as identifiers.)

Table 1-1   C# Reserved Keywords

abstract	float	return
as	for	sbyte
base	foreach	sealed
bool	goto	short
break	if	sizeof
byte	implicit	stackalloc
case	in	static
catch	int	string
char	interface	struct
checked	internal	switch
class	is	this
const	lock	throw
continue	long	true
decimal	namespace	try
default	new	typeof
delegate	null	uint
do	object	ulong
double	operator	unchecked
else	out	unsafe
enum	override	ushort
event	params	using
explicit	private	virtual
extern	protected	void
false	public	volatile
finally	readonly	while
fixed	ref	

A programming standard in C# is to begin class names with an uppercase letter and use other uppercase letters as needed to improve readability. Table 1-2 lists some valid and conventional class names you might use when creating classes in C#.

Table 1-2   Some Valid and Conventional Class Names in C#

Class Name	Description
Employee	Begins with an uppercase letter
FirstClass	Begins with an uppercase letter, contains no spaces, and has an initial uppercase letter that indicates the start of the second word
PushButtonControl	Begins with an uppercase letter, contains no spaces, and has an initial uppercase letter that indicates the start of all subsequent words
Budget2003	Begins with an uppercase letter and contains no spaces

Table 1-3 lists some class names that are valid, but unconventional.

 You should follow established conventions for C# so that other programmers can interpret and follow your programs. This book uses established C# programming conventions.

Table 1-3   Some Unconventional Class Names in C#

Class Name	Description
employee	Begins with a lowercase letter
First_Class	Although legal, the underscore is not commonly used to indicate new words
Pushbuttoncontrol	No uppercase characters are used to indicate the start of a new word, making the name difficult to read
BUDGET2003	Appears with all uppercase letters
Public	Although this identifier is legal because it is different than the keyword public, which begins with a lowercase "p", the similarity could cause confusion

Table 1-4 lists some illegal class names.

Table 1-4   Some Illegal Class Names in C#

Class Name	Description
an employee	Space character is illegal
Push Button Control	Space characters are illegal
class	"class" is a reserved word
2003Budget	Class names cannot begin with a digit
phone#	The # symbol is not allowed; identifiers consist of letters and digits

In Figure 1-1, the line `public class FirstClass` contains the keyword `class`, which identifies `FirstClass` as a class. The reserved word `public` is an access modifier. An **access modifier** defines the circumstances under which a class can be accessed. Public access is the most liberal type of access.

The simple program shown in Figure 1-1 has many pieces to remember. For now, you can use the program shown in Figure 1-3 as a shell, where you replace the identifier AnyLegalClassName with any legal class name, and the line /*********/ with any statements that you want to execute.

```
public class AnyLegalClassName
{
     public static void Main()
     {
          /*********/;
     }
}
```

Figure 1-3   Shell program

WRITING YOUR FIRST C# PROGRAM

Now that you understand the basic framework of a program written in C#, you are ready to enter your first C# program into a text editor so you can execute it. It is a tradition among programmers that the first program you write in any language produces "Hello, world!" as its output. You will create such a program now. To create a C# program, you can use the editor that is included as part of the Microsoft Visual Studio Integrated Development Environment (IDE). (The C# compiler, other language compilers, and many development tools also are contained in the IDE.) Alternatively, you can use any text editor. There are advantages to using the C# editor to write your programs, but to get started, using a plain text editor is simpler.

To write your first C# program:

1. Start any text editor, such as Notepad, WordPad, or any word processing program. Open a new document, if necessary.

2. Type the class header **public class Hello**. In this example, the class name is `Hello`.

3. Press the **Enter** key and type the class-opening curly brace **{**.

4. Press **Enter** again, then press the **Tab** key to indent.

5. Write the `Main()` method header: **public static void Main()**. Press **Enter** and then press **Tab**.

6. Type **{**, press **Enter**, and then press the **Tab** key to indent. Type the one executing statement in this program: `System.Console.Out.WriteLine ("Hello, world!");`.

7. Press **Enter**, press **Tab**, type a closing curly brace for the `Main()` method, press **Enter**, and type a closing curly brace for the class. Your code should look like Figure 1-4.

```
public class Hello
{
    public static void Main()
    {
        System.Console.Out.WriteLine("Hello, world!");
    }
}
```

Figure 1-4   The Hello class

8. Save the program as **Hello.cs** in the Chapter.01 folder on your Student Disk. It is important that the file extension be .cs, which stands for *C Sharp*. If the file has a different extension, the compiler for C# will not recognize the program as a C# program.

Many text editors attach their own filename extension (such as .txt or .doc) to a saved file. Double-check your saved file to ensure that it does not have a double extension (as in Hello.cs.txt). If the file has a double extension, rename it. If you explicitly type quotes surrounding a filename (as in "Hello.cs"), most editors will save the file as you specify, without adding their own extension. If you use a word processing program as your editor, select the option to save the file as a plain text file.

COMPILING AND EXECUTING A PROGRAM FROM THE COMMAND LINE

After you write and save a program, you must perform two more steps before you can view the program output:

1. You must compile the program you wrote (called the **source** code) into **intermediate language (IL)**.

2. You must use the C# **just in time (JIT)** compiler to translate the intermediate code into executable statements.

When you compile a C# program, you translate your source code into intermediate language. The JIT compiler converts IL instructions into native code at the last moment, and appropriately for each different type of computer on which the code might eventually be executed. In other words, the same set of IL can be JIT-compiled and executed on any supported architecture.

To compile your source code from the command line, you type **csc** followed by the name of the file that contains the source code. The command csc stands for "C Sharp compiler." For example, to compile a file named Hello.cs, you would type **csc Hello.cs** and then press the Enter key. There will be one of three outcomes:

- You receive an operating system error message such as "Bad command or file name" or "csc is not recognized as an internal or external command."

- You receive one or more program language error messages.

- You receive no error messages (only a copyright statement from Microsoft), indicating that the program has compiled successfully.

If you receive an operating system message such as "Bad command or file name," "csc is not recognized...," or "Source file could not be found," it may mean that:

- You misspelled the command **csc**.

- You misspelled the filename.

- You forgot to include the extension .cs with the filename.

- You didn't use the correct case. If your filename is **Hello.cs**, then **csc hello.cs** will not compile.

- You are not within the correct subdirectory or folder on your command line.

- The C# compiler was not installed properly.

- You need to set a path command. To locate the C# compiler whose name is csc.exe, use Explorer or click Start and then click Search. At the command line, type **path =**, followed by the complete path name that describes where csc.exe is stored; then try to execute the Hello program again. For example, you might type **path = c:\winnt\Microsoft.net\framework\v1.0.2914** and press Enter. Next, you would type **csc Hello.cs** and press Enter again.

If you receive a programming language error message, it means that the source code contains one or more syntax errors. A **syntax error** occurs when you introduce typing errors into your program. For example, if the first line within your program begins with "Public" (with an uppercase *P*), you will get an error message such as **A namespace does not directly contain members such as fields or methods** after compiling the program, because the compiler won't recognize Hello as a class with a **Main()** method. If this problem occurs, you must reopen the text file that contains the source code and make the necessary corrections.

The C# compiler issues warnings as well as errors. A warning is less serious than an error; it means that the compiler has determined that you have done something unusual, but not illegal. If you have purposely introduced a warning situation to test a program, then you can ignore the warning. Usually, however, you should treat a warning message just as you would an error message and attempt to remedy the situation.

If you receive no error messages after compiling the code in a file named Hello.cs, then the program compiled successfully and a file named Hello.exe is created and saved in the same folder as the program text file. To run the program from the command line, you simply type the program name **Hello**.

To compile and execute your Hello program from the command line:

1. Go to the command prompt on your system. In Windows 2000, click **Start**, point to **Programs**, point to **Accessories**, and then click **Command Prompt**. (In Windows XP, you point to All Programs instead of Programs.) Change the current directory to the name of the folder that holds your program (Chapter.01).

If your command prompt indicates a path other than the one you want, you can type cd\ and then press the Enter key to return to the root directory. You can then type cd Chapter.01 to change the path to the one where your program resides. The command cd is short for *change directory*.

2. Type the command that compiles your program: **csc Hello.cs**. If you do not receive any error messages and the prompt returns, it means that the compile operation was successful, that a file named Hello.exe has been created, and that you can execute the program. If you do receive error messages, check every character of the program you typed to make sure it matches Figure 1-4. Remember, C# is case sensitive, so all casing must match exactly. When you have corrected the errors, compile the program again.

3. You can verify that a file named Hello.exe was created in several ways:

   ■ At the command prompt, type **dir** to view a directory of the files stored in your Chapter.01 folder. Both Hello.cs and Hello.exe should appear in the list.

   ■ Use Windows Explorer to view the contents of the Chapter.01 folder.

   ■ Double-click the **My Computer** icon, find and double-click the **Chapter.01** folder, and view the contents.

4. At the command prompt, type the name of the program (the name of the executable file), **Hello**, and then press **Enter**. Alternatively, you can type the full filename **Hello.exe**, but typing the .exe extension isn't necessary. The output should look like Figure 1-5.

You can use the **/out** compiler option between the csc command and the name of the .cs file to indicate the name of the output file. For example, if you type csc /out:Hello.exe Hello.cs, you will create an output file named Hello.exe. By default, the name of the output file is the same as the name of the .cs file. Usually, this is your intention, so most often you omit the /out option. You will learn to add other options to the command line in Chapter 3.

Figure 1-5   Output of Hello program

ADDING COMMENTS TO A PROGRAM

As you can see, even the simplest C# program takes several lines of code and contains somewhat perplexing syntax. Large programs that perform many tasks include much more code. As you write longer programs, it becomes increasingly difficult to remember why you included steps and how you intended to use particular variables. **Program comments** are nonexecuting statements that you add to document a program. Programmers use comments to leave notes for themselves and for others who might read their programs in the future. At the very least, your programs should include comments indicating the author of the program, the date of its creation, and the program's name or function.

 We suggest that as you work through this book you add comments as the first three lines of every program. The comments should contain your name, the date, and the name of the program. Your instructor might want you to include additional comments.

Comments also can be useful when you are developing a program. If a program is not performing as expected, you can **comment out** various statements and subsequently run the program to observe the effect. When you comment out a statement, you turn it into a comment so that the compiler will not execute its command. This approach helps you pinpoint the location of errant statements in malfunctioning programs.

There are three types of comments in C#:

- **Line comments** start with two forward slashes (//) and continue to the end of the current line. Line comments can appear on a line by themselves, or at the end of a line following executable code.

- **Block comments** start with a forward slash and an asterisk (/*) and end with an asterisk and a forward slash (*/). Block comments can appear on a line by themselves, on a line before executable code, or after executable code. They can also extend across as many lines as needed.

- C# also supports a special type of comment used to create documentation from within a program. These comments, called **XML-documentation format**, involve using a special set of tags within angle brackets. (XML stands for Extensible Markup Language.) You will learn more about this type of comment as you continue your study of C#.

 The forward slash (/) and the backslash (\) characters often are confused, but they are distinct characters. You cannot use them interchangeably.

Figure 1-6 shows how comments can be used in code. The program covers 12 lines of type, yet only seven are part of the executable C# program, and the only line that actually *does* anything is the one that prints "Message".

```
public class ClassWithOneExecutingLine
/* This class has only one line that executes */
{
    public static void Main()
      {
           // The next line writes the message
           System.Console.Out.WriteLine("Message");   // Comment
      }
/* This program serves
   to demonstrate that a program
  can "look" a lot longer than it really is */
}
```

Figure 1-6   Using comments within a program

Next, you will add comments to your Hello.cs program.

To add comments to your program:

1. Position your cursor at the top of the file, press the **Enter** key to insert a new line, press the **Up** arrow key to go to that line, and then type the following comments at the top of the file. Press **Enter** after typing each line. Insert your name and today's date where indicated.

```
// Filename Hello.cs
// Written by <your name>
// Written on <today's date>
```

2. Scroll to the line that reads `public class Hello` and press the **End** key to position the insertion point at the end of the line. Press **Enter**, and then type the following block comment in the program.

```
/*  This program demonstrates the use of the WriteLine()
method to print the message Hello, world!  */
```

3. Save the file, replacing the old Hello.cs file with this new, commented version.

4. At the command line, compile the program using the command **csc Hello.cs**. When the program compiles successfully, execute it with the command **Hello**. Adding program comments does not make any difference in the execution of the program.

COMPILING AND EXECUTING A PROGRAM USING THE VISUAL STUDIO IDE

As an alternative to using the command line, you can compile and write your program within the Visual Studio Integrated Development Environment. There are several advantages to this approach:

- Some of the code you need is already created for you.

- The code is displayed in color, so you can more easily identify parts of your program. Reserved words appear in blue, comments in green, and identifiers in black.

- If error messages appear when you compile your program, you can double-click on an error message and the cursor will move to the line of code that contains the error.

- Other debugging tools are available. You will become more familiar with these tools as you develop more sophisticated programs.

Next, you will use the C# compiler environment to compile and execute the same Hello program you ran from the command line.

To compile and execute the Hello program:

1. Within the text editor you used to write the Hello program, select the entire program. In Notepad, for example, you can highlight all the lines of text with your mouse or press **Ctrl+A**. Next, copy the text to the Clipboard for temporary storage by clicking **Edit** on the menu bar and then clicking **Copy**, or by pressing **Ctrl+C**.

2. Open Visual Studio. If there is a shortcut icon on your desktop, you can double-click it. Alternatively, in Windows 2000, you can click the **Start** button, point to **Programs**, point to Microsoft Visual Studio.NET, and click **Microsoft Visual Studio.NET**, as shown in Figure 1-7.

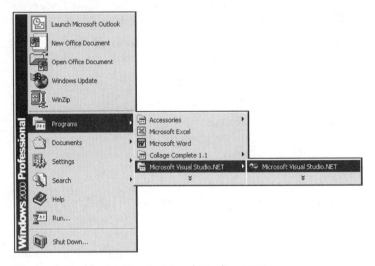

Figure 1-7   Navigating to Visual Studio .NET

3. If you see a Start Page, click **New Project**. If you do not see a Start Page, click **File** on the menu bar, point to **New**, and then click **Project**, as shown in Figure 1-8.

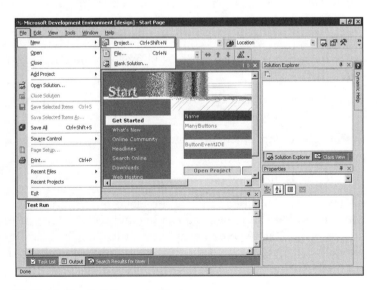

Figure 1-8   Creating a project

4. In the New Project window, click **Visual C# Projects** in the Project Types list. Under Templates, click **Console Application**. Enter **Hello** as the name for this project. For the location, select the **Chapter.01** folder on your Student Disk. Finally, click **OK**. See Figure 1-9.

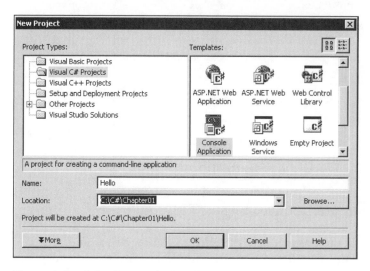

Figure 1-9   Selecting project options

5. The Hello application editing window appears, as shown in Figure 1-10. A lot of code is already written for you in this window, including a class named Hello, a `Main( )` method, many comments, and other features. You could leave the class header, `Main( )` method header, and other features, and just add the specific statements you need. You would save a lot of typing and prevent typographical errors. In this case you have already written a functioning Hello program, so you will replace the prewritten code with your Hello code. Select all the code in the editor window by highlighting it with your mouse or by pressing **Ctrl+A**. Then press **Delete**. Paste the previously copied Hello program into the editor by pressing **Ctrl+V** or by clicking **Edit** on the menu bar and then clicking **Paste**.

6. Save the file by clicking **File** on the menu bar and then clicking **Save Class1.cs**, or by clicking the **Save** button on the toolbar.

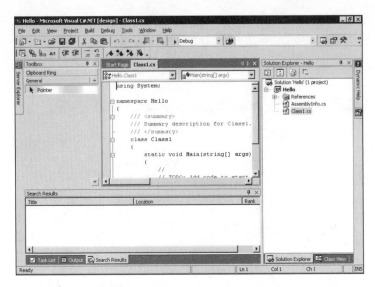

Figure 1-10   The console application template

7. To compile the program, click **Build** on the menu bar and then click the **Build** or **Build Hello** option. You should receive no error messages, as shown in Figure 1-11.

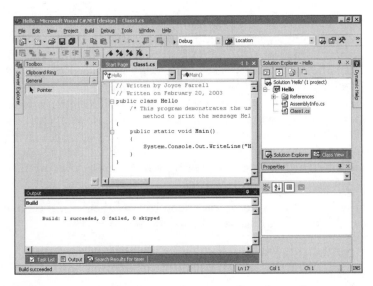

Figure 1-11   Output screen after compiling the Hello program

8. Click **Debug** on the menu bar, and then click **Start Without Debugging**. The output that appears in Figure 1-12 is identical to that when running the program from the command line.

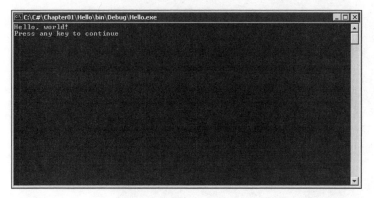

Figure 1-12   Output of the Hello program as run from the Visual Studio IDE

9. Close Visual Studio .NET by clicking **File** on the menu bar and then clicking **Exit**, or by clicking the **Close** box in the upper-right corner of the Visual Studio window.

10. When you create a C# program using an editor such as Notepad and compiling with the csc command, only two files are created—Hello.cs and Hello.exe. When you create a C# program using the Visual Studio editor, many additional files are created. You can view their filenames in several ways:

   ■ At the command prompt, type **dir** to view a directory of the files stored in your Chapter.01 folder. Within the Chapter.01 folder, a new folder named Hello has been created. Type the command **cd Hello** to change the current path to include this new folder, then type **dir** again. Figure 1-13 shows the list created using this method.

   ■ Use Windows Explorer to view the contents of the Hello folder within the Chapter.01 folder.

   ■ Double-click the **My Computer** icon, find and double-click the **Chapter.01** folder, double-click the **Hello** folder, and view the contents.

The Hello folder contains a bin folder, an obj folder, and several additional files. If you explore further, you will find that the Bin folder contains a Debug folder, which includes additional files. Using the Visual Studio editor to compile your programs creates a lot of overhead. These additional files will become important as you create more sophisticated C# projects. For now, while you learn C# syntax, using the command line to compile programs is simpler.

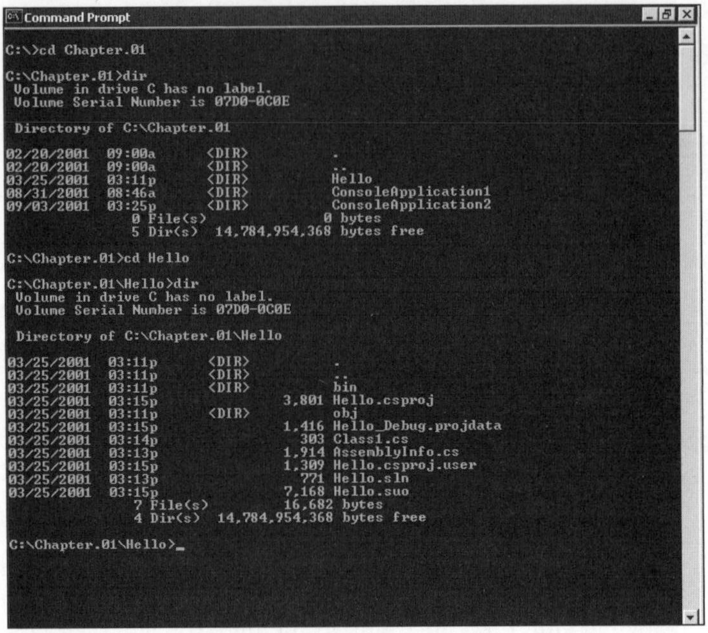

Figure 1-13   List of Hello program files

ELIMINATING THE REFERENCE TO OUT BY USING THE SYSTEM NAMESPACE

A program can contain as many statements as you want. For example, the program in Figure 1-14 produces the three lines of output shown in Figure 1-15. A semicolon separates each program statement.

```
public class ThreeLines
{
    public static void Main()
     {
          System.Console.Out.WriteLine("Line one");
          System.Console.Out.WriteLine("Line two");
          System.Console.Out.WriteLine("Line three");
     }
}
```

Figure 1-14   A program that produces three lines of output

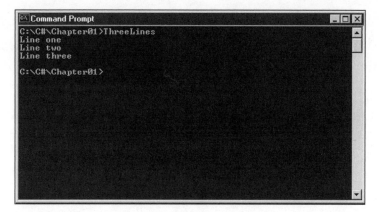

Figure 1-15   Output of ThreeLines program

The program in Figure 1-14 shows a lot of repeated code—the phrase "System.Console.Out.WriteLine" appears three times. When you use the name of the object Out, you are indicating the console screen. However, Out is the default output object. That is, if you write `System.Console.WriteLine("Hi");` without specifying a Console object, the message "Hi" goes to the default Console object, which is Out. Most C# programmers usually use the `WriteLine()` method without specifying the Out object.

When you need to repeatedly use a class from the same namespace, you can shorten the statements you type by using a clause that indicates a namespace where the class can be found. You use a namespace with a using clause, as shown in the program in Figure 1-16. By typing `using System;` prior to the class definition, the compiler knows to use the System namespace when it encounters the Console class. The output of the program in Figure 1-16 is identical to that in Figure 1-14, in which `System` was repeated with each `WriteLine()` statement.

```
using System;
public class ThreeLines
{
    public static void Main()
    {
        Console.WriteLine("Line one");
        Console.WriteLine("Line two");
        Console.WriteLine("Line three");
    }
}
```

Figure 1-16   A program that produces three lines of output and uses a using
              System clause

At this point, the clever programmer will say, "I'll shorten my typing tasks even further by typing `using System.Console;` at the top of my programs, and producing output with statements like `WriteLine("Hi");`." However, `using` cannot be used with a class name like System—only with a namespace name. Another option is to assign an alias to a class with a using clause. An **alias** is an alternative name for a class. You might assign one as a convenience when a fully qualified class name is very long. For example, Figure 1-17 shows a program that uses an alias for System.Console. The lines of code within the program are shorter, but more difficult for another programmer to read. While you are learning C#, you should avoid using aliases to simply reduce typing.

```
using SC = System.Console;
public class ThreeLines
{
   public static void Main()
     {
           SC.WriteLine("Line one");
           SC.WriteLine("Line two");
           SC.WriteLine("Line three");
     }
}
```

Figure 1-17   Using an alias for System.Console

CHAPTER SUMMARY

- A computer program is a set of instructions that you write to tell a computer what to do. Programmers write their programs, then use a compiler to translate their high-level language statements into intermediate language and machine code. A program works correctly when both its syntax and logic are correct.

- Procedural programming involves creating computer memory locations, called variables, and sets of operations, called procedures. In object-oriented programming, you envision program components as objects that are similar to concrete objects in the real world; then you manipulate the objects to achieve a desired result. Objects exist as members of classes and are made up of states and methods.

- The C# programming language was developed as an object-oriented and component-oriented language. It contains many features similar to those in Visual Basic, Java, and C++.

- To write a C# program that produces a line of console output, you must pass a literal string as a parameter to the `System.Console.Out.WriteLine()` method. System is a namespace, Console is a class, and Out is an object. The `WriteLine()` method call appears within the `Main()` method of a class you create.

- You can define a C# class or variable by using any name or identifier that begins with an underscore or a letter, that contains only letters or digits, and that is not a C# reserved keyword.

❐ To create a C# program, you can use the Microsoft Visual Studio environment. You can also use any text editor, such as Notepad, WordPad, or any word processing program.

❐ After you write and save a program, you must compile the source code into intermediate and machine language. From the command line, you use the csc command to create an executable file. Then you type the program's name to execute it.

❐ Program comments are nonexecuting statements that you add to document a program or to disable statements when you test a program. There are three types of comments in C#: line comments that start with two forward slashes (//) and continue to the end of the current line, block comments that start with a forward slash and an asterisk (/*) and end with an asterisk and a forward slash (*/), and XML-documentation comments.

❐ As an alternative to using the command line, you can compile and write your program within the Visual Studio IDE. The compiler provides some prewritten code, uses color to identify program components, and provides easier debugging.

❐ When you need to repeatedly use a class from the same namespace, you can shorten the statements you type by using a clause that indicates a namespace where the class can be found.

REVIEW QUESTIONS

1. A computer program written as a series of on and off switches is written in
   _____.

   a. machine language

   b. a low-level language

   c. a high-level language

   d. a compiled language

2. A program that translates high-level programs into intermediate or machine code is a(n)_____.

   a. mangler

   b. compiler

   c. analyst

   d. logician

3. The grammar and spelling rules of a programming language constitute its
   _____.

   a. logic

   b. variables

   c. syntax

   d. vortex

4. Variables are _____.

    a. procedures

    b. named memory locations

    c. grammar rules

    d. operations

5. Programs in which you create and use objects that have attributes similar to their real-world counterparts are known as _____ programming.

    a. procedural

    b. logical

    c. authentic

    d. object-oriented

6. Which of the following pairs is an example of a class and an object?

    a. robin and bird

    b. chair and desk

    c. university and Harvard

    d. Beefsteak and tomato

7. The technique of packaging an object's attributes into a cohesive unit that can be used as an undivided entity is _____.

    a. inheritance

    b. encapsulation

    c. polymorphism

    d. interfacing

8. Of the following languages, which is least similar to C#?

    a. Java

    b. Visual Basic

    c. C++

    d. COBOL

9. A series of characters that appears within double quotation marks is a(n) _____.

    a. parameter

    b. interface

    c. argument

    d. literal string

10. The C# method that prints a line of output on the screen and then positions the cursor on the next line is _____.

    a. WriteLine()

    b. PrintLine()

    c. DisplayLine()

    d. OutLine()

11. Which of the following is an object?

    a. System

    b. Console

    c. Out

    d. WriteLine

12. In C#, a scheme that groups similar classes is a(n) _____.

    a. superclass

    b. method

    c. namespace

    d. identifier

13. Every method in C# contains a _____.

    a. header and a body

    b. header and a footer

    c. variable and a class

    d. class and an object

14. Which of the following is a method?

    a. namespace

    b. public

    c. Main()

    d. static

15. Which of the following statements is true?

    a. An identifier must begin with an underscore.

    b. An identifier can contain digits.

    c. An identifier must be no more than 16 characters long.

    d. An identifier can contain only lowercase letters.

16. Which of the following identifiers is not legal in C#?

    a. per cent increase

    b. annualReview

    c. HTML

    d. alternativetaxcredit

17. The text of a program you write is called _____.

    a. object code

    b. source code

    c. machine language

    d. executable documentation

18. Programming errors such as using incorrect punctuation or misspelling words are collectively known as _____ errors.

    a. syntax

    b. logical

    c. executable

    d. fatal

19. A comment in the form `/* this is a comment */` is a(n) _____.

    a. XML comment

    b. block comment

    c. executable comment

    d. line comment

20. If a programmer inserts `using System;` at the top of a C# program, which of the following can the programmer use as an alternative to `System.Console.Out.WriteLine("Hello");`?

    a. System("Hello");

    b. WriteLine("Hello");

    c. Console.WriteLine("Hello");

    d. Console.Out("Hello");

EXERCISES

1. Indicate whether each of the following C# programming language identifiers is legal or illegal.

   a. WeeklySales _____

   b. last character _____

   c. class _____

   d. MathClass _____

   e. myfirstinitial _____

   f. phone# _____

   g. abcdefghijklmnop _____

   h. 23jordan _____

   i. my_code _____

   j. 90210 _____

   k. year2000problem _____

   l. αβφSorority _____

2. Name some attributes that might be appropriate for each of the following classes:

   a. TelevisionSet: _____

   b. EmployeePaycheck: _____

   c. PatientMedicalRecord: _____

3. Name a class to which each of these objects might belong:

   a. your red bicycle _____

   b. Albert Einstein _____

   c. last month's credit card bill _____

4. Using an Internet search engine, find at least three definitions for *object-oriented programming*. (Try searching with and without the hyphen in *object-oriented*.) Compare the definitions with each other and compile them into one "best" definition.

5. Write, compile, and test a program that displays your first name on the screen. Save the program as **Name.cs** in the Chapter.01 folder on your Student Disk.

6. Write, compile, and test a program that displays your full name, street address, and city and state on three separate lines on the screen. Save the program as **Address.cs** in the Chapter.01 folder on your Student Disk.

7. Write, compile, and test a program that displays your favorite quotation on the screen. Include the name of the person to whom the quote is attributed. Use as many display lines as you feel are appropriate. Save the program as **Quotation.cs** in the Chapter.01 folder on your Student Disk.

8. Write, compile, and test a program that displays a pattern similar to the following on the screen:

```
    X
   XXX
  XXXXX
 XXXXXXX
    X
```

Save the program as **Tree.cs** in the Chapter.01 folder on your Student Disk.

9. Each of the following files in the Chapter.01 folder on your Student Disk has syntax and/or logical errors. In each case, determine the problem and fix the program. After you correct the errors, save each file using the same filename preceded with "Fixed". For example, DebugOne1.cs will become FixedDebugOne1.cs.

   a. DebugOne1.cs

   b. DebugOne2.cs

   c. DebugOne3.cs

   d. DebugOne4.cs

2

USING DATA

In this chapter you will learn:

♦ About variable types and how to declare variables

♦ How to display variable values

♦ About the integral data types

♦ How to use standard binary arithmetic operators

♦ How to use shortcut arithmetic operators

♦ About the Boolean data type

♦ About floating-point data types

♦ How to format floating-point values

♦ About numeric type conversion

♦ About the char data type

♦ About the string data type

♦ How to define named constants

♦ How to accept console input

In Chapter 1, you learned about programming in general and the C# programming language in particular. You wrote, compiled, and ran a C# program that produces output. In this chapter, you build on your basic C# programming skills by learning how to manipulate data, including variables, data types, and constants. As you'll see, using variables makes writing computer programs worth the effort.

DECLARING VARIABLES

You can categorize data as variable or constant. A data item is **constant** when it cannot be changed after a program is compiled—in other words, when it cannot vary. For example, if you use the number 347 within a C# program, then 347 is a constant. Every time you execute this program, the value 347 will be used. You can refer to the number 347 as a **literal constant**, because its value is taken literally at each use.

 You will learn to create named constants later in this chapter.

On the other hand, when you want a value to be able to change, you can create a variable. A **variable** is a named location in computer memory that can hold different values at different points in time. For example, if you create a variable named `heatingBill` and include it in a C# program, `heatingBill` might contain the value 347, or it might contain 200. Different values might be used when the program is executed multiple times, or different values might even be used at different times during the same execution of the program. Using variables makes writing computer programs worth the effort. For example, because you can use a variable to hold `heatingBill` within a utility company's billing system, you can write one set of instructions to compute `heatingBill`, yet use thousands of different `heatingBill` values for thousands of utility customers during one execution of the program.

Whether it is stored as a constant or in a variable, all data you use in a C# program has a data type. A **data type** describes the format and size of a piece of data. C# provides for 14 basic or **intrinsic types** of data, as shown in Table 2-1. Of these built-in data types, the ones most commonly used are int, double, char, string, and bool. Each C# intrinsic type is an **alias**, or other name for, a class in the System namespace.

 The maximum long is 922,372,036,854,775,807. The maximum ulong is 18,446,744,073,709,551,615. The maximum float is 3.40282346638528859e38. The notation e38 means "times 10 to the 38th power." The maximum double is 1.7976931348623157E+308. The maximum decimal is 79,228,162,514,264,337,593,543,950,335. The minimum for each of these types is the negative value whose absolute value is one more than the positive maximum.

 The highest char value, 0xFFFF, represents the character in which every bit is turned on. The lowest value, 0x0000, represents the character in which every bit is turned off. Any value that begins with "0x" represents a hexadecimal, or base 16, value.

Table 2-1   C# Data Types

Type	System Type	Bytes	Description	Largest Value	Smallest Value
byte	Byte	1	Unsigned byte	255	0
sbyte	Sbyte	1	Signed byte	127	−128
short	Int16	2	Signed short	32,767	−32,768
ushort	UInt16	2	Unsigned short	65,535	0
int	Int32	4	Signed integer	2,147,483,647	−2,147,483,648
uint	UInt32	4	Unsigned integer	4,294,967,295	0
long	Int64	8	Signed long integer	Greater than 900,000 trillion	Less than negative 900,000 trillion
ulong	UInt64	8	Unsigned long integer	Greater than 18 million trillion	Less than negative 18 million trillion
float	Single	4	Floating-point number	A number that is greater than 3 followed by 38 zeros	A number that is less than negative 3 followed by 38 zeros
double	Double	8	Double-precision floating-point number	A number that is greater than 1 followed by 308 zeros	A number that is less than negative 1 followed by 308 zeros
decimal	Decimal	8	Fixed precision number	A number that is greater than 7 followed by 28 zeros	A number that is less than negative 7 followed by 28 zeros
string	String		Unicode string	There is no highest String value; for any two Strings, the one with the higher Unicode character value in an earlier position is considered higher than the other	Although the String type has no true minimum, you can think of the empty String "" as being the "lowest" String
char	Char		Unicode character	0xFFFF	0x0000
bool	Boolean		Boolean value (true or false)	Although the Boolean type has no true maximum, you can think of true as the "highest" Boolean value	For the same reason, you can think of false as the "lowest" Boolean value

2

You name variables using the same rules for identifiers as you use for class names. Basically, variable names must start with a letter, cannot include embedded spaces, and cannot be a reserved keyword. You must declare all variables you want to use in a program. A **variable declaration** includes

- The data type that the variable will store

- An identifier that is the variable's name

- An optional assignment operator and assigned value when you want a variable to contain an initial value

- An ending semicolon

 Variable names usually begin with lowercase letters to distinguish them from class names, and you should follow this convention when naming your variables. However, variable names *can* begin with either an uppercase or lowercase letter.

For example, the variable declaration `int myAge = 25;` declares a variable of type `int` named `myAge` and assigns it an initial value of 25. The declaration is a complete statement that ends in a semicolon. The equal sign (=) is the assignment operator. Any value to the right of the **assignment operator** is assigned to, or taken on by, the variable to the left of the equal sign. An assignment made when a variable is declared is an **initialization**; an assignment made later is simply an **assignment**. Thus, `int myAge = 25;` initializes myAge to 25, and a subsequent statement, such as `myAge = 42;`, assigns a new value to the variable. Note that the expression `25 = myAge;` is illegal, because assignment always takes place from right to left. By definition, a constant cannot be altered, so it is illegal to place one (such as 25) on the left side of an assignment operator.

Instead of using a name from the Type column of Table 2-1, you can use the fully qualified type name from the System namespace that is listed in the System Type column. For example, instead of using the type name `int`, you can use the full name `System.Int32`. It's better to use the shorter alias `int`, however, for several reasons— it's easier to type and easier to read, it resembles type names used in other languages such as Java and C++, and other C# programmers expect it.

 The number 32 in the name `System.Int32` represents the number of bits of storage allowed for the data type.

The variable declaration `int myAge;` declares a variable of type `int` named `myAge`, but no value is assigned at the time of creation. You can make an assignment later in the program, but you cannot use the variable in an arithmetic statement or display the value of the variable until you assign a value to it.

You can declare multiple variables of the same type in separate statements on different lines. For example, the following statements declare two variables. The first variable is named **myAge** and its value is 25. The second variable is named **yourAge** and its value is 19.

```
int myAge = 25;
int yourAge = 19;
```

You also can declare two variables of the same type in a single statement, by using the type once and separating the variable declarations with a comma, as shown in the following statement:

```
int myAge = 25, yourAge = 19;
```

Some programmers prefer to use the data type once, but break the declaration across multiple lines, as in the following example:

```
int     myAge = 25,
        yourAge = 19;
```

When you declare multiple variables of the same type, a comma separates the variable names and a single semicolon appears at the end of the declaration statement, no matter how many lines the declaration occupies. However, when declaring variables of different types, you must use a separate statement for each type. The following statements declare two variables of type int (**myAge** and **yourAge**) and two variables of type double (**mySalary** and **yourSalary**), without assigning initial values to any of them:

```
int myAge, yourAge;
double mySalary, yourSalary;
```

Similarly, the following statements declare two ints and two doubles, assigning values to two of the four named variables:

```
int     myZipCode = 54482,
        yourZipCode;
double myCarsMpg,
        yourCarsMpg = 31.5;
```

DISPLAYING VARIABLE VALUES

You can display variable values by using the variable name within a **WriteLine()** method call. For example, Figure 2-1 shows a C# program that displays the value of the variable **someMoney**. Figure 2-2 shows the output of the program.

You first used the **WriteLine()** method to display strings in Chapter 1.

```
using System;
public class DisplaySomeMoney
{
    public static void Main()
    {
        double someMoney = 39.45;
        Console.WriteLine(someMoney);
    }
}
```

Figure 2-1   Program that displays a variable value

Figure 2-2   Output of `DisplaySomeMoney` program

The output shown in Figure 2-2 is rather stark. It is usually best to include a string of explanation along with numeric output. The program in Figure 2-3 produces the output in Figure 2-4. This program used the **Write( )** method to display the string "The money is" before displaying the value of **someMoney**. Because the program uses **Write( )** instead of **WriteLine( )**, the second output appears on the same line as the first output. The space after "The money is" and before the closing quotation mark provides a space preceding the variable value. Without the space, the word "is" would run right into the displayed value.

```
using System;
public class DisplaySomeMoney2
{
    public static void Main()
    {
        double someMoney = 39.45;
        Console.Write("The money is ");
        Console.WriteLine(someMoney);
    }
}
```

Figure 2-3   Program that displays a string and a variable value

2

Figure 2-4   Output of `DisplaySomeMoney2` program

If you want to display several strings and several variables, you can end up with quite a few `Write()` and `WriteLine()` statements. To make producing output easier, you can combine strings and variable values into a single `Write()` or `WriteLine()` statement by using a format string. A **format string** is a string of characters that contains one or more placeholders for variable values. A **placeholder** consists of a pair of curly braces containing a number that indicates the desired variable's position in a list that follows the string. The first position is always position 0. For example, if you remove the `Write()` and `WriteLine()` statements from the program in Figure 2-3 and replace them with the following statement, the program produces the output shown in Figure 2-5. The placeholder `{0}` holds a position into which the first variable after the string (`someMoney`) is inserted.

```
Console.WriteLine("The money is {0} exactly",someMoney);
```

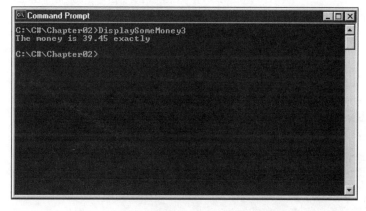

Figure 2-5   Output of `DisplaySomeMoney3` program

To display two variables within a single call to `Write()` or `WriteLine()`, you can use a statement like the following:

```
Console.WriteLine
    ("The money is {0} and my age is {1}",someMoney, myAge);
```

The number within the curly braces in the format string must be less than the number of values you list after the format string. In other words, if you list six values to be displayed, valid format position numbers are 0 through 5. You do not have to use the positions in order. For example, you can choose to display the value in position 2, then 1, then 0. You also can display a specific value multiple times, as in the following example. The output is shown in Figure 2-6.

```
Console.WriteLine
    ("The money is {0}. ${0} is a lot for my age which is {1}.",
    someMoney, myAge);
```

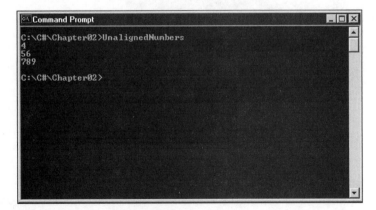

Figure 2-6   Output of `DisplaySomeMoney4` program

When you use a series of `WriteLine()` statements to display a list of variable values, the values are not right-aligned as you normally expect numbers to be. For example, the following code produces the output shown in Figure 2-7:

```
int num1 = 4, num2 = 56, num3 = 789;
Console.WriteLine("{0}",num1);
Console.WriteLine("{0}",num2);
Console.WriteLine("{0}",num3);
```

Figure 2-7   Unaligned output

If you use a second number within the curly braces in a number format, you can specify alignment and field size. For example, the following code produces the output shown in Figure 2-8. The output created by each `WriteLine()` statement is right-aligned in a field that is five characters wide. Alternatively, you can use a negative value for the second number to left-align the values.

```
int num1 = 4, num2 = 56, num3 = 789;
Console.WriteLine("{0,5}",num1);
Console.WriteLine("{0,5}",num2);
Console.WriteLine("{0,5}",num3);
```

```
Command Prompt                                    _ □ ×

C:\C#\Chapter02>AlignedNumbers
    4
   56
  789

C:\C#\Chapter02>
```

Figure 2-8   Aligned output

USING THE INTEGRAL DATA TYPES

In C#, nine data types are considered **integral** data types—that is, types that store whole numbers. The nine types are `byte`, `sbyte`, `short`, `ushort`, `int`, `uint`, `long`, `ulong`, and `char`. The first eight always represent whole numbers, and the ninth type, `char`, is used for characters like 'A' or 'B'. Actually, you can think of all nine types as numbers because every Unicode character, including the letters of the alphabet and punctuation marks, can be represented as a number. For example, the character 'A' is stored within your computer as a 65. Because you more commonly think of the `char` type as holding alphabetic characters instead of their numeric equivalents, the `char` type will be discussed in its own section later in this chapter.

 You first learned about Unicode in Chapter 1.

The most basic of the other eight integral types is `int`. You use variables of type `int` to store (or hold) **integers**, or whole numbers. An `int` uses four bytes of memory and can hold any whole number value ranging from 2,147,483,647 to -2,147,483,648. If you want to save memory and know you need only a small value, you can use one of the shorter integer types—`byte`, `sbyte` (signed byte), `short` (short int), or `ushort` (unsigned short int). For example, a payroll program might contain a variable named `numberOfDependents` that is declared as type `byte`, because `numberOfDependents` will never need to hold a negative value or a value exceeding 255; for that reason, you can allocate just one byte of storage to hold the value.

When you declare variables, you always make a judgment about which type to use. If you use a type that is too large, you waste storage. If you use a type that is too small, your program won't compile. Many programmers simply use `int` for most whole numbers.

The unsigned version of a type can hold twice as high a value as the signed type can. For example, a `byte` can hold twice the positive value that an `sbyte` can, because no storage is needed for the sign (plus or minus) of the stored value.

When you assign a value to any numeric variable, you do not type any commas; you type only digits. You can also type a plus or minus sign to indicate a positive or negative integer. In the next steps, you will write a program that declares several integral variables, assigns values to them, and displays the results.

To write a program with integral variables:

1. Open a new file in the text editor you are using to write your C# programs. Create the beginning of a program that will demonstrate variable use. Use the System namespace, name the class **DemoVariables**, and type the class-opening curly brace.

```
using System;
public class DemoVariables
{
```

Recall from Chapter 1 that you can write C# programs in any editor with which you are comfortable.

2. In the `Main()` method, declare two variables (an integer and an unsigned integer) and assign values to them.

```
public static void Main()
{
    int anInt = -123;
    uint anUnsignedInt = 567;
```

3. Add a statement to display the two values.

```
Console.WriteLine
    ("The int is {0} and the unsigned int is {1}.",
    anInt, anUnsignedInt);
```

4. Add two closing curly braces—one that closes the `Main()` method, and one that closes the `DemoVariables` class. Align each closing curly brace vertically with the opening brace that is its partner. In other words, the first closing brace aligns with the brace that opens `Main()`, and the second aligns with the brace that opens `DemoVariables`.

          }

     }

5. Save the program as **DemoVariables.cs** and compile it. If you receive any error messages, correct the errors and compile the program again. When the file is error-free, execute the program. The output should look like Figure 2-9.

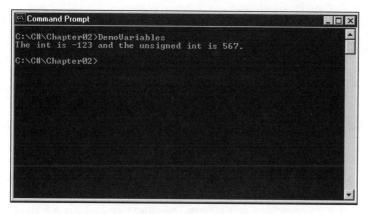

Figure 2-9   Output of DemoVariables.cs

6. Experiment with the program by introducing invalid values for the named variables. For example, change the value of `anUnsignedInt` to **−567** by typing a minus sign in front of the constant value. Compile the program. You receive an error message: *Constant value '-567' cannot be converted to a 'uint'.* Correct the error either by removing the minus sign or by changing the data type of the variable to **int**, and compile the program again. You should not receive any error messages. Remember to save your program file after you make each change and before you compile.

7. Change the value of `anInt` from −123 to **−123456789000**. When you compile the program, the following error message appears: *Cannot implicitly convert type 'long' to 'int'.* The value is a `long` because it is greater than the highest allowed int value. Correct the error either by using a lower value or by changing the variable type to **long**, and compile the program again. You should not receive any error messages.

8. Experiment with other changes to the variables. Include some variables of type `short`, `ushort`, `byte`, and `sbyte`, and experiment with their values.

USING THE STANDARD BINARY ARITHMETIC OPERATORS

Table 2-2 describes the five most commonly used binary arithmetic operators. You use these operators to manipulate values in your programs. The operators are called **binary** because you use two arguments with each—one value to the left of the operator and another value to the right of it.

 Several shortcut arithmetic operators will be discussed in the next section.

Table 2-2 Binary Arithmetic Operators

Operator	Description	Example
+	Addition	45 + 2: the result is 47
−	Subtraction	45 − 2: the result is 43
*	Multiplication	45 * 2: the result is 90
/	Division	45 / 2: the result is 22 (not 22.5)
%	Remainder (modulus)	45 % 2: the result is 1 (that is, 45 / 2 = 22 with a remainder of 1)

The operators / and % deserve special consideration. When you divide two integers, whether they are integer constants or integer variables, the result is an *integer*. In other words, any fractional part of the result is lost. For example, the result of 45 / 2 is 22, even though the result is 22.5 in a mathematical expression. When you use the remainder operator with two integers, the result is an integer with the value of the remainder after division takes place—so the result of 45 % 2 is 1 because 2 "goes into" 45 twenty-two times with a remainder of 1.

 In older languages, such as assembler, you had to perform division before you could take a remainder. In C#, you do not need to perform a division operation before you can perform a remainder operation. In other words, a remainder operation can stand alone.

In the following steps, you will add some arithmetic statements to the DemoVariables.cs program.

To use arithmetic statements in a program:

1. Open a new C# program file named **DemoVariables2** and enter the following statements to start a program that demonstrates arithmetic operations:

```
using System;
public class DemoVariables2
```

2

```
{
    public static void Main()
    {
```

2. Write a statement that will declare seven integer variables. You will assign initial values to two of the variables; the values for the other five variables will be calculated. Because all of these variables are the same type, you can use a single statement to declare all seven integers, insert commas between variable names, and place a single semicolon at the end. You can place line breaks wherever you want for readability. (Alternatively, you could use as many as seven separate declarations.)

```
int value1 = 43, value2 = 10,
        sum, diff, product, quotient, remainder;
```

3. Write the arithmetic statements that calculate the sum of, difference between, product of, quotient of, and remainder of the two assigned variables.

```
sum = value1 + value2;
diff = value1 - value2;
product = value1 * value2;
quotient = value1 / value2;
remainder = value1 % value2;
```

Instead of declaring the variables sum, diff, product, quotient, and remainder and assigning values later, you could declare and assign all of them at once, as in int sum = value1 + value2;. The only requirement is that value1 and value2 must be assigned values before you can use them in a calculation.

4. Include five WriteLine() statements to display the results.

```
Console.WriteLine
    ("The sum of {0} and {1} is {2}",value1,value2,sum);
Console.WriteLine
    ("The difference between {0} and {1} is {2}",
    value1,value2,diff);
Console.WriteLine("The product of {0} and {1} is {2}",
    value1,value2,product);
Console.WriteLine
    ("{0} divided by {1} is {2}",value1,value2,quotient);
Console.WriteLine
    ("and the remainder is {0}",remainder);
```

5. Add two closing curly braces—one for the Main() method and the other for the DemoVariables2 class.

```
    }

}
```

6. Save the file. Compile and execute the program. The output should look like Figure 2-10.

```
Command Prompt                                          _ □ ×

C:\C#\Chapter02>DemoVariables2
The sum of 43 and 10 is 53
The difference between 43 and 10 is 33
The product of 43 and 10 is 430
43 divided by 10 is 4
and the remainder is 3

C:\C#\Chapter02>_
```

Figure 2-10   Output of DemoVariables2 program

7. Change the values of the `value1` and `value2` variables and run the program again. Analyze the output to make sure you understand the arithmetic operations.

When you combine mathematical operations in a single statement, you must understand **operator precedence**, or the order in which parts of a mathematical expression are evaluated. Multiplication, division, and remainder always take place prior to addition or subtraction in an expression. For example, the expression `int result = 2 + 3 * 4;` results in 14, because the multiplication (3 * 4) occurs before adding 2. You can override normal operator precedence by putting the operation that should be performed first in parentheses. The statement `int result = (2 + 3) * 4;` results in 20, because the addition within the parentheses takes place first, and then that result (5) is multiplied by 4.

 Appendix A contains a chart describing the precedence of every C# operator.

USING SHORTCUT ARITHMETIC OPERATORS

Increasing the value held in a variable is a common programming task. Assume that you have declared a variable named `counter` that counts the number of times an event has occurred. Each time the event occurs, you want to execute a statement like `counter = counter + 1;`. Such a statement looks incorrect to an algebra student, but remember that the equal sign is not used to compare values in C#; it is used to assign values. The statement `counter = counter +1;` says "Take the value of counter, add 1 to it, and assign the result to counter."

Because increasing the value of a variable is so common, C# provides you with several shortcut ways to count and accumulate. The statement `counter += 1;` is identical in meaning to `counter = counter + 1;`. The `+=` operator adds and assigns in one step. Similarly, `bankBal += bankBal * intRate;` increases `bankBal` by a rate stored in `intRate`.

Besides the shortcut operator `+=`, you can use `–=`, `*=`, and `/=`. Each of these operators is used to perform an operation and assign the result in one step. For example:

- `balanceDue -= payment;` subtracts a payment from `balanceDue` and assigns the result to `balanceDue`.

- `rate * = 100` multiplies a rate by 100, converting a fractional value like 0.27 to a whole number like 27.

- `payment /= 12` changes a payment value from an annual to a monthly amount due.

You cannot place any spaces between the two symbols used in any of the shortcut arithmetic operators.

When you want to increase a variable's value by exactly 1, you can use two other shortcut operators—the **prefix** `++` and the **postfix** `++`. To use a prefix `++`, you type two plus signs before the variable name. The statement `someValue = 6;` followed by `++someValue` results in `someValue` holding 7, or 1 more than it held before the `++` operator was applied. To use a postfix `++`, you type two plus signs just after a variable name. Executing the statements `anotherValue = 56; anotherValue++;` results in anotherValue containing 57.

You can use the prefix ++ and postfix ++ with variables, but not with constants. An expression such as **++84** is illegal because 84 is constant and must always remain as 84. However, you can create a variable as in `int val = 84;`, and then write **++val** or **val++** to increase the variable's value to 85.

The prefix and postfix increment operators are **unary** operators because you use them with one value. Most arithmetic operators, like those used for addition and multiplication, are binary operators that operate on two values.

When you only want to increase a variable's value by 1, there is no apparent difference between using the prefix and postfix increment operators. However, these operators function differently. When you use the prefix `++`, the result is calculated and stored, and then the variable is used. For example, if `b = 4`, then `c = ++b` results in both `b` and `c` holding the value 5. When you use the postfix `++`, the variable is used, and then the result is calculated and stored. For example, if `b = 4;` and then `c = b++;`, first 4 will be assigned to `c`; *then* after the assignment, `b` is increased and takes the value 5. In other words, if `b = 4`, then the value of `b++` is also 4, but after the statement is completed, the value of `b` will be 5.

Besides the prefix and postfix increment operators, you can use a prefix or postfix **decrement operator** (--) that reduces a variable's value by 1. For example, if s and t are both assigned the value 34, then --s has the value 33 and t-- has the value 34, but t becomes 33.

USING THE BOOLEAN DATA TYPE

Boolean logic is based on true-or-false comparisons. An int variable can hold millions of different values at different times, but a **Boolean variable** can hold only one of two values—true or false. You declare a Boolean variable by using type bool. The following statements declare and assign appropriate values to two Boolean variables:

```
bool isItMonday = false;
bool areYouTired = true;
```

You also can assign values based on the result of comparisons to Boolean variables. A **comparison operator** compares two items; an expression containing a comparison operator has a Boolean value. Table 2-3 describes the six comparison operators that C# supports.

Table 2-3   Comparison Operators

Operator	Description	true Example	false Example
<	Less than	3 < 8	8 < 3
>	Greater than	4 > 2	2 > 4
==	Equal to	7 == 7	3 == 9
<=	Less than or equal to	5 <=5	8 <= 6
>=	Greater than or equal to	7 >= 3	1 >= 2
!=	Not equal to	5 != 6	3 != 3

When you use any of the operators that require two keystrokes (==, <=, >=, or !=), you cannot place any whitespace between the two symbols.

Legal, but somewhat useless, declaration statements might include the following, which compare two values directly:

```
bool isSixBigger = 6 > 5;   // Value stored would be true
bool isSevenSmallerOrEqual = 7 <= 4;
    // Value stored would be false
```

 If you begin a bool variable name with a form of the verb "to be" or "to do," such as "is" or "are," then you can more easily recognize the identifiers as Boolean variables when you encounter them within your programs.

Using Boolean values is more meaningful when you use variables (that have been assigned values) rather than constants in the comparisons, as in the following examples. In the first statement, the `hoursWorked` variable is compared to a constant value of 40. If the `hoursWorked` variable holds a value less than or equal to 40, then the expression is evaluated as false. In the second statement, the `annualIncome` variable value must be greater than 100000 for the expression to be true.

```
bool doesEmployeeReceiveOvertime = hoursWorked > 40;
bool isEmployeeInHighTaxBracket = annualIncome > 100000;
```

Next, you will write a program that demonstrates how Boolean variables operate.

To write a program that uses Boolean variables:

1. Open a new file in your editor and name it **DemoVariables3.cs**.

2. Enter the following code. In the `Main()` method, you declare an integer value, then assign different values to a Boolean variable. Notice that when you declare `value` and `isSixMore`, you assign types. When you reassign values to these variables later in the program, you do not redeclare them by using a type name. Instead, you simply assign new values to the already declared variables.

```
using System;
public class DemoVariables3
{
    public static void Main()
    {
            int value = 4;
            bool isSixMore = 6 > value;
            Console.WriteLine
              ("When value is {0} isSixMore is {1}",
              value,isSixMore);
            value = 35;
            isSixMore = 6 > value;
            Console.WriteLine
              ("When value is {0} isSixMore is {1}",
              value,isSixMore);
    }
}
```

3. Save and compile and run the program. The output looks like Figure 2-11.

4. Change the value of the variable named `value` and predict the outcome. Run the program to confirm your prediction.

Boolean variables become more useful after you learn to make decisions within C# programs.

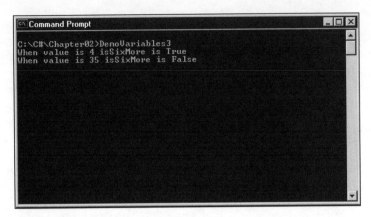

Figure 2-11 Output of DemoVariables3 program

USING FLOATING-POINT DATA TYPES

A **floating-point** number is one that contains decimal positions. C# supports three floating-point data types: float, double, and decimal. A **float** data type can hold as many as seven significant digits of accuracy. A **double** data type can hold 15 or 16 significant digits of accuracy. The term **significant digits** refers to the mathematical accuracy of a value. For example, a double given the value 123456789.987654321 will appear as 123456789.98765433 (notice the rightmost digit) because it is accurate to only the sixteenth digit, or the seventh digit to the right of the decimal point. Compared to floats and doubles, the **decimal** type has a greater precision and a smaller range, which makes it suitable for financial and monetary calculations. For example, a decimal given the value 123456789.987654321 will appear as 123456789.987654321 (notice that it is accurate to the rightmost digit). A decimal cannot hold as large a value as a double can, but the decimal will be more accurate to more decimal places.

Just as an integer constant such as 178 is an int by default, a floating-point number constant such as 18.23 is a double by default. To explicitly store a value as a float, you may place an *F* after the number, as in `float pocketChange = 4.87F;`. Either a lowercase or uppercase *F* can be used. You can also place a *D* (or *d*) after a floating-point value to indicate that it is a double; even without the *D*, however, it will be stored as a double by default. To explicitly store a value as a decimal, use an *M* (or *m*) after the number. (*M* stands for monetary; *D* can't be used for decimals because it indicates double.)

As with ints, you can add, subtract, multiply, and divide with floating-point numbers. Unlike with ints, however, you cannot perform modulus operations with such numbers. (Floating-point division results in a floating-point answer, so there is no remainder.)

If you store a value that is too large in a floating-point variable, you will see output expressed in **scientific notation**. Values expressed in scientific notation include an *E* (for exponent). For example, if you declare `float f = 1234567890f;`, the value will appear as 1.234568E9, meaning that it is approximately 1.234568 times 10 to the ninth power, or 1.234568 with the decimal point moved nine positions to the right.

2

FORMATTING FLOATING-POINT VALUES

By default, C# always displays floating-point numbers in the most concise way it can while maintaining the correct value. For example, if you declare a variable as `double myMoney = 14.00;` and then display it on screen with a statement such as `Console.WriteLine("The amount is {0}", myMoney);`, the output will appear as "The amount is 14". The two zeros to the right of the decimal point will not appear because they add no mathematical information. To see the decimal places, you can convert the floating-point value to a String using a standard numeric format string.

Standard numeric format strings are strings of characters expressed within double quotation marks that indicate a format for output. They take the form *X0*, where *X* is the format specifier and *0* is the precision specifier. The **format specifier** can be one of nine built-in format characters that define the most commonly used numeric format types. The **precision specifier** controls the number of significant digits or zeros to the right of the decimal point. Table 2-4 lists the nine format specifiers.

Table 2-4   Format Specifiers

Format Character	Description	Default Format (if no precision is given)
C or c	Currency	$XX,XX.XX ($XX,XXX.XX)
D or d	Decimal	[-]XXXXXXX
E or e	Scientific (exponential)	[-]X.XXXXXXE+xxx [-]X.XXXXXXe+xxx [-]X.XXXXXXE-xxx [-]X.XXXXXXe-xxx
F or f	Fixed-point	[-]XXXXXXX.XX
G or g	General	Variable; either general or scientific
N or n	Number	[-]XX,XXX.XX
P or p	Percent	Represents a passed numeric value as a percentage
R or r	Round trip	Ensures that numbers converted to strings will have the same values when they are converted back into numbers
X or x	Hexadecimal	Minimum hexadecimal (base 16) representation

You can use a format specifier with the `ToString()` method to convert a number into a string that has the desired format. For example, you can use the *F* format specifier to insert a decimal to the right of a nondecimal number, followed by the number of zeros indicated by the precision specifier. (If no precision specifier is supplied, two zeros will be inserted.) For example, the first `WriteLine()` statement in the following code produces 123.00, and the second produces 123.000:

```
double someMoney = 123;
string moneyString;
moneyString = someMoney.ToString("F");
Console.WriteLine(moneyString);
moneyString = someMoney.ToString("F3");
Console.WriteLine(moneyString);
```

You will learn more about strings later in this chapter.

You will learn more about creating and using methods in Chapter 3.

You use C as the format specifier when you want to represent a number as a currency value. Currency values appear with a dollar sign and appropriate commas as well as the desired number of decimal places, and negative values appear within parentheses. The integer you use following the *C* indicates the number of decimal places. If you do not provide a value for the number of decimal places, then two digits are shown after the decimal separator by default. For example, both of the following `WriteLine()` statements produce $456,789.00:

```
double moneyValue = 456789;
string conversion;
conversion = moneyValue.ToString("C");
Console.WriteLine(conversion);
conversion = moneyValue.ToString("C2");
Console.WriteLine(conversion);
```

Currency appears with a dollar sign and commas in the English **culture**, a set of rules that determines how culturally dependent values such as money and dates are formatted. You can change a program's culture by using the CultureInfoClass. The .NET framework supports more than 200 culture settings, such as Japanese, French, Urdu, and Sanskrit.

To display a numeric value as a formatted string, you are not required to create a separate String object. You also can make the conversion in a single statement; for example, the following code displays $12,345.00:

```
double payAmount = 12345;
Console.WriteLine(payAmount.ToString("c2"));
```

UNDERSTANDING NUMERIC TYPE CONVERSION

When performing arithmetic with variables or constants of the same type, the result of the arithmetic retains the same type. For example, when you divide two integers, the result is an integer; when you subtract two doubles, the result is a double. Often, however, you need to perform mathematical operations on different types. For example, in the following code you multiply an integer by a double:

```
int hoursWorked = 36;
double payRate = 12.35;
double grossPay = hoursWorked * payRate;
```

 An operand is any value used in an arithmetic or logical operation.

When you perform arithmetic operations with operands of dissimilar types, C# chooses a **unifying type** for the result and **implicitly** (or automatically) converts nonconforming operands to the unifying type. For example, if you multiply an int and a double, the result is implicitly a double. This requirement means the result must be stored in a double; if you attempt to assign the result to an int, you will receive a compiler error message.

The implicit numeric conversions are

- From `sbyte` to `short`, `int`, `long`, `float`, `double`, or `decimal`
- From `byte` to `short`, `ushort`, `int`, `uint`, `long`, `ulong`, `float`, `double`, or `decimal`
- From `short` to `int`, `long`, `float`, `double`, or `decimal`
- From `ushort` to `int`, `uint`, `long`, `ulong`, `float`, `double`, or `decimal`
- From `int` to `long`, `float`, `double`, or `decimal`
- From `uint` to `long`, `ulong`, `float`, `double`, or `decimal`
- From `long` to `float`, `double`, or `decimal`
- From `long` to `float`, `double`, or `decimal`
- From `char` to `ushort`, `int`, `uint`, `long`, `ulong`, `float`, `double`, or `decimal`
- From `float` to `double`.

 Conversions from `int`, `uint`, or `long` to `float` and from `long` to `double` may cause a loss of precision, but will never cause a loss of magnitude.

A constant expression of type `int`, such as 25, can be converted to `sbyte`, `byte`, `short`, `ushort`, `uint`   or   `ulong`. For example, `sbyte age = 19;` is legal. However, you must make sure that the value of the constant expression is within the range of the destination type.

You may **explicitly** (or purposefully) override the unifying type imposed by C# by performing a cast. A **cast** involves placing the desired result type in parentheses followed by the variable or constant to be cast. For example, two casts are performed in the following code:

```
double bankBalance = 189.66;
float weeklyBudget = (float) bankBalance / 4;
        // weeklyBudget is 47.415, one-fourth of bankBalance
int dollars = (int) weeklyBudget;
        // dollars is 47, the integer part of weeklyBudget
```

The value of `bankBalance / 4` is implicitly a double because a double divided by an int produces a double. The double result is then converted to a float before it is stored in `weeklyBudget`, and the float value `weeklyBudget` is converted to an int before it is stored in dollars. When the float value is converted to an int, the decimal-place values are lost.

 It is easy to lose data when performing a cast. For example, the largest byte value is 255 and the largest int value is 2,147,483,647, so the following statements produce distorted results:

```
int anOkayInt = 345;
byte aBadByte = (byte)anOkayInt;
```

 The highest value that a byte can hold is 255. If you attempt to store 256 in a byte, you will receive an error message unless you place the statement in a block preceded by the keyword `unchecked`, which tells the compiler not to check for invalid data. If you use the unchecked mode and store 256 in a byte, the results will look the same as storing 0; if you store 257, the result will appear as 1. You will see 89 when you store 345 in a byte variable and display the results, because the value 89 is exactly 256 less than 345.

USING THE CHAR DATA TYPE

You use the **char** data type to hold any single character. You place constant character values within single quotation marks because the computer stores characters and integers differently. For example, the statements `char aCharValue = '9';` and `int aNumValue = 9;` are both legal. The statements `char aCharValue = 9;` and `int aNumValue = '9'` are both illegal. A number can be a character, in which case it must be enclosed in single quotation marks and declared as a char type. An alphabetic letter, however, cannot be stored in a numeric type variable. The following code shows how you can store several characters using the char data type:

```
char myInitial = 'J';
char percentSign = '%';
char numThatIsAChar = '9';
```

 A variable of type char can hold only one character. To store a string of characters, such as a person's name, you must use a string. You will learn about strings later in this chapter.

You can store any character—including nonprinting characters such as a backspace or a tab—in a char variable. To store these characters, you use an **escape sequence**, which always begins with a backslash. For example, the following code stores a backspace character and a tab character in the char variables **aBackspaceChar** and **aTabChar**, respectively:

```
char aBackspaceChar = '\b';
char aTabChar = '\t';
```

In the preceding code, the escape sequence indicates a unique value for each character—a backspace or tab instead of the letter *b* or *t*. Table 2-5 describes some common escape sequences that are used in C#.

Table 2-5   Common Escape Sequences

Escape Sequence	Character Name
\'	Single quotation mark
\"	Double quotation mark
\\	Backslash
\0	Null
\a	Alert
\b	Backspace
\f	Form feed
\n	Newline
\r	Carriage return
\t	Horizontal tab
\v	Vertical tab

The characters used in C# are represented in **Unicode**, which is a 16-bit coding scheme for characters. For example, the letter *A* actually is stored in computer memory as a set of 16 zeros and ones—namely, 0000 0000 0100 0001. (The spaces are inserted here after every set of four digits for readability.) Because 16-digit numbers are difficult to read, programmers often use a shorthand notation called **hexadecimal**, or **base 16**. In hexadecimal shorthand, 0000 becomes 0, 0100 becomes 4, and 0001 becomes 1. Thus the letter *A* is represented in hexadecimal as 0041. You tell the compiler to treat the four-digit hexadecimal 0041 as a single character by preceding it with the \u escape sequence. Therefore, there are two ways to store the character *A*:

```
char letter = 'A';
char letter = '\u0041';
```

For more information about Unicode, go to *www.unicode.org*.

The second option for using hexadecimal obviously is more difficult and confusing than the first option, so it is not recommended that you store letters of the alphabet using the hexadecimal method. However, you can produce some interesting values using the Unicode format. For example, letters from foreign alphabets that use characters instead of letters (Greek, Hebrew, Chinese, and so on) and other special symbols (foreign currency symbols, mathematical symbols, geometric shapes, and so on) are not available on a standard keyboard, so you should know how to use Unicode characters.

Next, you will write a short program to demonstrate the use of escape sequences.

To write a program using escape sequences:

1. Open a new file in your text editor and name it **DemoEscapeSequences**.

2. Enter the following code. The three `WriteLine()` statements demonstrate using tabs, a newline, and alerts.

```
using System;
public class DemoEscapeSequences
{
    public static void Main()
    {
        Console.WriteLine
          ("This line\tcontains two\ttabs");
        Console.WriteLine
          ("This statement\ncontains a new line");
        Console.WriteLine
          ("This statement sounds three alerts\a\a\a");
    }
}
```

3. Save, compile, and test the program. Your output should look like Figure 2-12. Additionally, if your system has speakers, you should hear three "beep" sounds caused by the three '\a' characters.

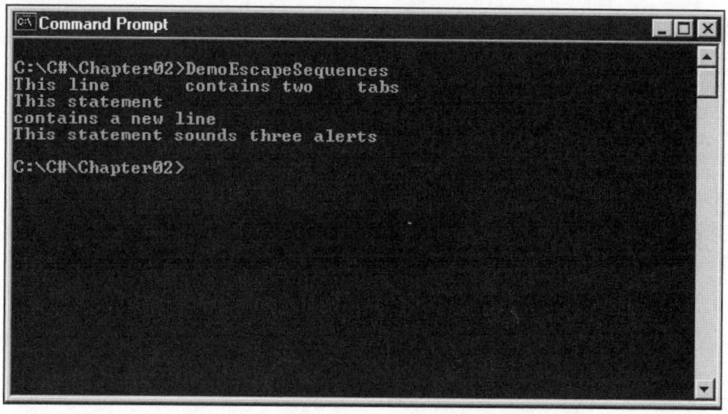

Figure 2-12   Output of DemoEscapeSequences

USING THE STRING DATA TYPE

In C#, you use the **string** data type to hold a series of characters. The value of a string is always expressed within double quotation marks. For example, the following statement declares a string named **firstName** and assigns "Jane" to it:

```
string firstName = "Jane";
```

When you assign a literal (such as "Jane") to a string, you can compare the string to another string using the == operator in the same way that you compare numeric or character variables. For example, the program in Figure 2-13 declares three string variables. Figure 2-14 shows the results: strings that contain "Amy" and "Amy" are considered equal, but strings that contain "Amy" and "Matthew" are not.

```
using System;
public class CompareNames1

{
    public static void Main()
    {
        string name1 = "Amy";
        string name2 = "Amy";
        string name3 = "Matthew";
        Console.WriteLine("compare {0} to {1}: {2}",
            name1,name2,name1==name2);
        Console.WriteLine("compare {0} to {1}: {2}",
            name1,name3,name1==name3);
    }
}
```

Figure 2-13   Program that compares two strings using ==

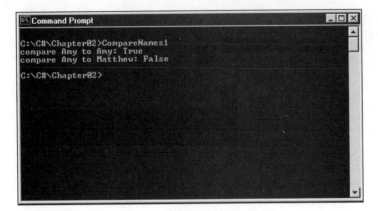

Figure 2-14 Output of CompareNames1 program that uses ==

You can use the == comparison operator with strings that are assigned literal values, but you cannot use it with strings that are created through several other methods. Also, the comparison operators == and != are the only two you can use with strings. The greater than and less than operators (>, <, >=, and <=) do not work with string arguments. For these reasons, the creators of C# recommend that you not use the comparison operators with strings, but instead use the **Equals()** or **Compare()** methods that belong to the String class.

The **Equals()** method requires two string arguments. As when you use the == operator, the **Equals()** method returns true or false. The **Compare()** method also requires two string arguments. When it returns a zero, the two strings are equivalent; when it returns a positive number, the first string is greater than the second; and when it returns a negative value, the first string is less than the second. A string is considered greater than another string when it is greater **lexically**, which in the case of letter values means alphabetically. That is, when you compare two strings, you compare each character in turn from left to right. If each Unicode value is the same, then the strings are equivalent. If any corresponding character values are different, the string that has the greater Unicode value earlier in the string is considered greater. Figure 2-15 shows a program that makes several comparisons using the **Equals()** and **Compare()** methods. Figure 2-16 shows the program's output.

The **Equals()** and **Compare()** methods are case sensitive. In other words, "Amy" does not equal "amy". In Unicode, all uppercase letters have lower values than their lowercase equivalents.

2

```
using System;
public class CompareNames2
{
    public static void Main()
    {
        string name1 = "Amy";
        string name2 = "Amy";
        string name3 = "Matthew";
        Console.WriteLine("compare {0} to {1}: {2}",
            name1,name2,String.Equals(name1,name2));
        Console.WriteLine("compare {0} to {1}: {2}",
            name1,name3,String.Equals(name1,name3));
        Console.WriteLine("compare {0} to {1}: {2}",
            name1,name2,String.Compare(name1,name2));
        Console.WriteLine("compare {0} to {1}: {2}",
            name1,name3,String.Compare(name1,name3));
    }
}
```

Figure 2-15   Program that compares two strings using `Equals()` and `Compare()`

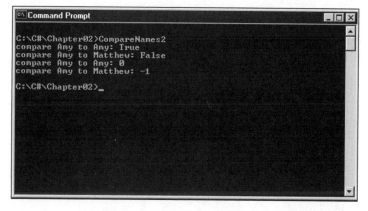

Figure 2-16   Output of CompareNames2 program that uses `Equals()` and `Compare()`

In C#, a string is **immutable**. That is, a string's value is not actually modified when you assign a new value to it. For example, when you write `name = "Amy";` followed by `name = "Donald";`, the first characters "Amy" still exist in computer memory, but the name variable no longer refers to their memory address. The situation is different than with numbers; when you assign a new value to a numeric variable, the value at the named memory address actually changes.

DEFINING NAMED CONSTANTS

By definition, a variable's value can vary, or change. Sometimes you want to create a **named constant** (often called simply a constant), an identifier whose contents cannot change. You create a named constant similarly to the way in which you create a named variable but by using the keyword `const`. Although there is no requirement to do so, programmers usually name constants using all uppercase letters, inserting underscores for readability. This convention makes constant names stand out so that the reader is less likely to confuse them with changeable variable names. For example, `const double TAX_RATE = .06;` declares a constant named **TAX_RATE** that is assigned a value of .06. You must assign a value to a constant when you create it. You can use a constant just as you would use a variable of the same type—for example, display it or use it in a mathematical equation—but you cannot assign any new value to it. Figure 2-17 shows a program that uses a **TAX_RATE** constant to calculate the tax on two different-priced items. Figure 2-18 shows the output.

```
using System;
public class SalesTax
{
        public static void Main()
        {
                const double TAX_RATE = .06;
                double itemPrice = 3.99;
                double total;
                total = itemPrice * TAX_RATE;
                Console.WriteLine("With {0} tax, a {1} item costs {2} more",
                        TAX_RATE, itemPrice.ToString("C"), total.ToString("C"));
                itemPrice = 145.65;
                total = itemPrice * TAX_RATE;
                Console.WriteLine("With {0} tax, a {1} item costs {2} more",
                        TAX_RATE, itemPrice.ToString("C"), total.ToString("C"));
        }
}
```

Figure 2-17   SalesTax program

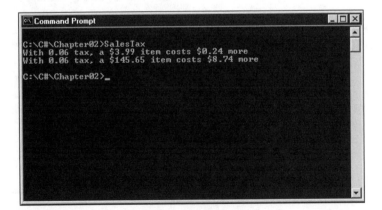

Figure 2-18   Output of SalesTax program

It's good programming practice to declare constants for any value that should never change; doing so makes your programs clearer. For example, when you declare a constant `const int INCHES_IN_A_FOOT = 12;` within a program, then you can use a statement such as `lengthInInches = lengthInFeet * INCHES_IN_A_FOOT;`. This statement is **self-documenting**; that is, even without a program comment, it is easy for someone reading your program to tell why you performed the calculation in the way you did.

ACCEPTING CONSOLE INPUT

When you write a program in which you assign values to variables and then manipulate those values, the output of the program is always the same. For example, no matter how many times you execute the SalesTax program in Figure 2-17, the two tax values are always calculated as $0.24 and $8.74. A more useful program would allow a user to input any price for which the tax could be calculated. A program that allows user input is an **interactive program**.

You can use the `Console.ReadLine()` method to accept user input from the keyboard. This method accepts all of the characters entered by a user until the user presses Enter. The characters can be assigned to a string. For example, the statement `myString = Console.ReadLine();` accepts a user's input and stores it in the variable `myString`. If you want to use the data as a string—for example, if the input is a word—then you simply use the variable to which you assigned the value. If you want to use the data as a number, then you must use a `Convert()` method to convert the input string to the proper type.

 The `Console.Read()` method is similar to the `Console.ReadLine()` method. `Console.Read()` reads just one character from the input stream, whereas `Console.ReadLine()` reads every character in the input stream until the user presses the Enter key.

Figure 2-19 shows an interactive program that prompts the user for a price and calculates a 6 percent sales tax. The program displays "Enter the price of an item" on the screen. Such an instruction to the user to enter data is called a **prompt**. After the prompt appears, the `Console.ReadLine()` statement accepts a string of characters and assigns them to the variable itemPriceAsString. Before the tax can be calculated, this value must be converted to a number. This conversion is accomplished with the statement `itemPrice = Convert.ToDouble(itemPriceAsString);`. Figure 2-20 shows a typical run of the program. (In this execution, the user typed 67.12 as the input value.)

```
using System;
public class InteractiveSalesTax
{
      public static void Main()
      {
            const double taxRate = .06;
            string itemPriceAsString;
            double itemPrice;
            double total;
            Console.WriteLine("Enter the price of an item");
            itemPriceAsString = Console.ReadLine();
            itemPrice = Convert.ToDouble(itemPriceAsString);
            total = itemPrice * taxRate;
            Console.WriteLine("With {0} tax, a {1} item costs {2} more",
                  taxRate, itemPrice.ToString("C"), total.ToString("C"));

      }
}
```

Figure 2-19   InteractiveSalesTax program

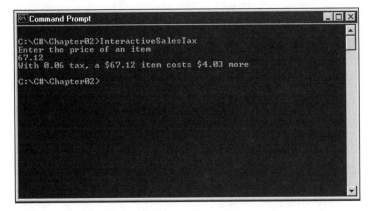

Figure 2-20   Output of InteractiveSalesTax program

Table 2-6 shows Convert class methods you can use to change strings into more useful data types. The methods use the class types (also called run-time types) in their names. For example, recall from Table 2-1 that the "formal" name for an int is Int32, so the method you use to convert a string to an integer is named `Convert.ToInt32()`.

Table 2-6   Selected Convert Class Methods

Method	Description
ToBoolean()	Converts a specified value to an equivalent Boolean value
ToByte()	Converts a specified value to an 8-bit unsigned integer
ToChar()	Converts a specified value to a Unicode character

Table 2-6   Selected Convert Class Methods (continued)

Method	Description
ToDecimal()	Converts a specified value to a decimal number
ToDouble()	Converts a specified value to a double-precision floating-point number
ToInt16()	Converts a specified value to a 16-bit signed integer
ToInt32()	Converts a specified value to a 32-bit signed integer
ToInt64()	Converts a specified value to a 64-bit signed integer
ToSByte()	Converts a specified value to an 8-bit signed integer
ToSingle()	Converts a specified value to a single-precision floating-point number
ToString()	Converts the specified value to its equivalent String representation
ToUInt16()	Converts a specified value to a 16-bit unsigned integer
ToUInt32()	Converts a specified value to a 32-bit unsigned integer
ToUInt64()	Converts a specified value to a 64-bit unsigned integer

In the next steps, you will write an interactive program that allows the user to enter two integer values. The program then calculates and displays their sum.

To write the interactive addition program:

1. Open a new file in your editor. Type the first few lines needed for the Main() method of an InteractiveAddition class:

```
using System;
public class InteractiveAddition
{
  public static void Main()
  {
```

2. Add variable declarations for two strings that will accept the user's input values. Also, declare three integers for the numeric equivalents of the string input values and their sum.

```
string name, firstString, secondString;
int first, second, sum;
```

3. Prompt the user for his or her name, accept it into the name string, and then display a personalized greeting to the user, along with the prompt for the first integer value.

```
Console.WriteLine("Enter your name");
name = Console.ReadLine();
Console.WriteLine("Hello {0}! Enter the first integer",
  name);
```

4. Accept the user's input as a string, and then convert the input string to an integer.

```
firstString = Console.ReadLine();
first = Convert.ToInt32(firstString);
```

5. Add statements that prompt for and accept the second integer and convert it to a string.

```
Console.WriteLine("Enter the second integer");
secondString = Console.ReadLine();
second = Convert.ToInt32(secondString);
```

6. Assign the sum of the two integers to the sum variable and display all of the values. Add the closing curly brace for the `Main()` method and the closing curly brace for the class.

```
sum = first + second;
Console.WriteLine("{0}, the sum of {1} and {2} is {3}",
   name, first, second, sum);
   }
}
```

7. Save the file as **InteractiveAddition.cs** in the Chapter.02 folder of your Student Disk. Compile and run the program. When you are prompted to do so, supply your name and any integers you want, and confirm that the result appears correctly. Figure 2-21 shows a typical run of the program.

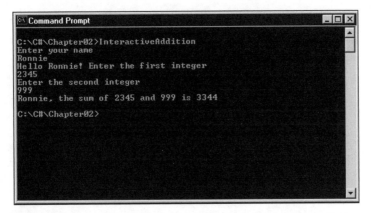

Figure 2-21   Typical run of InteractiveAddition program

CHAPTER SUMMARY

❑ Data is constant when it cannot be changed after a program is compiled; data is variable when it might change. C# provides for 14 basic built-in types of data. A variable declaration includes a data type, an identifier, an optional assigned value, and a semicolon.

❑ You can display variable values by using the variable name within a `WriteLine()` or `Write()` method call. To make producing output easier, you can combine strings and variable values into a single `Write()` or `WriteLine()` statement by using a format string.

2

❑ In C#, nine data types are considered integral data types—byte, sbyte, short, ushort, int, uint, long, ulong, and char.

❑ You use the binary arithmetic operators +, -, *, /, and % to manipulate values in your programs. When you combine mathematical operations in a single statement, you must understand operator precedence, or the order in which parts of a mathematical expression are evaluated. Multiplication, division, and remainder always take place prior to addition or subtraction in an expression, unless you use parentheses to override the normal precedence.

❑ Because increasing the value of a variable is a common task, C# provides you with several shortcut arithmetic operators. They include +=, -=, *=, /=, and the prefix and postfix increment and decrement operators.

❑ A Boolean variable can hold only one of two values—true or false. C# supports six comparison operators: >, <, >=, <=, ==, and !=. An expression containing a comparison operator has a Boolean value.

❑ C# supports three floating-point data types: float, double, and decimal. You can perform the mathematical operations of addition, subtraction, multiplication, and division with floating-point data, but not modulus. You can use format and precision specifiers to display floating-point data to a specified number of decimal places.

❑ When you perform arithmetic with variables or constants of the same type, the result of the arithmetic retains the same type. When you perform arithmetic operations with operands of different types, C# chooses a unifying type for the result and implicitly converts nonconforming operands to the unifying type. You may explicitly override the unifying type imposed by C# by performing a cast.

❑ You use the char data type to hold any single character. You place constant character values within single quotation marks. You can store any character—including nonprinting characters such as a backspace or a tab—in a char variable. To store these characters, you must use an escape sequence, which always begins with a backslash.

❑ In C#, you use the string data type to hold a series of characters. The value of a string is always expressed within double quotation marks. Although the == and != comparison operators can be used with strings that are assigned literal values, you should instead use the Equals() and Compare() methods that belong to the String class.

❑ Named constants are program identifiers you cannot change.

❑ You can use the Console.ReadLine() method to accept user input. Often you must use a Convert class method to change the input string into a usable data type.

REVIEW QUESTIONS

1. When you use a number like 45 in a C# program, the number is a
   _____.

   a. literal constant

   b. figurative constant

   c. literal variable

   d. figurative variable

2. A variable declaration must contain all of the following *except* a(n)
   _____.

   a. data type

   b. identifier

   c. assigned value

   d. ending semicolon

3. Which of the following is true of variable declarations?

   a. Two variables of the same type can be declared in the same statement.

   b. Two variables of different types can be declared in the same statement.

   c. Two variables of the same type must be declared in the same statement.

   d. Two variables of the same type cannot coexist in a program.

4. Assume you have two variables declared as int var1 = 3; and
   int var2 = 8;. Which of the following would display *838*?

   a. `Console.WriteLine("{0}{1}{2}",var1, var2);`

   b. `Console.WriteLine("{0}{1}{0}",var1, var2);`

   c. `Console.WriteLine("{0}{1}{2}",var2, var1);`

   d. `Console.WriteLine("{0}{1}{0}",var2, var1);`

5. Assume you have a variable declared as int var1 = 3;. Which of the following
   would display *X 3X?*

   a. `Console.WriteLine("X{0}X",var1);`

   b. `Console.WriteLine("X{0,2}X",var1);`

   c. `Console.WriteLine("X{2,0}X",var1);`

   d. `Console.WriteLine("X{0}{2}",var1);`

6. Assume you have a variable declared as int var1 = 3;. What is the value of
   `22 % var1`?

   a. 0

   b. 1

   c. 7

   d. 21

7. Assume you have a variable declared as `int var1 = 3;`. What is the value of `22 / var1`?

    a. 0

    b. 1

    c. 7

    d. 21

8. What is the value of the expression `4 + 2 * 3`?

    a. 0

    b. 10

    c. 18

    d. 36

9. Assume you have a variable declared as `int var1 = 3;`. If `var2 = ++var1`, what is the value of `var2`?

    a. 2

    b. 3

    c. 4

    d. 5

10. Assume you have a variable declared as `int var1 = 3;`. If `var2 = var1++`, what is the value of `var2`?

    a. 2

    b. 3

    c. 4

    d. 5

11. A variable that can hold the two values `true` and `false` is of type
    _____.

    a. integer

    b. Boolean

    c. character

    d. barbarian

12. Which of the following is *not* a C# comparison operator?

    a. `=>`

    b. `!=`

    c. `==`

    d. `<`

13. What is the value of the expression 6 >= 7?

    a. 0

    b. 1

    c. true

    d. false

14. Which of the following C# types *cannot* contain floating-point numbers?

    a. float

    b. double

    c. decimal

    d. int

15. Assume you have declared a variable as `double hourly = 13.00;`. What will the statement `Console.WriteLine(hourly);` display?

    a. 13

    b. 13.0

    c. 13.00

    d. 13.000000

16. Assume you have declared a variable as `double salary = 45000.00;`. Which of the following will display `$45,000.00`?

    a. `Console.WriteLine(salary.toString( "f", null ));`

    b. `Console.WriteLine(salary.toString("c",null));`

    c. `Console.WriteLine(salary);`

    d. two of these

17. When you perform arithmetic operations with operands of different types, such as adding an int and a float, _____.

    a. C# chooses a unifying type for the result

    b. you must choose a unifying type for the result

    c. you must provide a cast

    d. you receive an error message

18. Unicode is _____.

    a. an object–oriented language

    b. a subset of the C# language

    c. a 16-bit coding scheme

    d. another term for hexadecimal

19. Which of the following declares a variable that can hold the word *computer*?
    a. `string device = 'computer';`
    b. `string device = "computer";`
    c. `char device = 'computer';`
    d. `char device = "computer";`

20. Which of the following is the best way to compare two string variables named `string1` and `string2` to determine if their contents are equal?
    a. string1 = string2
    b. string1 == string2
    c. Equals.String(string1,string2)
    d. String.Equals(string1,string2)

EXERCISES

1. What is the numeric value of each of the following expressions, as evaluated by the C# programming language?
    a. 4 + 2 * 3 _____
    b. 6 / 4 * 7 _____
    c. 16 / 2 + 14 / 2 _____
    d. 18 / 2 _____
    e. 17 / 2 _____
    f. 32 / 5 _____
    g. 14 % 2 _____
    h. 15 % 2 _____
    i. 28 % 5 _____
    j. 28 % 4 * 3 + 1 _____
    k. (2 + 6) * 4 _____
    l. 20 / (4 + 1) _____

2. What is the value of each of the following Boolean expressions?
    a. 5 > 2 _____
    b. 6 <= 18 _____
    c. 49 >= 49 _____
    d. 2 == 3 _____
    e. 2 + 6 == 7 _____
    f. 3 + 7 <= 10 _____

g. 3 != 9 _____

h. 12 != 12 _____

i. −2 != 2 _____

j. 2 + 5 * 3 ==21 _____

3. Are any of the following expressions illegal? For the legal expressions, what is the numeric value of each statement, as evaluated by the C# programming language?

a. 2.2 * 1.4

b. 6.78 − 2

c. 24.0 / 6.0

d. 7.0 % 3.0

e. 9 % 2.0

4. Choose the best data type for each of the following, so that no memory storage is wasted. Give an example of a typical value that would be held by the variable and explain why you chose the type you did.

a. your age

b. the U.S. national debt

c. your shoe size

d. your middle initial

5. Write a C# program that declares variables to represent the length and width of a room in feet. Assign appropriate values to the variables, such as `length = 15` and `width = 25`. Compute and display the floor space of the room in square feet (area = length * width). As output, do not display only a value; instead, display explanatory text with the value, such as `The floor space is 375 square feet..` Save the program as **Room.cs** in the Chapter.02 folder on your Student Disk.

6. Write a C# program that declares variables to represent the length and width of a room in feet, and the price of carpeting *per square foot* in dollars and cents. Assign appropriate values to the variables. Compute and display, with explanatory text, the cost of carpeting the room. Save the program as **Carpet.cs** in the Chapter.02 folder on your Student Disk.

7. Write a program that declares variables to represent the length and width of a room in feet, and the price of carpeting *per square yard* in dollars and cents. Assign the value 25 to the length variable and the value 42 to the width variable. Compute and display the cost of carpeting the room. (*Hint:* There are nine square feet in one square yard.) Save the program as **Yards.cs** in the Chapter.02 folder on your Student Disk.

8. Write a program that declares a `minutes` variable to represent minutes worked on a job, and assign a value to it. Display the value in hours and minutes. For example, 197 minutes becomes 3 hours and 17 minutes. Save the program as **HoursAndMinutes.cs** in the Chapter.02 folder on your Student Disk.

2

9. Write a program that declares four variables to hold the number of eggs produced in a month by each of four chickens, and assign a value to each variable. Sum the eggs, then display the total in dozens and eggs. For example, a total of 127 eggs is 10 dozen and 7 eggs. Save the program as **Eggs.cs** in the Chapter.02 folder on your Student Disk.

10. Modify the Eggs program in Exercise 9 so it accepts a number of eggs for each chicken from the user. Save the program as **EggsInteractive.cs** in the Chapter.02 folder on your Student Disk.

11. Write a program that declares five variables to hold scores for five tests you have taken, and assign a value to each variable. Display the average of the tests, to two decimal places. Save the program as **Tests.cs** in the Chapter.02 folder on your Student Disk.

12. Modify the Tests program in Exercise 11 so it accepts five test scores from a user. Save the program as **TestsInteractive.cs** in the Chapter.02 folder on your Student Disk.

13. Write a program that declares two variables to hold the names of two of your friends, and assign a value to each variable. Display the result of using the `String.Compare()` method with your friends' names. Save the program as **TwoFriends.cs** in the Chapter.02 folder on your Student Disk.

14. Modify the TwoFriends program in Exercise 13 so it accepts your friends' names from the keyboard. Save the program as **TwoFriendsInteractive.cs** in the Chapter.02 folder on your Student Disk.

15. Each of the following files in the Chapter.02 folder on your Student Disk has syntax and/or logical errors. In each case, determine the problem and fix the program. After you correct the errors, save each file using the same filename preceded with "Fixed". For example, DebugTwo1.cs will become FixedDebugTwo1.cs.

    a. DebugTwo1.cs

    b. DebugTwo2.cs

    c. DebugTwo3.cs

    d. DebugTwo4.cs

3

USING METHODS

In this chapter you will learn:

♦ How to write methods with no arguments and no return value
♦ About implementation hiding and how to use multiple files
♦ How to write methods that require a single argument
♦ How to write methods that require multiple arguments
♦ How to write methods that return a value
♦ How to use reference and output parameters with methods
♦ How to overload methods
♦ How to avoid ambiguous methods

In Chapters 1 and 2, you learned to create C# programs containing `Main()` methods that declare variables, accept input, perform arithmetic, and produce output. As your programs grow in complexity, their `Main()` methods will contain many additional statements. Rather than creating increasingly long `Main()` methods, most programmers prefer to modularize their programs, placing instructions in smaller "packages". In this chapter, you learn to create many types of C# methods. You will gain the ability to send data to these methods, and to receive information back from them.

WRITING METHODS WITH NO ARGUMENTS AND NO RETURN VALUE

A **method** is a series of statements that carry out a task. Any class can contain an unlimited number of methods. So far, you have written classes that contain a `Main()` method, but no others. All of these classes have **invoked**, or **called**, a method named `WriteLine()`. For example, consider the simple HelloClass shown in Figure 3-1. The `Main()` method contains a statement that calls the `Console.WriteLine()` method. You can easily identify method names because they are always followed by a set of parentheses. Depending on the method, there might be an **argument** within the parentheses. The call to the `WriteLine()` method within the HelloClass in Figure 3-1 contains the string argument "Hello". The simplest methods you can invoke don't require any arguments.

 Methods are similar to the procedures, functions, and subroutines used in other programming languages.

```
using System;
public class HelloClass
{
      public static void Main()
      {
            Console.WriteLine("Hello");
      }
}
```

Figure 3-1   The HelloClass

When you call the `WriteLine()` method within the HelloClass in Figure 3-1, you use a method that has already been created for you. Because the creators of C# knew you would often want to write a message to the output screen, they created a method that you could call. This method takes care of all the hardware details of producing a message on the output device; you simply call the method and pass the desired message to it. The creators of C# were able to anticipate many of the methods you would need for your programs; you will use many of these methods throughout this book. However, your programs often will require custom methods that the creators of C# could not have expected.

For example, the output of the program in Figure 3-1 is simply the word "Hello". Suppose you want to add three more lines of output to display a standard welcoming message when users execute your program. Of course, you can add three new `WriteLine()` statements to the existing program, but you also can create a method to display the three new lines.

There are two major reasons to create a method instead of adding three lines to the existing program:

- If you add a method call instead of three new lines, the `Main()` method will remain short and easy to follow. The `Main()` method will contain just one statement that calls a method rather than three separate `WriteLine()` statements.

- More importantly, a method is easily *reusable*. After you create the welcoming method, you can use it in any program. In other words, you do the work once, and then you can use the method many times.

In C#, a method must include:

- A method declaration (or header or definition)

- An opening curly brace

- A method body

- A closing curly brace

The method declaration contains:

- Optional declared accessibility

- An optional `static` modifier

- The return type for the method

- The method name

- An opening parenthesis

- An optional list of method arguments (you separate the arguments with commas if there is more than one)

- A closing parenthesis

The optional declared accessibility for a method can be any of the following modifiers:

- **Public**, which you select by including a `public` modifier in the member declaration. This modifier allows unlimited access to a method.

- **Protected internal**, which you select by including both a `protected` and an `internal` modifier in the member declaration. This modifier limits method access to the containing program or types derived from the containing class.

- **Protected**, which you select by including a `protected` modifier in the member declaration. This modifier limits method access to the containing class or types derived from the containing class.

- **Internal**, which you select by including an `internal` modifier in the member declaration. This modifier limits method access to the containing program.

- **Private**, which you select by including a `private` modifier in the member declaration. This modifier limits method access to the containing type.

If you do not provide an accessibility modifier for a method, it is private by default. As you study C#, deciding which access modifier to choose will become clearer; for example, when you begin to create your own class objects, you usually will provide them with public methods, but sometimes you will make methods private. For now, we will create methods to be public.

Additionally, you can declare a method to be static or nonstatic. If you use the keyword modifier `static`, you indicate that a method can be called without referring to an object. If you do not indicate that a method is static, it is nonstatic by default. When you begin to create your own class objects, you will write many nonstatic methods and your understanding of the use of these terms will become clearer. For now, all methods you create will be static.

Every method has a return type, indicating what kind of value that the method will return to any other method that calls it. If a method does not return a value, its return type is `void`. If you do not indicate a return type for a method, its return type is `int` by default. Later in this chapter, you will create methods that return values; for now, the methods will be `void` methods.

Every method has a name that must be a legal C# identifier; that is, it must not contain spaces and must begin with a letter of the alphabet or an underscore.

Every method name is followed by a set of parentheses. Sometimes these parentheses contain arguments, but in the simplest methods, the parentheses are empty.

In summary, the first methods you write will be `public`, `static`, and `void`, and have empty argument lists. Therefore, you can write the `WelcomeMessage()` method as it is shown in Figure 3-2. According to its declaration, it is public and static. It returns nothing, so its return type is `void`. Its identifier is `WelcomeMessage`, and it receives nothing, so its parentheses are empty. Its body, consisting of three `WriteLine()` statements, appears within curly braces.

```
public static void WelcomeMessage()
   {
        Console.WriteLine("Welcome");
        Console.WriteLine("It's a pleasure to serve you");
        Console.WriteLine("Enjoy the program");
   }
```

Figure 3-2 The `WelcomeMessage()` method

You can place a method in its own file (as you will do in the next section) or within the file of a program that will use it, but not within any other method. Figure 3-3 shows the two locations where you can place the `WelcomeMessage()` method within the Hello program file.

```
using System;
public class HelloClass
{
     // The WelcomeMessage() method could go here
     public static void Main()
     {
          Console.WriteLine("Hello");
     }
     // Alternatively, the WelcomeMessage() method could go here
     // But it cannot go in both places
}
```

Figure 3-3   Placement of methods

If the `Main()` method calls the `WelcomeMessage()` method, then you simply use the `WelcomeMessage()` method's name as a statement within the body of the `Main()` method. Figure 3-4 shows the complete program.

```
using System;
public class HelloClass
{
    public static void Main()
    {
       WelcomeMessage();
       Console.WriteLine("Hello");
    }
    public static void WelcomeMessage()
      {
          Console.WriteLine("Welcome");
          Console.WriteLine("It's a pleasure to serve you");
          Console.WriteLine("Enjoy the program");
      }
}
```

Figure 3-4   HelloClass with `Main()` method calling the `WelcomeMessage()` method

The output from the program shown in Figure 3-4 appears in Figure 3-5. When the `Main()` method executes, it calls the `WelcomeMessage()` method, then it prints "Hello". Because the `Main()` method calls the `WelcomeMessage()` method before it prints "Hello", the three lines that make up the welcome message appear first in the output.

 Each of two different classes can have its own method named `WelcomeMessage()`. Such a method in the second class would be entirely distinct from the identically named method in the first class.

Figure 3-5 Output of CallWelcomeMessage program containing HelloClass with call to `WelcomeMessage()` method

In the next steps, you will create a DemoLogo program in which a `Main()` method calls another method that displays a company's logo.

1. Open a new file in your text editor. Enter the statement that uses the System namespace, then type the class header for the DemoLogo class and type the class-opening curly brace.

```
using System;
public class DemoLogo
{
```

2. Type the `Main()` method for the `DemoLogo()` class. This method prints a line, then calls the `PrintCompanyLogo()` method.

```
public static void Main()
{
    Console.Write("Our company is ");
    PrintCompanyLogo();
}
```

3. Add a method that prints a two-line logo for a company.

```
public static void PrintCompanyLogo()
{

    Console.WriteLine("See Sharp Optical");

    Console.WriteLine("We prize your eyes");

}
```

4. Add the closing curly brace for the class (`}`), then save the file as **DemoLogo.cs** in the Chapter03 folder of your Student Disk.

5. Compile and execute the program. The output should look like Figure 3-6.

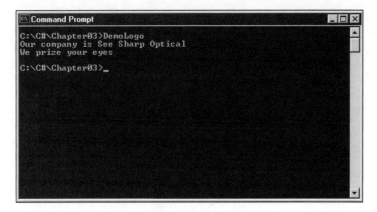

Figure 3-6   Output of DemoLogo program

HIDING IMPLEMENTATION BY USING MULTIPLE FILES

An important principle of object-oriented programming is the notion of **implementation hiding**. When you make a request to a method, you don't need to know the details of how the method is executed. For example, when you make a dental appointment, you do not need to know how the appointment is actually recorded at the dental office—perhaps it is written in a book, marked on a large chalkboard, or entered into a computerized database. The implementation details are of no concern to you as a client, and if the dental office changes its methods from one year to the next, the change does not affect your use of the appointment method. Your only concern is the way you **interface** or interact with the dental office, not how the office records appointments. Similarly, if you use a thermostat to raise the temperature in your apartment or house, you do not need to know whether the heat is generated by natural gas, electricity, solar energy, or a hamster on a wheel. As long as you receive heat, the implementation details can remain hidden.

With well-written program methods, the invoking program must know the name of the method (and what type of information to send it), but the program does not need to know how the method works. You later can substitute a new, improved method for the old one, and if the interface to the method does not change, you won't need to make any changes in programs invoking the method.

Hidden implementation methods often are said to exist in a **black box**.

For example, suppose you rewrite the **WelcomeMessage()** method as shown in Figure 3-7. The method is constructed differently from the one with the identical name shown in Figure 3-4—the new method uses two statements instead of three, uses a **Write()**

method for a portion of its output instead of all `WriteLine()` methods, and uses two newline escape sequences ('\n'). Nevertheless, if you substitute the new version for the old one, any program that uses the method does not need to be altered, and the output is identical.

```
public static void WelcomeMessage()
{
    Console.Write("Welcome\nIt's a pleasure ");
    Console.WriteLine("to serve you\nEnjoy the program");
}
```

Figure 3-7   Alternate `WelcomeMessage()` method

You should not alter the `WelcomeMessage()` method arbitrarily. However, as you learn to program, you will encounter many opportunities to substitute an improved method for an older, less efficient one. Also, you often will use methods written by others or that you "borrow" from other applications you have written. To more easily incorporate methods into a program, it is common practice to store methods (or groups of associated methods) in their own classes and files. Then you can add them into any application that uses them. The resulting compound program is called a **multifile assembly**. To create a multifile assembly, you need to create a namespace and use some additional command-line options when you compile your program.

In the next steps, you will create two files to use in a multifile assembly.

You first learned about namespaces when you used the System namespace in Chapter 1. A namespace is a scheme that provides a way to group similar classes.

1. Open the DemoLogo class file that you saved in the previous set of steps in the Chapter.03 folder of your Student Disk.

2. Cut the **PrintCompanyLogo()** method from the file.

Use your editor's Cut feature rather than simply deleting the method. That way, you can use your editor's Paste feature to paste the method into a new file, thereby saving typing. In many editors, you can use your mouse to highlight the text you want to cut and use **Ctrl+X** to cut it. When you are ready to paste the text to a new location, you can use **Ctrl+V**.

3. As the second line in the file, add the statement that will tell the compiler to use a new namespace you will create:

   using LogoNamespace;

4. Change the name of the class from DemoLogo to **DemoLogo2**.

5. Change the `PrintCompanyLogo()` method to use Logo, the name of the new class you will create to hold the method.

```
Logo.PrintCompanyLogo();
```

6. Save the file as **DemoLogo2.cs** in the Chapter.03 folder of your Student Disk. For your convenience, Figure 3-8 shows the contents of the altered file.

```
using System;
using LogoNamespace;
public class DemoLogo2
{
   public static void Main()
     {
        Console.Write("Our company is ");
        Logo.PrintCompanyLogo();
     }
}
```

Figure 3-8   DemoLogo2 class

7. Open a new file in your text editor. Paste the `PrintCompanyLogo()` method that you cut from the DemoLogo.cs file in this new file.

8. Place the `PrintCompanyLogo()` method in its own class by typing **public class Logo** and an opening curly brace above the method. Add a closing curly brace below the method.

9. At the top of the file, type **using System;** so the program recognizes the `WriteLine()` methods.

10. Wrap the entire file in a namespace by inserting **namespace LogoNamespace** and an opening curly brace at the top of the file and a closing curly brace at the bottom. The finished product should look like Figure 3-9.

```
namespace LogoNamespace
{
     using System;
     public class Logo
     {
           public static void PrintCompanyLogo()
           {
                Console.WriteLine("See Sharp Optical");
                Console.WriteLine("We prize your eyes");
           }
     }
}
```

Figure 3-9   The LogoNamespace namespace

Normally you do not include the word *Namespace* within the name of a namespace. A more conventional namespace name would be *Logo*. This example uses *LogoNamespace* to help you remember that the name refers to a namespace rather than a class or a file.

11. Save the file as **LogoNamespace.cs** in the Chapter.03 Folder of your Student Disk.

The Logo class you created in the last steps is different from any you have created so far with this book, because it does not contain a `Main()` method to act as an entry point for the class. If you attempt to compile the file using the command `csc LogoNamespace.cs`, you receive the following error message: "LogoNamespace.exe does not have an entry point defined." Your intention is not to have the class act as a stand-alone program; rather, you want the class to contain a method that other programs can use. To compile the Logo class file, you must use a command that tells the compiler to create a **netmodule** file—that is, a file that contains modules to be used as part of another program rather than one that contains an executable program. When you compile the program that contains the `Main()` method for the multifile assembly, you must include a command that adds the netmodule to the `Main()` program.

In the following steps you will compile the LogoNamespace file as a netmodule and use the **addmodule** command to associate the netmodule file with the DemoLogo2 program.

1. At the command prompt, type the following command:

   ```
   csc /t:module LogoNamespace.cs
   ```

   Press **Enter**. The command prompt should return. If you see compiler error messages, correct the errors and try the compile again.

2. Use the DOS **dir** command or Windows Explorer to confirm that a file named LogoNamespace.netmodule was created.

3. Compile the DemoLogo2 program to include the LogoNamespace module by typing the following command and pressing **Enter**:

   ```
   csc DemoLogo2.cs  /addmodule:LogoNamespace.netmodule
   ```

4. Using **dir** or Explorer, confirm that the DemoLogo2.exe file was created. Then execute the program by typing its name, **DemoLogo2**. Figure 3-10 shows the results.

Figure 3-10   Output of DemoLogo2

Tip As an alternative to compiling the module file and then compiling the program file using a separate command, you can accomplish both tasks by typing a single command: `csc /out:DemoLogo2.exe DemoLogo.cs /out:LogoNamespace.netmodule LogoNamespace.cs`.

Tip The Visual Studio .NET IDE for C# can only be used to create single-file assemblies. If you want to create multifile assemblies, you must use the command-line compiler.

As you become more proficient using C#, you will find additional reasons to create multifile assemblies besides including methods stored in separate files. Probably the most common reason you create a multifile assembly is to combine modules written in different languages, such as Visual C++ or Visual Basic.

WRITING METHODS THAT REQUIRE A SINGLE ARGUMENT

Some methods require additional information. If a method could not receive communications from you, called **arguments** or **parameters**, then you would have to write an infinite number of methods to cover every possible situation. For example, when you make a dental appointment, you do not need to employ a different method for every date of the year at every possible time of day. Rather, you can supply the date and time as information to the method, which then is carried out in the same manner, no matter what date and time are involved. If you design a method to triple numeric values, it makes sense that you can supply the `Triple()` method with an argument representing the value to be tripled, rather than having to develop a `Triple1()` method, a `Triple2()` method, and so on.

You already have used a method to which you supplied a wide variety of parameters. At any call, the `System.WriteLine()` method can receive any one of an infinite number of arguments—"Hello", "Goodbye", and so on. No matter what message you send to the `WriteLine()` method, the messages will be displayed correctly.

When you write the declaration for a method that can receive an argument, you need to include the following items within the method declaration parentheses:

- The type of the argument
- A local name for the argument

For example, consider a public method named `ComputeSevenPercentSalesTax()`, which displays the result of multiplying a value that represents a selling price by 7%. The method header for a usable `ComputeSevenPercentSalesTax()` method could be `public void ComputeSevenPercentSalesTax(double saleAmount)`. You can think of the parentheses in a method declaration as a funnel into the method—data parameters listed there are "dropping in" to the method.

The argument `double saleAmount` within the parentheses indicates that the `ComputeSevenPercentSalesTax()` method will receive a value of type double. Within the method, the value will be known as `saleAmount`. Figure 3-11 shows a complete method.

```
public static void ComputeSevenPercentSalesTax(double saleAmount)
{
        double tax;
        tax = saleAmount * 0.07;
        Console.WriteLine("The tax on {0} is {1}",
                saleAmount, tax.ToString("f"));
}
```

Figure 3-11   The `ComputeSevenPercentSalesTax()` method

Within the `ComputeSevenPercentSalesTax()` method, you must use the format string and `ToString()` method if you want figures to display to exactly two decimal positions. You learned how to display values to a fixed number of decimal places in Chapter 2; recall that using the fixed format with no number defaults to two decimal places.

The `ComputeSevenPercentSalesTax()` method is a void method (has a void return type) because it does not need to return any value to any method that uses it—its only function is to receive the `saleAmount` value, multiply it by 0.07, and then display the result. It is a static method because you do not create an object with which to use it.

Within a program, you can call the `ComputeSevenPercentSalesTax()` method by using either a constant value or a variable as an argument. Thus, both `ComputeSevenPercentSalesTax(12.99);` and `ComputeSevenPercentSales Tax(myPurchase);` would invoke the `ComputeSevenPercentSalesTax()` method correctly (assuming that myPurchase was declared as a double variable and assigned an appropriate value). You can call the `ComputeSevenPercentSalesTax()` method any number of times, with a different constant or variable argument each time. Each of these arguments becomes known as saleAmount within the method. The identifier saleAmount holds any double value passed into the method. Interestingly, if the value in the method call is a variable, it might possess the same identifier as saleAmount or a different one, such as myPurchase. The identifier saleAmount is simply the name the value "goes by" while being used within the method, no matter what name it "goes by" in the calling program. That is, the variable saleAmount is a **local** variable to the `ComputeSevenPercentSalesTax()` method. The variable saleAmount is also an example of a **formal parameter**, a parameter within a method header that accepts a value. In contrast, arguments within a method *call* often are referred to as **actual parameters**.

The variable `saleAmount` is also an example of a value parameter, or a parameter that receives a copy of the value passed to it. You will learn more about value parameters as well as other types of parameters later in this chapter.

Should a programmer change the way in which the tax value is calculated—for example, by coding `tax = saleAmount * 7 / 100;` or `tax = 0.07 * saleAmount;`—no program that uses the `ComputeSevenPercentSalesTax()` method will ever know the difference. No matter how the tax is calculated, a calling program passes a value into the `ComputeSevenPercentSalesTax()` method, and a calculated result appears on the screen.

Figure 3-12 shows a complete program called UseSevenPercentSalesTax. It uses the `ComputeSevenPercentSalesTax()` method twice, first with a variable argument, and then with a constant argument. The program's output appears in Figure 3-13.

```
using System;
public class UseSevenPercentSalesTax
{
        public static void Main()
        {
                double myPurchase = 12.99;
                ComputeSevenPercentSalesTax(myPurchase);
                ComputeSevenPercentSalesTax(35.67);
        }
        public static void ComputeSevenPercentSalesTax(double saleAmount)
        {
                double tax;
                tax = saleAmount * 0.07;
                Console.WriteLine("The tax on {0} is {1}",
                        saleAmount, tax.ToString("f"));
        }
}
```

Figure 3-12   Complete program using the `ComputeSevenPercentSalesTax()` method

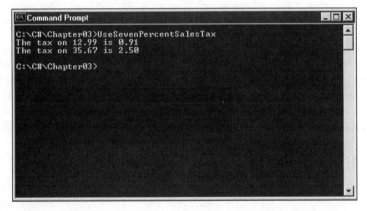

Figure 3-13   Output of UseSevenPercentSalesTax program

WRITING METHODS THAT REQUIRE MULTIPLE ARGUMENTS

A method can require more than one argument. You can pass multiple arguments to a method by listing the arguments within the call to the method and separating them with commas. For example, rather than creating a `ComputeSevenPercentSalesTax()` method that multiplies an amount by 0.07, you might prefer to create a more flexible method to which you can pass two values—the value on which the tax is calculated and the tax percentage by which it should be multiplied. Figure 3-14 shows a method that uses two such arguments.

A declaration for a method that receives two or more arguments must list the type for each argument separately, even if the arguments have the *same* type.

```
public static void ComputeSalesTax(double saleAmount, double taxRate)
{
        double tax;
        tax = saleAmount * taxRate;
        Console.WriteLine("The tax on {0} is {1}",
           saleAmount, tax.ToString("F"));
}
```

Figure 3-14 The `ComputeSalesTax()` method

In Figure 3-14, two arguments (double saleAmount and double taxRate) appear within the parentheses in the method header. A comma separates the arguments, and each argument requires its own named type (in this case, both arguments are of type double) as well as an identifier. When you pass values to the method in a statement such as `ComputeSalesTax(myPurchase,localRate);`, the first value passed will be referenced as `saleAmount` within the method, and the second value passed will be referenced as `taxRate`. Therefore, it is very important that arguments be passed to a method in the correct order. The call `ComputeSalesTax(200.00, 0.10);` results in output stating that "The tax on 200 is 20.00." The call `ComputeSalesTax(0.10, 200.00);` results in output stating that "The tax on 0.10 is 20.00," which is clearly incorrect.

If two method arguments are of the same type—for example, two doubles— passing them to a method in the wrong order results in a logical error. If a method expects arguments of diverse types, then passing arguments in reverse order constitutes a syntax error.

Figure 3-15 shows a complete program that calls the `ComputeSalesTax()` method two times. Figure 3-16 shows the output.

You can write a method to take any number of arguments in any order. When you call the method, however, the arguments you send to it must match in both number and type with the arguments listed in the method declaration. Thus, a method to compute an automobile salesperson's commission might require arguments such as an integer value of a car sold, a double percentage commission rate, and a character code for the vehicle type. The correct method will execute only when three arguments of the correct types are sent in the correct order.

```
using System;
public class UseSalesTax
{
        public static void Main()
        {
                double myPurchase = 239.11;
                double myRate = 0.10;
                ComputeSalesTax(myPurchase, myRate);
                ComputeSalesTax(16.55, 0.02);
        }
        public static void ComputeSalesTax(double saleAmount, double taxRate)
        {
                double tax;
                tax = saleAmount * taxRate;
                Console.WriteLine("The tax on {0} is {1}",
                    saleAmount, tax.ToString("F"));
        }
}
```

Figure 3-15   The UseSalesTax program

Figure 3-16   Output of UseSalesTax program

WRITING METHODS THAT RETURN VALUES

The return type for a method can be any type used in the C# programming language, which includes the basic built-in types int, double, char, and so on, as well as class types (including class types you create). Of course, a method also can return nothing, in which case the return type is void.

In addition to the primitive types, a method can return a class type. If a class named BankLoan exists, a method might return an instance of a BankLoan as in `public BankLoan ApprovalProcess()`. In other words, a method can return anything from a simple int to a complicated BankLoan that contains 20 data fields. You will create classes like BankLoan in Chapter 4.

3

A method's return type is known more succinctly as a method's type. For example, the declaration for the `WelcomeMessage()` method shown in Figure 3-2 is `public static void WelcomeMessage()`. This method is public and returns no value, so it is of type void. A method that returns true or false depending on whether an employee worked overtime hours might be `public bool IsOvertimeEarned()`. This method is public and returns a bool value, so it is of type bool.

The header for a method that calculates and displays your gross pay is `public static void CalcAndShowPay(double hours, double rate)`. This method receives hours and rate as arguments, prints the results, and does not need to return any value to the method that calls it. If you want to create a method to return the calculated gross pay value rather than displaying it, the header would be `public static double CalcPay(double hours, double rate)`. Figure 3-17 shows this method.

```
public static double CalcPay(double hours, double rate)
{
        double gross;
        gross = hours * rate;
        return gross;
}
```

Figure 3-17   The `CalcPay()` method

Notice the return type **double** in the method header. Also notice the return statement, which is the last statement within the method. The **return** statement causes the value stored in **gross** to be sent back to any method that calls the `CalcPay()` method.

If a method returns a value and you call the method, you typically will want to use the returned value, although it is not required. For example, when you invoke the `CalcPay()` method, you might want to assign the value to a double variable named `grossPay`, as in `grossPay = CalcPay(myHours, myRate);`. The `CalcPay()` method returns a double, so it is appropriate to assign the returned value to a double variable. Figure 3-18 shows a program that uses the `CalcPay()` method, and Figure 3-19 shows the output.

```
using System;
public class UseCalcPay
{
        public static void Main()
        {
                double myHours = 37.5;
                double myRate = 12.75;
                double grossPay;
                grossPay = CalcPay(myHours, myRate);
                Console.WriteLine("I worked {0} hours at {1} per hour",
                    myHours, myRate);
                Console.WriteLine("My gross pay is {0}",
                    grossPay.ToString("C"));
        }
        public static double CalcPay(double hours, double rate)
        {
                double gross;
                gross = hours * rate;
                return gross;
        }
}
```

Figure 3-18   Program using the `CalcPay()` method

Figure 3-19   Output of UseCalcPay program

Alternatively, you can choose to display a method's returned value directly without storing it in any variable, as in the following:

```
Console.WriteLine("My gross pay is {0}",
    CalcPay(myHours, myRate).ToString("C"));
```

In this statement, the call to the `CalcPay()` method is made from within the `WriteLine()` method call. Because `CalcPay()` returns a double, you can use the method call `CalcPay()` in the same way you would use any simple double value. For example, besides printing it, you can perform math with it, assign it, and so on. The method call `CalcPay()` has a double value in the same way a double variable has a value.

Next, you will write a method named `CalcPhoneCallPrice()` that both receives arguments and returns a value. The purpose of the method is to take the length of a phone call in minutes and the rate charged per minute and then calculate the price of a phone call, assuming each call includes a 25-cent connection charge in addition to the per-minute charge. After writing the `CalcPhoneCallPrice()` method, you will write a `Main()` method that calls the `CalcPhoneCallPrice()` method using four different sets of data as arguments.

To create a class containing a method that receives two arguments and returns a value:

1. Open your text editor and type the **using System;** statement.

2. Add the class header for **public class PhoneCall**, and add an opening curly brace.

3. Type the following `CalcPhoneCallPrice()` method. It receives an integer and a double as arguments. The fee for a call is calculated as 0.25 plus the minutes times the rate per minute. The method returns the phone call fee to the calling method.

```
public static double CalcPhoneCallPrice
    (int minutes, double rate)
{
    double callFee;
    callFee = .25 + minutes  * rate;
    return callFee;
}
```

4. Add the `Main()` method header for the PhoneCall class. Begin the method by declaring two call lengths, `call1` and `call2`, and two call rates, `rate1` and `rate2`. Also, declare a double `priceOfCall` that will hold the result of a calculated call price.

```
public static void Main()
{
  int call1 = 2, call2 = 5;
  double rate1 = .03, rate2 = .12;
  double priceOfCall;
```

5. Add a statement that prints column headings under which you can list combinations of call lengths, rates, and prices. The three column headings are right-aligned, each in a field ten characters wide.

```
Console.WriteLine("{0,10}{1,10}{2,10}",
    "Minutes","Rate","Price");
```

Add a statement that calls the `CalcPhoneCallPrice()` method, passing in one of the call lengths (call1) and one of the calling rates (rate1). The value returned from `CalcPhoneCallPrice()` is stored in the `priceOfCall` variable.

```
priceOfCall = CalcPhoneCallPrice(call1, rate1);
```

Print the call length, its rate, and the calculated `priceOfCall` converted to a currency string.

```
Console.WriteLine("{0,10}{1,10}{2,10}",
    call1,rate1,priceOfCall.ToString("C"));
```

6. Add three pairs of statements that calculate and print all other possible length and rate combinations—`call1` with `rate2`, `call2` with `rate1`, and `call2` with `rate2`.

```
priceOfCall = CalcPhoneCallPrice(call1, rate2);
Console.WriteLine("{0,10}{1,10}{2,10}",
    call1,rate2,priceOfCall.ToString("C"));
priceOfCall = CalcPhoneCallPrice(call2, rate1);
Console.WriteLine("{0,10}{1,10}{2,10}",
    call2,rate1,priceOfCall.ToString("C"));
priceOfCall = CalcPhoneCallPrice(call2, rate2);
Console.WriteLine("{0,10}{1,10}{2,10}",
    call2,rate2,priceOfCall.ToString("C"));
```

Add a closing curly brace for the `Main()` method and another for the PhoneCall class.

7. Save the file as **PhoneCall.cs**. Compile and run the program. The output looks like Figure 3-20. It shows how a single method can produce a variety of results when you use different values for the arguments.

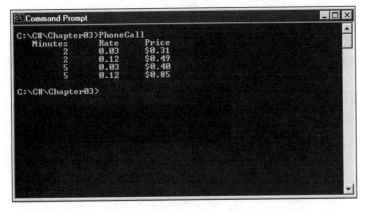

Figure 3-20   Output of PhoneCall program

USING ref AND out PARAMETERS WITHIN METHODS

In C#, you can write methods with four kinds of formal parameters listed within the parentheses in the method header. These four types are:

- Value parameters, which are declared without any modifiers
- Reference parameters, which are declared with the **ref** modifier
- Output parameters, which are declared with the **out** modifier
- Parameter arrays, which are declared with the **params** modifier

 This chapter discusses value, reference, and output parameters. You will learn about parameter arrays in Chapter 6.

So far, all of the method parameters you have created have been value parameters. When you use a value parameter in a method header, you indicate the parameter's type and name, and the method receives a copy of the value passed to it. This copy—the formal parameter—is stored at a different memory address than the variable that was used as the parameter in the method call—the actual parameter. In other words, the actual parameter and the formal parameter refer to two separate memory locations, and any change to the formal parameter value within the method has no effect on the actual parameter value back in the calling method. Changes to value parameters never affect the original argument in the calling method.

 Using a real-world analogy, you know that people with the same name living in different places are not the same person. Changes in the life of Jane Doe in Maine, such as a raise or a department transfer, have no effect on Jane Doe in Vermont. The same is true of like-named variables located in different methods.

Figure 3-21 shows a program that declares a variable named **var**, assigns 4 to it, prints it, and passes it to a method that accepts a value parameter. The method assigns a new value, 777, to the formal, passed parameter and prints it. When control returns to the **Main()** method, the value of **var** remains 4. Changing the value of **var** within the **MethodWithValueParam()** method has no effect on **var** in **Main()**. Even though both methods contain a variable named **var**, they represent two separate variables, each with its own memory location. Figure 3-22 shows the output.

```
using System;
public class ParameterDemo1
{
        public static void Main()
        {
                int var = 4;
                Console.WriteLine("In Main var is {0}",var);
                MethodWithValueParam(var);
                Console.WriteLine("In Main var is {0}",var);
        }
        public static void MethodWithValueParam(int var)
        {
                var = 777;
                Console.WriteLine("In MethodWithValueParam, param is {0}",var);
        }
}
```

Figure 3-21   Program calling method with a value parameter

Figure 3-22   Output of a program that passes a value parameter to a method

 Programmers say that a value parameter is used for "in" parameter passing—that is, parameters whose values go into a method, but modifications to which do not come "out."

In the `MethodWithValueParam()` method, it makes no difference whether you use the name `var` as the `Main()` method's actual parameter or use some other name. In either case, the passed and received variables occupy separate memory locations.

On occasion, you might want a method to be able to alter a value you pass to it. In that case, you can use a reference parameter or an output parameter. Both **reference** and **output parameters** have memory addresses that are passed to a method, allowing it to alter the original variables. When you use a reference parameter to a method, the parameter must have been assigned a value before you use it in the method call. When you use an output parameter, it need not contain an original value. Neither reference nor output parameters occupy their own memory locations. Rather, both reference and output parameters act as **aliases**, or other names, for the same memory location occupied by the original passed variable. You use the keyword **ref** as a modifier to indicate a reference parameter, and the keyword **out** as a modifier to indicate an output parameter.

Using an alias for a variable is similar to using an alias for a person. Jane Doe might be known as "Ms. Doe" at work but "Sissy" at home. Both names refer to the same person.

Figure 3-23 shows a **Main()** program that calls a **MethodWithRefParam()** method. The **Main()** method declares a variable, displays its value, and then passes the variable to the **MethodWithRefParam()** method. The modifier **ref** precedes the variable name **var** in both the method call and the method header. The method's parameter **param** holds the memory address of **var**, making **param** an alias for **var**. When the method changes the value of **param**, the change persists in the **var** variable within **Main()**. Figure 3-24 shows the output of the program.

```
using System;
public class ParameterDemo2
{
        public static void Main()
        {
                int var = 4;
                Console.WriteLine("In Main var is {0}",var);
                MethodWithRefParam(ref var);  // notice use of ref
                Console.WriteLine("In Main var is {0}",var);
        }
        public static void MethodWithRefParam(ref int param)
           // notice use of ref
        {
                param = 888;
                Console.WriteLine("In MethodWithRefParam, param is {0}",param);
        }
}
```

Figure 3-23   Program calling method with a reference parameter

In the header for the **MethodWithRefParam()** method, it makes no difference whether you use the same name as the **Main()** method's passed variable (**var**) or some other name, such as **param**. In either case, the passed and received variables occupy the same memory location—the address of one is the address of the other.

Figure 3-24 Output of a program that passes a reference parameter to a method

When you use a reference parameter, the passed variable must have an assigned value. Using an output parameter is convenient when the passed variable doesn't have a value yet. For example, the program in Figure 3-25 uses `InputMethod()` to obtain values for two parameters. The parameters get their values from the method, so it makes sense to provide them with no values going in, but to have them retain values coming out. Figure 3-26 shows a typical execution of the program.

```
using System;
public class InputMethodDemo
{
        public static void Main()
        {
                int first, second;
                InputMethod(out first, out second); // notice use of out
                Console.WriteLine
                   ("After InputMethod first is {0} and second is {1}",
                   first, second);
        }
        public static void InputMethod(out int one, out int two)
          // notice use of out
        {
                string s1, s2;
                Console.Write("Enter first integer ");
                s1 = Console.ReadLine();
                Console.Write("Enter second integer ");
                s2 = Console.ReadLine();
                one = Convert.ToInt32(s1);
                two = Convert.ToInt32(s2);
        }
}
```

Figure 3-25 InputMethodDemo program

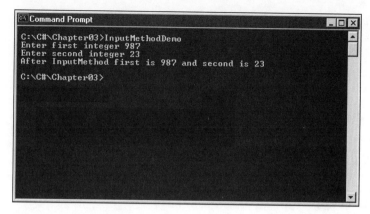

Figure 3-26 Output of typical run of InputMethodDemo program

In summary, when you need a method to alter a single value, you have two options:

- You can send a value parameter to a method, alter the local version on the variable within the method, return the altered value, and assign the return value to the original variable back in the calling module.

- You can send a reference or output parameter and alter the original value from within the method.

A major advantage to using reference or output parameters exists when you want a method to change multiple variables. Any method can have only a single return type and can return at most only one value. By using reference or output parameters to a method, you can change multiple values.

In the next steps, you will write a program that uses a method to swap two values.

1. Open your editor and begin the Swap program as follows:

```
using System;
public class SwapProgram
{
        public static void Main()
        {
```

2. Declare two integers and display their values. Call the `Swap()` method and pass in the addresses of the two variables so that their contents can be altered. Because the parameters already have assigned values, you can use reference parameters. After the method call, display the two values again. Add the closing curly brace for the `Main()` method.

```
int first = 34, second = 712;
Console.WriteLine
    ("Before swap first is {0} and second is {1}",
    first, second);
Swap(ref first, ref second);
```

```
Console.WriteLine
   ("After swap first is {0} and second is {1}",
   first, second);
}
```

3. Create the `Swap()` method as shown. You can swap two values by storing the first value in a temporary variable, then assigning the second value to the first variable. At this point, both variables hold the value originally held by the second variable. When you assign the temporary variable's value to the second variable, the two values are reversed.

```
public static void Swap(ref int one, ref int two)
{
   int temp;
   temp = one;
   one = two;
   two = temp;
}
```

4. Add the closing curly brace for the class. Save the file as **SwapProgram.cs**. Compile and execute the program. Figure 3-27 shows the output.

Figure 3-27   Output of SwapProgram

OVERLOADING METHODS

Overloading involves using one term to indicate diverse meanings. When you use the English language, you frequently overload words. When you say "open the door," "open your eyes," and "open a computer file," you describe three very different actions using different methods and producing different results. However, anyone who speaks English fluently has no trouble comprehending your meaning because the verb "open" is understood in the context of the noun that follows it.

Overloading a method is an example of polymorphism—the ability of a method to act appropriately depending on the context. You first learned the term *polymorphism* in Chapter 1.

When you overload a C# method, you write multiple methods with a shared name. The compiler understands your meaning based on the arguments you use with the method. For example, suppose you create a method to apply a simple interest rate to a bank balance. The method receives two double arguments—the balance and the interest rate—and displays the multiplied result. Figure 3-28 shows the method.

```
public static void CalculateInterest(double bal, double rate)
{
        double interest;
        interest = bal * rate;
        Console.WriteLine("{0} interest on {1} earns {2}",
            rate, bal.ToString("C"), interest.ToString("C"));
}
```

Figure 3-28   The `CalculateInterest()` method with two double arguments

When a program calls the `CalculateInterest()` method and passes double values, as in `CalculateInterest(1000.00, 0.04)`, the simple interest will be calculated correctly as 4% of 1000.00. Assume, however, that the interest rate passed to the `CalculateInterest()` method comes from inconsistent user input. Some users who want to indicate an interest rate of 4% might type .04, and others might assume they are indicating a value of 4% by typing 4. When the `CalculateInterest()` method is called with arguments 1000.00 and .04, the interest is calculated correctly as 40.00. When the method is called using 1000.00 and 4, the interest is calculated incorrectly as 4000.00.

The `CalculateInterest()` method can receive integer arguments even though it is defined as needing double arguments, because integers will be promoted or cast automatically to doubles, as you learned in Chapter 2.

A solution to this problem is to overload the `CalculateInterest()` method. Overloading methods involves writing multiple methods with the same name, but with different arguments. For example, in addition to the `CalculateInterest()` method shown in Figure 3-28, you could use the method shown in Figure 3-29.

In Figure 3-29, the rateDouble value is calculated by dividing by 100.0, not by 100. If two integers are divided, the result is a truncated integer; dividing by a double 100.0 causes the result to be a double. Alternatively, you could use a cast.

```
public static void CalculateInterest(double bal, int rate) //rate is an int
{
        double interest, rateDouble;
        rateDouble = rate / 100.0;
        interest = bal * rateDouble;
        Console.WriteLine("{0} interest on {1} earns {2}",
                rateDouble, bal.ToString("C"), interest.ToString("C"));
}
```

Figure 3-29   The `CalculateInterest()` method with a double and an integer argument

If you call the `CalculateInterest()` method using two double arguments, as in `CalculateInterest(1000.00, .04)`, the first version of the `CalculateInterest()` method shown in Figure 3-28 executes. If you use an integer as the second parameter in the call to `CalculateInterest()`, as in `CalculateInterest(1000.00, 4)`, then the method shown in Figure 3-29 executes, and the whole-number rate value will be divided by 100.0 correctly before it is used to determine the interest earned.

Of course, you could use methods with different names to solve the dilemma of producing an accurate simple interest figure—for example, `CalculateInterestRateUsingDouble()` and `CalculateInterestRateUsingInt()`. Using this approach would require that you place a decision within your program to determine which of the two methods to call, but it is more convenient to use one method name and then let the compiler determine which method to use. Overloading the `CalculateInterest()` method makes it more convenient for other programmers to use your method in the future. Whether their application assumes an interest rate is expressed as a double or as an integer, the interest will be calculated correctly. Also, it is easier to remember one reasonable name for tasks that are functionally identical except for argument types.

 You will learn about making decisions within programs in Chapter 5.

In the next steps you will overload a method that correctly triples an integer, a double, or a string, depending on how you call the method.

1. Open a new file in your text editor. Create a method that triples and displays an integer argument as follows:

```
public static void Triple(int num)
{
  const int three = 3;
  Console.WriteLine("{0} times {1} is {2}\n",
    num, three, num * three);
}
```

2. Create a similar method that triples a double argument:

```
public static void Triple(double num)
{
        const int three = 3;
        Console.WriteLine("{0} times {1} is {2}\n",
            num, three, num * three);
}
```

3. Create a third method with the same name that takes a string argument.
   Define tripling a message as printing it three times, separated by tabs.

```
public static void Triple(string message)
{
        Console.WriteLine("{0} times 3 is:",message);
        Console.WriteLine("{0}\t{0}\t{0}\n",message);
}
```

4. Position your cursor at the top of the file and add a using statement, class
   header, and opening curly brace so the three overloaded `Triple()` methods
   will be contained in a class named `OverloadedTriples`.

```
using System;
public class OverloadedTriples
{
```

5. Position your cursor at the bottom of the file and add the closing curly brace
   for the OverloadedTriples class.

6. Position your cursor after the opening curly brace for the class and insert a
   `Main()` method that declares an integer, a double, and a string and, in turn,
   passes each to the appropriate `Triple()` method.

```
public static void Main()
{
        int iNum = 20;
        double dNum = 4.5;
        string message = "Go team!";
        Triple(iNum);
        Triple(dNum);
        Triple(message);
}
```

7. Save the file as **OverloadedTriples.cs** in the Chapter.03 folder on your
   Student Disk. Compile and execute the program. Figure 3-30 shows the output.

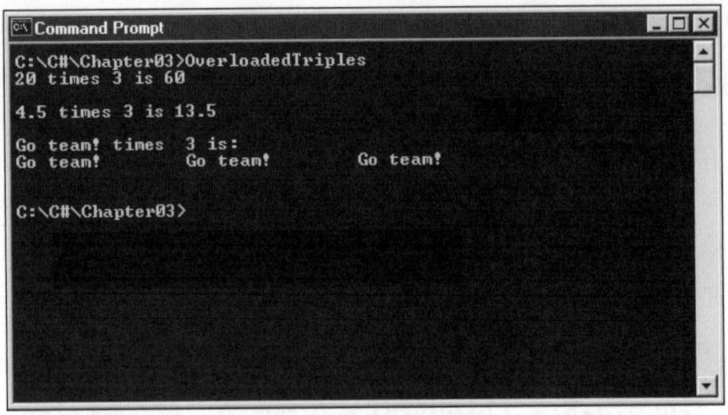

Figure 3-30   Output of OverloadedTriples program

AVOIDING AMBIGUOUS METHODS

When you overload a method, you run the risk of creating an **ambiguous** situation—one in which the compiler cannot determine which method to use. Every time you call a method, the compiler decides whether a suitable method exists; if so, the method executes, and if not, you receive an error message.

For example, the simple method shown in Figure 3-31 accepts two arguments—a double and an integer. When you call the method using double and integer parameters, it works correctly, displaying its message. When you write a single version of a method like this one, there is no possibility of ambiguity.

```
public static void SimpleMethod(double d, int i)
    // notice double and int parameters
{
        Console.WriteLine("Method receives double and integer");
}
```

Figure 3-31   The SimpleMethod() method

If you write a Main() method as in Figure 3-32, in which you declare dNum as a double variable and iNum as an integer variable, both method calls SimpleMethod(dNum, iNum); and SimpleMethod(iNum, iNum); result in the output "Method receives double and integer," as shown in Figure 3-33. When you call the method using dNum and iNum as the actual parameters, the method works as expected. When you call the method using iNum twice, then the second integer is cast as (or promoted to) a double, and the method works as well. Even though there is no exact match for a call to SimpleMethod() using two integers, the method that takes a double and an integer is "close enough." The compiler uses its rules regarding unifying types, promotes the

integer argument to a double, and assumes that it was your intention to use the
`SimpleMethod()` method with the arguments you supplied.

 You learned about casts and unifying types in Chapter 2.

```
public static void Main()
{
        int iNum = 20;
        double dNum = 4.5;
        SimpleMethod(dNum, iNum);
        SimpleMethod(iNum, iNum);
}
```

Figure 3-32   The `Main()` method that calls `SimpleMethod()` two ways

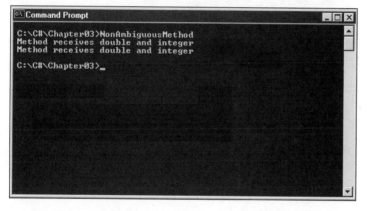

Figure 3-33   Output when `Main()` calls `SimpleMethod()` two ways

When you write a second version of `SimpleMethod()` to accept two integers, as shown
in Figure 3-34, then `SimpleMethod()` becomes overloaded. When you rerun the `Main()`
method in Figure 3-32, there is a "better match" for the call with two integers, so each
method calls the version of `SimpleMethod()` that is an exact match. Figure 3-35 shows
the output; each call to `SimpleMethod()` executes a different version of the method.

```
public static void SimpleMethod(int i, int i2)
    // notice two integer parameters
{
        Console.WriteLine("Method receives two integers");
}
```

Figure 3-34   The `SimpleMethod()` method with an integer argument

A more complicated and potentially ambiguous situation arises when the compiler cannot determine which of several versions of a method to use. Consider the program in Figure 3-36. The class contains two versions of `SimpleMethod()`—one that takes a double and integer, and one that takes an integer and double.

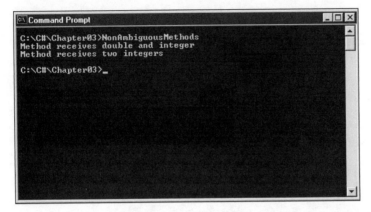

Figure 3-35   Output of program using overloaded `SimpleMethod()`

```
using System;
public class AmbiguousMethods
{
        public static void Main()
        {
        int iNum = 20;
        double dNum = 4.5;
        SimpleMethod(iNum, dNum);  // calls first version
        SimpleMethod(dNum, iNum);  // calls second version
        SimpleMethod(iNum, iNum);  // error! Call is ambiguous.
        }
        public static void SimpleMethod(int i, double d)
        {
                Console.WriteLine("Method receives int and double");
        }
        public static void SimpleMethod(double d, int i)
        {
                Console.WriteLine("Method receives double and int");
        }
}
```

Figure 3-36   Program containing ambiguous method call

In the `Main()` method in Figure 3-36, a call to `SimpleMethod()` with an integer argument first and a double argument second executes the first version of the method, and a call to `SimpleMethod()` with a double argument first and an integer argument second executes the second version of the method. With each of these calls, the compiler can find an exact match for the arguments you send. However, if you call `SimpleMethod()` using two integer arguments, an ambiguous situation arises because there is no exact match for the method call. Because the first integer could be promoted to a double (matching the second version of the overloaded method), or the second integer could be promoted to a double (matching the first version), the compiler does not know which version of the `SimpleMethod()` method to use, and the program will not execute.

 An overloaded method is not ambiguous on its own—it becomes ambiguous only if you create an ambiguous situation. A program with potentially ambiguous methods will run without problems if you make no ambiguous method calls. For example, if you remove the `SimpleMethod()` call that contains two integers from the program in Figure 3-36, the program runs.

Methods can be overloaded correctly by providing different argument lists for methods with the same name. Methods with identical names that have identical argument lists but different return types are not overloaded—they are illegal. For example, `public static int AMethod(int x)` and `public static void AMethod(int x)` cannot coexist within a program. The compiler determines which of several versions of a method to call based on argument lists. When the method call `AMethod(17);` is made, the compiler will not know which method to execute because both possibilities take an integer argument.

CHAPTER SUMMARY

❑ A method is a series of reusable statements that carry out a task. In C#, a method must include a method declaration (or header or definition), an opening curly brace, a method body, and a closing curly brace. A method declaration contains optional declared accessibility, an optional `static` modifier, the return type for the method, the method name, an opening parenthesis, an optional list of method arguments, and a closing parenthesis.

❑ Invoking programs must know the interface to methods but need not understand the hidden implementation. This concept allows you to substitute new methods for old ones and to use methods written by other programmers. To more easily incorporate methods into a program, it is common practice to store methods (or groups of associated methods) in their own classes and files. Then you can add them into any application that uses them, creating a multifile assembly.

❑ Methods receive data in the form of arguments or parameters. When you write the method declaration for a method that can receive an argument, you need to include a type and local name for the argument within the method declaration parentheses. When you call a method that requires an argument, you can use either a constant value or a variable. The argument within a method call is an actual parameter; the local argument within a method that accepts the value from the call is a formal parameter.

❑ You can pass multiple arguments to a method by listing the arguments within the call to the method and separating them with commas. You can write a method to take any number of arguments in any order. When you call the method, however, the arguments you send to it must match in number, type, and order with the arguments listed in the method declaration.

❑ The return type for a method can be any type used in the C# programming language, which includes the basic types `int`, `double`, `char`, and so on, as well as class types (including class types you create). A method also can return nothing, in which case the return type is `void`. A method's return type is known more succinctly as a method's type. A method's return statement causes a value to be sent back to the calling method.

❑ In C#, you can write methods with four kinds of formal parameters listed within the parentheses in the method header: value parameters, reference parameters, output parameters, and parameter arrays. When you use a value parameter in a method header, you indicate the parameter's type and name, and the method receives a copy of the value passed to it. Both reference and output parameters have memory addresses that are passed to a method, allowing it to alter the original values. When you use a reference parameter to a method, the parameter must have been assigned a value before you use it in the method call. When you use an output parameter, it does not need to contain an original value.

❑ Overloading a method involves writing multiple methods with the same name, but with different arguments.

❑ The compiler determines which of several versions of a method to call based on argument lists. When you overload a method, you run the risk of creating an ambiguous situation—one in which the compiler cannot determine which method to use.

REVIEW QUESTIONS

1. At most, a class can contain _____ method(s).

    a. 0

    b. 1

    c. 2

    d. any number of

2. What is the most important reason for creating methods within a program?

    a. Methods are easily reusable.

    b. Because all methods must be stored in the same class, they are easy to find.

    c. The `Main()` method becomes more detailed.

    d. All of these are true.

3

3. In C#, a method must include all of the following *except* a(n) _____.

a. method declaration

b. argument list

c. body

d. closing curly brace

4. A method declaration must contain _____.

a. a statement of purpose

b. declared accessibility

c. the static modifier

d. a return type

5. If you use the keyword modifier **static** in a method header, you indicate that the method _____.

a. can be called without referring to an object

b. cannot be copied

c. cannot be overloaded

d. can be ambiguous

6. If you do not indicate a return type for a method, its return type is _____ by default.

a. void

b. int

c. public

d. private

7. In C#, you can store a group of methods in a separate file from the class that uses them. When you compile both files together, you create a _____.

a. compiler composition

b. multifile assembly

c. method pact

d. composite file gathering

8. When you write the method declaration for a method that can receive an argument, you need to include all of the following items *except* _____.

a. a pair of parentheses

b. the type of the argument

c. a local name for the argument

d. an initial value for the argument

9. Suppose you have declared a variable as int myAge = 21;. Which of the following is a legal call to a method with the declaration public static void AMethod(int num)?

a. AMethod(int*f*55);

b. AMethod(myAge);

c. AMethod(int myAge);

d. AMethod( );

10. Suppose you have declared a method named public static void CalculatePay(double rate). Which is true of a method that calls the CalculatePay() method?

a. The calling method must contain a declared double named rate.

b. The calling method might contain a declared double named rate.

c. The calling method cannot contain a declared double named rate.

d. The calling method can contain no declared double variables.

11. In the method call PrintTheData(double salary);, salary is the _____ parameter.

a. formal

b. actual

c. proposed

d. preferred

12. A program contains the method call PrintTheData(double salary);. In the method definition, the name of the formal parameter must be _____.

a. salary

b. any legal identifier other than salary

c. any legal identifier

d. omitted

13. What is a correct method declaration for a method that receives two double arguments and calculates the difference between them?

a. public static void CalcDifference(double price1, price2)

b. public static void CalcDifference(double price1, double price2)

c. public static void CalcDifference(double price1, double anotherPrice)

d. Two of these are correct.

14. A method is declared as `double CalcPay(int hoursWorked)`. Suppose you write a method containing `int hours = 35;` and `double pay;`. Which of the following represents the correct way to use the `CalcPay()` method?

    a. `hours = CalcPay();`

    b. `hours = CalcPay(pay);`

    c. `pay = CalcPay(hoursWorked);`

    d. `pay = CalcPay(hours);`

15. Which is *not* a type of method parameter in C#?

    a. value

    b. reference

    c. forensic

    d. output

16. Which type of method parameter receives the address of the variable passed in?

    a. a value parameter

    b. a reference parameter

    c. an output parameter

    d. two of the above

17. Assume you declare a variable as `int x = 100;` and correctly pass it to a method with the declaration `public static void IncreaseValue(ref int x)`. There is a single statement within the `IncreaseValue()` method: `x = x + 25;`. Back in the `Main()` method, after the method call, what is the value of x?

    a. 100

    b. 125

    c. impossible to tell

    d. program will not run

18. Assume you declare a variable as `int x = 100;` and correctly pass it to a method with the declaration `public static void IncreaseValue(int x)`. There is a single statement within the `IncreaseValue()` method: `x = x + 25;`. Back in the `Main()` method, after the method call, what is the value of x?

    a. 100

    b. 125

    c. impossible to tell

    d. program will not run

19. What is the difference between a reference parameter and an output parameter?

   a. A reference parameter receives a memory address; an output parameter does not.

   b. A reference parameter occupies a unique memory address; an output parameter does not.

   c. A reference parameter must have an initial value; an output parameter need not.

   d. A reference parameter need not have an initial value; an output parameter must.

20. Which of the following pairs of method declarations represent overloaded methods?

   a.
```
public static void Method(int a)
public static void Method(int b)
```

   b.
```
public static void Method(double d)
public static int Method()
```

   c.
```
public static double Method(int e)
public static int Method(int f)
```

   d. Two of these are overloaded methods.

EXERCISES

1. Name any device you use every day. Discuss how implementation hiding is demonstrated in the way this device works. Is it a benefit or a drawback to you that implementation hiding exists for methods associated with this object?

2. a. Create a class named Numbers whose `Main()` method holds two integer variables. Assign values to the variables. Within the class, create two methods, `Sum()` and `Difference()`, that compute the sum of and difference between the values of the two variables, respectively. Each method should perform the computation and display the results. In turn, call each of the two methods from `Main()`, passing the values of the two integer variables. Save the program as **Numbers.cs** in the Chapter.03 folder on your Student Disk.

   b. Add a method named `Product()` to the Numbers class. This method should compute the multiplication product of two integers, but not display the answer. Instead, it should return the answer to the calling `Main()` program, which displays the answer. Save the program as **Numbers2.cs** in the Chapter.03 folder on your Student Disk.

3. a. Create a class named ConvertInches. Its `Main()` method holds an integer variable named `inches` to which you will assign a value. Create a method to which you pass `inches`. The method displays the inches in feet and inches. For example, 67 inches is 5 feet 7 inches. Save the program as **InchesToFeet.cs** in the Chapter.03 folder on your Student Disk.

b. Add a second method to the ConvertInches class. This method displays a passed argument as yards, feet, and inches. For example, 67 inches is 1 yard, 2 feet, and 7 inches. Add a statement to the `Main()` method so that after it calls the method to convert inches to feet and inches, it passes the same variable to the new method to convert the same value to yards, feet, and inches. Save the program as **InchesToYards.cs** in the Chapter.03 folder on your Student Disk.

3

4. Create a class named Monogram. Its `Main()` method holds six character variables that hold your first, middle, and last initials, and a friend's first, middle, and last initials, respectively. Create a method named `DisplayMonogram()` to which you pass three initials. The method displays the initials surrounded by two asterisks on each side and with periods following each initial, as shown in the following example:

    ** J. M. F. **

Within the `Main()` method, call the `DisplayMonogram()` method twice—once using your initials and once using your friend's initials. Save the program as **Monogram.cs** in the Chapter.03 folder on your Student Disk.

5. Create a class named Exponent. Its `Main()` method holds an integer value and, in turn, passes the value to a method that squares the number and to a method that cubes the number. The `Main()` method prints the results returned from each of the other methods. Save the program as **Exponent.cs** in the Chapter.03 folder on your Student Disk.

6. Create a class named Square. In the `Main()` method, declare an integer and assign a value. Display the value of the integer, then pass it to a method that accepts the value as a reference parameter and prints its square (the number times itself). In `Main()`, print the value again. Save the program as **Square.cs** in the Chapter.03 folder on your Student Disk.

7. a. Create a class named Reverse3. Within its `Main()` method, declare three integers named `firstInt, middleInt,` and `lastInt.` Assign values to the variables, display them, and then pass them to a method that places the first value in the `lastInt` variable and the last value in the `firstInt` variable. In the `Main()` method, display the three variables again, demonstrating that their positions have been reversed. Save the program as **Reverse3.cs** in the Chapter.03 folder on your Student Disk.

    b. Create a new class named Reverse4, which contains a method that reverses the positions of four variables. Write a `Main()` method that demonstrates the method works correctly. Save the program as **Reverse4.cs** in the Chapter.03 folder on your Student Disk.

8. Create a class named Area. Include three overloaded methods that compute the area of a square when two dimensions are passed to it. One method takes two integers as arguments, one takes two doubles, and the third takes an integer and a double. Write a `Main()` method that demonstrates each method works correctly. Save the program as **Area.cs** in the Chapter.03 folder on your Student Disk.

9. Create a class named ComputeWeeklySalary. Include two overloaded methods—one that accepts your annual salary as an integer and one that accepts your annual salary as a double. Each method should calculate and display your weekly salary, assuming 52 weeks in a year. Include a `Main()` method that demonstrates both overloaded methods work correctly. Save the program as **ComputeWeeklySalary.cs** in the Chapter.03 folder on your Student Disk.

10. Create a class named TaxCalculation. Include two overloaded methods—one that accepts a price and a tax rate expressed as doubles (for example, 79.95 and .06, where .06 represents 6%), and one that accepts a price as a double and a tax rate as an integer (for example, 79.95 and 6, where 6 represents 6%). Include a `Main()` method that demonstrates each method calculates the same tax amount appropriately. Save the program as **TaxCalculation.cs** in the Chapter.03 folder on your Student Disk.

11. Each of the following files in the Chapter.03 folder on your Student Disk has syntax and/or logical errors. In each case, determine the problem and fix the program. After you correct the errors, save each file using the same filename preceded with "Fixed". For example, DebugThree1.cs will become FixedDebugThree1.cs.

    a. DebugThree1.cs

    b. DebugThree2.cs

    c. DebugThree3.cs

    d. DebugThree4.cs

CREATING AND USING CLASSES

In this chapter you will learn:

♦ About class concepts

♦ How to create a class from which objects can be instantiated

♦ About instance variables and methods

♦ How to declare objects

♦ How to compile and run a program that instantiates class objects

♦ How to organize your classes

♦ About public fields and private methods

♦ About the `this` reference

♦ How to write constructor methods

♦ How to pass parameters to constructors

♦ How to overload constructors

♦ How to write destructor methods

Much of your understanding of the world comes from your ability to categorize objects and events into classes. As a young child, you learned the concept of "animal" long before you knew the word. Your first encounter with an animal might have been with the family dog, a neighbor's cat, or a goat at a petting zoo. As you developed speech, you might have used the same term for all of these creatures, gleefully shouting, "Doggie!" as your parents pointed out cows, horses, and sheep in picture books or along the roadside on drives in the country. As you grew more sophisticated, you became able to distinguish dogs from cows; still later, you became able to distinguish breeds. Your understanding of the class "animal" helps you see the similarities between dogs and cows, and your understanding of the class "dog" helps you see the similarities between a Great Dane and a Chihuahua. Understanding classes gives you a framework for categorizing new experiences. You might not know the term "okapi," but when you learn it's an animal, you begin to develop a concept of what an okapi might be like.

Classes are also the basic building blocks of object-oriented programming. You already understand that differences exist between the `Double`, `Int32`, and `Float` classes, yet at the same time you understand that items that are members of these classes possess similarities—they are all data types, you can perform arithmetic with all of them, they all can be converted to strings, and so on. Understanding classes enables you to see similarities in objects and increases your understanding of the programming process. In this chapter, you will discover how C# handles classes and learn to create your own classes and construct objects that are members of those classes.

UNDERSTANDING CLASS CONCEPTS

When you write programs in C#, you create two distinct types of classes:

- Classes that are application programs, containing a `Main()` method
- Classes from which you instantiate objects

All of the classes you have created so far in this book have been application programs containing a `Main()` method that executes when you run the program in which it resides. Many classes do not contain a `Main()` method; instead, you use these classes to create program objects.

When you think in an object-oriented manner, everything is an object, and every object is a member of a class. You can think of any inanimate physical item as an object—your desk, your computer, and the building in which you live are all called "objects" in everyday conversation. You can think of living things as objects, too—your houseplant, your pet fish, and your sister are objects. Events also are objects—the stock purchase you made, the mortgage closing you attended, or a graduation party that was held in your honor are all objects.

 In C#, an application program you write to use other classes is a class itself.

Everything is an object, and every object is a member of a more general class. Your desk is a member of the class that includes all desks, and your pet fish is a member of the class that contains all fish. An object-oriented programmer would say that your desk is an instance of the Desk class and your fish is an instance of the Fish class. These statements represent **is-a relationships** because you can say, "My oak desk with the scratch on top *is a* Desk and my goldfish named Moby *is a* Fish." The difference between a class and an object parallels the difference between abstract and concrete. An object is an **instantiation** of a class; an object is one tangible example of a class. Your goldfish, my guppy, and the zoo's shark each constitute one instantiation of the Fish class.

The concept of a class is useful because of its reusability. Objects receive their attributes from classes. For example, if you invite me to a graduation party, I automatically know many things about the object (the party). I assume there will be a starting time, a number of guests, some quantity of food, and some nature of gifts. I understand parties because of my previous knowledge of the `Party` class, of which all parties are members. I don't know the number of guests or the date or time of this particular party, but I understand that because all parties have a date and time, then this one must as well. Similarly, even though every stock purchase is unique, each must have a dollar amount and a number of shares. All objects have predictable attributes because they are members of certain classes.

The data components of a class often are called the **instance variables** of that class. Also, class object attributes often are called **fields** to help distinguish them from other variables you might use. The contents of a class object's instance variables also are known as its **states**. For example, the current states of a particular party include 8 p.m. and Friday; the states of a particular stock purchase include $10 and five shares.

In addition to their attributes, class objects have methods associated with them, and every object that is an instance of a class is assumed to possess the same methods. For example, at some point you must set the date and time for any party you host. You might name these methods `SetDate()` and `SetTime()`. For party guests, it would be useful to find out the date and time; the guests might use methods named `GetDate()` and `GetTime()` to do so.

Your graduation party, then, might possess the identifier `myGraduationParty`. As a member of the `Party` class, it might have data members for the date and time, like all parties, and methods to `SetDate()` and `SetTime()`. When you use them, the `SetDate()` and `SetTime()` methods require arguments, or information passed to them. For example, `myGraduationParty.SetDate("May 12")` and `myGraduationParty.SetTime("6 p.m.")` invoke methods that are available for `myGraduationParty` and send it arguments. When you think of an object and its methods, it's as though you can send a message to the object to direct it to accomplish some task—you can tell the party object named `myGraduationParty` to set the time and date you request. Even though `yourAnniversaryParty` also is a member of the `Party` class, and even though it also has `SetDate()` and `SetTime()` methods, you will want to send different arguments to `yourAnniversaryParty` than I want to send to `myGraduationParty`. Within any object-oriented program, you continuously make requests to objects' methods, often including arguments as part of those requests.

Additionally, some methods used in a program must return a message or value. If one of your party guests calls the `GetDate()` method, she hopes it will respond with the desired information. Similarly, within object-oriented programs, methods often are called upon to return a piece of information to the source of the request. For example, a method within a `Payroll` class that calculates the federal withholding tax might return a tax figure in dollars and cents, and a method within an `Inventory` class might return true or false depending on its determination of whether the quantity of an item has reached the reorder point.

When you program in C#, you create two types of classes—applications with a `Main()` method and object classes. You create the classes from which objects will be instantiated (or other programmers create them for you), and then you write applications to use the objects, along with their data and methods. Often, you will write programs that use classes created by others, as you have used the **Console** class; similarly, you might create a class that other programmers will use to instantiate objects within their own programs. A program or class that instantiates objects of another prewritten class is a **class client** or **class user**.

CREATING A CLASS FROM WHICH OBJECTS CAN BE INSTANTIATED

When you create a class, you first must assign a name to it, and then you must determine what data and methods will be part of the class. Suppose you decide to create a class named **Employee**. One instance variable of **Employee** might be an employee number, and two necessary methods might set (or provide a value for) the employee number and then get (or retrieve) it. To begin, you create a **class header** or **class definition** containing three parts:

1. An optional access modifier
2. The keyword **class**
3. Any legal identifier you choose for the name of your class

 You will learn other optional components you can add to a class definition as you continue to study C#.

For example, a header for an **Employee** class is **internal class Employee**. The keyword **internal** is a class access modifier. You can declare a class to be one of the following:

- **public**, meaning access to the class is not limited.
- **protected**, meaning access to the class is limited to the class and to any classes derived from the class. You will learn about deriving classes in Chapter 7.
- **internal**, meaning access is limited to the assembly (a group of code modules compiled together) to which the class belongs.
- **private**, meaning access is limited to another class to which the class belongs. In other words, a class can be **private** if it is contained within another class, and only that containing class should have access to the **private** class.

Private and protected classes have limited uses. Furthermore, when you declare a class using a namespace, you only can declare it to be **public** or **internal**. For now, you will always use one of those two modifiers with your classes. If you do not explicitly include an access specifier, class access is **internal** by default. Because most classes you create will have **internal** access, typing an access specifier is often unnecessary.

You learned about creating namespaces in Chapter 3.

In addition to the class header, classes you create must have a class body enclosed between curly braces. Figure 4-1 shows a shell for an `Employee` class.

```
class Employee
{
        // Instance variables and methods go here
}
```

Figure 4-1   `Employee` class shell

CREATING INSTANCE VARIABLES AND METHODS

When you create a class, you define both its attributes and its methods. You declare the **instance variables**, which are the attributes or fields, for a class within the curly braces using the same syntax you use to declare other variables—you provide a type and an identifier. When you create an instance variable, you create an attribute to hold a value that describes a feature of every object of that class. For example, within the `Employee` class you can declare an integer ID number; when you create `Employee` objects, each will have its own `idNumber`. You can define the ID number simply as `int idNumber;`. However, programmers frequently include an access modifier for each of the class fields and declare the `idNumber` as `private int idNumber;`. Figure 4-2 shows the `Employee` class containing the `idNumber` field.

```
class Employee
{
        private int idNumber;
}
```

Figure 4-2   `Employee` class containing `idNumber` field

If you do not provide an access specifier for a class field, its access is `private` by default.

The allowable field modifiers are `new`, `public`, `protected`, `internal`, `private`, `static`, `readonly`, and `volatile`. Most class fields are `private`, which provides the highest level of security. Identifying a field as `private` means that no other class can access the field's values, and only methods of the same class will be allowed to set, get, or otherwise use the field. Using private fields within classes is an example of **information hiding**, a feature found in all object-oriented languages. The private data of a class should be changed or manipulated only by its own methods, not by methods that belong to other classes.

 A benefit of information hiding is the ability to validate data. A method that sets a variable's value can ensure that the value falls within a specified range. For example, perhaps an **Employee**'s salary should not be below the federal minimum wage, or a department number should not be negative or greater than 10.

In contrast to a class's private data fields, most class methods are not usually private; they are public. The resulting private data/public method arrangement provides a means to control outside access to your data—only a class's nonprivate methods can be used to access a class's private data. The situation is similar to having a "public" receptionist who controls the messages passed in and out of your private office. The way in which the nonprivate methods are written controls how you will use the private data.

For example, one method you need for an **Employee** class that contains an **idNumber** is the method to retrieve (or return) any **Employee**'s **idNumber** for use by a program. A reasonable name for this method is **GetId()**, and its declaration is **public int GetId()**, because it will have public access, return an integer (the employee ID number), and possess the identifier **GetId()**. The **GetId()** method contains just one statement: the statement that accesses the value of the private **idNumber** field. Figure 4-3 shows the **Employee** class with the addition of the **GetId()** method.

```
class Employee
{
        private int idNumber;
        public int GetId()
        {
              return idNumber;
        }
}
```

Figure 4-3 Employee class with `idNumber` field and `GetId()` method

Notice that the `GetId()` method does not employ the `static` modifier, unlike many other methods you have created. The keyword `static` is used for class-wide methods, but not for instance methods that "belong" to objects. If you are creating a program with a `Main()` method that you will execute to perform some task, then many of your methods will be static. You can call the static methods from within `Main()` without creating an object. However, if you are creating a class from which objects will be instantiated, most methods will probably be nonstatic, as you will be associating the methods with individual objects. Methods used with object instantiations are called **instance methods**.

You can call class methods without creating an instance of the class. Instance methods require an instantiated object; class methods do not.

The counterpart to the `GetId()` method is the method you create to provide a value for an Employee's ID number. A method with the definition `void SetId(int id)` provides a means to pass an integer into the class instance method, where it will be used to assign a value to the `Employee`'s `idNumber`. The `SetId()` method does not need to return any value to a calling method, so its return type can be void. Its only statement assigns the passed parameter to the Employee's ID number. Figure 4-4 shows the complete `Employee` class, including the `SetId()` method.

```
class Employee
{
        private int idNumber;
        public int GetId()
        {
                return idNumber;
        }
        public void SetId(int id)
        {
                idNumber = id;
        }
}
```

Figure 4-4   The `Employee` class with `idNumber` field and `GetId()` and `SetId()` methods

The `Employee` class in Figure 4-4 is not a program that will run; it contains no `Main()` method. Rather, it is simply a description of what `Employee` objects will have (an `idNumber`) and be able to do (set and get the `idNumber`) when you write a program that contains `Employee` objects.

At this point, declaring get and set methods that do nothing except retrieve or assign a value might seem like a lot of work for very little payoff. Soon, however, you will learn to write methods that provide more functionality. For example, you could write a `SetId()` method that ensures that an `Employee's idNumber` always contains exactly four digits or that the `idNumber` is returned only to authorized personnel.

DECLARING OBJECTS

Declaring a class does not create any actual objects. A class is just an abstract description of what an object will be like if any objects are ever actually instantiated. Just as you might understand all the characteristics of an item you intend to manufacture long before the first item rolls off the assembly line, you can create a class with fields and methods long before you instantiate any objects that are members of that class.

A two-step process creates an object that is an instance of a class. First, you supply a type and an identifier, just as when you declare any variable. Second, you allocate computer memory for that object. For example, you might define an integer as `int someValue;` and you might define an `Employee` as `Employee myAssistant;`, where `myAssistant` could be any legal identifier you choose to represent an `Employee`.

Every object name is also a reference—that is, a computer memory location.

When you declare an integer as `int myInteger;`, you notify the compiler that an integer named `myInteger` will exist, and you reserve computer memory for it at the same time. When you declare the `myAssistant` instance of the `Employee class`, you are notifying the compiler that you will use the identifier `myAssistant`. However, you are not yet setting aside computer memory in which the `Employee` named `myAssistant` can be stored—that is done only for the built-in, predefined variable types. To allocate the needed memory, you must use the **new operator**. After defining `myAssistant` with the `Employee myAssistant;` statement, you must use the statement that actually sets aside enough memory to hold `myAssistant: myAssistant = new Employee();`. You also can define and reserve memory for `myAssistant` in one statement, as in `Employee myAssistant = new Employee();`. In this statement, `Employee` is the object's type (as well as its class), and `myAssistant` is the name of the object. The equal sign is the assignment operator, so a value is being assigned to `myAssistant`. The `new` operator is allocating a new, unused portion of computer memory for `myAssistant`. The value being assigned to `myAssistant` is a memory address at which it will be located. You need not be concerned with the actual memory address—when you refer to `myAssistant`, the compiler will locate it at the appropriate address for you—but `myAssistant` does need to know its own address.

Because class objects hold their memory addresses, you can call any class a **reference type**—in other words, a type that refers to a specific memory location. A reference type is a type that holds an address as opposed to the predefined types like `int`, `double`, and `char`, which are **value types**.

The last portion of the statement, `Employee()`, looks suspiciously like a method name with its parentheses. In fact, it is the name of a method that constructs an `Employee` object. `Employee()` is a **constructor method**. You will write your own constructor methods later in this chapter. For now, note that when you don't write a constructor method for a class object, C# writes one for you, and the name of the constructor method is always the same as the name of the class whose objects it constructs.

After an object has been instantiated, its public methods can be accessed using the object's identifier, a dot, and a method call. For example, if you declare an **Employee** named **myAssistant**, you can access **myAssistant**'s **SetId( )** method with the statement **myAssistant.SetId(345);**. The statement changes the **Employee**'s **idNumber** to the integer 345 by passing the value into the **SetId( )** method, where it is assigned to the **idNumber** for the **myAssistant** object. No class client (for example, a **Main( )** method) can access **myAssistant**'s **idNumber** directly; the only way a client can access the **private** data is by sending a message through one of the object's **public** methods. Figure 4-5 shows a class named **CreateEmployee** whose **Main( )** method declares an **Employee**, sets the **idNumber**, and retrieves the **idNumber** within a **WriteLine( )** statement. Figure 4-6 shows the execution of the program.

4

```
using System;
public class CreateEmployee
{
      public static void Main()
      {
              Employee myAssistant = new Employee();
              myAssistant.SetId(345);
              Console.WriteLine("ID # is {0}",myAssistant.GetId());
      }
}
class Employee
{
      private int idNumber;

      public int GetId()
      {
              return idNumber;
      }
      public void SetId(int id)
      {
              idNumber = id;
      }
}
```

Figure 4-5 The `CreateEmployee` class

Next, you will create a **Student** class. This class contains an ID number, last name, and grade-point average for the **Student**. It also contains methods that get and set each of these fields.

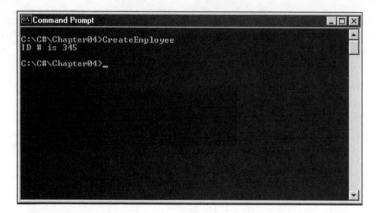

Figure 4-6 Output of CreateEmployee class

To create a Student class:

1. Open a new file in your text editor. Begin the Student class by declaring the class name **Student**. Insert an opening curly brace and declare the three fields that will hold an ID number, last name, and grade-point average, as follows:

```
class Student
    {
        private int idNumber;
        private string lastName;
        private double gradePointAverage;
```

2. Add three methods that retrieve or get each of the three fields. Each method must have a return type that corresponds to the type of variable it returns.

```
public int GetId()
{
        return idNumber;
}
public string GetName()
{
        return lastName;
}
public double GetGPA()
{
        return gradePointAverage;
}
```

3. Add three more methods that set each of the Student fields by assigning a passed parameter.

```
public void SetId(int id)
{
        idNumber = id;
}
```

```
public void SetName(string name)
{
        lastName = name;
}
public void SetGPA(double gpa)
{
        gradePointAverage = gpa;
}
```

4. Add a closing curly brace for the class. Save the file as **Student.cs** in the Chapter.04 folder of your Student Disk.

5. Open a new file in your text editor and begin a program that creates a `Student` object, assigns some values, and displays the `Student`.

```
using System;
public class CreateStudent
{
```

6. Add a `Main()` method that declares a `Student` named `oneSophomore`. Use the three set methods that belong to the `Student` class to set the field values.

```
public static void Main()
{
        Student oneSophomore = new Student();
        oneSophomore.SetId(951);
        oneSophomore.SetName("Ross");
        oneSophomore.SetGPA(3.5);
```

7. Include a `WriteLine()` statement that will allow you to see the contents of the oneSophomore's fields.

```
Console.WriteLine
   ("The student named {0} has ID # {1} and a gpa of {2}",
        oneSophomore.GetName(), oneSophomore.GetId(),
        oneSophomore.GetGPA());
```

8. Add a closing curly brace for the `Main()` method and another for the `CreateStudent` class. Save the file as **CreateStudent.cs** in the Chapter.04 folder on your Student Disk.

COMPILING AND RUNNING A PROGRAM THAT INSTANTIATES CLASS OBJECTS

When you create a class that describes objects you will instantiate, and another class that instantiates those objects, you physically can contain the two classes within a single file or place each class in its own file.

The advantages to placing both classes within the same file are that your development time typically is shorter and that the compilation process is simpler. When you first develop classes, you are likely to introduce both syntax and logical errors into each file you use. By placing your classes in the same file, you reduce the time needed to navigate through multiple files and check issues such as consistent spelling of variable and method names and consistent use of data types. Also, when you compile only a single file, the sources of any error messages you receive are easier to locate.

Advantages also come from placing classes in separate files. One advantage is simply organization. In a workshop, you can store all your nuts, bolts, and nails in one large box. Just as a multi-drawer storage cabinet makes it easier to find a quarter-inch bolt when you need it, containing each class in its own file makes the classes more manageable and easier to locate. More importantly, when a class resides within its own file, the class is easier to reuse within additional programs you create in the future.

In the next steps, you will compile and execute the **Student** class and its program both ways: as a single file and separated into two files. When you write programs in the future, you can use whichever method suits you at the time.

1. In your text editor, open the **CreateStudent.cs** file that you saved in the last set of steps.

2. Resave the file as **CreateAndUseStudent.cs**.

3. Open the **Student.cs** file and select its entire contents. In most editors you can accomplish this by pressing **Ctrl+A** or by dragging your mouse across the entire body of text. In your editor, select **Copy** to copy the **Student** class. (In many text editors, you can press **Ctrl+C** to copy.)

4. At the bottom of the newly created **CreateAndUseStudent** file, **Paste** the **Student** class. (In many text editors, you can press **Ctrl+V** to paste.) The **CreateAndUseStudent** file now contains two complete classes: **CreateStudent** and **Student**. Save the file.

5. At the command line, you can compile the file using the command **csc CreateAndUseStudent.cs**. After the file compiles successfully, execute it using the command **CreateAndUseStudent**. Figure 4-7 shows the output.

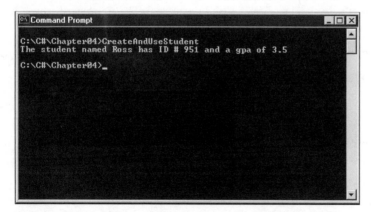

Figure 4-7   Output of `CreateAndUseStudent`

6. As an alternative to using the combined **CreateAndUseStudent** file, you can retain each class in its own file. Open the **Student.cs** file you created in the last set of steps. This file contains just the **Student** class. Provide a namespace for the class by typing **namespace StudentNamespace** and an opening curly brace at the top of the file, and a closing curly brace at the bottom of the file. Save the file (as **Student.cs**).

7. Open the **CreateStudent.cs** file you created earlier in this chapter. This file contains the program that instantiates a **Student** object. As the second line of the file, after **using System;**, insert the statement that uses the **Student** file: **using StudentNamespace;**. Save the file as **UseStudent.cs**.

8. At the command line, issue the command to compile the **Student** class as a netmodule:

   csc /t:module Student.cs

9. Compile the **UseStudent** program so it includes the Student netmodule:

   csc UseStudent.cs /addmodule:Student.netmodule

10. Execute the program using the command **UseStudent**. The output is the same as shown in Figure 4-7. Figures 4-8 and 4-9 show the completed **Student** and **CreateStudent** classes, respectively.

```
namespace StudentNamespace
{
    class Student
    {
        private int idNumber;
        private string lastName;
        private double gradePointAverage;
        public int GetId()
        {
            return idNumber;
        }
        public string GetName()
        {
            return lastName;
        }
        public double GetGPA()
        {
            return gradePointAverage;
        }
        public void SetId(int id)
        {
            idNumber = id;
        }
```

Figure 4-8   Student class

```
                public void SetName(string name)
                {
                        lastName = name;
                }
                public void SetGPA(double gpa)
                {
                        gradePointAverage = gpa;
                }
        }
}
```

Figure 4-8   Student class (continued)

```
using System;
using StudentNamespace;
public class CreateStudent
        {
                public static void Main()
                {
                        Student oneSophomore = new Student();
                        oneSophomore.SetId(951);
                        oneSophomore.SetName("Ross");
                        oneSophomore.SetGPA(3.5);
                        Console.WriteLine
                          ("Student named {0} has ID # {1} and a gpa of {2}",
                                oneSophomore.GetName(),
                                oneSophomore.GetId(), oneSophomore.GetGPA());

                }
        }
```

Figure 4-9   CreateStudent class

ORGANIZING YOUR CLASSES

Most classes you create will have more than a few data fields and more methods than just get and set methods for each field. For example, a typical `Employee` class would contain more than an `idNumber` field—a few of the many possibilities include `firstName`, `lastName`, `address`, `phoneNumber`, `salary`, `departmentNumber`, `hireDate`, `numberOfDependents`, and so on. Although there is no requirement to do so, most programmers place data fields in some logical order at the beginning of a class. For example, the `idNumber` field is most likely used as a unique identifier for each `Employee` (which database users often call a **primary key**), so it makes sense to list the employee ID number first in the class. An employee's last name and first name "go together," so it makes sense to store these two `Employee` components adjacently. Despite these common-sense rules, there is a lot of flexibility in how you position your data fields within any class.

A unique identifier must have no duplicates within an application. In other words, although an organization might have many employees with the last name "Johnson" or a salary of 400.00, only one employee will have ID number 128.

Even if the only methods created for the **Employee** class include one set method and one get method for each instance variable, quite a few methods are required. Finding ~~list~~ of methods can become a formidable task. For ease in locat- ~~y~~ programmers prefer to store them in alphabetical order. If you ~~get~~ values so they begin with "Get" and name all methods that ~~n~~ with "Set," then placing all the methods in alphabetical order ~~al~~ groupings. Another reasonable course of action is to pair the ~~r~~ a particular field. In other words, you can place the **GetId( )** ~~ds~~ adjacently, and do the same for **GetLastName( )** and

~~eeping~~ your classes organized is to use comments liberally. Every ~~ne~~ well-placed comments. Figure 4-10 shows the beginning of ~~taining~~ several data fields, methods, and documenting comments.

~~l~~ program comments are crucial to creating understandable ~~e~~ been left out of many examples in this book to save space. ~~should~~ contain many comments that identify your program ~~d~~ explain the purpose and structure of your methods.

```
     Farrell
8, 2003
     employee data
e

ta members
ate int idNumber;
private string lastName;
private string firstName;
private double salary;

// GetId method returns employee number
    public int GetId()
    {
           return idNumber;
    }
// GetLastName method returns employee name
    public String GetLastName()
    {
           return lastName;
    }
```

Figure 4-10   **Employee** class with data fields, methods, and comments

Get into the habit of documenting your programs with your name, today's date, and a brief explanation of what the program does. Your instructor might ask you to insert other information as comment text as well.

USING PUBLIC FIELDS AND PRIVATE METHODS

Most of the time, class data fields are private and class methods are public. This technique ensures that data will be used and changed only in the ways provided in your methods. Novice programmers might make a data field public to avoid having to call the get and set methods. For example, Figure 4-11 shows a **Desk** class that contains two public fields. Because the fields are public, no get or set methods are needed. The program that instantiates a **Desk** can set and retrieve the values in the fields without "bothering" with the awkward syntax of the object name, dot, and method call needed if the fields are private. Although it is easy to work with, the **Desk** class in Figure 4-11 violates a basic principle of object-oriented programming. That is, data should be hidden when at all possible, and access to it should be controlled by well-designed methods.

```
using System;
class Desk
{
        public string wood;
        public int drawers;
}
public class TestDesk
{
        public static void Main()
        {
                Desk myDesk = new Desk();
                myDesk.wood = "mahogany";  // notice wood and drawers
                myDesk.drawers = 4;        // are accessed directly
                Console.WriteLine("My {0} desk has {1} drawers",
                        myDesk.wood, myDesk.drawers);
        }
}
```

Figure 4-11   Poorly designed `Desk` class and program that instantiates a `Desk`

Although private fields and public methods are the norm, occasionally you will want to create public fields and private methods. Consider the **Carpet** class shown in Figure 4-12. Although it contains several private data fields, this class also contains one public data field. Following the four public method declarations, one private method is defined.

```
class Carpet
{
        public const string motto =  "made from the finest materials";
        private int length;
        private int width;
        private int area;
        public int GetLength()
        {
                return length;
        }
        public int GetWidth()
        {
                return width;
        }
        public int GetArea()
        {
                return area;
        }
        public void SetDimensions(int side1, int side2)
        {
                length = side1;
                width = side2;
                calcArea();
        }
        private void CalcArea()
        {
                area = length * width;
        }
}
```

Figure 4-12   The Carpet class

A legitimate reason to create a public data field occurs when you want all objects of a class to contain the same value. When you create Carpet objects from the class in Figure 4-12, each Carpet will have its own length, width, and area, but all Carpet objects will have the same motto. The field motto is preceded with the keyword const, meaning the motto is constant. That is, no program can change its value. When you define a named constant within a class, it is always static. That is, the field belongs to the entire class, not to any particular instance of the class. When you create a static field, only one copy is stored for the entire class, no matter how many objects you instantiate. On the other hand, multiple copies of nonstatic fields exist—one for each object instantiated. When you use a constant field, you use the class name, a dot, and the constant name, as in Carpet.motto, rather than an object, a dot, and the constant name.

 You learned to create named constants in Chapter 2.

Throughout this book, you have been using `static` to describe the `Main()` method of a class. You do not need to create an object of any class that contains a `Main()` to be able to use `Main()`.

Figure 4-13 shows a program that instantiates and uses a `Carpet` object, and Figure 4-14 shows the results when the program executes. Notice that although the `Console.WriteLine()` statement requires get methods for the `length`, `width`, and `area` of the `Carpet` object, the `motto` is referenced using the class name only.

```
using System;
public class TestCarpet
{
        public static void Main()
        {
                Carpet aRug = new Carpet();
                aRug.SetDimensions(12,14);
                Console.WriteLine
                    ("The {0} X {1} Carpet has an area of {2} and is {3}",
                    aRug.GetLength(), aRug.GetWidth(),
                    aRug.GetArea(), Carpet.motto);
        }
}
```

Figure 4-13   The `TestCarpet` class

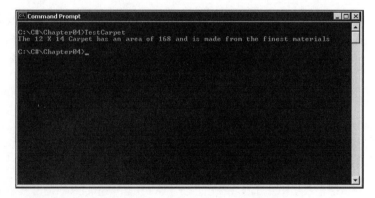

Figure 4-14   Output of `TestCarpet`

The `Carpet` class contains one private method named `CalcArea()`. As you examine the code in the `TestCarpet` class in Figure 4-13, notice that two parameters are passed to the `SetDimensions()` method. Within `SetDimensions()`, these two parameters respectively are assigned to the `length` and `width` of a `Carpet` object. The `TestCarpet` class can call the `SetDimensions()` method because it is a public method. In turn, the `SetDimensions()` method calls the private `CalcArea()` method. The `CalcArea()` method is defined as private because there is no reason for a client class like `TestCarpet` to call `CalcArea()`. The `Carpet` class's own `SetDimensions()` method should call `CalcArea()` only after valid values have been assigned to the `length` and `width` fields. You create a method to be private when it should be called only by other methods within the class, and not by outside classes.

Understanding the this Reference

4

After you create a class, you might eventually create thousands of objects from that class. When you create each object, you provide storage for each of the object's instance variables. For example, Figure 4-15 shows part of a `Book` class that contains only three fields and two methods. When you declare several `Book` objects, as in the statements `Book myBook = new Book()` and `Book yourBook = new Book()`, each `Book` object requires separate memory locations for its `title`, `numPages`, and `price`.

```
class Book
{
        private string title;
        private int numPages;
        private double price;
        public int GetPages()
        {
                return numPages;
        }
        public void SetPages(int pages)
        {
                numPages = pages;
        }
}
```

Figure 4-15   Partial Book Class

Storing a single `Book` object requires allocating storage space for three separate fields; the storage requirements for `Book` objects used by a library or retail bookstore would be far more considerable, but necessary—each `Book` must be able to "hold" its own data. If each `Book` object also required its own copy of each method contained in the class, the storage requirements would multiply. It makes sense that each `Book` needs space to store its unique title and other data, but because every `Book` uses the same methods, storing multiple copies seems wasteful and unnecessary.

Fortunately, each `Book` object does not need to store its own copy of each method. Whether you make the method call `myBook.GetPages()` or `yourBook.GetPages()`, you access the same `GetPages()` method. However, there must be a difference between the two method calls, because each returns a different value. The difference lies in an implicit, or invisible, reference that is passed to every instance method. When you call the method myBook.GetPages(), you automatically pass a reference to (the memory address of) myBook into the method. The implicitly passed reference is the **this reference**.

You can explicitly refer to the this reference within an instance method, as in the two methods in Figure 4-16. When you refer to numPages within a Book class method, you are referring to the numPages field of "this" Book—the Book whose name you used in the method call—perhaps myBook or yourBook. The use of the keyword this in the two methods in Figure 4-16 is not required; the versions of the two methods shown in Figure 4-15 work just as well.

```
public int GetPages()
{
        return this.numPages;
}
public void SetPages(int pages)
{
        this.numPages = pages;
}
```

Figure 4-16   Book class methods explicitly using this references

Figure 4-17 illustrates a situation in which using the this reference is required. In this version of the SetPages() method, the local argument that accepts an integer into the method possesses the identifier numPages. If the assignment statement within the method was written as numPages = numPages, the value of the local parameter numPages would be assigned to itself—a useless action. The local numPages within the SetPages() method would override the numPages field that is part of the Book class, and the Book class field would never be set. By explicitly naming the field this.numPages as the one that receives the value, the Book class numPages field is correctly assigned a value. Of course, you could avoid having to use the this reference by simply using a different identifier for the parameter to the method. However, as you continue to write more sophisticated C# programs, you will encounter situations in which you need to refer to the this reference to access an object's fields. Additionally, you may want to include the this reference within a method for clarity, so the reader has no doubt when you are referring to a class instance variable.

```
public void SetPages(int numPages)
{
        this.numPages = numPages;
}
```

Figure 4-17   Book class method that requires explicit this references

UNDERSTANDING CONSTRUCTOR METHODS

When you create a class such as `Employee`, and instantiate an object with a statement such as `Employee aWorker = new Employee();`, you are actually calling a method named `Employee()` that is provided by C#. A **constructor method** is a method that establishes an object. Every class you create is automatically supplied with a public constructor method with no parameters. The constructor method named `Employee()` establishes one `Employee` with the identifier `aWorker`, and provides the following initial values to the `Employee`'s data fields:

- Numeric fields are set to 0 (zero).

- Character fields are set to '\0', or null.

- Boolean fields are set to false.

- Object-type fields, such as `string` or any class object, are set to `null` (or empty).

 You will learn to create constructors with parameters in the next section of this chapter.

If you do not want an `Employee`'s fields to hold these default values, or if you want to perform additional tasks when you create an `Employee`, then you can write your own constructor method to replace the automatically supplied version. Any constructor method you write must have the same name as its class, and constructor methods cannot have a return type. For example, if you create an `Employee` class that contains a salary field and you want every new `Employee` object to have a salary of 300.00, then you could write the constructor method for the `Employee` class that appears in Figure 4-18. Any instantiated `Employee` will have a default salary figure of 300.00.

```
Employee()
{
      salary = 300.00;
}
```

Figure 4-18   Employee class constructor

You can write any statement in a constructor. Although you usually would have no reason to do so, you could print a message from within a constructor or perform any other task. Next, you will create a `Cake` class containing a constructor and demonstrate that it is called when a `Cake` object is instantiated.

To create the Cake class:

1. Open a new file in your text editor and enter the first few lines of the file that holds the Cake class. Every Cake object will have an integer number of layers, a string flavor, and a Boolean field that holds a value indicating whether the Cake object is frosted.

```
using System;
class Cake
{
    int layers;
    string flavor;
    bool isFrosted;
```

2. Add a constructor that does nothing except announce that a Cake has been created.

```
public Cake()
{
    Console.WriteLine("Cake created!");
}
```

3. Add three get methods. Each returns one of the Cake's field values.

```
public int GetLayers()
{
    return layers;
}
public string GetFlavor()
{
    return flavor;
}
public bool GetFrosted()
{
    return isFrosted;
}
```

4. Add a closing curly brace for the Cake class.

5. Add a short CreateCake class to the file. This program will contain a Main() method that creates a single Cake object and displays its values. Notice that the method does not contain any statement that sets the Cake's values; the values displayed will be the default values automatically set by the constructor.

```
public class CreateCake
{
    public static void Main()
    {
        Cake myBirthdayCake = new Cake();
        Console.WriteLine
            ("The {0} cake has {1} layers. Frosted is {2}.",
```

```
            myBirthdayCake.GetFlavor(),
            myBirthdayCake.GetLayers(),
            myBirthdayCake.GetFrosted());
    }
}
```

6. Save the file as **Cake.cs** in the Chapter.04 folder on your Student Disk. When you compile the program, you receive the three warning messages shown in Figure 4-19. When the compiler issues warning messages, it is suggesting changes to your program, but it will not stop the program from executing. These warning messages indicate that no start-up values have been supplied for the `Cake`'s fields. Usually, you want to make changes to programs until all warnings are eliminated. In this case, however, you want to see the automatically stored `Cake` values even though they are meaningless.

Depending on the spacing you used when writing your program, the line numbers for your errors might differ from those in Figure 4-19.

Figure 4-19 Warning messages after compiling `Cake` class

7. Execute the program. Figure 4-20 shows the output. When the `Cake` is created, the constructor message appears, and then the values are displayed. The gap between "The" and "cake" is the null value that represents the unassigned flavor for the `Cake`. The numeric field contains 0, and the Boolean field contains `false`.

8. Next, you will modify the `Cake` constructor to initialize every `Cake`'s data fields. Within the `Cake` constructor, after the statement that displays "Cake created!", insert three assignment statements as follows:

```
layers = 2;
flavor = "chocolate";
isFrosted = true;
```

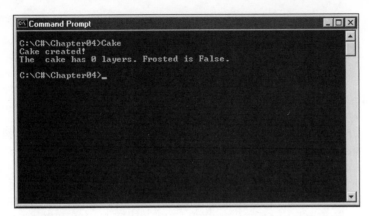

Figure 4-20   Output of Cake program using default values

9. Save the file as **Cake2.cs** in the Chapter.04 folder on your Student Disk. Compile the program; no warning messages are displayed because every field has been provided with an initial value.

10. Execute the program. The output appears as in Figure 4-21.

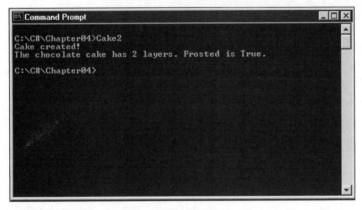

Figure 4-21   Output of Cake2 program

PASSING PARAMETERS TO CONSTRUCTORS

You can create a constructor method to ensure that all objects of a class are initialized with the same values in their data fields. After construction, you might change the value in an individual object's fields by using the appropriate set methods. Alternatively, you might create objects that hold unique field values right from the start by writing constructors to which you pass one or more parameters. You then can use the parameter values to set fields for individual object instantiations. For example, consider the **Employee** class with two data fields shown in Figure 4-22. Its constructor method assigns 999 to each potentially instantiated **Employee**'s idNumber. Any time an **Employee** object is created using a statement such as `Employee partTimeWorker = new Employee();`, even if no other data-assigning methods are ever used, you are ensured that the Employee's `idNumber` holds a default value. The `partTimeWorker Employee`, like all `Employee`s, will have an initial `idNumber` of 999.

```
public class Employee
{
        private int idNumber;
        private double salary;
        public Employee()
        {
                idNumber = 999;
        }
        //   Other methods go here
}
```

Figure 4-22   Employee class

As an alternative, you might choose to create `Employee`s with initial `idNumber` fields that differ for each `Employee`. To accomplish this task within a constructor, you need to pass an employee number to the constructor. Figure 4-23 shows an `Employee` constructor that receives a parameter. With this constructor, an integer is passed in using a statement such as `Employee partTimeWorker = new Employee(876);`. When the constructor executes, the integer used as the actual parameter within the method call is passed to `Employee()` and assigned to the `Employee`'s `idNumber`.

```
public Employee(int empID)
{
                idNumber = empID;
}
```

Figure 4-23   Employee constructor method with parameter

Next, you will alter the `Cake` class constructor to accept parameters to use as initial values for a `Cake`'s fields.

1. Open the **Cake2.cs** file in your text editor and immediately save it as **Cake3.cs** in the Chapter.04 folder of your Student Disk. Replace the existing constructor with a new version that accepts three parameters and assigns each to the appropriate `Cake` field, as follows:

```
public Cake(int cakeLayers, string cakeFlavor,
   bool cakeFrosting)
{
   layers = cakeLayers;
   flavor = cakeFlavor;
   isFrosted = cakeFrosting;
}
```

2. Within the `Main()` method of the `CreateCake` class, remove the statement that declares the `Cake` object using the parameterless constructor, and replace it with one that uses the three-parameter constructor, as follows:

```
Cake myBirthdayCake = new Cake(3,"Strawberry",false);
```

3. Save the program, and then compile and execute it. The output looks like Figure 4-24; each field has correctly been assigned the value you provided.

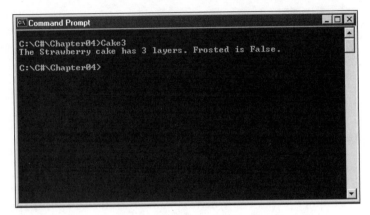

Figure 4-24   Output of Cake3 program

OVERLOADING CONSTRUCTORS

If you create a class from which you can instantiate objects, C# automatically provides a default constructor. As soon as you create your own constructor, whether it has parameters or not, you no longer have access to the automatically created version. However, if you want a class to have both parameter and parameterless versions of a constructor, you can create them. Like any other C# methods, constructors can be overloaded. You can write as many constructors for a class as you want as long as their argument lists do not cause ambiguity. For example, the `Employee` class in Figure 4-25 contains five constructors. The `Main()` method within the `CreateSomeEmployees` class shows how different types of `Employee`s might be instantiated. Notice that one version of the `Employee` constructor—the one that supports a character parameter—doesn't even use the parameter; sometimes you might create a constructor with a specific parameter type simply to force that constructor to be the version that executes.

```
using System;

class Employee
{
        int idNumber;
        double salary;
```

Figure 4-25   Employee class with five constructors

```
            public Employee()
            {
                    idNumber = 999;
                    salary = 0;
            }
            public Employee(int empID)
            {
                    idNumber = empID;
            }
            public Employee(double empSal)
            {
                    salary = empSal;
            }
            public Employee(int empID, double empSal)
            {
                    idNumber = empID;
                    salary = empSal;
            }
            public Employee(char code)
            {
                    idNumber = 1;
                    salary = 100000;
            }
    }

public class CreateSomeEmployees
{
        public static void Main()
        {
                Employee aWorker = new Employee();
                Employee anotherWorker = new Employee(234);
                Employee aThirdWorker = new Employee(45500.95);
                Employee aFourthWorker = new Employee(471, 24655.00);
                Employee theBoss = new Employee('B');
        }
}
```

Figure 4-25   Employee class with five constructors (continued)

UNDERSTANDING DESTRUCTOR METHODS

A **destructor method** contains the actions you require when an instance of a class is destroyed. Most often, an instance of a class is destroyed when it goes out of scope. As with constructors, if you do not explicitly create a destructor method for a class, C# automatically provides one.

To explicitly declare a destructor method, you use an identifier that consists of a tilde (~) followed by the class name. You cannot provide any parameters to a destructor; it must have an empty argument list. As a consequence, destructors cannot be overloaded; a class can have at most one destructor.

Figure 4-26 shows an `Employee` class that contains only one field, `idNumber`, and two methods, a constructor and a destructor. When you execute the `Main()` method in the `DemoEmployeeDestructor` class, you instantiate two `Employee` objects, each with its own `idNumber` value. When the `Main()` method ends, the two `Employee` objects go out of scope, and the destructor method for each object is called. Figure 4-27 shows the output.

```
using System;
class Employee
{
        int idNumber;
        public Employee(int empID)
        {
                idNumber = empID;
                Console.WriteLine("Employee object {0} created", idNumber);
        }
        ~Employee()
        {
                Console.WriteLine("Employee object {0} destroyed!", idNumber);
        }
}
public class DemoEmployeeDestructor
{
        public static void Main()
        {
                Employee aWorker = new Employee(101);
                Employee anotherWorker = new Employee(202);
        }
}
```

Figure 4-26 Employee class with destructor method

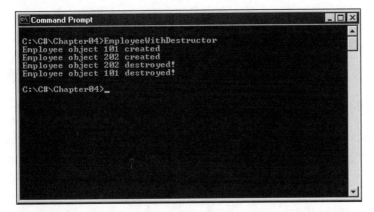

Figure 4-27 Output of `DemoEmployeeDestructor` class

The program in Figure 4-26 never explicitly calls the destructor method, yet you can see from the output that the destructor executes twice. Destructors are invoked automatically; you cannot explicitly call one. Interestingly, the last object created is the first object destroyed; the same relationship would hold true no matter how many objects the program instantiated.

 An instance of a class becomes eligible for destruction when it is no longer possible for any code to use it—that is, when it goes out of scope. The actual execution of the destructor method for an object might occur at any time after the object becomes eligible for destruction.

For now, you have little reason to create a destructor method except to demonstrate how it is called automatically. Later, when you write more sophisticated C# programs that work with files, databases, or large quantities of computer memory, you might want to perform specific clean-up or close-down tasks when an object goes out of scope. Then you will place appropriate instructions within a destructor method.

CHAPTER SUMMARY

- ❏ When you write programs in C#, you create two distinct types of classes: application programs containing a `Main()` method, and classes from which you instantiate objects. When you think in an object-oriented manner, everything is an object, and every object is an instantiation of a class. Classes contain data or attributes in fields, and classes contain methods.

- ❏ When you create a class, you create a class header (or class definition) and a class body.

- ❏ You declare the attributes and instance variables (or fields) for a class within the curly braces using the same syntax you use to declare other variables—you provide a type and an identifier. Instance data fields usually are declared to be private, while instance methods most often are declared to be public.

- ❏ Declaring a class does not create any actual objects. When you create an instance of a class, you supply a type and an identifier, just as when you declare any variable, and then you allocate computer memory for that object using the **new** operator. When you don't write a constructor method for a class object, C# writes one for you; the name of the constructor method is always the same as the name of the class whose objects it constructs.

- ❏ After an object has been instantiated, its public methods can be accessed using the object's identifier, a dot, and a method call.

- ❏ When you create a class that describes objects you will instantiate, and another class that instantiates those objects, you physically can contain both classes within the same file or place each class in its own file.

- ❏ Although there is no requirement to do so, most programmers place data fields in some logical order at the beginning of a class. For ease in locating class methods, many programmers prefer to store them in alphabetical order. Another reasonable approach is to pair the get and set methods for each field. Also, you can keep your classes organized by using comments liberally.

❑ Most of the time, class data fields are private and class methods are public. When at all possible, data should be hidden, and access to it should be controlled by well-designed methods. However, you might create a public static data field when you want all objects to contain the same value, and you might create a private method when it should be called only by other methods within the class.

❑ When you create an object, you provide storage for each of the object's instance variables, but not for each instance method. When you call an instance method, it receives an implicitly passed `this` reference.

❑ A constructor method establishes an object. Every class you create is automatically supplied with a public, parameterless constructor method that initializes its fields to default values. You can write your own constructor method to replace the automatically supplied version. Any constructor method you write must have the same name as its class. Also, constructor methods cannot have a return type.

❑ You can create objects that hold unique field values right from the start by writing constructors to which you pass one or more parameters.

❑ Like any other C# methods, constructors can be overloaded. You can write as many constructors for a class as you want as long as their argument lists do not cause ambiguity.

❑ A destructor method contains the actions you require when an instance of a class is destroyed. To explicitly declare a destructor method, you use an identifier that consists of a tilde (~) followed by the class name. You cannot provide any parameters to a destructor. Destructors cannot be overloaded; a class can have at most one destructor. Destructors are invoked automatically.

REVIEW QUESTIONS

1. When you write programs in C#, you create two distinct types of classes: classes that are application programs, and classes _____.

   a. that are overloaded

   b. from which you instantiate objects

   c. that are clients of application programs

   d. that contain a `Main()` method

2. Which of the following represents an is-a relationship?

   a. a School and a Teacher

   b. a Hospital and a Building

   c. a Car and a Truck

   d. all of these

3. An object is a(n) _____ of a class.
   a. child
   b. institution
   c. instantiation
   d. relative

4. The data components of a class often are called the _____.
   a. instance variables
   b. fields
   c. states
   d. all of these

5. A class header or class definition can contain all of the following *except* _____.
   a. an optional access modifier
   b. the keyword `class`
   c. an identifier
   d. initial field values

6. The fields that belong to every object of a class are _____ variables.
   a. instance
   b. static
   c. common
   d. class

7. Most class fields are created with the _____ modifier.
   a. `public`
   b. `protected`
   c. `new`
   d. `private`

8. Most class methods are created with the _____ modifier.
   a. `public`
   b. `protected`
   c. `new`
   d. `private`

9. Instance methods that belong to individual class objects are _____ static methods.
   a. always
   b. usually
   c. occasionally
   d. never

10. To allocate memory for an object instantiation, you must use the _____ operator.

    a. `mem`

    b. `alloc`

    c. `new`

    d. `instant`

11. Assume you have created a class named `MyClass`. The name of the `MyClass` constructor method is _____.

    a. `MyClass()`

    b. `MyClassConstructor()`

    c. Either of these can be the constructor method name.

    d. Neither of these can be the constructor method name.

12. Assume you have created a class named `DemoLogo`. Within the `Main()` method of this class, the following statement executes correctly: `Console.WriteLine("My company is {0}", Company.logo);`. Within the `Company` class, you know `logo` must be a(n) _____.

    a. integer field

    b. static field

    c. private field

    d. constant field

13. Assume you have created a class named `DemoCar`. Within the `Main()` method of this class, you instantiate a `Car` object named `myCar` and the following statement executes correctly: `Console.WriteLine("The Car gets {0} miles per gallon", myCar.GetMpg());`. Within the `Car` class, the `GetMpg()` method must be _____.

    a. `public` and `static`

    b. `public` and `non-static`

    c. `private` and `static`

    d. `private` and `non-static`

14. A `this` reference is _____.

    a. implicitly passed to nonstatic methods

    b. implicitly passed to static methods

    c. explicitly passed to nonstatic methods

    d. explicitly passed to static methods

15. When you use an instance variable within a class's nonstatic methods, you _____ explicitly refer to the method's `this` reference.

    a. must

    b. can

    c. cannot

    d. should (even though it is not required)

16. A class's default constructor _____.

    a. sets numeric fields to 0

    b. sets Boolean values to `true`

    c. both of these

    d. none of these

17. Which of the following constructor methods for the `Chair` class could coexist with the `Chair(int height)` constructor method without ambiguity?

    a. `Chair(int legs)`

    b. `Chair(int height, int legs)`

    c. both of these

    d. none of these

18. Which of the following statements correctly instantiates a `House` object if the `House` class contains a single constructor with the declaration `House(int bedrooms, double price)`?

    a. `House myHouse = new House();`

    b. `House myHouse = new House(3,125000.00);`

    c. `House myHouse = House(4, 200,000.00);`

    d. two of these

19. You explicitly call a destructor method _____.

    a. when you are done using an object

    b. when an object goes out of scope

    c. when a class is destroyed

    d. You cannot explicitly call a destructor method.

20. In a program that creates five object instances of a class, the constructor executes _____ time(s) and the destructor executes _____ time(s).

    a. one; one

    b. one; five

    c. five; one

    d. five; five

EXERCISES

1. a. Create a class named `Pizza`. Data fields include a string for toppings (such as pepperoni), an integer for diameter in inches (such as 12), and a double for price (such as 13.99). Include methods to get and set values for each of these fields. Save this class as **Pizza.cs** in the Chapter.04 folder of your Student Disk.

   b. Create a class named `TestPizza` that instantiates one `Pizza` object and demonstrates the use of the `Pizza` set and get methods. Save this class as **TestPizza.cs** in the Chapter.04 folder of your Student Disk.

2. a. Create a class named `HousePlant`. A `HousePlant` has fields for a name (for example, Philodendron), a price (for example, 29.99), and a value indicating whether the plant has been fed in the last month (for example, true). Include get and set methods for each field. Save the file as **HousePlant.cs** in the Chapter.04 folder on your Student Disk.

   b. Create a class named `DisplayHousePlants` that instantiates three `HousePlant` objects. Demonstrate the use of the get and set methods for each field for each object. Save the file as **DisplayHousePlants.cs** in the Chapter.04 folder of your Student Disk.

3. a. Create a class named `Circle` with fields named `radius`, `area`, and `diameter`. Include a constructor that sets the `radius` to 1. Also include public methods named `SetRadius()`; `GetRadius()`; `GetDiam()`; `GetArea()`; `ComputeDiameter()`, which computes a circle's diameter; and `ComputeArea()`, which computes a circle's area. (The diameter of a circle is twice its radius; the area is 3.14 multiplied by the square of the radius.) Save the class as **Circle.cs** in the Chapter.04 folder of your Student Disk.

   b. Create a class named `TestCircle` whose `Main()` method declares three `Circle` objects. Using the `SetRadius()` method, assign a small radius value to one Circle and assign a larger radius value to another Circle. Do not assign a value to the radius of the third circle; instead, retain the value assigned at construction. Call `ComputeDiameter()` and `ComputeArea()` for each `Circle` and display the results. Save the program as **TestCircle.cs** in the Chapter.04 folder on your Student Disk.

4. a. Create a class named `Square` that contains fields for length of side and area, and whose constructor requires a parameter for the length of one side of a `Square`. The constructor assigns its parameter to the length of the `Square`'s side field, and calls a private method that computes the area field. Also include methods to get each `Square` field. Save the class as **Square.cs** in the Chapter.04 folder of your Student Disk.

   b. Create a class named `DemoSquares` that instantiates two `Square` objects and displays their field values. Save the class as **DemoSquares.cs** in the Chapter.04 folder of your Student Disk.

5. a. Create a class named `GirlScout` that contains fields for a `GirlScout`'s name, troop number, and dues owed. Include a constant static field that contains the last words of the `GirlScout` motto ("to obey the Girl Scout law"). Include a constructor that allows you to set all three nonstatic `GirlScout` fields with parameter values. Also include get methods for each field. Save the class as **GirlScout.cs** in the Chapter.04 folder of your Student Disk.

    b. Create a class named `DemoScout` that instantiates two `GirlScout` objects and displays their values. Also display the `GirlScout` motto. Save the class as **DemoScout.cs** in the Chapter.04 folder of your Student Disk.

6. a. Create a class named after your state (for example, `Alaska` or `Wisconsin`). No objects will be instantiated from this class; instead, the class includes only public static fields that contain the state's capital city, population, and state bird. Save the class as **MyStateFacts.cs** in the Chapter.04 folder on your Student Disk.

    b. Create a class named `DisplayStateFacts` that displays the content of each field in your `StateFacts` class. Save the class as **DisplayStateFacts.cs** in the Chapter.04 folder on your Student Disk.

7. a. Create a class named `City`. Objects will be instantiated from this class. Include fields that hold the `City`'s name, its state, and its population. Include a constructor that accepts arguments to assign to all three fields. Also include methods to get and set each field. Save the class as **City.cs** in the Chapter.04 folder of your Student Disk.

    b. Create a class named `MovingHistory`. Instantiate two `City` objects— `myCity` and `myFriendsCity`. When you declare each object, provide constructor parameters that set appropriate `City` values for the birthplaces of you and your friend. Display the `City` objects. Then use the set methods to change each `City` object and reflect a `City` to which you relocated later in life. Display the `City` objects again. Save the class as **MovingHistory.cs** in the Chapter.04 folder of your Student Disk.

8. Each of the following files saved in the Chapter.04 folder on your Student Disk has syntax and/or logical errors. In each case, determine the problem and fix the program. After you correct the errors, save each file using the same filename preceded with "Fixed." For example, DebugFour1.cs will become FixedDebugFour1.cs.

    a. DebugFour1.cs

    b. DebugFour2.cs

    c. DebugFour3.cs

    d. DebugFour4.cs

5

SELECTION AND REPETITION

In this chapter you will learn:

- How to make decisions using the `if` statement
- How to make decisions using the `if-else` statement
- How to use compound expressions in `if` statements
- How to make decisions using the `switch` statement
- How to use the conditional operator
- How to use the NOT operator
- How to loop using the `while` statement
- How to loop using the `for` statement
- How to loop using the `do` statement
- How to use nested loops

A major reason that computer programs seem so powerful is their ability to make decisions. Programs that decide which travel route will afford the best weather conditions, which Web site will provide the closest match to search criteria, or which recommended medical treatment has the highest probability of success all rely on a program's decision making. In this chapter you will learn to make decisions in C# programs.

MAKING DECISIONS USING THE if STATEMENT

The if and if-else statements are the two most commonly used decision-making statements in C#. You use an **if statement** to make a single-alternative decision. In other words, you use an if to determine whether an action will occur. The if statement takes the form

```
if (expression)
        statement;
```

where *expression* represents any C# expression that can be evaluated as true or false and *statement* represents the action that will take place if the expression evaluates as true. You must place the if statement's evaluated expression between parentheses.

Usable expressions in an if statement include conditional expressions like amount > 5 and month == "May" as well as the value of Boolean variables such as isValidIDNumber. If the expression evaluates as true, then the statement executes. Whether the expression evaluates as true or false, the program continues with the next statement following the if.

You learned about Boolean expressions in Chapter 2. Table 2-3 summarizes how you use the comparison operators.

In some programming languages, such as C++, nonzero numbers evaluate as true and 0 evaluates as false. In C#, only Boolean expressions evaluate as true and false.

For example, the following code displays 'A' and 'B'. The expression number < 5 evaluates as true, so the statement that displays 'A' executes. Then the independent statement that displays 'B' executes.

```
int number = 3;
if (number < 5)
        Console.WriteLine("A");
Console.WriteLine("B");
```

You are not required to leave a space between the keyword if and the opening parentheses, but if you do, the statement is easier to read and is less likely to be confused with a method call.

Notice there is no semicolon at the end of the line containing if (number < 5). The statement does not end at that point; it ends after Console.WriteLine("A");.

The following code segment displays 'B' only. Because the expression `number < 5` is `false`, the statement that displays 'A' never executes.

```
int number = 12;
if (number < 5)
        Console.WriteLine("A");
Console.WriteLine("B");
```

Although it is customary, and good style, to indent the statement that executes when an `if` Boolean expression evaluates as `true`, the C# compiler does not pay any attention to the indentation. Each of the following `if` statements displays 'A' when `number` is less than 5. The first shows an `if` written on a single line; the second shows an `if` on two lines but with no indentation.

```
if (number < 5) Console.WriteLine("A");
if (number < 5)
        Console.WriteLine("A");
```

When you want to execute two or more statements conditionally, you must place the statements within a block defined by curly braces. For example, the following code displays both 'C' and 'D' when `number` is less than 5, and neither when `number` is not less than 5.

```
if (number < 5)
{
        Console.WriteLine("C");
        Console.WriteLine("D");
}
```

You can place any number of statements within the block contained by the curly braces, including another `if` statement. Figure 5-1 shows a **nested if** statement—one in which a second `if`'s Boolean expression is tested only when the first `if`'s Boolean expression evaluates as `true`. In the program in Figure 5-2, when a user enters a number greater than 5, the first `if` evaluates as `true` and the `if` that tests whether the number is greater than 10 executes. When the second `if` evaluates as `true`, the `Console.WriteLine()` statement executes. However, if the second `if` is `false`, no output occurs. When the user enters a number less than or equal to 5, the second `if` is never even tested, and again no output occurs. Figure 5-2 shows the output after the program is executed three times using three different input values.

```
using System;
public class NestedDecision
{
      public static void Main()
      {
            const int HIGH = 10, LOW = 5;
            string numberString;
            int number;
            Console.Write("Enter an integer ");
            numberString = Console.ReadLine();
            number = Convert.ToInt32(numberString);
            if (number > 5)
                  if (number < 10)
                        Console.WriteLine("{0} is between {1} and {2}",
                              number, LOW, HIGH);
      }
}
```

Figure 5-1   Program using nested `if`

Figure 5-2   Three executions of program containing nested `if` statements

MAKING DECISIONS USING THE `if-else` STATEMENT

Some decisions you make are **dual-alternative decisions**; they have two possible outcomes. If you want to perform one action when a Boolean expression evaluates as `true` and an alternate action when it evaluates as `false`, you can use an `if-else` statement. The `if-else` statement takes the form

```
if (expression)
        statement1;
else
        statement2;
```

You can code an `if` without an `else`, but it is illegal to code an `else` without an `if`.

For example, Figure 5-3 shows a program containing an `if-else` statement. With every execution of the program, one or the other of the two `WriteLine()` statements executes. Figure 5-4 shows two executions of the program.

```
using System;
public class IfElseDecision
{
        public static void Main()
        {
                const int HIGH = 10;
                string numberString;
                int number;
                Console.Write("Enter an integer ");
                numberString = Console.ReadLine();
                number = Convert.ToInt32(numberString);
                if(number > HIGH)
                        Console.WriteLine("{0} is greater than {1}", number, HIGH);
                else
                        Console.WriteLine("{0} is not greater than {1}", number, HIGH);
        }
}
```

Figure 5-3   Dual-alternative `if-else`

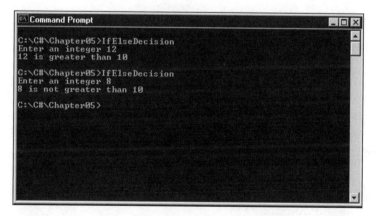

Figure 5-4   Output of `IfElseDecision` program

The indentation shown in the `if-else` example in Figure 5-3 is not required, but is standard usage. You vertically align the keyword `if` with the keyword `else`, and then indent the action statements that depend on the evaluation.

Just as you can block several statements so they all execute when an expression within an if is true, you can block multiple statements after an else so that they will all execute when the evaluated expression is false.

When you create a block using curly braces, you do not have to place multiple statements within it. It is perfectly legal to block a single statement. Blocking a single statement can be a useful technique to help prevent future errors. When a program later is modified to include multiple statements that depend on the if, it is easy to forget to add curly braces. You will naturally place the additional statements within the block if the braces are already in place.

Next, you will write a program that requires using multiple, nested if-else statements to accomplish its goal—determining whether any of the three integers entered by a user are equal.

1. Open a new text file and then enter the following method, which prompts a user for an integer and then returns it. The Main() program can call this method three times to get each of the three integers that you will compare.

```
public static int GetANumber()
{
    string numberString;
    int number;
    Console.Write("Enter an integer ");
    numberString = Console.ReadLine();
    number = Convert.ToInt32(numberString);
    return number;
}
```

2. Above the GetANumber() method, at the top of the file, write the first lines necessary for a CompareThreeNumbers class:

```
using System;
public class CompareThreeNumbers
{
```

3. Begin a Main() method by declaring three integers and obtaining values for them using the GetANumber() method.

```
public static void Main()
{
    int num1, num2, num3;
    num1 = GetANumber();
    num2 = GetANumber();
    num3 = GetANumber();
```

4. If the first number and the second number are equal, there are two possibilities: either the first is also equal to the third, in which case all three numbers are equal, or the first is not equal to the third, in which case only the first two numbers are equal. Insert the following code:

```
if(num1 == num2)
   if(num1 == num3)
      Console.Out.WriteLine
         ("All three numbers are equal ");
   else
      Console.Out.WriteLine
         ("The first two numbers are equal ");
```

 Often, programmers mistakenly use a single equal sign rather than the double equal sign when attempting to determine equivalency. For example, the expression `number = HIGH` does not compare number to HIGH. Instead, it attempts to assign the value HIGH to the number variable. When it is part of an `if` statement, this assignment is illegal.

5. If the first two numbers are not equal, but the first and third are equal, print an appropriate message. For clarity, the `else` should vertically align under `if(num1 == num2)`.

```
else
   if(num1 == num3)
      Console.Out.WriteLine
         ("The first and last numbers are equal");
```

6. When `num1` and `num2` are not equal, and `num1` and `num3` are not equal, but `num2` and `num3` are equal, display an appropriate message. For clarity, the `else` should vertically align under `if(num1 == num3)`.

```
else
      if(num2 == num3)
         Console.Out.WriteLine
            ("The last two numbers are equal");
```

7. Finally, if none of the pairs (num1 and num2, num1 and num3, or num2 and num3) is equal, display an appropriate message. For clarity, the `else` should vertically align under `if(num2 == num3)`.

```
      else
         Console.Out.WriteLine
            ("No two numbers are equal");
```

8. Add a closing curly brace for the `Main()` method. At the end of the file, below the closing brace for the `GetANumber()` method, add a closing curly brace for the class.

9. Save the file as **CompareThreeNumbers.cs** in the Chapter.05 folder on your Student Disk. Compile the program, then execute it several times,

providing different combinations of equal and non-equal integers when prompted. Figure 5-5 shows several executions of the program.

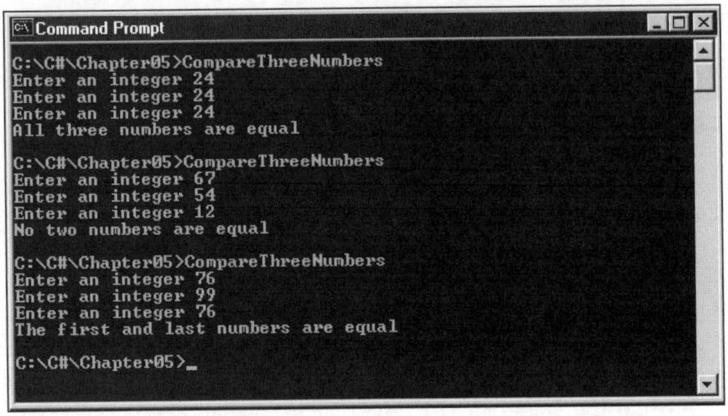

```
Command Prompt                                          _ □ X

C:\C#\Chapter05>CompareThreeNumbers
Enter an integer 24
Enter an integer 24
Enter an integer 24
All three numbers are equal

C:\C#\Chapter05>CompareThreeNumbers
Enter an integer 67
Enter an integer 54
Enter an integer 12
No two numbers are equal

C:\C#\Chapter05>CompareThreeNumbers
Enter an integer 76
Enter an integer 99
Enter an integer 76
The first and last numbers are equal

C:\C#\Chapter05>_
```

Figure 5-5   Three executions of `CompareThreeNumbers`

USING COMPOUND EXPRESSIONS IN if STATEMENTS

In many programming situations you encounter, you need to make multiple decisions. For example, suppose a specific college scholarship is available:

- if your high school class rank is higher than 75 percent

- and if your grade-point average is higher than 3.0

- and if you are a state resident

- or if you are a resident of a cooperating state

- or if one of your parents went to the college

No matter how many decisions must be made, you can decide on the scholarship eligibility for any student by using a series of if statements to test the appropriate variables. For convenience and clarity, however, you can combine multiple decisions into a single if statement using a combination of AND and OR operators.

Using the AND Operator

As an alternative to nested if statements, you can use the **conditional AND operator** (or simply the **AND operator**) within a Boolean expression to determine whether two expressions are both true. The AND operator is written as two ampersands (&&). For example, the two code samples shown in Figure 5-6 work exactly the same way. The age variable is tested, and if it is greater than or equal to 0 and less than 120, a message prints to explain that the value is valid.

```
// using &&
if(age >= 0 && age < 120)
      Console.Out.WriteLine("Age is valid");
// using nested ifs
if(age >= 0)
      if(age < 120)
            Console.Out.WriteLine("Age is valid");
```

Figure 5-6   Using the AND operator or nested `if` statements

You are never required to use the AND operator because nested `if` statements always achieve the same result, but using the AND operator often makes your code more concise, less error-prone, and easier to understand.

It is important to note that when you use the AND operator, you must include a complete Boolean expression on each side of the && operator. If you want to set a bonus to $400 when a `saleAmount` is both over 1000 and under 5000, the correct statement is `if(saleAmount > 1000 && saleAmount < 5000) bonus = 400;`. The statement `if(saleAmount > 1000 && < 5000) bonus = 400;` is incorrect and will not compile, because the `saleAmount` variable is not used on both sides of the AND expression.

With the AND operator, both Boolean expressions must be `true` before the action in the statement can occur. If the first expression is `false`, the second expression is never evaluated, because its value does not matter. The program in Figure 5-7 illustrates this phenomenon. The program assigns values to length and width variables, and contains two Boolean methods. Each method receives a package dimension and returns `true` or `false`, indicating whether the package dimension meets the requirements for shipping. The `if` statement in the `Main()` module appears to test the return values of the two methods. If the package passes both tests (that is, if `isLengthOK()` and `isWidthOK()` both return `true`), then the package is "OK to ship." Figure 5-8 shows the execution of the program.

The output in Figure 5-8 shows that the `isLengthOK()` method is called correctly because the "Checking length" message is displayed. Because the length exceeds the `LIMIT` constant, the return value of `isLengthOK()` is false, and the second method call in the `Main()` method `if` statement never executes. (The output confirms this fact; the "Checking width" message never displays.) In this example, exceeding the maximum length is enough to disqualify a package from shipping, so there is no need to test whether the width is valid. If the second method in the `if` statement, `isWidthOK()`, performed some other necessary task, it might never be executed.

```
using System;
public class ShipPackage
{
      public static void Main()
      {
             int length, width;
             length = 12;
             width = 4;
             if(isLengthOK(length) && isWidthOK(width));
                    Console.Out.WriteLine("OK to ship");
             else
                    Console.Out.WriteLine("Size too large");
      }
      static bool isLengthOK(int length)
      {
             const int LIMIT = 10;
             bool isOk = false;
             Console.WriteLine("Checking length {0}", length);
             if (length < LIMIT)
             isOk = true;
      return isOk;
}
static bool isWidthOK(int width)
{
      const int LIMIT = 8;
      bool isOk = false;
      Console.WriteLine("Checking width {0}", width);
      if(width < LIMIT)
             isOk = true;
      return isOk;
      }
}
```

Figure 5-7   Demonstrating nonevaluation of second Boolean expression in a compound AND expression

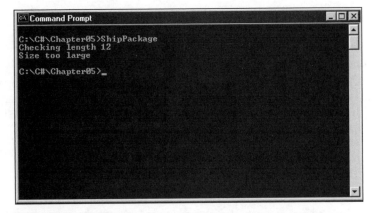

Figure 5-8   Output of `ShipPackage`

When you test multiple Boolean method results using && and the first result is false, it is easy to forget that the method to the right of the && operator will not execute. If the right-hand method performs important tasks, it would be prudent to insert a program comment advising those who read your code that execution of the second method is purposely bypassed under specific conditions.

Using the OR Operator

You can use the **conditional OR operator** (or simply the **OR operator**) when you want some action to occur even if only one of two conditions is `true`. The OR operator is written as `||`. For example, if you want to print a message indicating an invalid age when the variable is less than 0 or is 120 or greater, you can use either code sample in Figure 5-9.

You create the OR operator by using two vertical pipes. On most keyboards, the pipe is found above the backslash key; typing it requires that you also hold down the Shift key.

```
// using ||
if(age < 0 || age >= 120)
        Console.Out.WriteLine("Age is not valid");
// using nested ifs
if(age < 0)
        Console.Out.WriteLine("Age is not valid");
else
        if(age >= 120)
                Console.Out.WriteLine("Age is not valid");
```

Figure 5-9   Using the OR operator or nested `if` statements

A common use of the OR operator is to decide to take action whether a character variable is uppercase or lowercase. For example, in `if(selection == 'A' || selection == 'a')` ..., the subsequent action occurs whether the selection variable holds an uppercase or lowercase 'A'.

When the OR operator is used in an `if` statement, only one of the two Boolean expressions in the `if` needs to be true for the resulting `true` statement to execute. When you use the OR operator and the first Boolean expression is `true`, the second expression is never evaluated, because it doesn't matter whether it is `true` or `false`.

Combining AND and OR Operators

You can combine as many AND and OR operators in an expression as you need. For example, when three conditions must be `true` before performing an action, you can use an expression like `if (a && b && c)`. When you combine AND and OR operators within the same Boolean expression, the AND operators take precedence, meaning their Boolean values are evaluated first.

For example, consider a program that determines whether a movie theater patron can purchase a discounted ticket. Assume discounts are allowed for children (age 12 and younger) and for senior citizens (age 65 and older) who attend G-rated movies. The following code looks reasonable but produces incorrect results, because the && evaluates before the ||.

```
if(age <= 12 || age >= 65 && rating == 'G')
    Console.Out.WriteLine("Discount applies");
```

For example, assume a movie patron is 10 years old and the movie rating is 'R'. The patron should not receive a discount (or be allowed to see the movie!). However, within the if statement above, the expression age >= 65 && rating == 'G' evaluates first. It is false, so the if becomes the equivalent of if(age <= 12 || false). Because age <= 12 is true, the if becomes the equivalent of if(true || false), which evaluates as true, and the statement "discount applies" incorrectly displays.

You can use parentheses to correct the logic and force the expression age <=12 || age >= 65 to evaluate first, as shown in the following code.

```
if((age <= 12 || age >= 65) && rating == 'G')
    Console.Out.WriteLine("Discount applies");
```

With the added parentheses, if age is 12 or less OR 65 or greater, the expression is evaluated as if(true && rating == 'G'); when the age value qualifies a patron for a discount, then the rating value must also be acceptable. Figure 5-10 shows the if within a complete program. Figure 5-11 shows the execution before the parentheses surrounding age <=12 || age >= 65 were added, and Figure 5-12 shows the output after the inclusion of the parentheses.

```
using System;
public class MovieDiscount
{
    public static void Main()
    {
        int age = 10;
        char rating = 'R';
        if((age <= 12 || age >= 65) && rating == 'G')
            Console.Out.WriteLine("Discount applies");
        else
            Console.Out.WriteLine("Full price");
    }
}
```

Figure 5-10   Movie ticket discount program using parentheses to alter precedence of Boolean evaluations

Figure 5-11   Output of MovieDiscount program before adding parentheses to alter precedence

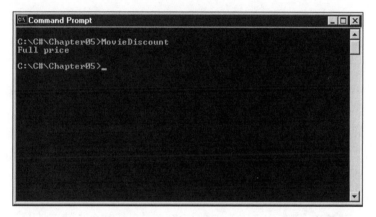

Figure 5-12   Output of MovieDiscount program after adding parentheses to alter precedence

 In Chapter 2, you controlled arithmetic operator precedence by using parentheses.

 You can use parentheses for clarity even when they are not required. For example, a && b || c and (a && b) || c both evaluate a && b first. However, if the version with parentheses makes your intentions clearer, you should use it.

 Appendix A describes the precedence of every C# operator. For example, in Appendix A you can see that the comparison operators <= and >= have higher precedence than both && and ||.

In the next steps you will create an interactive program that allows you to test AND and OR logic for yourself. The program decides whether a delivery charge applies to a shipment. If the customer lives in Zone 1 or Zone 2, then shipping is free as long as the order contains fewer than 10 boxes. If the customer lives in another zone, or if the order is too large, then a delivery charge applies. First, you will create a program with incorrect logic; then you will fix it to demonstrate correct use of parentheses when combining ANDs and ORs.

To create the delivery charge program:

1. Open a new file in your text editor and enter the first few lines of the program. Define constants for ZONE1, ZONE2, and the LOWQUANTITY limit, as well as variables to hold the customer's zone and number of boxes in the shipment.

```
using System;
public class DemoORAndANDWrongLogic
{
    public static void Main()
    {
        const int ZONE1 = 1, ZONE2 = 2;
        const int LOWQUANTITY = 10;
        int quantity;
        int deliveryZone;
```

2. Enter statements that describe the delivery charge criteria to the user and accept keyboard values for the customer's delivery zone and shipment size. You will write the GetInt() method shortly; for now, understand that it accepts a string prompt and returns an integer value.

```
Console.Out.WriteLine
    ("Delivery is free for zone {0} or  {1}",
    ZONE1, ZONE2);
Console.WriteLine
    ("...when the number of boxes is less than {0}",
    LOWQUANTITY);
deliveryZone = GetInt("Enter delivery zone ");
quantity = GetInt
    ("Enter the number of boxes in the shipment ");
```

3. Write a compound if statement that appears to test whether the customer lives in Zone 1 or 2 and has a shipment consisting of fewer than 10 boxes.

```
if(deliveryZone == ZONE1 || deliveryZone == ZONE2
    && quantity < LOWQUANTITY)
        Console.Out.WriteLine("Delivery is free");
else
    Console.Out.WriteLine("A delivery charge applies");
```

4. Add a closing curly brace for the Main() method. Then add the GetInt() method as follows:

```
public static int GetInt(string prompt)
{
  string inputString;
  int num;
  Console.Write(prompt);
  inputString = Console.ReadLine();
  num = Convert.ToInt32(inputString);
  return num;
}
```

5. Add the closing curly brace for the class and save the file as **DemoORAndANDWrongLogic.cs** in the Chapter.05 folder on your Student Disk. Compile and execute the program. Enter values for the zone and shipment size. The program appears to run correctly until you enter a shipment for Zone 1 that exceeds nine boxes. Such a shipment should not be free, but the output indicates that it is. Figure 5-13 shows the output.

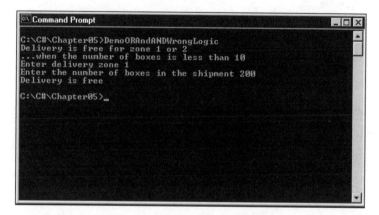

Figure 5-13   Output of DemoORAndANDWrongLogic when deliveryZone is 1 and quantity is not less than or equal to 10

6. To remedy the problem, insert parentheses around the expression deliveryZone == ZONE1 || deliveryZone == ZONE2 within the if statement in the Main() method. Change the class name to DemoORAndAND (removing *WrongLogic*). Save the new version of the program as **DemoORAndAND.cs**. When you compile and execute this version of the program, every combination of zone and quantity values should work correctly. Figure 5-14 shows the output for a Zone 1 delivery of 200 boxes. For reference, Figure 5-15 shows the complete, working program.

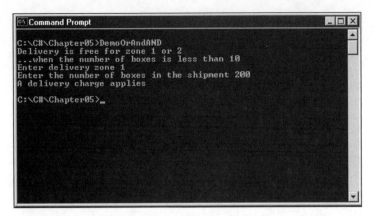

Figure 5-14   Output of DemoORAndAND when deliveryZone is 1 and quantity is not less than or equal to 10

```csharp
using System;
public class DemoORAndAND
{
    public static void Main()
    {
        const int ZONE1 = 1, ZONE2 = 2;
        const int LOWQUANTITY = 10;
        int quantity;
        int deliveryZone;
        Console.Out.WriteLine("Delivery is free for zone {0} or {1}",
            ZONE1, ZONE2);
        Console.WriteLine("...when the number of boxes is less than {0}",
            LOWQUANTITY);
        deliveryZone = GetInt("Enter delivery zone ");
        quantity = GetInt("Enter the number of boxes in the shipment ");
        if((deliveryZone == ZONE1 || deliveryZone == ZONE2)
                && quantity < LOWQUANTITY)
                    Console.Out.WriteLine("Delivery is free");
        else
                Console.Out.WriteLine("A delivery charge applies");
    }
    public static int GetInt(string prompt)
    {
        string inputString;
        int num;
        Console.Write(prompt);
        inputString = Console.ReadLine();
        num = Convert.ToInt32(inputString);
        return num;
    }
}
```

Figure 5-15   DemoORAndAND program

MAKING DECISIONS USING THE switch STATEMENT

By nesting a series of if and else statements, you can choose from any number of alternatives. For example, suppose you want to execute different methods based on a student's class year. Figure 5-16 shows the logic using nested if statements. The program segment tests the **year** variable four times and executes one of four methods, or displays an error message.

An alternative to the series of nested if statements in Figure 5-16 is to use the **switch statement**. The **switch** statement tests a single variable against a series of exact matches.

```
if(year == 1)
      FreshmanMethod();
else if(year == 2)
      SophomoreMethod();
else if(year == 3)
      JuniorMethod();
else if(year == 4)
      SeniorMethod();
else Console.WriteLine("Invalid year");
```

Figure 5-16   Executing multiple alternatives using a series of if statements

 The switch statement is not as flexible as the if because you can test only one variable and it must be tested for equality.

The **switch** structure uses four new keywords:

- The keyword **switch** starts the structure and is followed immediately by a test expression (called the **switch expression**) enclosed in parentheses.

- The keyword **case** is followed by one of the possible values that might equal the switch expression. A colon follows the value. The entire expression—for example, **case 1:**—is a **case label**. Most switch structures contain several case labels.

- The keyword **break** optionally terminates a **switch** structure at the end of each **case**. Although other statements can end a **case**, **break** is the most commonly used.

- The keyword **default** optionally is used prior to any action that should occur if the test expression does not match any **case**.

 You are not required to list the case label values in ascending order, as shown in Figure 5-17. It is most efficient to list the most common case first, instead of the case with the lowest value.

For example, Figure 5-17 shows the `switch` structure used to execute one of the school year's methods (or the error method).

```
switch (year)
{
      case 1:
             FreshmanMethod();
             break;
      case 2:
             SophomoreMethod();
             break;
      case 3:
             JuniorMethod();
             break;
      case 4:
             SeniorMethod();
             break;
      default:
             Console.WriteLine("Invalid year");
             break;
}
```

Figure 5-17   Example `switch` structure

The `switch` structure shown in Figure 5-17 begins by evaluating the `year` variable shown in the `switch` statement. If the year is equal to the first `case` label value, which is 1, then the statement that calls the `FreshmanMethod()` will execute. The `break` statement causes a bypass of the rest of the `switch` structure, and execution continues with any statement after the closing curly brace of the `switch` structure.

If the `year` variable is not equivalent to the first `case` label value of 1, then the next `case` label value is compared, and so on. If the `year` variable does not contain the same value as any of the `case` label expressions, then the `default` statement or statements execute.

If the end point of the statement list of a `switch` section is reachable, a compiler error occurs. For example, the following code is not allowed, because when the `year` value is 1, the `FreshmanMethod()` executes and the code reaches the end of the `case`.

```
switch (year)
{
  case 1:
        FreshmanMethod();
  case 2:
        SophomoreMethod();
        break;
}
```

Not allowing code to reach the end of a **case** is known as the "no fall through rule" because in other programming languages, such as Java and C++, this syntax would be allowed; when **year** equals 1, it would result in execution of both the **FreshmanMethod( )** and **SophomoreMethod( )**. Falling through to the next **case** is not allowed in C#; the most common way to avoid this error is to use a **break;** statement at the end of each **case**.

> The **governing type** of a **switch** statement is established by the **switch** expression. The governing type can be **sbyte, byte, short, ushort, int, uint, long, ulong, char, string,** or an enum type. You will learn about the enum type later.

A **switch** does not need to contain a **default** case. If the test expression in a **switch** does not match any of the **case** label values, and there is no **default** value, then the program simply continues with the next executable statement.

You can use multiple labels to govern a list of statements. For example, in the code in Figure 5-18, the **UpperClassMethod( )** executes whether the **year** value is 3 or 4.

> You receive a compiler error if two or more **case** label values in a **switch** statement are the same.

```
switch (year)
{
      case 1:
              FreshmanMethod();
              break;
      case 2:
              SophomoreMethod();
              break;
      case 3:
      case 4:
              UpperClassMethod();
              break;
      default:
              Console.WriteLine("Invalid year");
              break;
}
```

Figure 5-18   Example **switch** structure using multiple labels to execute a single statement block

You are never required to use a **switch** structure; you can always achieve the same results with nested **if** statements. The **switch** structure is simply a convenience you can use when there are several alternative courses of action depending on a single integer or character variable. Additionally, it makes sense to use a **switch** only when there are a reasonable number of specific matching values to be tested. For example, if every sale amount from 1 to 500 requires a 5 percent commission, it is not reasonable to test every possible dollar amount using the following code:

```
switch (saleAmount)
{
    case 1:
            commRate = .05;
            break;
    case 2:
            commRate = .05;
            break;
    case 3:
            commRate = .05;
            break;
    // ...and so on for several hundred more cases
```

With 500 different dollar values resulting in the same commission, one test—`if(saleAmount <= 500)`—is far more reasonable than listing 500 separate cases.

USING THE CONDITIONAL OPERATOR

The **conditional operator** is used as an abbreviated version of the `if-else` statement; it requires three expressions separated with a question mark and a colon. Like the `switch` structure, you never are required to use the conditional operator. Rather, it is simply a convenient shortcut. The syntax of the conditional operator is `testExpression ? trueResult : falseResult;`.

The conditional operator `?:` is *ternary* because it requires three arguments: a test expression and `true` and `false` result expressions.

The first expression, `testExpression`, is evaluated as `true` or `false`. If it is `true`, then the entire conditional expression takes on the value of the expression following the question mark (`trueResult`). If the value of the `testExpression` is `false`, then the entire expression takes on the value of `falseResult`. For example, `biggerNum = (a > b) ? a : b;` evaluates `a > b`. If `a` is greater than `b`, then the entire conditional expression takes the value of `a`, which then is assigned to `biggerNum`. If `a` is not greater than `b`, then the expression assumes the value of `b`, and `b` is assigned to `biggerNum`.

USING THE **NOT** OPERATOR

You use the **NOT operator**, which is written as an exclamation point (!), to negate the result of any Boolean expression. Any expression that evaluates as `true` becomes `false` when preceded by the NOT operator, and any `false` expression preceded by the NOT operator becomes `true`.

For example, suppose a monthly car insurance premium is $200 if the driver is younger that age 26, and $125 if the driver is age 26 or older. Each of the following `if` statements (which have been placed on single lines for convenience) correctly assigns the premium values.

```
if(age < 26) premium = 200;    else premium = 125;
if(!(age < 26)) premium = 125;    else premium = 200;
if(age >= 26) premium = 125;    else premium = 200;
if(!(age>= 26)) premium = 200;    else premium = 125;
```

The statements with the NOT operator are somewhat more difficult to read, particularly because they require the double set of parentheses, but the result is the same in each case. Using the NOT operator is clearer when the value of a Boolean variable is tested. For example, a variable initialized as `bool oldEnough = (age >= 25);` can become part of the relatively easy-to-read expression `if(!oldEnough)`....

USING THE while LOOP

Making decisions is what makes programs seem smart; looping is what makes programs powerful. A **loop** is a structure that allows repeated execution of a block of statements. Within a looping structure, a Boolean expression is evaluated. If it is `true`, a block of statements called the **loop body** executes, and then the Boolean expression is evaluated again. As long as the expression is `true`, the statements in the loop body continue to execute. When the Boolean evaluation is `false`, the loop ends.

One execution of any loop is called an iteration.

You can use a **while loop** to execute a body of statements continuously while some condition continues to be `true`. A `while` loop consists of the keyword `while` followed by a Boolean expression within parentheses, followed by the body of the loop, which can be a single statement or a block of statements surrounded by curly braces.

Just as within an `if` statement, the evaluated Boolean expression in a `while` statement can be a compound expression that uses ANDs and ORs.

For example, the code shown in Figure 5-19 causes the message "Hello" to display (theoretically) forever because there is no code to end the loop. Such a loop that never ends is called an **infinite loop**.

An infinite loop does not actually execute infinitely. All programs run with the help of computer memory and hardware, both of which have finite capacities.

```
int number = 1;
while (number > 0)
        Console.WriteLine("Hello");
```

Figure 5-19   An infinite loop

In Figure 5-19, the expression `number > 0` evaluates as `true`, and "Hello" is displayed. The expression `number > 0` evaluates as `true` again and "Hello" is displayed again. Because nothing ever alters the value of `number`, the loop runs forever, evaluating the same Boolean expression and printing "Hello".

It is always a bad idea to write an infinite loop, although even experienced programmers write them by accident. If you ever find yourself in the midst of an infinite loop, you can break out by holding down the Ctrl key and then pressing the C key or the Break (Pause) key.

To make a `while` loop end, three separate actions should occur:

- Some variable, the **loop control variable**, is initialized.
- The loop control variable is tested in the `while` statement.
- The body of the `while` statement must take some action that alters the value of the loop control variable.

For example, the code shown in Figure 5-20 shows a loop that displays "Hello" four times. The variable `number` is initialized to 1. Then the `while` loop compares `number` to 5, finds it is less than 5, and the loop body executes. The loop body shown in Figure 5-20 consists of two statements made into a block by surrounding them with curly braces. The first statement prints "Hello" and then the second statement adds 1 to `number`. The next time `number` evaluates, its value is 2, which is still less than 5, so the loop body executes again. "Hello" prints a third time when `number` becomes 4, and a fourth time when `number` becomes 5. Now when the expression `number < 5` evaluates, it is `false`, so the loop ends. Program execution would continue with any subsequent statements.

```
int number = 1;
while (number < 5)
{
    Console.WriteLine("Hello");
    number = number + 1;
}
```

Figure 5-20   A while loop whose body executes four times

 To an algebra student, a statement such as number = number + 1; looks wrong—a value can never be one more than itself. In C# (and many other programming languages), however, number = number + 1; takes the value of number, adds 1 to it, and then assigns the new value back into number.

5

If the curly braces are omitted from the code shown in Figure 5-20, the while loop ends at the end of the "Hello" statement. Adding 1 to number is no longer part of the loop body, so an infinite loop is created.

Also, if a semicolon is mistakenly placed at the end of the partial statement while (number < 5), the loop is also infinite—this loop has an **empty body**, or a body with no statements in it. In this case, number is initialized to 1, the Boolean expression number < 5 evaluates, and because it is true, the loop body is entered. Because the loop body is empty, ending at the semicolon, no action takes place, and the Boolean expression evaluates again. It is still true (nothing has changed), so the empty body is entered and the infinite loop continues.

Within a loop, you can change the value of the loop control variable in a number of ways. Many loop control variable values are altered by incrementing, or adding 1 to them, as in Figure 5-20. Other loops are controlled by reducing, or decrementing, a variable and testing whether the value remains greater than some benchmark value. Often, the value of a loop control variable is not altered by arithmetic, but instead is altered by user input. For example, perhaps you want to continue performing some task while the user indicates a desire to continue. In that case you do not know when you write the program whether the loop will be executed two times, 200 times, or no times at all.

Consider a program that displays a bank balance and asks if the user wants to see what the balance will be after one year of interest has accumulated. Each time the user indicates she wants to continue, an increased balance appears. When the user finally indicates she has had enough, the program ends. The program appears in Figure 5-21, and a typical execution appears in Figure 5-22.

```
using System;
public class LoopingBankBal
{
      public static void Main()
      {
            double bankBal = 1000;
            double intRate = 0.04;
            char response;
            Console.Write("Do you want to see your balance? Y or N ...");
            response = GetChar();
            while (response == 'Y')
            {
                  Console.WriteLine("Bank balance is {0}",
                     bankBal.ToString("C"));
                  bankBal = bankBal + bankBal * intRate;
                  Console.Write
                     ("Do you want to see next year's balance? Y or N ...");
                  response = GetChar();
            }
            Console.WriteLine("Have a nice day!");
      }
      public static char GetChar()
      {
            string inputString;
            char answer;
            inputString = Console.ReadLine();
            answer = Convert.ToChar(inputString);
            return answer;
      }
}
```

Figure 5-21   LoopingBankBal program

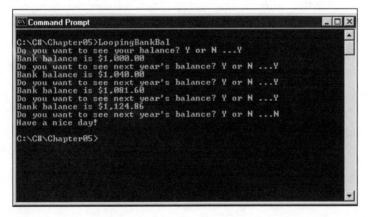

Figure 5-22   Output of typical execution of LoopingBankBal program

The program shown in Figure 5-21 continues to display bank balances while the response is *Y*. It could also be written to display while the response is not *N*, as in while (response != 'N').... A value that a user must supply to stop a loop is called a **sentinel value**.

The program shown in Figure 5-21 contains three variables: a bank balance, an interest rate, and a response. The program asks the user, "Do you want to see your balance?" and reads the response. The loop in the program begins with while (response == 'Y'). If the user types any response other than *Y*, then the loop body never executes; instead, the next statement to execute is the "Have a nice day!" statement at the bottom of the program. However, if the user enters *Y*, then all four statements within the loop body execute. The current balance is displayed, and the program increases the balance by the interest rate value; this value will never be displayed unless the user requests another loop repetition. Within the loop, the program then prompts the user and reads in a new value for response. The loop ends with a closing curly brace, and program control returns to the top of the loop where the Boolean expression in the while is tested again. If the user typed *Y* at the last prompt, then the loop is entered and the increased bankBal value that was calculated during the last loop cycle is finally displayed.

In C#, character data is case sensitive. If a program tests response == 'Y', a user response of *y* will result in a false evaluation.

USING THE for LOOP

You can use a while loop when you need to perform a task some predetermined number of times. A loop that executes a specific number of times is a **definite loop** or a **counted loop**. To write a definite loop, you initialize a loop control variable, and as long as it does not pass a limit, you continue to execute the body of the while loop. To avoid an infinite loop, the body of the while loop must contain a statement that alters the loop control variable.

Because you need definite loops so frequently when you write programs, C# provides a shorthand notation that you can use to create such a loop. When you use a **for statement**, you can indicate the starting value for the loop control variable, the test condition that controls loop entry, and the expression that alters the loop control variable, all in one convenient place.

You begin a **for** statement with the keyword **for** followed by a set of parentheses. Within the parentheses there are three sections separated by exactly two semicolons. The three sections are usually used for:

- Initializing the loop control variable

- Testing the loop control variable

- Updating the loop control variable

The body of the **for** statement follows the parentheses. As with an **if** or a **while**, you can use a single statement as the body of a **for** loop, or you can use a block of statements enclosed in curly braces. The **while** and **for** statements shown in Figure 5-23 produce the same output—the integers 1 through 10.

```
// Declare loop control variable
int x;
// Using a while loop to display 1 through 10
x = 1;
while(x < 11)
{
      Console.WriteLine(x);
      ++x;
}
// Using a for loop to display 1 through 10
for(x = 1; x < 11; ++x)
      Console.WriteLine(x);
```

Figure 5-23   Printing integers 1 through 10 with `while` and `for` loops

 Recall that ++x increases the value of x by 1. You learned about the shortcut arithmetic operators in Chapter 2.

Within the parentheses of the **for** statement shown in Figure 5-23, the first section prior to the first semicolon sets a variable named **x** to 1. The program will execute this statement once, no matter how many times the body of the **for** loop eventually executes.

After the initialization expression executes, program control passes to the middle, or test, section of the **for** statement. If the Boolean expression found there evaluates to **true**, then the body of the **for** loop is entered. In the program segment shown in Figure 5-23, **x** is set to 1, so when **x < 11** is tested, it evaluates to **true** and the loop body prints the value of **x**.

After the loop body executes, the final one-third of the **for** executes, and **x** increases to 2. Following the third section, program control returns to the second section, where **x** is compared to 11 a second time. Because the value of **x** is 2, it is still less than 11, so the body of the **for** loop executes. The value of **x** is displayed. Then the third, altering portion of the **for** statement executes again. The variable **x** increases to 3, and the **for** loop continues.

Eventually, when **x** is *not* less than 11 (after 1 through 10 have printed), the **for** loop ends, and the program continues with any statements that follow the **for** loop.

Although the three sections of the `for` loop are most commonly used for initializing, testing, and incrementing, you can also perform other tasks:

- You can initialize more than one variable by placing commas between the separate statements, as in `for(g = 0, h = 1; g < 6; ++g)`.

- You can perform more than one test by evaluating compound conditions, as in `for(g = 0; g < 3 && h > 1; ++g)`.

- You can decrement, or perform some other task, as in `for(g = 5; g >= 1; --g)`.

- You can even leave one or more portions of the `for` empty, although the two semicolons are still required as placeholders.

Generally, you should use the `for` loop for its intended purpose, which is a shorthand way of programming a definite loop.

You will learn about a similar loop, the `Foreach` loop, when you study arrays in Chapter 6.

USING THE do LOOP

With all the loops you have written so far, the loop body might execute many times, but it is also possible that the loop will not execute at all. For example, recall the bank balance program that displays compound interest, part of which is shown in Figure 5-24.

The program segment in Figure 5-24 begins with the prompt, "Do you want to see your balance? Y or N …". If the user does not reply by typing Y, the loop body never executes. The `while` loop checks a value at the "top" of the loop before the body has a chance to execute.

```
Console.Write("Do you want to see your balance? Y or N ...");
response = GetChar();
while (response == 'Y')
{
    Console.WriteLine("Bank balance is {0}", bankBal.ToString("C"));
    bankBal = bankBal + bankBal * intRate;
    Console.Write("Do you want to see next year's balance? Y or N ...");
    response = GetChar();
}
```

Figure 5-24   Part of the bank balance program using a `while` loop

Sometimes you might need a loop body to execute at least one time. If so, you want to write a loop that checks at the "bottom" of the loop after the first iteration. The **do loop** checks the bottom of the loop after one repetition has occurred.

Figure 5-25 shows a do loop for a bank balance program. The loop starts with the keyword do. The body of the loop follows and is contained within curly braces. The Boolean expression that controls loop execution is written using a while statement placed after the loop body. The bankBal variable is output before the user has any option of responding. At the end of the loop, the user is prompted "Do you want to see next year's balance? Y or N". Now the user has the option of seeing more balances, but the first view of the balance was unavoidable. The user's response is checked at the bottom of the loop. If it is Y, then the loop repeats.

```
do
{
     Console.WriteLine("Bank balance is {0}", bankBal.ToString("C"));
     bankBal = bankBal + bankBal * intRate;
     Console.Write("Do you want to see next year's balance? Y or N ...");
     response = GetChar();
}while(response == 'Y');
```

Figure 5-25   Part of the bank balance program using a do loop

In any situation where you want to loop, you never are required to use a do loop. Within the bank balance example, you could unconditionally display the bank balance once, prompt the user, and then start a while loop that might not be entered. However, when you know you want to perform some task at least one time, the do loop is convenient.

USING NESTED LOOPS

Just as if statements can be nested, so can loops. You can place a while loop within a while loop, a for loop within a for loop, a while loop within a for loop, or any other combination you can think of.

In the next steps you will write a program that creates a tipping table. Restaurant patrons can use this table to approximate the correct tip for meal prices from $10 to $100, at tipping percentage rates from 10 percent to 25 percent. The program uses several loops.

To create the tipping table:

1. Open a new file in your text editor and enter the beginning of the program. It begins by declaring variables to use for the price of a dinner, a tip percentage rate, and the amount of the tip.

```
using System;
public class TippingTable
{
     public static void Main()
     {
          double dinnerPrice = 10.00;
          double tipRate = 0.10;
          double tip;
```

2. To create a heading for the table, display "Price". (For alignment, insert three spaces after the quotes and before the *P* in *Price*.) On the same line, use a loop that displays every tip rate from 0.10 through 0.25 in increments of 0.05. In other words, the tip rates are 0.10, 0.15, 0.20, and 0.25. Complete the heading for the table using a `WriteLine()` statement that advances the cursor to the next line of output and a `WriteLine()` statement that displays a dashed line.

```
Console.Write("   Price");
for(tipRate = 0.10; tipRate <= 0.25; tipRate += 0.05)
      Console.Write("{0,8}",tipRate.ToString("F"));
Console.WriteLine();
Console.WriteLine
("----------------------------------------");
```

 Recall that within a `for` loop, the expression before the first semicolon executes once, the middle expression is tested, the loop body executes, and then the expression to the right of the second semicolon executes. In other words, 0.05 is not added to `tipRate` until after the `tipRate` displays on each cycle through the loop.

 As an alternative to typing 40 dashes in the `WriteLine()` statement, you could use the following loop to display a single dash 40 times. When the 40 dashes are completed, use `WriteLine()` to advance the cursor to a new line.

```
for(int x = 0; x < 40; ++x)
    Console.Write("-");
Console.WriteLine();
```

3. Reset `tipRate` to 0.10.

```
tipRate = 0.10;
```

4. Create a nested loop that continues while the `dinnerPrice` remains 100.00 or less. Each iteration of this loop displays one row of the tip table. Within this loop, display the `dinnerPrice`, then loop to display four tips while the `tipRate` varies from 0.10 through 0.25. At the end of the loop, increase the `dinnerPrice` by 10.00, reset the `tipRate` to 0.10 so it is ready for the next row, and write a new line to advance the cursor.

```
while(dinnerPrice <= 100.00)
{
    Console.Write("{0,8}", dinnerPrice.ToString("C"));
    while(tipRate <= 0.25)
    {
            tip = dinnerPrice * tipRate;
            Console.Write("{0,8}",tip.ToString("F"));
            tipRate += 0.05;
    }
```

```
                    dinnerPrice += 10.00;
                    tipRate = 0.10;
                    Console.WriteLine();
        }
```

 Recall that the {0,8} format string in the Write() statements displays the first argument in fields that are eight characters wide. You learned about format strings in Chapter 2.

5. Add two closing curly braces—one for the Main() method and one for the class.

6. Save the file as **TippingTable.cs** in the Chapter.05 folder on your Student Disk. Compile and execute the program. The output looks like Figure 5-26.

```
Command Prompt                                              _ □ ×

C:\C#\Chapter05>TippingTable
   Price    0.10     0.15     0.20     0.25
───────────────────────────────────────────────
  $10.00    1.00     1.50     2.00     2.50
  $20.00    2.00     3.00     4.00     5.00
  $30.00    3.00     4.50     6.00     7.50
  $40.00    4.00     6.00     8.00    10.00
  $50.00    5.00     7.50    10.00    12.50
  $60.00    6.00     9.00    12.00    15.00
  $70.00    7.00    10.50    14.00    17.50
  $80.00    8.00    12.00    16.00    20.00
  $90.00    9.00    13.50    18.00    22.50
 $100.00   10.00    15.00    20.00    25.00

C:\C#\Chapter05>_
```

Figure 5-26   Output of TippingTable

CHAPTER SUMMARY

❑ You use an if statement to make a single-alternative decision. The if statement takes the form if (expression) statement;. When you want to execute multiple statements conditionally, you can place the statements within a block defined by curly braces.

❑ When you make a dual-alternative decision, you can use an if-else statement. The if-else statement takes the form if (expression) statement1; else statement2;. Just as you can block several statements so they all execute when an expression within an if is true, you can block multiple statements after an else so they all execute when the evaluated expression is false.

❑ You can use the conditional AND operator (or simply the AND operator) within a Boolean expression to determine whether two expressions are both true. The AND operator is written as two ampersands (&&). When you use the AND operator, you must include a complete Boolean expression on each side of the && operator.

❏ You can use the conditional OR operator (or simply the OR operator) when you want some action to occur when one or both of two conditions are **true**. The OR operator is written as | |.

❏ When you combine AND and OR operators within the same Boolean expression without parentheses, the AND operators take precedence, meaning their Boolean values are evaluated first.

❏ The **switch** statement tests a single variable against a series of exact matches.

❏ The conditional operator is used as an abbreviated version of the **if-else** statement. It requires three expressions separated with a question mark and a colon.

❏ You use the NOT operator, which is written as an exclamation point (!), to negate the result of any Boolean expression.

❏ You can use a **while** loop to execute a body of statements continuously while some condition continues to be **true**. A **while** loop consists of the keyword **while**, followed by a Boolean expression within parentheses, followed by the body of the loop, which can be a single statement or a block of statements surrounded by curly braces.

❏ When you use a **for** statement, you can indicate the starting value for the loop control variable, the test condition that controls loop entry, and the expression that alters the loop control variable, all in one convenient place. You begin a **for** statement with the keyword **for**, followed by a set of parentheses. Within the parentheses there are three sections separated by exactly two semicolons. The three sections are typically used to initialize, test, and update the loop control variable.

❏ The **do** loop checks the bottom of the loop after one repetition has occurred.

❏ You can nest any combination of loops to achieve desired results.

5

REVIEW QUESTIONS

1. What is the output of the following code segment?

```
int a = 3, b = 4;
if(a == b)
    Console.Write("Black");
    Console.Write("White");
```

a. Black

b. White

c. BlackWhite

d. nothing

2. What is the output of the following code segment?

```
int a = 3, b = 4;
if(a < b)
{
    Console.Write("Black");
    Console.Write("White");
}
```

a. Black

b. White

c. BlackWhite

d. nothing

3. What is the output of the following code segment?

```
int a = 3, b = 4;
if(a > b)
    Console.Write("Black");
else
    Console.Write("White");
```

a. Black

b. White

c. BlackWhite

d. nothing

4. If the following code segment compiles correctly, what do you know about the variable x?

```
if(x) Console.WriteLine("OK");
```

a. x is an integer variable

b. x is a Boolean variable

c. x is greater than 0

d. none of these

5. What is the output of the following code segment?

```
int c = 6, d = 12;
if(c > d);
    Console.Write("Green");
    Console.Write("Yellow");
```

a. Green

b. Yellow

c. GreenYellow

d. nothing

6. What is the output of the following code segment?

```
int c = 6, d = 12;
if(c < d)
        if (c > 8)
                    Console.Write("Green");
        else
                    Console.Write("Yellow");
    else
        Console.Write("Blue");
```

a. Green

b. Yellow

c. Blue

d. nothing

7. What is the output of the following code segment?

```
int e = 5, f = 10;
if(e < f && f < 0)
        Console.Write("Red");
else
        Console.Write("Orange");
```

a. Red

b. Orange

c. RedOrange

d. nothing

8. What is the output of the following code segment?

```
int e = 5, f = 10;
if(e < f || f < 0)
        Console.Write("Red");
else
        Console.Write("Orange");
```

a. Red

b. Orange

c. RedOrange

d. nothing

9. Which of the following expressions is equivalent to

```
if (g > h)
    if(g < k)
                Console.Write("Brown");
```

5

a. `if(g > h && g < k) Console.Write("Brown");`

b. `if(g > h && < k) Console.Write("Brown");`

c. `if(g > h || g < k) Console.Write("Brown");`

d. two of these

10. Which of the following expressions assigns `true` to a Boolean variable named `isIDValid` when the `idNumber` is greater than 1000, less than or equal to 9999, or equal to 123456?

a. `isIDValid = (idNumber > 1000 && idNumber <= 9999 && idNumber == 123456)`

b. `isIDValid = (idNumber >1000 && idNumber <=9999 || idNumber == 123456)`

c. `isIDValid = ((idNumber > 1000 && idNumber <= 9999) || idNumber == 123456)`

d. two of these

11. Which of the following expressions is equivalent to `a || b && c || d`?

a. `a && b || c && d`

b. `(a || b) && (c || d)`

c. `a || (b && c) || d`

d. two of these

12. How many case labels would a `switch` statement require to be equivalent to the following `if` statement?

```
if(v == 1)
      Module1();
else
      Module2();
```

a. zero

b. one

c. two

d. impossible to tell

13. Falling through a `switch case` is most often prevented by using the _____.

a. `break` statement

b. `default` statement

c. `case` statement

d. `end` statement

14. If the test expression in a `switch` does not match any of the `case` values, and there is no `default` value, then _____.

   a. a compiler error occurs

   b. a run-time error occurs

   c. the program continues with the next executable statement

   d. the expression is incremented and the `case` values are tested again

15. Which of the following is equivalent to the statement
   `if (m == 0) d = 0 ; else d = 1;?`

   a. `? m == 0 : d = 0, d = 1;`

   b. `m? d = 0; d = 1;`

   c. `m == 0 ; d = 0; d = 1?`

   d. `m == 0 ? d = 0 : d = 1;`

16. Which of the following C# expressions is equivalent to `a < b && b < c?`

   a. `c > b > a`

   b. `a < b && c >= b`

   c. `!(b <= a) && b < c`

   d. two of these

17. What is the output of the following code segment?

```
s = 1;
while (s < 4)
    ++s;
    Console.Write(s);
```

   a. 1

   b. 4

   c. 1234

   d. 234

18. What is the output of the following code segment?

```
j = 5;
while(j > 0)
{
    Console.Write(j);
    j--;
}
```

   a. 0

   b. 5

   c. 54321

   d. 543210

19. Which of the following is *not* one of the actions that must occur in a non-infinite loop?

    a. initialize a loop control variable

    b. display the loop control variable

    c. test the loop control variable

    d. alter the loop control variable

20. What does the following code segment display?

    ```
    for (t = 0; t < 3; ++t)
        Console.Write(t);
    ```

    a. 0

    b. 01

    c. 012

    d. 0123

EXERCISES

As you create each exercise, save the finished program in the Chapter.05 folder of your Student Disk.

1. Write a program that prompts the user for an hourly pay rate. If the value entered is less than $5.65, display an error message. Save the program as **CheckLowRate.cs**.

2. Write a program that prompts a user for an hourly pay rate. If the value entered is less than $5.65 or greater than $49.99, display an error message. Save the program as **CheckLowAndHighRate.cs**.

3. Write a program that prompts a user for an hourly pay rate. While the user enters values less than $5.65 or greater than $49.99, continue to prompt the user. Save the program as **EnsureValidPayRate.cs**.

4. Write a program for a furniture company. Ask the user to choose *P* for pine, *O* for oak, or *M* for mahogany. Show the price of a table manufactured with the chosen wood. Pine tables cost $100, oak tables cost $225, and mahogany tables cost $310. Save the program as **Furniture.cs**.

5. Write a program for a college's admissions office. The user enters a numeric high school grade-point average (for example, 3.2) and an admission test score. Print the message "Accept" if the student meets either of the following requirements:

    ❑ A grade-point average of 3.0 or higher and an admission test score of at least 60

    ❑ A grade-point average of less than 3.0 and an admission test score of at least 80

    If the student does not meet either of the qualification criteria, print "Reject". Save the program as **Admission.cs**.

6. Write a program that prompts the user for an hourly pay rate and hours worked. Compute gross pay (hours times pay rate), withholding tax, and net pay (gross pay minus withholding tax). Withholding tax is computed as a percentage of gross pay based on the following:

Gross Pay	**Withholding Percentage**
Up to and including 300.00	10%
300.01 and up	12%

Save the program as **Payroll.cs**.

5

7. Write a program that allows the user to enter two integers and a character. If the character is *A*, add the two integers. If it is *S*, subtract the second integer from the first. If it is *M*, multiply the integers. Display the results of the arithmetic. Save the file as **Calculate.cs**.

8. Write a program that allows the user to enter integer values continuously until the user enters 999. Display the sum of the values entered, not including 999. Save the file as **Sum.cs**.

9. Write a program that asks the user to type a vowel from the keyboard. If the character entered is a vowel, display "OK"; if it is not a vowel, display an error message. Be sure to allow both uppercase and lowercase vowels. The program continues until the user types '!'. Save the file as **GetVowel.cs**.

10. Three salespeople work at Sunshine Hot Tubs—Andrea, Brittany, and Eric. Write a program that prompts the user for a salesperson's initial ('A', 'B', or 'E'). While the user does not type 'Z', continue by prompting for the amount of a sale the salesperson made. Calculate the salesperson's commission as 10 percent of the sale amount, and add the commission to a running total for that salesperson. After the user types 'Z' for an initial, display each salesperson's total commission earned. Save the file as **TubSales.cs**.

11. Display a multiplication table that shows the product of every integer from 1 through 10 multiplied by every integer from 1 through 10. Save the file as **MultiplicationTable.cs**.

12. Write a program that prints all even numbers from 2 to 100, inclusive. Save the file as **EvenNums.cs**.

13. Write a program that prints every integer value from 1 to 20, along with its squared value. Save the file as **TableOfSquares.cs**.

14. Write a program that sums the integers from 1 to 50. Save the file as **Sum50.cs**.

15. Write a program that prints every perfect number from 1 through 1000. A number is perfect if it equals the sum of all the smaller positive integers that divide evenly into it. For example, 6 is perfect because 1, 2, and 3 divide evenly into it and their sum is 6. Save the file as **Perfect.cs**.

16. Each of the following files in the Chapter.05 folder on your Student Disk has syntax and/or logical errors. In each case, determine the problem and fix the program. After you correct the errors, save each file using the same filename preceded with *Fixed*. For example, save DebugFive1.cs as **FixedDebugFive1.cs**.

a. DebugFive1.cs

b. DebugFive2.cs

c. DebugFive3.cs

d. DebugFive4.cs

6

USING ARRAYS

In this chapter you will learn:

♦ How to declare an array and assign values to array elements

♦ How to initialize an array

♦ How to use subscripts to access array elements

♦ How to use the `Length` field

♦ How to use `foreach` to control array access

♦ How to manually search an array to find an exact match

♦ How to search an array to find a range match

♦ How to use the `BinarySearch()` method

♦ How to use the `Sort()` and `Reverse()` methods

♦ How to pass an array to a method

♦ How to use parameter arrays

♦ How to declare an array of objects

♦ How to use the `BinarySearch()` and `Sort()` methods with object arrays

Storing values in variables provides programs with flexibility—a program that uses variables to replace constants can manipulate different values each time the program executes. When you add loops to your programs, the same variable can hold different values during successive cycles through the loop within the same program execution. This ability makes the program even more flexible. Learning to use the data structure known as an array provides you with further flexibility—you can store multiple values in adjacent memory locations and access them by varying a value that indicates which of the stored values you want to use. In this chapter, you will learn to create and manage C# arrays.

DECLARING AN ARRAY AND ASSIGNING VALUES TO ARRAY ELEMENTS

Sometimes storing just one value in memory at a time isn't adequate. For example, a sales manager who supervises 20 employees might want to determine whether each employee has produced sales above or below the average amount. When you enter the first employee's sales figure into a program, you can't determine whether it is above or below average, because you won't know the average until you have entered all 20 figures. You might plan to assign 20 sales figures to 20 separate variables, each with a unique name, then sum and average them. That process is awkward and unwieldy, however—you need 20 prompts, 20 read statements using 20 separate storage locations, and 20 addition statements. This method might work for 20 salespeople, but what if you have 30, 40, or 10,000 salespeople?

A superior approach is to assign the sales value to the same variable in 20 successive cycles through a loop that contains one prompt, one read, and one addition statement. Unfortunately, when you read in the sales value for the second employee, that data item replaces the figure for the first employee, and the first employee's value is no longer available to compare to the average of all 20 values. When the data-entry loop finishes, the only sales value left in memory is the last one entered.

The best solution is to create an array. An **array** is a list of data items that all have the same type and the same name. You declare an array variable in the same way as you declare any other variable, but you insert a pair of square brackets after the type. For example, to declare an array of double values to hold sales figures for salespeople, you write `double[] salesFigure;`.

In some programming languages, such as C++ and Java, you also can declare an array variable by placing the square brackets after the array name, as in `double salesFigure[];`. This format is illegal in C#.

After you create an array variable, you still need to create the actual array. You use the same procedure to create an array as you use to create an object. Recall that when you create a class named `Employee`, you can declare an `Employee` object with a declaration such as `Employee oneWorker;`. That declaration does not actually create the `oneWorker` object. Instead, you create the `oneWorker` object when you use the keyword **new** and the constructor method, as in `oneWorker = new Employee();`. Similarly, declaring an array and actually reserving memory space for it are two distinct processes. To reserve memory locations for 20 `salesFigure` objects, you declare the array variable with `double[] salesFigure;`; you then create the array with `salesFigure = new double[20];`. Just as with objects, you also can declare and create an array in one statement, such as `double[] salesFigure = new double[20];`.

You learned about creating objects using the new operator in Chapter 2.

Some other languages, such as COBOL, BASIC, and Visual Basic, use parentheses rather than brackets to refer to individual array elements. By using brackets, the creators of C# made it easier for you to distinguish arrays from methods. C++ and Java also use brackets surrounding array subscripts.

The statement `double[] salesFigure = new double[20];` reserves 20 memory locations for 20 `salesFigure` objects. You can distinguish each `salesFigure` from the others with a subscript. A **subscript** (also called **an index**) is an integer contained within square brackets that indicates the position of one of an array's variables, or **elements**. In C#, any array's elements are numbered beginning with 0, so you can legally use any subscript from 0 through 19 when working with an array that has 20 elements. In other words, the first `salesFigure` array element is `salesFigure[0]` and the last `salesFigure` element is `salesFigure[19]`.

6

In C#, an array subscript must be an integer. For example, no array contains an element with a subscript of 1.5.

A common mistake is to forget that the first element in an array is element 0, especially if you know another programming language in which the first array element is element 1. Making this mistake means you will be "off by one" in your use of any array.

When accessing an array element, if you are "off by one" but still using a valid subscript, your program will produce incorrect output. If you are "off by one" so that your subscript becomes larger than the highest value allowed, you will cause a program error.

To remember that array elements begin with element 0, it might be helpful to think of the first array element as being "zero elements away from" the beginning of the array, the second element as being "one element away from" the beginning of the array, and so on.

When you work with any individual array element, you treat it no differently than you would treat a single variable of the same type. For example, to assign a value to the first `salesFigure` in an array, you use a simple assignment statement, such as `salesFigure[0] = 2100.00;`. To print the last `salesFigure` in a 20-element array, you write `Console.WriteLine(salesFigure[19]);`.

Next, you will create a small array to see how arrays are used. The array will hold salaries for four categories of employees.

To create a program that uses an array:

  1. Open a new text file in your text editor.

2. Begin the class that will demonstrate array use by typing the following:

```
using System;
public class ArrayDemo1
{
   public static void Main()
{
```

3. Declare and create an array that can hold four double values by typing:

```
double[] payRate;
payRate = new double[4];
```

4. One by one, assign four values to the four pay rate array elements by typing:

```
payRate[0] = 6.00;
payRate[1] = 7.35;
payRate[2] = 8.12;
payRate[3] = 12.45;
```

5. To confirm that the four values have been assigned, print the pay rates, one by one, using the following code:

```
Console.WriteLine("Pay rate {0} is {1}",
   0,payRate[0].ToString("C"));
Console.WriteLine("Pay rate {0} is {1}",
   1,payRate[1].ToString("C"));
Console.WriteLine("Pay rate {0} is {1}",
   2,payRate[2].ToString("C"));
Console.WriteLine("Pay rate {0} is {1}",
   3,payRate[3].ToString("C"));
```

6. Add the two closing curly brackets that end the Main() method and the ArrayDemo1 class.

7. Save the program as **ArrayDemo1.cs** in the Chapter.06 folder on your Student Disk.

8. Compile and run the program. The program's output appears in Figure 6-1.

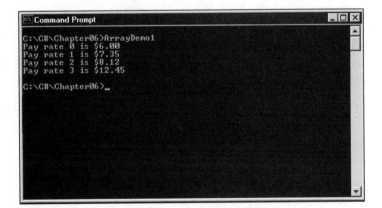

Figure 6-1 Output of the ArrayDemo1 program

You can change an array's size, if necessary. For example, if you declare `int[]` `array;`, you can assign five elements later with `array = new int[5];`; later in the program, you might again alter the array size to 100 with `array = new int[100];`. This feature is not allowed in most other programming languages.

INITIALIZING AN ARRAY

In C#, arrays are objects. When you declare an array name, you are declaring a specific instance of a class named **System.Array**. When you declare objects, their numeric fields initialize to 0, character fields are set to '\0' or **null**, Boolean fields are set to **false**, and object type fields (such as strings or any class object) are set to **null** (or empty); the same is true for arrays. For example, when you initialize an array with a statement such as `int[] someNums = new int[5];`, each of the five elements of `someNums` has a value of 0 because `someNums` is a numeric array object.

You learned about object field default values in Chapter 4.

You already know how to assign a different value to a single element of an array, as in `someNums[0] = 46;`. You also can assign nondefault values to array elements upon creation. To initialize an array to nondefault values, you use a list of values that are separated by commas and enclosed within curly braces. For example, if you want to create an array named **myScores** and store five test scores within the array, you can use any of the following declarations:

```
int[] myScores = new int[5] {100, 76, 88, 100, 90};
int[] myScores = new int[] {100, 76, 88, 100, 90};
int[] myScores = {100, 76, 88, 100, 90};
```

When you initialize an array by providing a size and list of values, as in the first example, the stated size and number of list elements must match. However, when you initialize an array by giving it values upon creation, you are not required to give the array a size, as shown in the second example; in that case, the size is assigned based on the number of values in the initializing list. The third example shows that when you initialize an array, you do not need to use the keyword **new** and repeat the type; instead, new memory is assigned based on the stated array type and the length of the list of provided values. Use whichever form of array initialization is clearest to you.

When you use curly braces at the end of a block of code, you do not follow the closing curly brace with a semicolon. Conversely, when you use curly braces to enclose a list of array values, you must complete the statement with a semicolon.

Programmers who have used other languages such as C++ and Java might expect that when an initialization list is shorter than the number of declared array elements, the "extra" elements will be set to default values. This is not the case in C#; if you declare a size, then you must list a value for each element.

Next, you will alter your `ArrayDemo1` program to initialize the array of doubles, rather than declaring the array in one step and assigning values later.

To initialize an array of doubles:

1. Open the **ArrayDemo1.cs** file in your text editor, and immediately save it as **ArrayDemo2.cs**. Change the class name from `ArrayDemo1` to `ArrayDemo2`.

2. Delete the first six lines within the `Main()` method; these lines declare the array, instantiate it, and assign four values. Replace them with a single statement that accomplishes the same tasks:

   ```
   double[] payRate = {6.00, 7.35, 8.12, 12.45};
   ```

3. Save, compile, and execute the program. The output looks the same as Figure 6-1.

USING SUBSCRIPTS TO ACCESS ARRAY ELEMENTS

If you treat each array element as an individual entity, then there isn't much of an advantage to declaring an array over declaring individual variables. The power of arrays becomes apparent when you begin to use subscripts that are variables rather constant values.

For example, when you declare an array of five integers, such as `int[] myScores = {100, 76, 88, 100, 90};`, you often want to perform the same operation on each array element. To increase each array element by 3, for example, you can write the following:

```
myScores[0] += 3;
myScores[1] += 3;
myScores[2] += 3;
myScores[3] += 3;
myScores[4] += 3;
```

With five array elements, this task is manageable. However, you can shorten the task by using a variable as the subscript. Then you can use a loop to perform arithmetic on each element in the array. For example:

```
for(sub = 0; sub < 5; ++sub)
        myScores[sub] += 3;
```

The variable `sub` is set to 0, then compared to 5. Because it is less than 5, the loop executes and `myScores[0]` increases by 3. The variable `sub` increments and becomes 1, which is still less than 5, so when the loop executes again, `myScores[1]` increases by

3, and so on. A process that took five statements now takes only one. Additionally, if the array had 100 elements, the first method of individually increasing the array values by 3 would require 95 additional statements. The only change required using the **for** loop would be to compare **sub** to 100 instead of 5.

Next, you will modify the **ArrayDemo2** program to use a **for** loop with the array.

1. Open the **ArrayDemo2.cs** file in your text editor, and immediately save it as **ArrayDemo3.cs**. Change the class name to **ArrayDemo3**.

2. Delete the four **WriteLine()** statements that print the four array values and replace them with the following **for** loop:

```
for(int x = 0; x  < 4; ++x)
   Console.WriteLine("Pay rate {0} is {1}", x,
      payRate[x].ToString("C"));
```

3. Save, compile, and run the program. Again, the output is the same as Figure 6-1.

USING THE Length FIELD

When you work with array elements, you must ensure that the subscript you use remains in the range 0 through one less than the length. If you declare an array with five elements and use a subscript that is negative or more than 4, you will receive an error message: "IndexOutOfRangeException". This message means the index, or subscript, does not hold a value that legally can access an array element. For example, when you declare an array of five integers, as in **int[] myScores = {100, 76, 88, 100, 90};**, you can access all five elements by coding the number 5 explicitly, as in **for(sub = 0; sub < 5; ++sub)....** If you modify your program to hold more or fewer array elements, you must remember to change every reference to the array size within the program. Many text editors have a "find and replace" feature that lets you change all of the 5s either simultaneously or one by one, but you must be careful not to change 5s that have nothing to do with the array; for example, the program might also have a stored interest rate variable holding 5 percent. A better technique is to use a variable that holds the array size and use it to control the loop, as in **for(sub = 0; sub < myArraysLength; ++sub)....** That way, if you change the size of the scores array, then the array always will use the correct maximum length.

Because every array automatically is a member of the class **System.Array**, you can use the fields and methods that are part of the **System.Array** class with any array you create. The **Length** field is a member of the **System.Array** class and automatically holds an array's length. Instead of creating your own variable, it is most efficient to use this field, which always updates to reflect any changes you make to your array's size. The following segment of code displays "Array size is 5":

```
int[] myScores = {100, 76, 88, 100, 90};
int scoresSize = myScores.Length;
Console.WriteLine("Array size is {0}",scoresSize);
```

An array's `Length` is a constant field—you cannot assign a new value to it.

Next, you will modify the **ArrayDemo3** program to use the `Length` field.

1. Open the **ArrayDemo3.cs** file in your text editor and immediately save it as **ArrayDemo4.cs**. Change the class name to **ArrayDemo4**.

2. Within the `for` statement that prints the array elements, change the 4 to **payRate.Length**.

3. Save, compile, and execute the program. The output is the same as in Figure 6-1.

4. At the end of the list of pay rates, insert a comma and a new, fifth rate of **22.22**.

5. Save the program, then compile and execute it again. The output looks like Figure 6-2. Even though all you did was add a new pay rate without making any other adjustments to the program, all five pay rates print correctly because C# adjusted the `Length` field.

```
Command Prompt                                          _ □ ✕

C:\C#\Chapter06>ArrayDemo4
Pay rate 0 is $6.00
Pay rate 1 is $7.35
Pay rate 2 is $8.12
Pay rate 3 is $12.45
Pay rate 4 is $22.22

C:\C#\Chapter06>_
```

Figure 6-2   Output of `ArrayDemo4` program

Using foreach to Control Array Access

You can easily navigate through arrays using a `for` or `while` loop that varies a subscript from 0 to `Array.Length - 1`. C# also supports a **foreach** statement that you can use to cycle through every array element without using subscripts. With the `foreach` statement, you provide a temporary variable that automatically holds each array value in turn.

For example, the following code prints each element in the **payRate** array in sequence:

```
double[] payRate = {6.00, 7.35, 8.12, 12.45, 22.22};
foreach(double money in payRate)
    Console.WriteLine("{0}", money.ToString("C"));
```

The variable money is declared as a double and during the execution of the loop, holds each payRate value in turn—first, payRate[0], then payRate[1], and so on. As a simple variable, money does not require a subscript, making it easier to work with. You use foreach only when you want to access every array element; to access only selected array elements, you must manipulate subscripts in some other way.

MANUALLY SEARCHING AN ARRAY FOR AN EXACT MATCH

When you want to determine whether some variable holds one of many possible valid values, one option is to use a series of if statements to compare the variable to a series of valid values. For example, suppose that a company manufactures 10 items. When a customer places an order for an item, you need to determine whether the item number is valid. If valid item numbers are sequential, say 101 through 110, then the following simple if statement that uses a logical AND operator can verify the order number and set a Boolean field to true: if(itemOrdered >= 101 && itemOrdered <= 110) isValidItem = true;. If the valid item numbers are nonsequential, however—for example, 101, 108, 201, 213, 266, 304, and so on—you must code the following deeply nested if statement or a lengthy OR comparison to determine the validity of an item number:

```
if(itemOrdered == 101)
        isValidItem = true;
else if(itemOrdered == 108)
        isValidItem = true;
else if(itemOrdered == 201)
        isValidItem = true;
// and so on
```

Instead of creating a long series of if statements, a more elegant solution is to compare the itemOrdered variable to a list of values in an array. You can initialize the array with the valid values by using the following statement:

```
int[] validValues = {101, 108, 201, 213, 266, 304, 311,
    409, 411, 412};
```

Next, you can use a for statement to loop through the array and set a Boolean variable to true when a match is found:

```
for(int x = 0; x < validValues.Length; ++x)
        if(itemOrdered == validValues[x])
                isValidItem = true;
```

 In place of the for loop, you could use a foreach loop as follows:

```
foreach(int validItem in validValues)
        if(itemOrdered == validItem)
                isValidItem = true;
```

This simple `for` loop replaces the long series of `if` statements. What's more, if a company carries 1,000 items instead of 10, then the only part of the `for` statement that changes is the comparison in the middle. As an added bonus, if you set up another array as a **parallel array** with the same number of elements and corresponding data, you can use the same subscript to access additional information. For example, if the 10 items your company carries have 10 different prices, then you can set up any array to hold those prices: `double[ ] prices = {0.89, 1.23, 3.50, 0.69…};` and so on. The prices must appear in the same order as their corresponding item numbers in the `validValues` array. Now the same `for` loop that finds the valid item number also finds the price, as shown in Figure 6-3. In other words, if the item number is found in the second position in the `validValues` array, then you can find the correct price in the second position in the prices array.

If you initialize parallel arrays, it is convenient to use spacing so that the corresponding values visually align on the screen or printed page.

```
int[] validValues = {101,  108,  201,  213,  266,  304,  311,  409,  411,  412};
double[] prices =    {0.89, 1.23, 3.50, 0.69, 5.79, 3.19, 0.99, 0.89, 1.26,
   8.00};
double itemPrice;
for(int x = 0; x < validValues.Length; ++x)
{
        if(itemOrdered == validValues[x])
        {
                isValidItem = true;
                itemPrice = prices[x];
        }
}
```

Figure 6-3   Accessing information in parallel arrays

In an array with many possible matches, it is most efficient to place the most common items first, so they are matched right away. For example, if item 311 is ordered most often, place 311 first in the `validValues` array and its price ($0.99) first in the `prices` array.

Within the code shown in Figure 6-3, you compare every `itemOrdered` with each of the 10 `validValues`. Even when an `itemOrdered` is equivalent to the first value in the `validValues` array (101), you always make nine additional cycles through the array. On each of these nine additional cycles, the comparison between `itemOrdered` and `validValues[x]` is always `false`. As soon as a match for an `itemOrdered` is found, it is most efficient to break out of the `for` loop early. An easy way to accomplish this task is to set `x` to a high value within the block of statements executed when a match is found. Then, after a match, the `for` loop will not execute again because the limiting comparison (`x < validValues.Length`) will have been surpassed. Figure 6-4 shows this approach.

```
for(int x = 0; x < validValues.Length; ++x)
{
        if(itemOrdered == validValues[x])
        {
                isValidItem = true;
                itemPrice = prices[x];
                x = validValues.Length;
                    // break out of loop when you find a match
        }
}
```

Figure 6-4 Breaking out of a for loop early

Instead of the statement that sets x to validValues.Length when a match is found, you could place a break; statement within the loop in its place. Some programmers disapprove of breaking out of a for loop early, whether by setting a variable's value or by using a break; statement. They argue that programs are easier to debug and maintain if each program segment has only one entry and one exit point. If you (or your instructor) agree with this philosophy, then select a method that uses a while statement, as described next.

As an alternative to using a for or foreach loop to search an array, you can use a while loop to search for a match. Using this approach, you set a subscript to 0 and, while the itemOrdered is not equal to a value in the array, increase the subscript and keep looking. You search only while the subscript remains lower than the number of elements in the array. If the subscript increases to match validValues.Length, then you never found a match in the 10-element array. If the loop ends before the subscript reaches validValues.Length, then you found a match and the correct price can be assigned to the itemPrice variable. Figure 6-5 shows this programming approach.

```
x = 0;
while(x < validValues.Length && itemOrdered != validValues[x])
        ++x;
if(x != validValues.Length)
{
        isValidItem = true;
        itemPrice = prices[x];
}
```

Figure 6-5 Searching with a while loop

SEARCHING AN ARRAY FOR A RANGE MATCH

Searching an array for an exact match is not always practical. For example, suppose your mail-order company gives customer discounts based on the quantity of items ordered. Perhaps no discount is given for any order of fewer than a dozen items, but increasing discounts are available for orders of increasing quantities, as shown in Figure 6-6.

Total Quantity Ordered	Discount
1 to 12	None
13 to 49	10%
50 to 99	14%
100 to 199	18%
200 or more	20%

Figure 6-6   Discount table for a mail-order company

One awkward, impractical option is to create a single array to store the discount rates. You could use a variable named `numOfItems` as a subscript to the array, but the array would need hundreds of entries, such as `double[] discount = {0, 0, 0, 0, 0, 0, 0, 0, 0, 0, 0, 0, 0, .10, .10, .10 ...};` and so on. When `numOfItems` is 3, for example, then `discount[numOfItems]` or `discount[3]` is 0. When `numOfItems` is 14, then `discount[numOfItems]` or `discount[14]` is .10. Because a customer might order thousands of items, the array would need to be ridiculously large.

Notice that 13 zeroes are listed in the discount array in the preceding example. The first array element has a zero subscript (and a zero discount for zero items). The next 12 discounts (1 through 12 items) also have zero discounts.

A better option is to create parallel arrays. One array will hold the five discount rates, and the other array will hold five discount range limits. The Total Quantity Ordered column in Figure 6-6 shows five ranges. If you use only the first figure in each range, then you can create an array that holds five low limits: `int[] discountRangeLimit = {1, 13, 50, 100, 200};`. A parallel array will hold the five discount rates: `double[] discount = {0, .10, .14, .18, .20};`. Then, starting at the last `discountRangeLimit` array element, for any `numOfItems` greater than or equal to `discountRangeLimit[4]`, the appropriate discount is `discount[4]`. In other words, for any `numOfItems` less than `discountRangeLimit[4]`, you should decrement the subscript and look in a lower range. Figure 6-7 shows the code.

```
// assume numOfItems is a declared integer for which a user has input a value
int[] discountRangeLimit =   {1, 13, 50, 100, 200};
double[] discount =          {0, .10, .14, .18, .20};
double customerDiscount;
int sub = 4;
while(sub >= 0 && numOfItems < discountRangeLimit[sub])
     --sub;
customerDiscount = discount[sub];
```

Figure 6-7   Searching an array of ranges

USING THE BinarySearch() METHOD

You have already learned that because every array in C# automatically is a member of the System.Array class, you can use the Length field. Additionally, the System.Array class contains a variety of useful, built-in methods.

The **BinarySearch() method** finds a requested value in a sorted array. Instead of employing the logic you used to find a match in the last section, you can take advantage of this built-in method to locate a value within an array, as long as the array items are organized in ascending order.

 A binary search is one in which a sorted list of objects is split in half repeatedly as the search gets closer and closer to a match. Perhaps you have played a guessing game, trying to guess a number from 1 to 100. If you asked, "Is it less than 50?," and upon hearing "Yes," asked, "Is it less than 25?," then upon hearing "No," asked, "Is it less than 37?," then you have performed a binary search.

Figure 6-8 shows a program that declares an array of integer idNumbers arranged in ascending order. The program prompts a user for a value, converts it to an integer, and, rather than using a loop to examine each array element and compare it to the entered value, simply passes the array and the entered value to the BinarySearch() method. The method returns −1 if the value is not found in the array; otherwise, it returns the array position of the sought value. Figure 6-9 shows several executions of this program.

```
using System;
public class BinarySearchDemo
{
      public static void Main()
      {
            int[] idNumbers = {122, 167, 204, 219, 345};
            int x;
            string entryString;
            int entryId;
            Console.Write("Enter an Employee ID ");
            entryString = Console.ReadLine();
            entryId = Convert.ToInt32(entryString);
            x = Array.BinarySearch(idNumbers, entryId);
            if(x < 0)
                  Console.WriteLine("ID {0} not found", entryId);
            else
                  Console.WriteLine("ID {0} was found at position {1} ",
                     entryId,x);
      }
```

Figure 6-8   BinarySearch program

Figure 6-9   Three executions of the BinarySearch program

In Figure 6-8, the single statement **x = Array.BinarySearch(idNumbers, entryId);** calls the method that performs the search, returning a −1 or the position where **entryId** was found. This single line of code is easier to write, less prone to error, and easier to understand than writing a loop to cycle through the **idNumbers** array looking for a match. Still, it is worthwhile to understand how to perform the manual search. You will need to use that technique under the following conditions, when the **BinarySearch()** method proves inadequate:

- If your array items are not arranged in ascending order, the **BinarySearch()** method does not work correctly.

- If your array holds duplicate values and you want to find all of them, the **BinarySearch()** method doesn't work—it can return only one value, so it returns the position of the first matching value it finds. This matching position is the one closest to the middle of the array.

- If you want to find a range match rather than an exact match, the **BinarySearch()** method does not work.

USING THE Sort() AND Reverse() METHODS

The **System.Array** class contains other useful methods you can use to manipulate your arrays. As with the **BinarySearch()** method, you could write all of these methods yourself. C# provides them as a convenience, however.

The **Sort() method** arranges array items in ascending order. Ascending order is lowest to highest; it works numerically for number types and alphabetically for characters and strings. To use the method, you pass the array name to **Array.Sort()**, and the element positions within the array are rearranged appropriately. Figure 6-10 shows a program that sorts an array of strings; Figure 6-11 shows its execution.

```
using System;
public class SortArray
{
      public static void Main()
      {
            string[] names = {"Olive", "Patty", "Richard", "Ned", "Mindy"};
            int x;
            Array.Sort(names);
            for(x=0; x< names.Length; ++x)
                  Console.WriteLine(names[x]);
      }
}
```

Figure 6-10   SortArray program

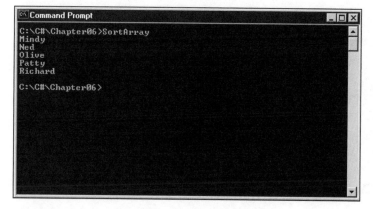

Figure 6-11   Output of SortArray program

The **Reverse() method** reverses the order of items in an array. In other words, for any array, the element that starts in position 0 is relocated to position Length — 1, the element that starts in position 1 is relocated to position Length — 2, and so on until the element that starts in position Length — 1 is relocated to position 0. You call the Reverse() method the same way you call the Sort() method—you simply pass the array name to the method. Figure 6-12 shows a program that uses Reverse() with an array of strings, and Figure 6-13 shows its execution.

When you Reverse() an array containing an odd number of elements, the middle element will remain in its original location.

```
using System;
public class ReverseArray
{
        public static void Main()
        {
                string[] names = {"Zach", "Wendy", "Rose", "Marcia"};
                int x;
                Array.Reverse(names);
                for(x=0; x< names.Length; ++x)
                        Console.WriteLine(names[x]);
        }
}
```

Figure 6-12   `ReverseArray` program

Figure 6-13   Output of `ReverseArray` program

In the next steps you will create an array of integers and use the **Sort()** and
Reverse() methods to manipulate it.

1. Open a new file in your text editor.

2. Type the beginning of a class named **MyTestScores** that includes an array
   of eight integer test scores, an integer you will use as a subscript, and a string
   that will hold user-entered data.

```
using System;
public class MyTestScores
{
  public static void Main()
  {
        int[] scores = new int[8];
        int x;
        string inputString;
```

3. Add a loop that prompts the user, accepts a test score, converts the score to an integer, and stores it as the appropriate element of the scores array.

```
for(x = 0; x < scores.Length; ++x)
{
    Console.Write("Enter your score on test {0} ", x + 1);
    inputString = Console.ReadLine();
    scores[x] = Convert.ToInt32(inputString);
}
```

4. Add a statement that creates a dashed line to visually separate the input from the output. Display "Scores in original order:", then use a loop to display each score in a field six characters wide.

```
Console.WriteLine("\n--------------------------------");
Console.WriteLine("Scores in original order:");
for(x = 0; x < scores.Length; ++x)
    Console.Write("{0,6}",scores[x]);
```

You learned to set display field sizes when you learned about format strings in Chapter 2.

5. Add another dashed line for visual separation, then pass the scores array to the Array.Sort() method. Print "Scores in sorted order:", then use a loop to display each of the newly sorted scores.

```
Console.WriteLine("\n--------------------------------");
Array.Sort(scores);
Console.WriteLine("Scores in sorted order:");
for(x = 0; x < scores.Length; ++x)
    Console.Write("{0,6}",scores[x]);
```

6. Add one more dashed line, reverse the array elements by passing scores to the Array.Reverse() method, display "Scores in reverse order:", and show the rearranged scores.

```
Console.WriteLine("\n--------------------------------");
Array.Reverse(scores);
Console.WriteLine("Scores in reverse order:");
for(x = 0; x < scores.Length; ++x)
    Console.Write("{0,6}",scores[x]);
```

7. Add two closing curly braces—one for the Main() method and one for the class. Save the file as **MyTestScores.cs** in the Chapter.06 folder of your Student Disk. Compile and execute the program. Figure 6-14 shows a typical execution of the program. The user-entered scores are not in order, but after the call to the Sort() method, they appear in ascending order. After the call to the Reverse() method, they appear in descending order.

```
Command Prompt                                              _ □ X
C:\C#\Chapter06>MyTestScores
Enter your score on test 1 76
Enter your score on test 2 89
Enter your score on test 3 65
Enter your score on test 4 32
Enter your score on test 5 100
Enter your score on test 6 90
Enter your score on test 7 84
Enter your score on test 8 48
------------------------------------------
Scores in original order:
    76     89     65     32    100     90     84     48

Scores in sorted order:
    32     48     65     76     84     89     90    100

Scores in reverse order:
   100     90     89     84     76     65     48     32
C:\C#\Chapter06>
```

Figure 6-14   Output of `MyTestScores` program

WRITING METHODS THAT ACCEPT ARRAY PARAMETERS

You already have seen that you can use any individual array element in the same manner as you would use any single variable of the same type. That is, if you declare an integer array as `int[] someNums = new int[12];`, then you can subsequently print `someNums[0]` or add one to `someNums[1]`, just as you would for any integer. Similarly, you can pass a single array element to a method in exactly the same manner as you would pass a variable.

Consider the program shown in Figure 6-15. This program creates an array of four integers and prints them. Next, the program calls a method named `MethodGetsOneInt()` four times, passing each of the array elements in turn. The method prints the passed value, changes the number to 999, and then prints the number again. Finally, back in the `Main()` method, the four numbers print again. Figure 6-16 shows the output.

As you can see in Figure 6-16, the program displays the four original values, then passes each to the `MethodGetsOneInt()` method, where it is displayed and then changed to 999. After the method executes four times, the `Main()` method displays the four values again, showing that they are unchanged by the assignments within `MethodGetsOneInt()`. The `oneVal` variable is local to the `MethodGetsOneInt()` method because it is not passed as a `ref` or `out` parameter; rather, it is a value parameter. Therefore, any changes to variables passed into the method are not permanent and are not reflected in the array in the `Main()` program. Each `oneVal` variable in the `MethodGetsOneInt()` method holds only a copy of the array element passed into the method, and the `oneVal` variable holding the assigned value of 999 exists only while the `MethodGetsOneInt()` method is executing.

 You learned about `ref` and `out` parameters in Chapter 3.

Instead of passing a single array element to a method, you can pass an entire array as a parameter. You indicate that a method argument is an array by placing square brackets after the data type in the method's parameter list. When you do pass an array to a method, changes you make to array elements within the method are permanent; that is, they are reflected in the original array that was sent to the method. Arrays, like all objects but unlike built-in types, are passed by reference; that is, the method receives the actual memory address of the array and has access to the actual values in the array elements.

6

```
using System;
public class PassArrayElement
{
        public static void Main()
        {
                int[] someNums = {10, 12, 22, 35};
                int x;
                Console.Write("\nAt beginning of Main() method...");
                for(x = 0; x < someNums.Length; ++x)
                        Console.Write("{0,6}", someNums[x]);
                Console.WriteLine();
                for(x = 0; x < someNums.Length; ++x)
                        MethodGetsOneInt(someNums[x]);
                Console.Write("At end of Main()method..........");
                for(x = 0; x < someNums.Length; ++x)
                        Console.Write("{0,6}", someNums[x]);
        }
        public static void MethodGetsOneInt(int oneVal)
        {
                Console.Write("In MethodGetsOneInt() {0}", oneVal);
                oneVal = 999;
                Console.WriteLine("     After change {0}", oneVal);
        }
}
```

Figure 6-15   `PassArrayElement` program

Figure 6-16   Output of the `PassArrayElement` program

You already have seen that methods can alter arrays passed to them. When you use the Sort() and Reverse() methods, the methods change the array contents.

You can create and pass an unnamed array to a method in a single step. For example, you can write MethodThatAcceptsArray(new int[] {45, 67, 89});.

The program shown in Figure 6-17 creates an array of four integers. After the integers are printed, the entire array is passed to a method named MethodGetsArray(). Within the method header, the parameter is declared as an array by using square brackets after the argument type. Within the method, the numbers are printed, which shows that they retain their values from Main() upon entering the method, but then the value 888 is assigned to each number. Even though MethodGetsArray() is a void method (meaning that nothing is returned to the Main() method), when the program prints the array for the second time within the Main() method, all of the values have been changed to 888, as you can see in Figure 6-18. Because arrays are passed by reference, the MethodGetsArray() method "knows" the address of the array declared in Main(), and makes its changes directly to the original array that was declared in the Main() method.

Next, you will modify the MyTestScores program so the test scores are displayed from within a module.

1. Open the **MyTestScores.cs** file you created earlier in this chapter. Save it as **MyTestScores2.cs**.

2. Change the class name to **MyTestScores2**.

3. Remove the following four lines, which together print a dashed line, print the message "Scores in original order:", and print the four scores in a loop:

```
Console.WriteLine("\n--------------------------------");
Console.WriteLine("Scores in original order:");
for(x = 0; x < scores.Length; ++x)
   Console.Write("{0,6}",scores[x]);
```

Replace these lines with a call to a method you will create named DisplayScores(). This method takes two arguments: the string to be displayed with the scores, and the array of scores.

```
DisplayScores("Scores in original order:", scores);
```

4. Remove the statement located just before Array.sort(scores); that prints a dashed line. After Array.sort(scores);, remove the next set of lines that print the message ("Scores in sorted order:") and the four scores, and replace them with a method call to DisplayScores(), including the string to display and the array name as parameters.

```
DisplayScores("Scores in sorted order:", scores);
```

```
using System;
public class PassArray
{
        public static void Main()
        {
                int[] someNums = {10, 12, 22, 35};
                int x;
                Console.Write("\nAt beginning of Main() method...");
                for(x = 0; x < someNums.Length; ++x)
                        Console.Write("{0,6}", someNums[x]);
                Console.WriteLine();
                MethodGetsArray(someNums);                // entire array is passed

                Console.Write("\n\nAt end of Main()method..........");
                for(x = 0; x < someNums.Length; ++x)
                        Console.Write("{0,6}", someNums[x]);
        }
        public static void MethodGetsArray(int[] one)
        {
                int x;
                Console.WriteLine("\nIn MethodGetsArray() method");
                for(x = 0; x < one.Length; ++x)
                {
                        Console.Write("\nBefore change {0,6}", one[x]);
                        one[x] = 888;
                        Console.Write("  After {0,6}", one[x]);
                }
        }
}
```

Figure 6-17 PassArray program

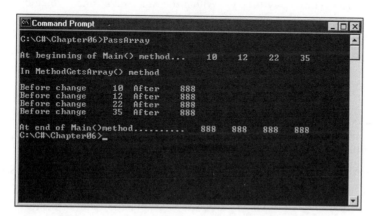

Figure 6-18 Output of the PassArray program

5. Remove the statement located just before `Array.Reverse(scores);` that prints a dashed line. After `Array.Reverse(scores);`, remove the next set

of lines that print the message ("Scores in reverse order:") and the four scores, and replace them with a method call to `DisplayScores()`.

```
DisplayScores("Scores in reverse order:", scores);
```

6. After the closing curly brace of the `Main()` method, include the following `DisplayScores()` method. It accepts a string and an array as arguments, writes a dashed line, displays the string message, and displays the scores in a loop.

```
public static void DisplayScores(string message, int[]
scores)
{
    int x;
    Console.WriteLine
("\n--------------------------------");
    Console.WriteLine(message);
    for(x = 0; x < scores.Length; ++x)
        Console.Write("{0,6}",scores[x]);
}
```

7. Save the program, then compile and execute it. The result is the same as that shown in Figure 6-14, but the output occurred within a method, making the `Main()` program shorter and allowing it to contain less repetitive code.

 Tip As with simple parameters, you can use `out` or `ref` when passing an array to a method. You do so when you want the method to create a new array by using the location of the named array in the calling method. For example, if a `Main()` method declares an array without assigning any values, as in `double[] payRate;`, then you can pass the array to a method with the header `AssignValues(out double[] money);` by using the statement `AssignValues(out payRate);`. Within the `AssignValues()` method, you can initialize the array as `money = new double[6];`, thereby creating a new array.

Using Parameter Arrays

When you don't know how many arguments you might eventually send to a method, you can declare a local array within the method header by using the keyword **params**. Such a method will accept any number of arguments.

For example, a method with the header `public static void DisplayStrings (params string[] people)` accepts an array of strings. In the call to this method, you can use one, two, or any other number of strings as actual parameters; within the method, they will be treated as an array. Figure 6-19 shows a program that calls `DisplayStrings()` three times—once with one string argument, once with three string arguments, and once with an array of strings. In each case, the method works correctly, treating the passed strings as an array and displaying them appropriately. Figure 6-20 shows the output.

```
using System;
public class ParamsDemo
{
        public static void Main()
        {
                string[] names = {"Mark", "Paulette", "Carol", "James"};
                DisplayStrings("Ginger");
                DisplayStrings("George", "Maria", "Thomas");
                DisplayStrings(names);
        }
        public static void DisplayStrings(params string[] people)
        {
                foreach(string person in people)
                        Console.Write("{0} ",person);
                Console.WriteLine("\n----------------");


        }
}
```

Figure 6-19   `ParamsDemo` program

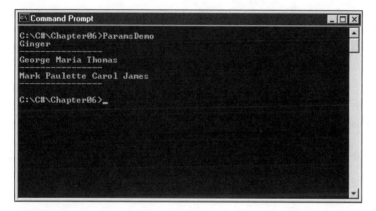

Figure 6-20   Output of the `ParamsDemo` program

 The four types of method parameters are value, reference, output, and params. You learned about value, reference, and output parameters in Chapter 3.

 You could create an even more flexible method by using a method header such as `Display(params Object[] things)`. Then the passed parameters could be any type—strings, integers, other classes, and so on. You will learn more about the `Object` class in Chapter 7.

DECLARING AN ARRAY OF OBJECTS

Just as you can declare arrays of integers or doubles, you can declare arrays that hold elements of any type, including objects. For example, Figure 6-21 shows an **Employee** class containing two data fields (**idNumber** and **salary**), and get and set methods for each field.

```
class Employee
{
        private int idNumber;
        private double salary;
        public int GetId()
        {
              return idNumber;
        }
        public double GetSalary()
        {
              return salary;
        }
        public void SetId(int id)
        {
              idNumber = id;
        }
        public void SetSalary(double pay)
        {
              salary = pay;
        }
}
```

Figure 6-21   A simple **Employee** class

 You created classes similar to the **Employee** class in Chapter 4.

Of course, you also can create separate **Employee** objects with unique names, such as **Employee painter, electrician, plumber;**. For many programs, however, it is far more convenient to create an array of **Employee** objects. An array named **empArray** that holds seven **Employee** objects is defined by **Employee[ ] empArray = new Employee[7];**. This statement reserves enough computer memory for seven **Employee** objects named **empArray[0]** through **empArray[6]**. It does not actually construct those Employees; instead, you must call the seven individual constructors to do so. Because the **Employee** class in Figure 6-21 contains a default constructor that requires no arguments, the loop following calls the constructor seven times:

```
for(int x = 0; x < empArray.Length; ++x)
        empArray[x] = new Employee();
```

As **x** varies from 0 through 6, each of the seven **empArray** objects is constructed.

When you create an array from a value type, such as int or char, the array holds the actual values. When you create an array from a reference type, such as a class you create, then the array holds the memory addresses of the objects. In other words, the array "refers to" the objects instead of containing the objects. You learned the terms *value* and *reference* type in Chapter 4.

 You can create an array of objects and provide default values to the elements' constructors in one step. For example, if an Inventory class contains a constructor that requires an integer argument, you can declare an array of Inventory objects by writing the following: Inventory[] items = {new Inventory(123), new Inventory(345), new Inventory(678)};.

To use a method that belongs to an object that is part of an array, you insert the appropriate subscript notation after the array name and before the dot-method. For example, to set all seven Employee idNumber fields to 999 and all seven Employee salary fields to 7.25, you can write the following:

```
for(int x = 0; x < empArray.Length; ++x)
{
        empArray[x].SetId(999);
        empArray[x].SetSalary(7.25);
}
```

 Pay attention to the syntax of the Employee objects' method calls, such as empArray[x].SetId(999);. Although you might be tempted to place the subscript at the end of the expression after the method name, as in empArray.SetId(999)[x];, you cannot do so—the values in x (0 through 6) refer to a particular empArray element, each of which has access to a single setId() method. The placement of the bracketed subscript following the empArray element means that the method "belongs" to a particular empArray instance and that the method will receive a this pointer to that instance.

 The curly braces are important in the preceding for loop. Without them, the seven Employee idNumber fields would be set, but the SetSalary() method call would be outside the loop. Not only would it execute just once, but the value of x would also have increased to 7 and exceed the end of the array, causing an error.

Next, you will create a class to hold student data, and then you will write a program to manipulate an array of Student objects.

To create a Student class:

    1. Open a new file in your text editor, and begin to create a Student class that contains private fields representing a student ID number, name, and grade-point average.

6

```
class Student
{
    private int idNumber;
    private string name;
    private double gpa;
```

2. Create three `get` methods that return each of the three private fields.

```
public int GetId()
{
  return idNumber;
}
public string GetName()
{
  return name;
}
public double GetGpa()
{
  return gpa;
}
```

3. Also include three public set methods that provide values for each private field.

```
public void SetId(int id)
{
  idNumber = id;
}
public void SetName(string studentName)
{
  name = studentName;
}
public void SetGpa(double pay)
{
  gpa = pay;
}
```

4. Add a closing curly brace for the class. Save the file as **StudentArrayDemo.cs** in the Chapter.06 folder of your Student Disk.

5. Insert a blank line at the top of the file where you will enter a class that will use the `Student` class you just created. Enter the first few lines of the program as follows:

```
using System;
public class StudentArrayDemo
{
  public static void Main()
  {
```

6. In this program, you will create an array of five `Student` objects. You will need a subscript to manipulate the array. Because you will assign data to the

objects interactively, you need a string to hold data entered from the keyboard as well as fields to hold the entered ID number, name, and grade-point average for each student. Declare these items as follows:

```
Student[] student = new Student[5];
int x;
string enteredData;
int enteredId;
string enteredName;
double enteredGpa;
```

7. Create the five `Student` objects in a loop that varies from zero to one less than the value in the `Length` field for the array, and that calls the `Student` class constructor five times.

```
for(x = 0; x < student.Length; ++x)
    student[x] = new Student();
```

8. Begin a loop that prompts the user to enter student data. First, prompt the user for an ID number. To enable the user to keep track of the number of students entered, include a number within the prompt. When the subscript `x` is 0, the user will be entering data for the first `Student` object; display `x + 1` rather than `x` because users will think of the first `Student` as "Student 1" instead of "Student 0." Read the data as a string, then convert it to an integer using the `Convert.ToInt32()` method. Finally, assign the entered integer to the `Student` object's private `idNumber` field using the `Student` class `public` method `setId()`.

```
for(x = 0; x < student.Length; ++x)
{
    Console.Write("Enter ID for student #{0} ",x + 1);
    enteredData = Console.ReadLine();
    enteredId = Convert.ToInt32(enteredData);
    student[x].SetId(enteredId);
```

You first used the `Console.ReadLine()` and `Convert.ToInt32()` methods in Chapter 5.

9. Continuing within the same loop, prompt for and receive `Student` names and grade point-averages.

```
Console.Write("Enter name for student {0} ",x + 1);
enteredName = Console.ReadLine();
student[x].SetName(enteredName);
Console.Write
   ("Enter grade point average for student #{0} ", x + 1);
enteredData = Console.ReadLine();
enteredGpa = Convert.ToDouble(enteredData);
student[x].SetGpa(enteredGpa);
```

The `enteredName` needs no conversion because it is intended to be a string.

10. Add a closing curly brace for the data entry `for` loop. Also, add a statement to display a dashed line on the screen and create visual separation between the data entry portion of the program and the output.

```
Console.WriteLine
    ("----------------------------------------------------");
```

11. Confirm that all of the data fields were set correctly by using a `for` loop to display each `Student` object in the array. You can display the grade-point average to two decimal places by using the `ToString()` method with the `GetGpa()` method as shown.

```
for(x = 0; x < student.Length; ++x)
    Console.WriteLine
    ("Student #{0} ID is {1}, name is {2}, and gpa is {3}",
    x + 1, student[x].GetId(), student[x].GetName(),
    student[x].GetGpa().ToString("F2"));
```

12. Add two closing curly braces—one for the `Main()` method and another for the `StudentArrayDemo` class. The completed code is shown in Figure 6-22.

```
using System;
public class StudentArrayDemo
{
    public static void Main()
    {
        Student[] student = new Student[5];
        int x;
        string enteredData;
        int enteredId;
        string enteredName;
        double enteredGpa;
        for(x = 0; x < student.Length; ++x)
            student[x] = new Student();
        for(x = 0; x < student.Length; ++x)
        {
            Console.Write("Enter ID for student #{0} ",x + 1);
            enteredData = Console.ReadLine();
            enteredId = Convert.ToInt32(enteredData);
            student[x].SetId(enteredId);
            Console.Write("Enter name for student {0} ",x + 1);
            enteredName = Console.ReadLine();
            student[x].SetName(enteredName);
            Console.Write
```

Figure 6-22   Completed `StudentArrayDemo` program

```
                              ("Enter grade point average for student #{0} ",
                                  x + 1);
                       enteredData = Console.ReadLine();
                       enteredGpa = Convert.ToDouble(enteredData);
                       student[x].SetGpa(enteredGpa);
                 }
                 Console.WriteLine
                 ("-------------------------------------------------");
                 for(x = 0; x < student.Length; ++x)
                   Console.WriteLine
                     ("Student #{0} ID is {1}, name is {2}, and gpa is {3}",
                      x + 1, student[x].GetId(), student[x].GetName(),
                      student[x].GetGpa().ToString("F2"));
           }
     }
}
class Student
{
        private int idNumber;
        private string name;
        private double gpa;

        public int GetId()
        {
                return idNumber;
        }
        public string GetName()
        {
                return name;
        }
        public double GetGpa()
        {
                return gpa;
        }
        public void SetId(int id)
        {
                idNumber = id;
        }
        public void SetName(string studentName)
        {
                name = studentName;
        }
        public void SetGpa(double pay)
        {
                gpa = pay;
        }
}
```

Figure 6-22   Completed `StudentArrayDemo` program (continued)

13. Save the file, then compile and execute it. When the program prompts you, enter ID numbers, names, and grade point averages for five students. Figure 6-23 shows a typical execution of the program.

```
Command Prompt                                              _ □ ×

C:\C#\Chapter06>StudentArrayDemo
Enter ID for student #1 101
Enter name for student 1 Arthur
Enter grade point average for student #1 2.3
Enter ID for student #2 202
Enter name for student 2 Latisha
Enter grade point average for student #2 3.5
Enter ID for student #3 303
Enter name for student 3 Enrico
Enter grade point average for student #3 2.8
Enter ID for student #4 404
Enter name for student 4 Allison
Enter grade point average for student #4 3.9
Enter ID for student #5 505
Enter name for student 5 Yolanda
Enter grade point average for student #5 4.0
_____
Student #1 ID is 101, name is Arthur, and gpa is 2.30
Student #2 ID is 202, name is Latisha, and gpa is 3.50
Student #3 ID is 303, name is Enrico, and gpa is 2.80
Student #4 ID is 404, name is Allison, and gpa is 3.90
Student #5 ID is 505, name is Yolanda, and gpa is 4.00

C:\C#\Chapter06>
```

Figure 6-23   Execution of the `StudentArrayDemo` program

USING THE `BinarySearch()` AND `Sort()` METHODS WITH OBJECT ARRAYS

You already have used the `System.Array` class's built-in `BinarySearch()` and `Sort()` methods with simple data types like `int`, `double`, and `string`. A complication arises when you consider searching or sorting arrays of objects you create. When you create an array of simple data items, there is no doubt as to ascending order. The classes that support simple data items each contain a method named `CompareTo()`, which provides the details of how the basic data types compare to each other. In other words, they define comparison facts such as "2 is more than 1" and "B is more than A." The `Sort()` and `BinarySearch()` methods use the `CompareTo()` method for the current type of data being sorted. In other words, `Sort()` uses the `Int32` version of `CompareTo()` when sorting integers and the `Char` version of `CompareTo()` when sorting characters.

You learned about the built-in data type class names in Chapter 2; they are summarized in Table 2-1.

When you create a class containing many fields, however, you must tell the compiler which field to use when making comparisons. For example, you logically might sort an organization's `Employee` class objects by ID number, salary, department number, last name, hire date, or any field contained in the class. To tell C# which field to use for placing

Employee objects in order, you must create an interface. An **interface** is a collection of methods (and perhaps other members) that can be used by any class, as long as the class provides a definition to override the interface's do-nothing, or abstract, definition. In other words, the methods in an interface are empty, and any class that uses them must provide the details. Interfaces define named behaviors that classes can implement, so that all classes can use the same method names but use them appropriately for the class. In this way, interfaces provide for polymorphism—the ability of different objects to use the same method names but act appropriately based on the context.

You first learned about polymorphism in Chapter 1.

You will learn more about abstract methods and classes in Chapter 7.

C# contains an interface named **`IComparable`**, which contains the definition for the **`CompareTo()`** method that compares one object to another and returns an integer. Figure 6-24 shows the definition of `IComparable`. The method does not contain any statements; you must override this statement definition in classes you create if you want the objects to be comparable.

C# supports many interfaces. You can identify an interface name by its initial letter I.

```
interface IComparable
{
        int CompareTo(Object o);
}
```

Figure 6-24 The `IComparable` interface

When you create a class whose members you will want to compare, you must include two additional features in your class:

- You must include a single colon and the interface name `IComparable` after the class name.

- You must write a method containing the header `int IComparable.CompareTo(Object o)`.

6

`Object` is a class—the most generic of all classes. Every `Employee` object you create is not only an `Employee`, but also an `Object`. (This concept is similar to "every banana is a fruit" or "every collie is a dog.") By using the type `Object` as a parameter, the `CompareTo()` method can accept anything. You will learn more about the `Object` class in Chapter 7.

To work correctly in methods such as `BinarySearch()` and `Sort()`, the `CompareTo()` method you create for your class must return an integer value. Figure 6-25 shows the return values that every version of `CompareTo()` should provide.

Return Value	Meaning
Negative	This instance is less than the compared object.
Zero	This instance is equal to the compared object.
Positive	This instance is greater than the compared object.

Figure 6-25   Return values of `IComparable.CompareTo()` method

When you create a class containing an `IComparable.CompareTo()` method, the method is an instance method and receives a `this` reference to the object used to call it. A second object is passed to the method; within the method you first must convert, or cast, the passed object to the same type as the calling object's class, and then compare the corresponding fields you want from the `this` object and the passed object. For example, Figure 6-26 shows a `CompareTo()` method you could use within an `Employee` class if you wanted to compare `Employee` objects based on the contents of their `idNumber` fields.

 You first learned about casting in Chapter 2.

 You first learned about the `this` reference when you created classes and objects in Chapter 4.

The method in Figure 6-25 is an instance method; that is, it "belongs" to an `Employee` object. When another `Employee` is passed in as `Object o`, it is cast as an `Employee` and stored in the `temp` variable. The `idNumber` values of the `this` `Employee` and the passed `Employee` are compared, and one of three integer values is returned.

```
int IComparable.CompareTo(Object o)
{
        int returnVal;
        Employee temp = (Employee)o;
        if(this.idNumber > temp.idNumber)
                returnVal = 1;
        else
                if(this.idNumber < temp.idNumber)
                        returnVal = -1;
                else
                        returnVal = 0;
        return returnVal;
}
```

Figure 6-26   `IComparable.CompareTo()` method for `Employee` class

Figure 6-27 shows a complete program that uses the `Employee` class in Figure 6-28. The `Employee` class contains a `CompareTo()` method that compares `Employee` `idNumber` values. The program in Figure 6-27 declares an array of three `Employee` objects with ID numbers of 333, 111, and 222. The program also declares a `seekEmp` object with an ID number of 222. The program sorts the array, displays the sorted elements, then finds the array element that matches the `seekEmp` object. Figure 6-29 shows the program execution.

```
using System;
public class ComparableEmployeeArray
{
        public static void Main()
        {
                Employee[] empArray = new Employee[]
                        {new Employee(333, 12.50), new Employee(111, 14.75),
                                new Employee(222, 22.35)};
                int x;
                Employee seekEmp = new Employee(222, 0.0);
                Array.Sort(empArray);
                Console.WriteLine("Sorted employees:");
                for(x = 0; x < empArray.Length; ++x)
                  Console.WriteLine("Employee #{0} ID is {1} and salary is {2}",
                   x,empArray[x].GetId(),empArray[x].GetSalary().ToString("C"));
                x = Array.BinarySearch(empArray, seekEmp);
                Console.WriteLine("Employee #{0} was found at position {1}",
                        seekEmp.GetId(), x + 1);
        }
}
```

Figure 6-27   `ComparableEmployeeArray` program

```
class Employee : IComparable
{
        private int idNumber;
        private double salary;
        public Employee(int id, double pay)
        {
                idNumber = id;
                salary = pay;
        }
        public int GetId()
        {
                return idNumber;
        }
        public double GetSalary()
        {
                return salary;
        }
        public void SetId(int id)
        {
                idNumber = id;
        }
        public void SetSalary(double pay)
        {
                salary = pay;
        }
        int IComparable.CompareTo(object o)
        {
                int returnVal;
                Employee temp = (Employee)o;
                if(this.idNumber > temp.idNumber)
                        returnVal = 1;
                else
                        if(this.idNumber < temp.idNumber)
                                returnVal = -1;
                        else
                                returnVal = 0;
                return returnVal;
        }
}
```

Figure 6-28   Comparable `Employee` class

Notice that the seekEmp object matches the Employee in the second array position based on the idNumber only—not the salary—because the CompareTo() method in the Employee class uses only idNumber values and not salaries to make comparisons. You *could* have written code that requires both the idNumber and salary values to match before returning a positive number.

Figure 6-29   Execution of the `ComparableEmployeeArray` program

In the next steps, you modify the `Student` class you created earlier so that it will become comparable.

1. Open the **StudentArrayDemo** file in your editor. Change the class name to **StudentCompare** and immediately save the file as **StudentCompare.cs** in the Chapter.06 folder on your Student Disk.

2. Within the `Main( )` method, insert a new line just before the last loop that prints the list of `Student` scores (in other words, five lines up from the end of the `Main( )` method right after the statement that prints a line of dashes). Enter the statement that will sort the entered `Student` values as follows:

   ```
   Array.Sort(student);
   ```

3. Make the necessary changes to the `Student` class to make it sortable. Change the `Student` class header to add the `IComparable` interface by adding a colon and the class name `IComparable`:

   ```
   class Student : IComparable
   ```

4. Add a `CompareTo( )` method to the `Student` class as follows. You can place the method anywhere in the `Student` class as long as it is not within the braces of any other method. The method accepts an object that is cast to a `Student` object. If the `idNumber` of the controlling `Student` object is greater than the argument's `idNumber`, then the return value is set to 1. If the `idNumber` of the controlling `Student` object is less than the argument's `idNumber`, then the return value is –1. Otherwise, the return value is 0.

   ```
   int IComparable.CompareTo(object o)
   {
       int returnVal;
       Student temp = (Student)o;
       if(this.idNumber > temp.idNumber)
           returnVal = 1;
       else
   ```

```
            if(this.idNumber < temp.idNumber)
                returnVal = -1;
            else
                returnVal = 0;
        return returnVal;
    }
```

5. Save the file, then compile and execute it. When you are prompted, enter any `Student` values you want. A typical execution appears in Figure 6-30. After the `Student` array is sorted, the `Student` objects appear in `idNumber` order.

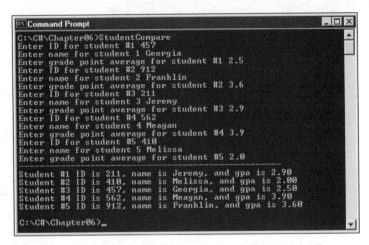

Figure 6-30   Output of the `StudentCompare` program

CHAPTER SUMMARY

❏ An array is a list of data items, all of which have the same type and the same name. You declare an array variable by inserting a pair of square brackets after the type. You reserve memory for an array by using the keyword **new**. A subscript (also called an index) is an integer contained within square brackets that indicates one of an array's variables, or elements. Any array's elements are numbered 0 through one less than the array's length.

❏ In C#, arrays are objects of a class named **System.Array**; like all objects, their fields are initialized to default values. To initialize an array to nondefault values, you use a list of values that are separated by commas and enclosed within curly braces.

❏ The power of arrays becomes apparent when you begin to use subscripts that are variables rather than constant values, and when you use loops to process array elements.

❐ When you work with array elements, you must ensure that the subscript you use remains in the range 0 through length -1. You can use the **Length** field, which is a member of the **System.Array** class, to automatically hold an array's length.

❐ You can use the **foreach** statement to cycle through every array element without using subscripts. With the **foreach** statement, you provide a temporary variable that automatically holds each array value in turn.

❐ When you want to determine whether some variable holds one of many possible valid values, you can compare the variable to a list of values in an array. If you set up a parallel array with the same number of elements and corresponding data, you can use the same subscript to access additional information.

❐ You can create parallel arrays to more easily perform a range match.

❐ The **BinarySearch()** method finds a requested value in a sorted array. The method returns −1 if the value is not found in the array; otherwise, it returns the array position of the sought value. You cannot use the **BinarySearch()** method if your array items are not arranged in ascending order, if the array holds duplicate values and you want to find all of them, or if you want to find a range match rather than an exact match.

❐ The **Sort()** method arranges array items in ascending order. The **Reverse()** method reverses the order of items in an array.

❐ You can pass a single array element to a method in exactly the same manner as you would pass a variable. Alternatively, instead of passing a single array element to a method, you can pass an entire array. When you do so, changes you make to array elements within the method are permanent; that is, they are reflected in the original array that was sent to the method. Arrays, like all objects but unlike built-in types, are passed by reference; that is, the method receives the actual memory address of the array and has access to the actual values in the array elements.

❐ When you don't know how many arguments you might eventually send to a method, you can declare a local array within the method header by using the keyword **params**. Such a method will accept any number of arguments.

❐ Just as you can declare arrays of integers or doubles, you can declare arrays that hold elements of any type, including objects.

❐ The classes that support simple data items each contain a method named **CompareTo()**, which provides the details of how the basic data types compare to each other. When you create a class containing fields, however, you must create an **IComparable** interface containing a **CompareTo()** method. This method tells the compiler which field to use when making comparisons, enabling you to use methods such as **Sort()** and **BinarySearch()**.

REVIEW QUESTIONS

1. Which of the following correctly declares an array of four integers?

   a. `int array[4];`

   b. `int[] array = 4;`

   c. `int[4] array;`

   d. `int[] array = new int[4];`

2. The value placed within square brackets after an array name is _____.

   a. a subscript

   b. an index

   c. always an integer

   d. All of these are correct.

3. If you define an array to contain seven elements, then the highest array subscript you can use is _____.

   a. 5

   b. 6

   c. 7

   d. 8

4. When you declare an array of six **double** elements and do not provide any initialization values, the value of element 1 is _____.

   a. 0

   b. 1

   c. 5

   d. unknown

5. Which of the following correctly declares an array of four integers?

   a. `int[] ages = new int[4] {20, 30, 40, 50};`

   b. `int[] ages = new int[] {20, 30, 40, 50};`

   c. `int[] ages = {20, 30, 40, 50};`

   d. All of these are correct.

6. When an **ages** array is correctly initialized using the values {20, 30, 40, 50} as in Question 5, then the value of **ages[4]** is _____.

   a. 0

   b. 4

   c. 50

   d. undefined

7. When you declare an array as `int[] temperature = {0, 32, 50, 90, 212, 451};`, the value of `temperature.Length` is _____.

   a. 5

   b. 6

   c. 7

   d. unknown

8. Which of the following doubles every value in a 10-element integer array named `amount`?

   a. `for(int x = 9; x >= 0; -x)    amount[x] *= 2;`

   b. `foreach(int number in amount) number *= 2;`

   c. both of these

   d. neither of these

9. Which of the following adds 10 to every value in a 15-element integer array named `points`?

   a. `for(int sub = 0; sub > 15; ++sub)    points[sub] +=10;`

   b. `foreach(int sub in points) points +=10;`

   c. both of these

   d. neither of these

10. Two arrays that store related information in corresponding element positions are _____.

    a. analogous arrays

    b. polymorphic arrays

    c. relative arrays

    d. parallel arrays

11. Which of the following traits do the `BinarySearch()` and `Sort()` methods have in common?

    a. Both methods take a single argument that must be an array.

    b. Both methods belong to the `System.Array` class.

    c. The array that each method uses must begin in ascending order.

    d. They both operate on arrays made up of simple data types but not class objects.

12. If you use the `BinarySearch()` method and the object you seek is not found in the array, _____.

    a. an error message is displayed

    b. a zero is returned

    c. the value `false` is returned

    d. a negative value is returned

6

13. The `BinarySearch()` method is inadequate when _____.

    a. array items are in ascending order

    b. the array holds duplicate values and you want to find them all

    c. you want to find an exact match for a value

    d. array items are not numeric

14. An array is declared as `char[] grades = {'A', 'B', 'C', 'D', 'F'};`. Which of the following method headers would work with the method call `displayGrades(grades);`?

    a. `void displayGrades(char[] grades);`

    b. `void displayGrades(char grades[]);`

    c. `void displayGrades(char grades[5]);`

    d. All of these would work.

15. An array is declared as `char[] grades = {'A', 'B', 'C', 'D', 'F'};`. Which of the following method headers would work with the method call `displayGrades(grades[0]);`?

    a. `void displayGrades(char grades);`

    b. `void displayGrades(char[0] grades);`

    c. `void displayGrades(char grades[0]);`

    d. All of these would work.

16. When you pass an array to a method, changes you make to array elements within the method _____.

    a. exist for the scope of that method only

    b. are reflected in the original array that was sent to the method

    c. are not allowed

    d. are treated just like changes made to individual data items that are passed as parameters

17. You can declare an array of 200 `Furniture` class objects with the declaration _____.

    a. `Furniture = new Furniture[200];`

    b. `Furniture[] = new myChairs[200];`

    c. `Furniture[] myChairs = new Furniture[200];`

    d. `Furniture myChairs[] = new Chairs[200];`

18. Suppose you declare a class named `Furniture` containing a method declared as `string GetWoodType();`, and you declare an array of 200 `Furniture` objects named `myChairs`. You can access the last `Furniture` object's wood type with a call to which of the following?

    a. `Furniture.GetWoodType(199)`

    b. `myChairs[199].GetWoodType()`

    c. `Furniture[199].GetWoodType`

    d. `myChairs.GetWoodType[199];`

19. A collection of methods (and perhaps other members) that can be used by any class, as long as the class provides a definition to override the collection's do-nothing, or abstract, definitions, is a(n) _____.

    a. superclass

    b. polymorph

    c. perimeter

    d. interface

20. When you create a class whose members you will want to compare, you must _____.

    a. include at least one numeric field within the class

    b. write a `CompareTo()` method for the class

    c. `Sort()` the class members before performing any other operations with them

    d. be careful not to override the existing `IComparable.CompareTo()` method

6

EXERCISES

As you work through each exercise, save the finished program in the Chapter.06 folder of your Student Disk.

1. Write a program containing an array that holds five integers. Assign values to the integers. Display the integers from first to last, and then display them from last to first. Save the program as **IntegerList.cs**.

2. Write a program for a package delivery service. The program contains an array that holds the 10 ZIP codes to which the company delivers packages. Prompt a user to enter a ZIP code and display a message indicating whether the ZIP code is one to which the company delivers. Save the program as **CheckZIPS.cs**.

3. Write another program for the package delivery service in Exercise 2. The program should again use an array that holds the 10 ZIP codes to which the company delivers packages. Create a parallel array containing 10 delivery charges that differ for each ZIP code. Prompt a user to enter a ZIP code and then display either a message indicating the price of delivery to that ZIP code or a message indicating that the company does not deliver to the requested ZIP code. Save the program as **DeliveryCharges.cs**.

4. The Chat-A-While phone company provides service to six area codes and charges the following per-minute rates for phone calls:

Area Code	Per-Minute Rate ($)
262	0.07
414	0.10
608	0.05
715	0.16
815	0.24
920	0.14

Write a program that allows a user to enter an area code and the length of time for a call in minutes, then display the total cost of the call. Save the program as **ChatAWhile.cs**.

5. The Whippet Bus Company charges prices for tickets based on distance traveled, as follows:

Distance (miles)	Ticket Price ($)
0 – 99	25.00
100 – 299	40.00
300 – 499	55.00
500 and farther	70.00

Write a program that allows a user to enter a trip distance. The output is the ticket price. Save the program as **WhippetBus.cs**.

6. Write a program that prompts the user to make a choice for a pizza size—*S*, *M*, *L*, or *X*—and then displays the price as $6.99, $8.99, $12.50, or $15.00, respectively. Save the program as **PizzaPrices.cs**.

7. Write a program that computes commissions for automobile salespeople based on the value of the car. Salespersons receive 5 percent of the sale price for any car sold for up to $15,000; 7 percent for any car over $15,000 and up to and including $24,000; and 10 percent of the sale price of any car over $24,000. Write a program that allows a user to enter a car price. The output is the salesperson's commission. Save the program as **Commission.cs**.

8. Create a class named **Taxpayer**. Data fields for **Taxpayer** objects include the Social Security number (use an int for the type, and do not use dashes within the Social Security number) and the yearly gross income. Methods include get and set methods for each data field. Write a program that declares an array of 10 **Taxpayer** objects. Prompt a user for data for each object, then display the 10 objects. Save the program as **Taxpayer.cs**.

9. Create an array that stores 20 prices. Prompt a user to enter 20 values, then display the sum of the values. Next, display all values less than $5.00. Finally, calculate the average of the prices, and display all values that are higher than the calculated average. Save the program as **Prices.cs**.

10. Create a method named `Sum()` that accepts any number of integer parameters and displays their sum. Write a `Main()` method that demonstrates the `Sum()` method works correctly when passed one, three, five, or an array of 10 integers. Save the program as **UsingSum.cs**.

11. Create a class named `Car` containing fields that hold a vehicle ID number, make, model, color, and value for a `Car` object. Include appropriate get and set methods for each field. Write a `DisplayFleet()` method that accepts any number of `Car` objects, displays their values, and displays the total value of all `Car` objects passed to the method. Write a `Main()` method that declares five `Car` objects and assigns values to each, then calls `DisplayFleet()` three times—passing three, four, and five `Car` objects in successive calls. Save the program as **Car.cs**.

12. a. Create a class named `School` that contains fields for the `School` name and number of students enrolled, and methods that get and set both fields. Also, include an `IComparable.CompareTo()` method so that `School` objects can be sorted by enrollment. Write a program that allows a user to enter information about eight `School` objects. Display the `School` objects in order of enrollment size from smallest to largest `School`. Save the program as **School.cs**.

    b. Modify the program created in part a so that after the `School` objects are displayed in order, the program prompts the user to enter a minimum enrollment figure. Then display all `School` objects that have an enrollment at least as large as the entered value. Save the program as **SchoolMinEnroll.cs**.

13. a. Create a class named `Friend`. Its fields include a `Friend`'s name, phone number, and three integer fields that together represent the `Friend`'s birthday—month, day, and year. Write a program that declares an array of eight `Friend` objects. Prompt the user to enter data about eight `Friend` objects. Then display the `Friend` objects in alphabetical order by first name. Save the program as **FriendList.cs**.

    b. Modify the program created in part a so that after the list of `Friend` objects is displayed, the program prompts the user for a `Friend`'s name, and the program returns the `Friend`'s phone number and birthday. Save the program as **FriendBirthday.cs**.

6

c. Modify the program in part b so that the **Friend**'s birth month displays as a word—for example, "January"—instead of as an integer. Save the program as **FriendBirthdayMonth.cs**.

d. Modify the program in part c so that after the requested **Friend**'s birthday displays, the program also displays a list of every **Friend** who has a birthday in the same month. Save the program as **AllFriendsInSameMonth.cs**.

14. Each of the following files in the Chapter.06 folder on your Student Disk has syntax and/or logical errors. In each case, determine the problem and fix the program. After you correct the errors, save each file using the same filename preceded with *Fixed*. For example, DebugSix01.cs will become FixedDebugSix01.cs.

a. DebugSix01.cs

b. DebugSix02.cs

c. DebugSix03.cs

d. DebugSix04.cs

7

INTRODUCTION TO INHERITANCE

In this chapter you will learn:

♦ About the concept of inheritance

♦ Inheritance terminology

♦ How to extend classes

♦ How to use the `protected` access specifier

♦ How to override superclass methods

♦ How to access superclass methods from a subclass

♦ How a subclass object "is an" instance of the superclass

♦ About the `Object` class

♦ How to work with superclasses that have constructors

♦ How to work with superclass constructors that require arguments

♦ How to create and use abstract classes

♦ How to create and use interfaces

♦ The benefits of inheritance

Understanding classes helps you organize objects in real life. Understanding inheritance helps you organize them more precisely. If you have never heard of a Braford, for example, you would have a hard time forming a picture of one in your mind. When you learn that a Braford is an animal, you gain some understanding of what it must be like. That understanding grows when you learn it is a mammal, and the understanding is almost complete when you learn it is a cow. As a cow, you know a Braford has many characteristics in common with all cows. To identify a Braford, you must learn only relatively minor details—its color or markings, for example. Most of a Braford's characteristics, however, derive from its membership in a particular hierarchy of classes: cow, mammal, and animal.

All object-oriented programming languages make use of inheritance for the same reasons—to organize the objects programs use, and to make new objects easier to understand based on your knowledge of their inherited traits. In this chapter you will learn to make use of inheritance with your C# objects.

UNDERSTANDING THE CONCEPT OF INHERITANCE

Inheritance is the principle that states you can apply your knowledge of a general category to more specific objects. You are familiar with the concept of inheritance from all sorts of situations. When you use the term *inheritance,* you might think of genetic inheritance. You know from biology that your blood type and eye color are the products of inherited genes; you can say that many other facts about you (your attributes) are inherited. Similarly, you often can attribute your behaviors to inheritance; for example, the way you handle money might be similar to the way your grandmother handles it, and your gait might be the same as your father's—so your methods are inherited, too.

 You first learned about inheritance in Chapter 1.

You also might choose to own plants and animals based on their inherited attributes. You plant impatiens next to your house because they thrive in the shade; you adopt a poodle because you know they don't shed. Every plant and pet has slightly different characteristics, but within a species, you can count on many consistent inherited attributes and behaviors. In other words, you can reuse the knowledge you gain about more general categories and apply it to more specific categories. Similarly, the classes you create in object-oriented programming languages can inherit data and methods from existing classes. When you create a class by making it inherit from another class, you are provided with data fields and methods automatically; you can reuse fields and methods that are already written and tested.

You already know how to create classes and how to instantiate objects that are members of those classes. For example, consider the `Employee` class in Figure 7-1. The class contains two data fields, `empNum` and `empSal`, as well as four methods—a get and set method for each field.

After you create the `Employee` class, you can create specific `Employee` objects, as in `Employee receptionist = new Employee();` and `Employee deliveryPerson = new Employee();`. These `Employee` objects can eventually possess different numbers and salaries, but because they are `Employee` objects, you know that each `Employee` possesses *some* number and salary.

Suppose you hire a new type of `Employee` that earns a commission as well as a salary. You can create a class with a name such as `CommissionEmployee`, and provide this class with three fields (`empNum`, `empSal`, and `empCommissionRate`) and six methods (get and set methods for each of the three fields). However, this work would duplicate much of the work that you already have done for the `Employee` class. The wise and efficient alternative is to create the class `CommissionEmployee` so it inherits all the attributes and methods of `Employee`. Then, you can add just the single field and two methods that are additions within `CommissionEmployee` objects. Figure 7-2 depicts these relationships.

```
public class Employee
{
        private int empNum;
        private double empSal;
        public int GetEmpNum()
        {
                return empNum;
        }
        public double GetEmpSal()
        {
                return empSal;
        }
        public void SetEmpNum(int num)
        {
                empNum = num;
        }
        public void SetEmpSal(double sal)
        {
                empSal = sal;
        }
}
```

Figure 7-1   An `Employee` class

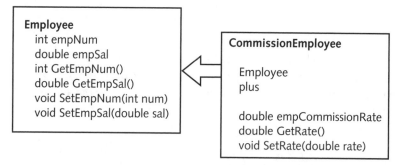

Figure 7-2   `CommissionEmployee` class inherits from `Employee`

When you use inheritance to create the `CommissionEmployee` class, you acquire the following benefits:

- You save time, because you need not recreate the `Employee` fields and methods.

- You reduce the chance of errors, because the `Employee` methods have already been used and tested.

- You make it easier for anyone who has used the `Employee` class to understand the `CommissionEmployee` class because such users can concentrate on the new features only.

Thus the ability to use inheritance makes programs easier to write, less error-prone, and easier to understand. Imagine that besides `CommissionEmployee`, you want to create several other specific `Employee` classes (perhaps `PartTimeEmployee`, including a field for hours worked, or `DismissedEmployee`, including a reason for dismissal). By using inheritance, you can develop each new class correctly and more quickly.

 In part, the concept of class inheritance is useful because it makes class code reusable. However, you do not use inheritance simply to save work. Properly used, inheritance always involves a general-to-specific relationship.

UNDERSTANDING INHERITANCE TERMINOLOGY

A class that is used as a basis for inheritance, like `Employee`, is called a **base class**. When you create a class that inherits from a base class (such as `CommissionEmployee`), it is a **derived class** or **extended class**. When confronted with two classes with a parent–child relationship, you can tell which class is the base class and which is the derived class by using the two classes in a sentence with the phrase "is a." A derived class always "is a" case or instance of the more general base class. For example, a `Tree` class may be a base class to an `Evergreen` class. An `Evergreen` "is a" `Tree`; however, it is not true that every `Tree` is an `Evergreen`. Thus `Tree` is the base class and `Evergreen` is the derived class. Similarly, a `CommissionEmployee` "is an" `Employee`—not the other way around—so `Employee` is the base class and `CommissionEmployee` is derived.

You can use the terms **superclass** and **subclass** as synonyms for base class and derived class. Thus, `Evergreen` can be called a subclass of the `Tree` superclass. You also can use the terms **parent class** and **child class**. A `CommissionEmployee` is a child to the `Employee` parent. Use the pair of terms with which you are most comfortable; all of these terms will be used interchangeably in this book.

As an alternative way to discover which of two classes is the base class and which is the subclass, you can try saying the two class names together (although this technique might not work with every base–subclass pair). In the English language, when people say their names together, they state the more specific name before the all-encompassing family name, such as "Ginny Kroening." Similarly, with classes, the order that "makes more sense" is the child–parent order. Thus, because "Evergreen Tree" makes more sense than "Tree Evergreen," you can deduce that `Evergreen` is the child class.

Finally, you usually can distinguish base classes from their subclasses by size. Although it is not required, a subclass is generally larger than a superclass, in the sense that it usually has additional fields and methods. A subclass description may look small, but any subclass contains all of its base class's fields and methods as well as its own more specific fields and methods.

Do not think of a subclass as a "subset" of another class—in other words, possessing only parts of its superclass. In fact, a subclass usually contains more than its parent.

A derived class can be further extended. In other words, a subclass can have a child of its own. For example, after you create a `Tree` class and derive `Evergreen`, you might derive a `Spruce` class from `Evergreen`. Similarly, a `Poodle` class might derive from `Dog`, `Dog` from `DomesticPet`, and `DomesticPet` from `Animal`. The entire list of superclasses from which a subclass is derived constitutes the **ancestors** of the subclass. Inheritance is **transitive**; that means a child inherits all the members of all its ancestors. In other words, when you declare a `Spruce` object, it contains all the attributes and methods of both an `Evergreen` and a `Tree`. As you work with C#, you will encounter many examples of such transitive chains of inheritance.

 When you create your own transitive inheritance chains, you want to place fields and methods at their most general level. In other words, a method named `Grow()` rightfully belongs in a `Tree` class whereas `LeavesTurnColor()` does not, because the method applies to only some of the `Tree` child classes. Similarly, a `LeavesTurnColor()` method would be better located in a `Deciduous` class than separately within the `Oak` or `Maple` child class.

EXTENDING CLASSES

When you create a class that is an extension or child of another class, you use a single colon between the derived class name and its base class name. For example, the class header `public class CommissionEmployee : Employee` creates a subclass–superclass relationship between `Employee` and `CommissionEmployee`. Each `CommissionEmployee` automatically contains the data fields and methods of the superclass; you then can add new fields and methods to the newly created subclass. Figure 7-3 shows a `CommissionEmployee` class.

```
class CommissionEmployee : Employee
{
     private double commissionRate;
     public double GetRate()
     {
          return commissionRate;
     }
     public void SetRate(double rate)
     {
          commissionRate = rate;
     }
}
```

Figure 7-3 `CommissionEmployee` class

For simplicity, the access modifier public has been omitted from the class header in Figure 7-3. In Chapter 4, you learned that the default access modifier is internal. Because this example uses CommissionEmployee within the same file where the class is created, internal access is adequate.

The CommissionEmployee class in Figure 7-3 contains three fields: empNum and empSal, inherited from Employee, and commissionRate, which is defined within the CommissionEmployee class. Similarly, the CommissionEmployee class contains six methods—four are inherited from Employee and two are defined within CommissionEmployee itself. When you write a program that instantiates an object using the statement CommissionEmployee salesperson = new CommissionEmployee();, then you can use any of the following statements to get field values for the salesperson:

- salesperson.GetEmpNum();

- salesperson.GetEmpSal();

- salesperson.GetRate();

The salesperson object has access to all three methods because it is both a CommissionEmployee and an Employee. Similarly, any of the following statements is legal:

- salesperson.SetEmpNum(3198);

- salesperson.SetEmpSal(200.00);

- salesperson.SetRate(0.07);

Figure 7-4 shows a Main() method that declares Employee and CommissionEmployee objects and shows all the methods that can be used with each. Figure 7-5 shows the program output.

Inheritance works only in one direction: A child inherits from a parent, and not the other way around. If a program instantiates an Employee object, as in Employee clerk = new Employee();, the Employee object does *not* have access to the CommissionEmployee fields or methods. Employee is the parent class, and clerk is an object of the parent class. It makes sense that a parent class object does not have access to its child's data and methods. When you create the parent class, you will not know how many future subclasses might be created, or what their data or methods might look like. In addition, subclasses are more specific. A HeartSurgeon class and an Obstetrician class are children of a Doctor class. You do not expect all members of the general parent class Doctor to have the HeartSurgeon's RepairValve() method or the Obstetrician's DeliverBaby() method. However, HeartSurgeon and Obstetrician objects have access to the more general Doctor methods TakeBloodPressure() and BillPatients().

```
using System;
public class DemoEmployees
{
        public static void Main()
        {
                Employee clerk = new Employee();
                CommissionEmployee salesperson = new CommissionEmployee();
                clerk.SetEmpNum(5612);
                clerk.SetEmpSal(425.00);
                salesperson.SetEmpNum(3198);
                salesperson.SetEmpSal(200.00);
                salesperson.SetRate(0.07);
                Console.WriteLine("\nClerk #{0} makes {1} per week",
                        clerk.GetEmpNum(),
                        clerk.GetEmpSal().ToString("C2"));
                Console.WriteLine("\nSalesperson #{0} makes {1} per week",
                        salesperson.GetEmpNum(),
                        salesperson.GetEmpSal().ToString("C2"));
                Console.WriteLine("...plus {0} percent commission on all sales",
                        salesperson.GetRate());
        }
}
```

Figure 7-4   Main() method with Employee and CommissionEmployee objects

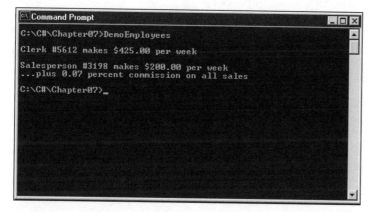

Figure 7-5   Output of DemoEmployees program

 As with doctors, it is convenient to think of subclasses as *specialists*.

Next, you will create a working example of inheritance. You will create this example in four parts:

1. You will create a general BankLoan class that holds data pertaining to a bank loan—a loan number, customer name, and amount borrowed.

2. After you create the general BankLoan class, you will write a program to instantiate and use a BankLoan object.

3. You will create a more specific CarLoan subclass that inherits the attributes of the BankLoan class but adds information about the automobile that serves as collateral for the loan.

4. You will modify the BankLoan demonstration program to add a CarLoan object and demonstrate its use.

To create the BankLoan class:

1. Open a new file in your text editor, and then enter the following first few lines for a BankLoan class. The class will host three data fields—the loan number, the last name of the customer, and the value of the loan.

```
using System;
public class BankLoan
{
   private int loanNumber;
   private string lastName;
   private double loanAmount;
```

2. Add three get methods. Each returns the value of one of the three data fields.

```
public int GetLoanNum()
{
   return loanNumber;
}
public string GetName()
{
   return lastName;
}
public double GetLoanAmount()
{
   return loanAmount;
}
```

3. Add three set methods. Each assigns a value to one of the three data fields.

```
public void SetLoanNum(int num)
{
   loanNumber = num;
}
public void SetName(string name)
```

```
{
   lastName = name;
}
public void SetLoanAmount(double amt)
{
   loanAmount = amt;
}
```

4. Add a closing curly brace for the class. Save the file as **DemoBankLoan.cs** in the Chapter.07 folder of your Student Disk. Compile the file and correct any errors other than the one error you expect telling you that the program does not define an entry point. The message means that you cannot execute the file because it doesn't contain a class with a Main() method yet.

5. Enter the following code to add a DemoBankLoan class that contains a Main() method. The class declares a BankLoan object and shows how to set each field and display the results.

```
public class DemoBankLoan
{
   public static void Main()
   {
      BankLoan aLoan = new BankLoan();
      aLoan.SetLoanNum(2239);
      aLoan.SetName("Mitchell");
      aLoan.SetLoanAmount(1000.00);
      Console.WriteLine("Loan #{0} for {1} is for {2}",
         aLoan.GetLoanNum(), aLoan.GetName(),
         aLoan.GetLoanAmount().ToString("C2"));
   }
}
```

6. Save the file, and then compile and execute the program. The output looks like Figure 7-6.

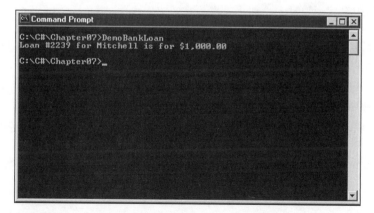

Figure 7-6   Output of DemoBankLoan program

Next, you will create a class named CarLoan. A CarLoan "is a" type of BankLoan. As such, it has all the attributes of a BankLoan plus the year and make of the car that the customer is using for collateral for the loan. Therefore, CarLoan is a subclass of BankLoan.

To create the CarLoan class that extends the BankLoan class:

1. Save the DemoBankLoan.cs file as **DemoCarLoan.cs** in the Chapter.07 folder of your Student Disk. Position your cursor after the closing brace for the BankLoan class, press **Enter** to start a new line, and begin the definition of the CarLoan class. It extends BankLoan and contains two fields: carYear and carMake.

```
class CarLoan : BankLoan
{
   private int carYear;
   private string carMake;
```

2. Include four methods—a get and set method for each of the new CarLoan attributes.

```
public int GetYear()
{
   return carYear;
}
public string GetMake()
{
   return carMake;
}
public void SetYear(int year)
{
   carYear = year;
}
public void SetMake(string make)
{
   carMake = make;
}
```

3. Add a closing curly brace for the class. Save the program, compile it, and correct any errors.

4. Modify the DemoBankLoan class to include a CarLoan object. First, change the name of the class from DemoBankLoan to **DemoCarLoan**.

5. Within the Main() method, just after the declaration of the BankLoan object, declare a CarLoan as follows:

```
CarLoan aCarLoan = new CarLoan();
```

6. After the three set method calls for the `BankLoan`, insert five set method calls for the `CarLoan`.

```
aCarLoan.SetLoanNum(3178);
aCarLoan.SetName("Jansen");
aCarLoan.SetLoanAmount(18000.00);
aCarLoan.SetYear(2002);
aCarLoan.SetMake("Ford");
```

7. Following the `WriteLine()` statement that displays the `BankLoan` object data, insert two `WriteLine()` statements that display the `CarLoan` object's data.

```
Console.WriteLine("Loan #{0} for {1} is for {2}",
   aCarLoan.GetLoanNum(), aCarLoan.GetName(),
   aCarLoan.GetLoanAmount().ToString("C2"));
Console.WriteLine("Loan #{0} is for a {1} {2}",
   aCarLoan.GetLoanNum(), aCarLoan.GetYear(),
   aCarLoan.GetMake());
```

8. Save the program, and then compile and execute it. The output looks like Figure 7-7. The `CarLoan` object correctly uses its own methods and those of the parent `BankLoan` class. For reference, Figure 7-8 shows the entire program.

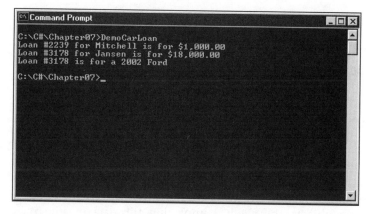

Figure 7-7   Output of `DemoCarLoan` program

```
public class DemoCarLoan
{
        public static void Main()
        {
                BankLoan aLoan = new BankLoan();
                CarLoan aCarLoan = new CarLoan();
                aLoan.SetLoanNum(2239);
                aLoan.SetName("Mitchell");
                aLoan.SetLoanAmount(1000.00);
                aCarLoan.SetLoanNum(3178);
                aCarLoan.SetName("Jansen");
                aCarLoan.SetLoanAmount(18000.00);
                aCarLoan.SetYear(2002);
                aCarLoan.SetMake("Ford");
                Console.WriteLine("Loan #{0} for {1} is for {2}",
                        aLoan.GetLoanNum(), aLoan.GetName(),
                        aLoan.GetLoanAmount().ToString("C2"));
                Console.WriteLine("Loan #{0} for {1} is for {2}",
                        aCarLoan.GetLoanNum(), aCarLoan.GetName(),
                        aCarLoan.GetLoanAmount().ToString("C2"));
                Console.WriteLine("Loan #{0} is for a {1} {2}",
                        aCarLoan.GetLoanNum(), aCarLoan.GetYear(),
                        aCarLoan.GetMake());

        }
}
```

Figure 7-8 Program listing for DemoCarLoan

USING THE protected ACCESS SPECIFIER

The Employee in Figure 7-1 is a typical C# class in that its data fields are private and its methods are public. In Chapter 3, you learned that this scheme provides for information hiding—protecting your private data from alteration by methods outside the data's own class. When a program is a client of the Employee class (that is, it instantiates an Employee object), the client cannot alter the data in any private field directly. For example, when you write a Main() method that creates an Employee as Employee clerk = new Employee();, you cannot change the Employee's empNum, idNum, or empSal directly using a statement such as clerk.empNum = 2222;. Instead, you must use the SetEmpNum() method with the clerk object.

When you employ information hiding, you are assured that your data will be altered only by the methods you choose and only in ways that you can control. If outside classes could alter an Employee's private fields, then the fields could be assigned values that the Employee class couldn't control. In such a case, the principle of information hiding would be destroyed.

Any subclass you create, such as `CommissionEmployee`, inherits all the data and methods of its superclass. However, even though a child of `Employee` has `empNum` and `empSal` fields, the `CommissionEmployee` methods cannot alter those `private` fields. If you could use private data outside of its class, the principle of information hiding would be destroyed. If you intend the `Employee` class data field `empNum` to be `private`, then you don't want any outside classes using the field. If a new class could simply extend your `Employee` class and "get to" its data fields without "going through the proper channels," then information hiding would not be operating.

On some occasions, you do want to access parent class data from within a subclass. For example, suppose that a `CommissionEmployee` draws commission only and no regular salary; that is, when you set a `CommissionEmployee`'s rate field, the `empSal` should become 0. If you want the subclass methods to be able to access `empSal`, then it cannot be `private`. However, if you don't want other, nonchild classes to access the field, then it cannot be `public`. The solution is to create the field using the modifier `protected`. Using the keyword **protected** provides you with an intermediate level of security between public and private access. A protected data field or method can be used within its own class or in any classes extended from that class, but it cannot be used by "outside" classes. In other words, protected members can be used "within the family"—by a class and its descendents.

Figure 7-9 shows how you can declare `empSal` as `protected` within the `Employee` class so that it becomes legal to access it directly within the `SetRate()` method of the `CommissionEmployee` derived class.

```
class Employee
{
      protected double empSal;  // empSal is protected, not private
      // rest of class would follow here
}
class CommissionEmployee : Employee
{
      private double commissionRate;
      public double GetRate()
      {
            return commissionRate;
      }
      public void SetRate(double rate)
      {
            commissionRate = rate;
            empSal = 0;    // If empSal was private, this would be illegal
      }
}
```

Figure 7-9   Declaring `empSal` as `protected` and accessing it within
`CommissionEmployee`

OVERRIDING SUPERCLASS METHODS

When you create a subclass by extending an existing class, the new subclass contains data and methods that were defined in the original superclass. Sometimes the superclass data fields and methods are not entirely appropriate for the subclass objects.

For example, suppose you have created a Student class as shown in Figure 7-10. Students have names, credits in which they are enrolled, and tuition amounts. You can set a Student's name and credits by using the set methods, but you cannot set a Student's tuition directly because there is no SetTuition() method. Instead, tuition is calculated based on a standard RATE (of $55.75) for each credit that the Student takes.

 In Figure 7-10, the Student fields that hold credits and tuition are declared as protected because a child class will use them.

```
class Student
{
        private const double RATE = 55.75;
        private string name;
        protected int credits;
        protected double tuition;
        public string GetName()
        {
                return name;
        }
        public int GetCredits()
        {
                return credits;
        }
        public double GetTuition()
        {
                return tuition;
        }
        public void SetName(string name)
        {
                this.name = name;
        }
        public void SetCredits(int creditHours)
        {
                credits = creditHours;
                tuition = credits * RATE;
        }
}
```

Figure 7-10   Student class

Suppose you derive a subclass from Student called ScholarshipStudent. A ScholarshipStudent has a name, credits, and tuition, but the tuition is not calculated in the same way as it is for a Student; instead, tuition for a ScholarshipStudent should be set to 0. You want to use the SetCredits() method to set a ScholarshipStudent's credits, but you want the method to behave differently than the parent class Student's SetCredits() method. Using the same method name to indicate different implementations is called polymorphism. The word *polymorphism* means "many forms"; it means many forms of action take place even though you use the same method name to describe the action. In other words, there are many forms of the same method depending on the object associated with the word.

 You first learned about polymorphism in Chapter 1.

The English language provides many examples of polymorphism:

- You *run* a race differently than you *run* a business.
- You *play* chess differently than you *play* a guitar.
- You *open* a door differently than you *open* a bank account.

You understand each use of these English verbs based on the context in which it is used. In a similar way, C# understands your use of the same method name based on the type of object associated with it. Figure 7-11 shows a ScholarshipStudent class. As a child of Student, a ScholarshipStudent possesses all the attributes and methods of a Student, but its SetCredits() method behaves differently.

```
class ScholarshipStudent : Student
{
        new public void SetCredits(int creditHours)
        {
                credits = creditHours;
                tuition = 0;
        }
}
```

Figure 7-11 ScholarshipStudent class

In the child ScholarshipStudent class in Figure 7-11, the SetCredits() method is declared as new because it has the same header as a method in its parent class—it overrides and **hides** its counterpart in the parent class. If you omit new, the program will still operate correctly, but you will receive a warning that you are hiding the method with the same name in the base class. Using the keyword new eliminates the warning and makes your intentions clear. When you call SetName() using a ScholarshipStudent object, it will use the parent class method because `SetName()` is not hidden; when you call `SetCredits()` using a `ScholarshipStudent` object, however, it will use the **new**, overriding method from its own class.

If `credits` and `tuition` had been declared as `private` within the Student class, then `ScholarshipStudent` would not be able to use them.

If a superclass and its subclass have methods with the same name but different argument lists, you are overloading methods, and not overriding them. You learned about overloading methods in Chapter 3.

A superclass member that is not hidden by the derived class is **visible** in the derived class.

Figure 7-12 shows a program that uses `Student` and `ScholarshipStudent` objects. Even though each object calls the `SetCredits()` method with the same number of credit hours, the calculated `tuition` values are different, because each object uses a different version of the `SetCredits()` method. Figure 7-13 shows the execution of the program.

```
class DemoStudents
{
    public static void Main()
    {
        Student payingStudent = new Student();
        ScholarshipStudent freeStudent = new ScholarshipStudent();
        payingStudent.SetName("Megan");
        payingStudent.SetCredits(15);
        freeStudent.SetName("Luke");
        freeStudent.SetCredits(15);
        Console.WriteLine("{0}'s tuition is {1}",
            payingStudent.GetName(),
            payingStudent.GetTuition().ToString("C"));
        Console.WriteLine("{0}'s tuition is {1}",
            freeStudent.GetName(),
            freeStudent.GetTuition().ToString("C"));
    }
}
```

Figure 7-12   DemoStudents program

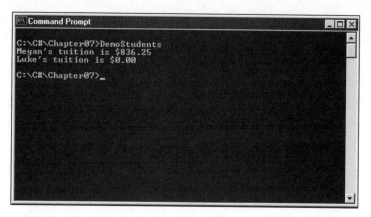

Figure 7-13   Output of `DemoStudents` program

ACCESSING SUPERCLASS METHODS FROM A SUBCLASS

A subclass can contain a method with the same name and arguments as a method in its parent class; when this happens, using the subclass method overrides the parent class method. In some situations, you might want to use the parent class method within a subclass. If so, you can use the keyword **base** to access the parent class method. For example, when both a base class `Employee` and its child `CommissionEmployee` contain a `SetEmpNum()` method, then within the `CommissionEmployee` class you can call `SetEmpNum()` to access the derived class method or `base.SetEmpNum()` to access the base class version of the method.

To demonstrate this idea, you will alter the `BankLoan` and `CarLoan` classes you created earlier in this chapter. Suppose the bank adopts new rules as follows:

- No loan will be made for any car year older than 1997.

- Although `BankLoan`s might have larger numbers, `CarLoan`s will have three-digit loan numbers. If a larger loan number is provided, the program will use only the last three digits for the loan number.

To implement the new `CarLoan` rules:

1. Open the DemoCarLoan.cs file and immediately save it as **DemoCarLoan2.cs**.

2. Within the `BankLoan` class, change the access modifier of `loanAmount` from **private** to **protected**. You do so to enable the `CarLoan` child class to change the `loanAmount` to zero if a car year is older than 1997.

3. Within the CarLoan class, replace the existing SetYear() method so that it not only sets the carYear field, but also when a car's year is less than 1997, the loanAmount becomes 0.

```
public void SetYear(int year)
{
   carYear = year;
   if(carYear < 1997)
       loanAmount = 0;
}
```

4. Also within the CarLoan class, change the inherited SetLoanNum method to accommodate the new rules. If a car loan number is three digits or fewer, pass it on to the superclass SetLoanNum() method. If not, obtain the last three digits by calculating the remainder when the loan number is divided by 1000 and pass the new number to the superclass method. Add the following method after the closing curly brace for the GetMake() method

```
new public void SetLoanNum(int num)
{
   if(num <= 999)
       base.SetLoanNum(num);
   else
   {
       num = num % 1000;
       base.SetLoanNum(num);
   }
}
```

 If you did not use the keyword base to access SetLoanNum() within the CarLoan class, you would be telling this version of SetLoanNum() to call itself. Although the program would compile, it would run continuously until it ran out of memory and issued an error message. A method that calls itself is a **recursive** method.

5. Save the file. Compile it and correct any errors.

6. Replace the existing DemoCarLoan class with a DemoCarLoan2 class. This class contains a Main() method that declares two CarLoan objects and supplies values for their fields. The year for one loan is set prior to 1997 so you can see that the loan amount is correctly reset to 0. The loan number for the other loan is set with five digits so you can see that the SetLoanNum() method will correctly reduce it to three digits.

```
public class DemoCarLoan2
{
 public static void Main()
 {
  CarLoan aCarLoan = new CarLoan();
  CarLoan anotherCarLoan = new CarLoan();
  aCarLoan.SetLoanNum(111);
  aCarLoan.SetName("Morris");
  aCarLoan.SetLoanAmount(12000.00);
  aCarLoan.SetYear(1992);
  aCarLoan.SetMake("Toyota");
  anotherCarLoan.SetLoanNum(88888);
  anotherCarLoan.SetName("Jefferson");
  anotherCarLoan.SetLoanAmount(18000.00);
  anotherCarLoan.SetYear(2002);
  anotherCarLoan.SetMake("Chevrolet");
  Console.WriteLine("Loan #{0} for {1} is for {2}",
   aCarLoan.GetLoanNum(), aCarLoan.GetName(),
   aCarLoan.GetLoanAmount().ToString("C2"));
  Console.WriteLine("Loan #{0} is for a {1} {2}",
   aCarLoan.GetLoanNum(), aCarLoan.GetYear(),
   aCarLoan.GetMake());
  Console.WriteLine("Loan #{0} for {1} is for {2}",
   anotherCarLoan.GetLoanNum(), anotherCarLoan.GetName(),
   anotherCarLoan.GetLoanAmount().ToString("C2"));
  Console.WriteLine("Loan #{0} is for a {1} {2}",
   anotherCarLoan.GetLoanNum(), anotherCarLoan.GetYear(),
   anotherCarLoan.GetMake());
 }
}
```

7. Save the file, and then compile and execute it. Figure 7-14 shows the results. Notice that the 1992 car loan amount is reduced to 0, and that when you attempt to assign 88888 to a loan number, it is altered to 888.

8. Change the assigned values within the DemoCarLoan2 class to combinations of early and late years and valid and invalid loan numbers. After each change, save the program, compile and execute it, and confirm that the program operates as expected.

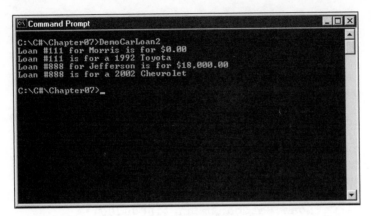

Figure 7-14 Output of DemoCarLoan2 program

UNDERSTANDING A SUBCLASS OBJECT "IS AN" INSTANCE OF THE SUPERCLASS

Every subclass object "is a" specific instance of both the subclass and the superclass. In other words, myCar "is a" Car as well as a Vehicle, and myDog "is a" Dog as well as a Mammal. You can assign a subclass object to an object of any of its superclass types. When you do so, C# makes an **implicit conversion** from subclass to superclass.

 C# also makes implicit conversions when casting one data type to another. For example, in the statement double money = 10;, the value 10 is implicitly converted (or cast) to a double.

To demonstrate that C# makes an implicit conversion from subclass to superclass:

1. Locate the **DemoStudents.cs** file in the Chapter.07 folder of your Student Disk and open it in your text editor. This file contains the three classes shown in Figures 7-10 through 7-12—the Student, ScholarshipStudent and DemoStudents classes. Immediately save the file as **DemoStudents2.cs**.

2. In the Main() method of the DemoStudents class, delete the two Console.WriteLine() statements and replace them with the following two method calls:

```
DisplayStudent(payingStudent);
DisplayStudent(freeStudent);
```

You pass both the payingStudent, who is a Student, and the freeStudent, who is a ScholarshipStudent, to the DisplayStudent() method. DisplayStudent() will accept both object types.

3. After the closing brace of the DemoStudents class's Main( ) method, and above the closing curly brace of the DemoStudents class, insert the following method that accepts a Student argument and displays Student data:

```
public static void DisplayStudent(Student stu)
{
   Console.WriteLine("{0}'s tuition is {1}",
      stu.GetName(),
      stu.GetTuition().ToString("C"));
}
```

4. Save the file, and then compile and execute the program. The output is the same as in Figure 7-13. The DisplayStudent( ) method works correctly whether you pass in a Student object or an object of its child class.

USING THE Object CLASS

Every class you create in C# derives from a single class named System.Object. In other words, the **object** (or Object) class type in the System namespace is the ultimate base class for all other types. The keyword object is an alias for the System.Object class. You can use the lowercase and uppercase versions of the class interchangeably.

When you create a class such as Employee, you usually use the class header class Employee, which implicitly, or automatically, descends from the Object class. Alternatively, you could use the header class Employee : Object to explicitly show the base class.

Because every class descends from Object, every object "is an" Object. As proof, you can write a method that accepts an argument of type Object; it will accept arguments of any type. Figure 7-15 shows a program that declares three objects—a Student, a ScholarshipStudent, and a BankLoan. Even though these types possess different attributes and methods (and one type, BankLoan, has nothing in common with the other two), each type can serve as an argument to the DisplayObjectMessage( ) because each type "is an" Object. Figure 7-16 shows the execution of the program.

7

```
class DiverseObjects
{
        public static void Main()
        {
                Student payingStudent = new Student();
                ScholarshipStudent freeStudent = new ScholarshipStudent();
                BankLoan aLoan = new BankLoan();
                Console.Write("Using Student:              ");
                DisplayObjectMessage(payingStudent);
                Console.Write("Using ScholarshipStudent:  ");
                DisplayObjectMessage(freeStudent);
                Console.Write("Using BankLoan:            ");
                DisplayObjectMessage(aLoan);
        }
        public static void DisplayObjectMessage(Object o)
        {
                Console.WriteLine("DisplayObjectMessage() successfully called");
        }
}
```

Figure 7-15   `DiverseObjects` program

Figure 7-16   Output of `DiverseObjects` program

When you create any child class, it inherits all the methods of its parent. Because all classes inherit from the `Object` class, all classes inherit the `Object` class methods. The `Object` class contains four `public` instance methods summarized in Table 7-1.

Table 7-1   The Four `public` Instance Methods of the `Object` Class

Method	Explanation
`Equals()`	Determines whether two `Object` instances are equal
`GetHashCode()`	Gets a unique code for each object; useful in certain sorting and data management tasks
`GetType()`	Returns the `Type`, or class, of an object
`ToString()`	Returns a `String` that represents the object

The Object class contains other nonpublic and noninstance (static) methods as well as the four methods listed in Table 7-1. The C# documentation can provide you with more details on these methods.

Using the Object Class's GetType() Method

The GetType() method returns an object's type, or class. For example, if you have created an Employee object named someWorker, then Console.WriteLine(someWorker.GetType()); displays Employee.

Using the Object Class's ToString() Method

The Object class methods are not terribly useful as they stand. For example, when you use the Object class's ToString() method with an object you create, it simply returns the name of the class. That is, if someWorker is an Employee, then Console.WriteLine(someWorker.ToString()); displays Employee. When you create a class such as Employee, you should override the Object class's ToString() method with your own, more useful version—perhaps one that returns an Employee's ID number, name, or combination of the two. Of course, you could create a differently named method to do the same thing, perhaps GetEmployeeIdentification() or ConvertEmployeeToString(). However, by naming your class method ToString(), you make the class easier for others to understand and use. Programmers know the ToString() method works with every object; when they use it with your objects, you can provide a useful set of information.

A class's ToString() method is often a useful debugging aid.

You have been using an overloaded version of the ToString() method to format numeric output since Chapter 2.

In the next steps you show how the Object class's ToString() method works with your Student class objects. You also create a new ToString() method for the Student class and show how it overrides the Object class version.

1. Open the **DemoStudents2.cs** file in your text editor. Immediately save it as **DemoStudents3.cs**.

2. Because this program won't use it, remove the entire DisplayStudent() method from the DemoStudents class. Also, remove the last two lines of the Main() method in the DemoStudents class—the ones that call the DisplayStudent() method.

3. Just before the closing curly brace of the `Main()` method in the `DemoStudents` class, insert two `WriteLine()` statements that use the `Object` class's `ToString()` method with the `Student` and `ScholarshipStudent` objects:

```
Console.WriteLine(payingStudent.ToString());
Console.WriteLine(freeStudent.ToString());
```

4. Save the program, and then compile and execute it. The output appears in Figure 7-17. Each object uses the `Object` class version of the `ToString()` method that simply displays the name of the class to which each object belongs.

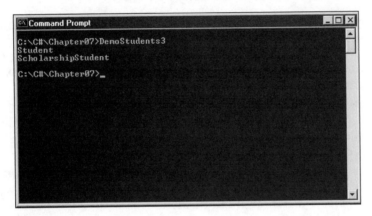

Figure 7-17 Output of `DemoStudents3` program

5. Next, you will override the `Object` class's `ToString()` method by providing the `Student` class with its own version. Save the DemoStudents3.cs file as **DemoStudents4.cs**.

6. Just before the closing curly brace of the `Student` class (after the closing brace of the `SetCredits()` method), insert a `ToString()` method for this class. It is `public`, is `new`, returns a `String`, and accepts no arguments. This method builds and returns an explanatory `String` containing the `Student`'s name and `credits` values.

```
public new String ToString()
{
   String stuString = "Student " + name + " has " +
      credits + " credits";
   return stuString;
}
```

7. Save the program, and then compile and execute it. The output appears in Figure 7-18. Now that the `Student` class has its own `ToString()` method, the method will be used by `Student` and `ScholarshipStudent` objects.

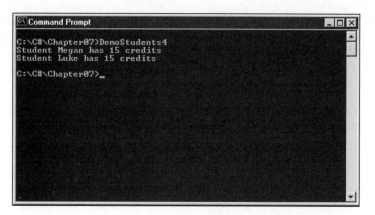

Figure 7-18 Output of DemoStudents4 program

Using the Object Class's Equals() Method

The Object class's Equals() method returns true if two Objects have the same memory address—that is, if one object is a reference to the other and both are literally the same object. Like the ToString() method, this method might not be useful to you. For example, you might prefer to think of two Employee objects as equal if their ID numbers or names are equal. You might want to override the Equals() method for any class you create if you anticipate wanting to compare objects based on any of their field values. When you override the Equals() method, you will receive a warning if you do not also override the GetHashCode() method (because Equals() uses GetHashCode()). A hash code is a number that uniquely identifies an object; you might use hash codes in some advanced C# applications. If you choose to override the GetHashCode() method, you should write this method so it returns a unique integer for every object—an Employee or Student ID number, for example.

You first used the Equals() method to compare String objects in Chapter 2. When you use Equals() with Strings, you use the String class's Equals() method that compares String contents as opposed to String addresses. In other words, the Object class's Equals() method has already been overridden in the String class.

WORKING WITH SUPERCLASSES THAT HAVE CONSTRUCTORS

When you create any object, as in SomeClass anObject = new SomeClass();, you are calling a class constructor method that has the same name as the class itself. When you instantiate an object that is a member of a subclass, you actually call two constructors: the constructor for the base class and the constructor for the extended, derived class. When you create any subclass object, the base class constructor must execute first; only then does the subclass constructor execute.

In the examples of inheritance you have seen so far in this chapter, each class contained default constructors, so their execution was transparent. However, you should realize that when you create an object using `CommissionEmployee salesperson = new CommissionEmployee();` (where `CommissionEmployee` is a subclass of `Employee`), both the `Employee()` and `CommissionEmployee()` constructors execute.

To demonstrate this idea, you can create a class whose constructor does nothing except print a message. Then, when you extend the class, you can create a subclass constructor that prints a different message. When you create an object that is a child class object, both messages appear.

To demonstrate that a subclass constructor calls the superclass constructor first:

1. Open a new file in your text editor.

2. Create a `Customer` for a store that wants to keep data on its customers. This class will serve as a base class. The `Customer` class contains fields for a `name` and `balanceDue`. The constructor prints a message on the screen announcing that execution is taking place.

```
using System;
class Customer
{
  protected string name;
  protected double balanceDue;
  public Customer()
  {
    Console.WriteLine
      ("Executing Customer() constructor");
  }
}
```

In a fully functional `Customer` class, you most likely would add get and set methods for each field. Additionally, you would never create a constructor whose only purpose is to announce its existence; most constructors initialize data fields. However, this abbreviated class is intended merely to demonstrate how superclass constructor methods are called.

3. Below the `Customer` class, add a `PreferredCustomer` child class. This class contains two new fields; with `PreferredCustomer`s, you store a discount rate and the year that the customer became a `PreferredCustomer`. The `PreferredCustomer` constructor announces its execution.

```
class PreferredCustomer : Customer
{
  private double discountRate;
  private int sinceYear;
  public PreferredCustomer()
  {
```

```
            Console.WriteLine
               ("Executing PreferredCustomer() constructor");
         }
      }
```

4. Add a demonstration program whose `Main()` method performs a single task: It declares a `PreferredCustomer` object.

```
class DemoPreferredCustomerConstructor
{
   public static void Main()
   {
         PreferredCustomer pc = new PreferredCustomer();
   }
}
```

5. Save the file as **DemoPreferredCustomerConstructor.cs** in the Chapter.07 folder of your Student Disk and compile it. When it executes, you receive four warning messages as shown in Figure 7-19. These warning messages let you know that you have created fields you never use. If you had created a working program using the `PreferredCustomer` class, perhaps one that produced bills to `PreferredCustomer`s, it would most likely be a mistake to leave these fields without useful values, and you would want to remedy the situation. In this program, however, you are creating a `PreferredCustomer` object merely to demonstrate its constructor's execution, so you can safely ignore the warning messages.

7

Figure 7-19   Warning messages issued by `DemoPreferredCustomerConstructor` program

6. Execute the program. The output appears in Figure 7-20. The `DemoPreferredCustomerConstructor` program declares a single `PreferredCustomer` object. The output in Figure 7-20 shows that both the base class and child class constructors execute, in that order.

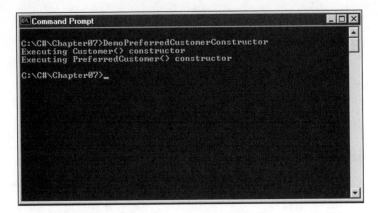

Figure 7-20 Output of `DemoPreferredCustomerConstructor` program

Of course, most constructors perform many more tasks than printing a message to inform you that they exist. When constructors initialize variables, you usually want the base class constructor to initialize the data fields that originate in the base class. The subclass constructor needs to initialize only the data fields that are specific to the subclass.

Next, you will modify the `Customer` and `PreferredCustomer` constructors to behave in a more usual (and more useful) manner.

1. Save the DemoPreferredCustomerConstructor.cs file as **DemoPreferredCustomerConstructor2.cs**.

2. Remove the `WriteLine` statement from the `Customer` constructor and replace it with statements that initialize the `name` and `balanceDue` fields to generic values.

   ```
   name = "XXX";
   balanceDue = 0;
   ```

3. Similarly, remove the `WriteLine()` statement from the `PreferredCustomer` constructor and replace it with statements that set the `PreferredCustomer` field values. Assume that the default `discountRate` is 0.08 and the default `sinceYear` value is 1977—the year the store was established.

   ```
   discountRate = 0.08;
   sinceYear = 1977;
   ```

4. After the closing curly brace of the `PreferredCustomer` constructor, but before the closing brace of the `PreferredCustomer` class, add a `ToString()` method that returns a `String` constructed of the four `PreferredCustomer` field values separated by spaces.

```
public new String ToString()
{
  String s = name + " " + balanceDue + " " +
        discountRate + " " + sinceYear;
  return s;
}
```

5. Within the `Main()` method of the `DemoPreferredCustomerConstructor()` class, add a single statement after the declaration of the `PreferredCustomer` that displays the `PreferredCustomer`'s values.

   ```
   Console.WriteLine("The preferred customer is {0}",
     pc.ToString());
   ```

6. Save the file, and then compile and execute it. As Figure 7-21 shows, each of the constructors has executed and successfully supplied default values for the `PreferredCustomer` object.

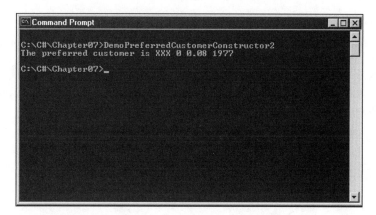

```
Command Prompt                                          _ □ ✕

C:\C#\Chapter07>DemoPreferredCustomerConstructor2
The preferred customer is XXX 0 0.08 1977

C:\C#\Chapter07>_
```

Figure 7-21   Output of `DemoPreferredCustomerConstructor2` program

USING SUPERCLASS CONSTRUCTORS THAT REQUIRE ARGUMENTS

When you create a class and do not provide a constructor, C# automatically supplies one that never requires arguments. When you write your own constructor for a class, you replace the automatically supplied version. Depending on your needs, the constructor you create for a class might require arguments. When you use a class as a superclass, and the class has a constructor that requires arguments, then you must make sure that any subclasses provide the superclass constructor with what it needs.

Don't forget that a class can have many constructors. As soon as you create at least one constructor for a class, you can no longer use the automatic version.

When a superclass constructor requires arguments, you must include a constructor for each subclass you create. Your subclass constructor can contain any number of statements, but within the header of the constructor, you must provide values for any arguments required by the base class constructor. Even if you have no other reason for creating a subclass constructor, you must write the subclass constructor so it can call its parent's constructor.

The format of the statement that calls a superclass constructor is `base(list of arguments)`. The keyword **base** always refers to the superclass of the class in which you use it. For example, if you create an `Employee` class with a constructor that requires two arguments—an integer and a string—and you create a `CommissionEmployee` class that is a subclass of `Employee`, then the following code shows a valid constructor for `CommissionEmployee`:

```
public CommissionEmployee() : base(1234, "XXXX")
{
     // Other statements can go here

}
```

In this example, the `CommissionEmployee` constructor requires no arguments, but it passes two arguments to its base class constructor. Every `CommissionEmployee` passes 1234 and "XXXX" to the `Employee` constructor. A different `CommissionEmployee` constructor might require arguments; then it could pass the appropriate arguments on to the superclass constructor, as in the following example:

```
public CommissionEmployee(int id, string name) :
  base(id, name)
{
   // Other statements can go here
}
```

Although it seems as though you should be able to use the superclass constructor name to call the superclass constructor, C# does not allow you to do so. You must use the keyword name base.

Yet another `CommissionEmployee` constructor might require three or more arguments. Some arguments might be passed to the base class constructor, and some might be used within `CommissionEmployee`. Consider the following example:

```
public CommissionEmployee(int id, string name,
     double rate) : base(id, name)
     // two parameters passed to base constructor
  {
     empCommissionRate = rate;
     // rate used within child constructor
     // Other statements can go here
  }
```

Next, you will modify the `Customer` and `PreferredCustomer` classes so their constructors require arguments.

1. Open the **DemoPreferredCustomerConstructor2.cs** file in your text editor. Immediately save it as **DemoPreferredCustomerConstructor3.cs**.

2. Remove the current no-argument version of the `Customer` class constructor and replace it with the following version, which requires and assigns values for the `name` and `balance` of a `Customer`:

```
public Customer(string name, double balance)
{
   this.name = name;
   balanceDue = balance;
}
```

3. Remove the current `PreferredCustomer` constructor that requires no arguments and replace it with the following version that needs four parameters. This version sends two parameters to the base class constructor and uses the other two parameters to assign fields that are specific to the child class.

```
public PreferredCustomer(string name, double balance,
   double rate, int year): base(name, balance)
{
   discountRate = rate;
   sinceYear = year;
}
```

4. Within the `Main()` method of the `DemoPreferredCustomerConstructor` class, remove the first line, which declares a `PreferredCustomer` using no arguments with the constructor. Replace it with a declaration statement that uses four arguments for the constructor:

```
PreferredCustomer pc =
   new PreferredCustomer("Harris", 2500, 0.04, 1999);
```

5. Save the file, and then compile and execute it. The output appears in Figure 7-22. The `PreferredCustomer` constructor accepts four arguments, passes two to the base class constructor, and uses the other two itself.

7

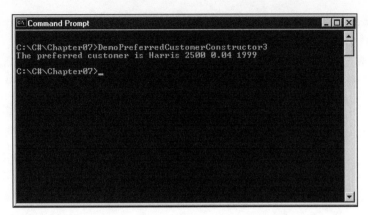

Figure 7-22 Output of `DemoPreferredCustomerConstructor3` program

CREATING AND USING ABSTRACT CLASSES

Creating classes is easier after you understand the concept of inheritance. When you create a child class, it inherits all the general attributes you need; you must create only the new, more specific attributes required by the child class. For example, a `Painter` and a `Sculptor` are more specific than an `Artist`. They can inherit general attributes of all `Artists`, but add specific attributes and methods.

Another way to think about a superclass is to notice that it contains the features shared by its subclasses. The subclasses are more specific examples of the superclass type; they add features to the shared, general features. Conversely, when you examine a subclass, you notice that its parent is more general. Sometimes a parent class is so general that you never intend to create any specific instances of the class. For example, you might never create "just" an `Artist`; each `Artist` is more specifically a `Painter`, `Sculptor`, `Illustrator`, and so on. A class that you create only to extend from, but not to instantiate from, is an abstract class. An **abstract class** is one from which you cannot create any concrete objects, but from which you can inherit. You use the keyword `abstract` when you declare an abstract class.

 Nonabstract classes from which objects *can* be instantiated are called **concrete** classes.

Abstract classes are like regular classes in that they can contain data fields and methods. The difference is that you cannot create instances of abstract classes by using the **new** operator. Rather you create abstract classes simply to provide a superclass from which other objects may be derived. Abstract classes usually contain abstract methods, although they are not required. An **abstract method** has no method statements; any class derived from a class containing an abstract method must override the abstract method by providing a body (that is, an implementation) for it. (Alternatively, the derived class can declare the method to be abstract; in that case, the derived class's children must implement the method.)

When you create an abstract method, you provide the keyword **abstract** and the intended method type, name, and arguments, but you do not provide statements within the method. (You do not even supply curly braces.) When you create a subclass that inherits an abstract method from a parent, then you must use the keyword **override** in the method header and provide the actions, or implementation, for the inherited method within the subclass. In other words, you are required to code a subclass method to override the empty superclass method that is inherited.

If you attempt to instantiate an object from an abstract class, you will receive a compiler error message.

An abstract method also is known as a **virtual method**.

For example, suppose you want to create classes to represent different animals, such as **Dog** and **Cat**. You can create a generic abstract class named **Animal** so you can provide generic data fields, such as the animal's name, only once. An **Animal** is generic, but each specific **Animal** makes a unique sound that differs from **Animal** to **Animal**. If you code an abstract **Speak()** method in the abstract **Animal** class, then you require all future **Animal** subclasses to override the **Speak()** method and provide an implementation that is specific to the subclass. Figure 7-23 shows an abstract **Animal** class containing a data field for the name, a constructor that assigns a name, a **GetName()** method, and an abstract **Speak()** method.

```
abstract class Animal
{
    protected string name;
    public Animal(string name)
    {
        this.name = name;
    }
    public string GetName()
    {
        return name;
    }
    public abstract string Speak();
}
```

Figure 7-23   Animal class

The `Animal` class in Figure 7-23 is declared to be `abstract`. You cannot place a statement such as `Animal myPet = new Animal("Murphy");` within a program, because the program will not execute. `Animal` is an `abstract` class, so no `Animal` objects can exist.

You create an abstract class like `Animal` so that you can extend it. For example, you can create `Dog` and `Cat` classes as shown in Figure 7-24. Because the `Animal` class contains a constructor that requires a `string` argument, both `Dog` and `Cat` must contain constructors that provide `string` arguments for their base class.

```
class Dog : Animal
{
     public Dog(string name) : base(name)
     {
     }
     public override string Speak()
     {
          return "woof";
     }
}
class Cat : Animal
{
     public Cat(string name) : base(name)
     {
     }
     public override string Speak()
     {
          return "meow";
     }
}
```

Figure 7-24   `Dog` and `Cat` classes

 You can create an abstract class with no abstract methods, but you cannot create an abstract method outside of an abstract class.

The `Dog` and `Cat` constructors perform no tasks other than passing out the name to the `Animal` constructor. The overriding `Speak()` methods within `Dog` and `Cat` are required because the abstract parent `Animal` class contains an abstract `Speak()` method. You can code any statements you like within the `Dog` and `Cat` class `Speak()` methods, but the `Speak()` methods must exist first.

Figure 7-25 shows a program that implements `Dog` and `Cat` objects, and Figure 7-26 shows the output. `Speak()` operates polymorphically; that is, each object acts appropriately using the correct `Speak()` method.

```
using System;
class DemoAnimals
{
    public static void Main()
    {
        Dog spot = new Dog("Spot");
        Cat puff = new Cat("Puff");
        Console.WriteLine("{0} says {1}", spot.GetName(), spot.Speak());
        Console.WriteLine("{0} says {1}", puff.GetName(), puff.Speak());
    }
}
```

Figure 7-25   `DemoAnimals` program

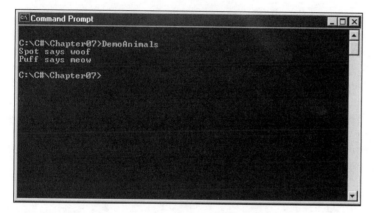

Figure 7-26   Output of `DemoAnimals` program

CREATING AND USING INTERFACES

Some object-oriented programming languages, notably C++, allow a subclass to inherit from more than one parent class. For example, you might create an `Employee` class that contains data fields pertaining to each employee in your organization. You also might create a `Product` class that holds information about each product your organization manufactures. When you create a `Patent` class for each product for which your company holds a patent, you might want to include product information as well as information about the employee who was responsible for the invention. In this situation, it would be convenient to inherit fields and methods from both the `Product` and `Employee` classes. The ability to inherit from more than one class is called **multiple inheritance**.

Multiple inheritance is a difficult concept, and programmers encounter many problems when they use it. For example, variables and methods in the parent classes may have identical names, which creates a conflict when the child class uses one of the names. Additionally, as you already have learned, a child class constructor must call its parent class constructor. When two or more parents exist, this becomes a more complicated task: To which class should **base** refer when a child class has multiple parents?

For all of these reasons, multiple inheritance is prohibited in C#. C# does provide an alternative to multiple inheritance, known as an interface. Much like an abstract class, an interface is a collection of methods (and perhaps other members) that can be used by any class as long as the class provides a definition to override the interface's abstract definitions. Within an abstract class, some methods can be abstract, while others need not be. Within an interface, all methods are abstract.

You learned about interfaces in Chapter 6 when you used the `IComparable` interface.

You create an interface much as you create an abstract class definition, except that you use the keyword **interface** instead of **abstract class**. For example, suppose you create an **IWorking** interface as shown in Figure 7-27. For simplicity, give the **IWorking** interface a single method named **Work()**.

Although not required, in C# it is customary to start interface names with an uppercase "I" and end them with "ing". Other languages follow different conventions. For example, in Java, interfaces usually end with "able"; the `IWorking` interface, therefore, would likely be named `Workable`.

```
public interface IWorking
{
   string Work();
}
```

Figure 7-27 The `IWorking` interface

When any class implements **IWorking**, it must also include a **Work()** method that returns a **string**. Figure 7-28 shows two classes that implement **IWorking**: the **Employee** class and the **Animal** class. Because each implements **IWorking**, each must declare a **Work()** method. The **Employee** class implements **Work()** to return the string "I do my job". The abstract **Animal** class defines **Work()** as an abstract method, meaning that descendents of **Animal** must implement **Work()**. Figure 7-28 also shows two child classes of **Animal**, **Dog** and **Cat**; note how **Work()** is defined differently for each.

```
using System;
public interface IWorking
{
     string Work();
}
class Employee : IWorking
{
     private string name;
     public Employee(string name)
     {
          this.name = name;
     }
     public string GetName()
     {
          return name;
     }
     public string Work()
     {
          return "I do my job";
     }
}
abstract class Animal : IWorking
{
     protected string name;
     public Animal(string name)
     {
          this.name = name;
     }
     public string GetName()
     {
          return name;
     }
     public abstract string Work();
}
class Dog : Animal
{

     public Dog(string name) : base(name)
     {
     }
     public override string Work()
     {
          return "I watch the house";
     }
}
```

Figure 7-28   Using the IWorking interface

```
class Cat : Animal
{

    public Cat(string name) : base(name)
    {
    }
    public override string Work()
    {
        return "I catch mice";
    }
}
```

Figure 7-28 Using the IWorking interface (continued)

When you create a program that instantiates an **Employee**, a **Dog**, or a **Cat**, as in the **DemoWorking** program in Figure 7-29, each object type knows how to "Work()" appropriately. Figure 7-30 shows the output.

```
class DemoWorking
{
    public static void Main()
    {
        Employee bob = new Employee("Bob");
        Dog spot = new Dog("Spot");
        Cat puff = new Cat("Puff");
        Console.WriteLine("{0} says {1}",
            bob.GetName(), bob.Work());
        Console.WriteLine("{0} says {1}",
            spot.GetName(), spot.Work());
        Console.WriteLine("{0} says {1}",
            puff.GetName(), puff.Work());
    }
}
```

Figure 7-29 DemoWorking program

Abstract classes and interfaces are similar in that you cannot instantiate concrete objects from either one. Abstract classes differ from interfaces in that abstract classes can contain nonabstract methods, but all methods within an interface must be abstract. A class can inherit from only one superclass (whether abstract or not), but it can implement any number of interfaces. For example, if you want to create a **Child** that inherits from a **Parent** class and implements two interfaces, **IWorking** and **IPlaying**, you would define the class name and list the base class and interfaces separated by commas: **class Child : Parent, IWorking, IPlaying**.

Figure 7-30 Output of DemoWorking program

Beginning programmers sometimes find it difficult to decide when to create an abstract superclass and when to create an interface. Typically, you would create an abstract class when you want to provide some data or methods that subclasses can inherit, but you want the subclasses to override some specific methods that you declare to be **abstract**. You would create an interface when you want subclasses to override every method. Use a superclass when the class you want to create "is a" subtype of another class; use an interface when the class you want to create will act like the interface.

Interfaces provide you with a way to exhibit polymorphic behavior. If diverse classes implement the same interface in unique ways, then you can treat each class type in the same way using the same language. When different classes use the same interface, you know the names of the methods that are available with those classes and C# classes adopt a more uniform functionality; this consistency helps you to understand new classes you encounter more easily. If you know, for example, the method names contained in the **IWorking** interface and you see that a class implements **IWorking**, then you have a head start in understanding how the class functions.

 Now that you understand how to construct your own interfaces, you will benefit from rereading the section describing the **IComparable** interface in Chapter 6.

RECAPPING THE BENEFITS OF USING INHERITANCE

When an automobile company designs a new car model, it does not build every component from scratch. The car might include a new feature—for example, some model contained the first air bag—but many of a new car's features are simply modifications of existing features. The manufacturer might create a larger gas tank or a more comfortable seat, but these new features still possess many of the properties of their predecessors from older models. Most features of new car models are not even modified; instead, existing components such as air filters and windshield wipers are included on the new model without any changes.

Similarly, you can create powerful computer programs more easily if many of their components are used either "as is" or with slight modifications. Extending classes and using interfaces do not give you the ability to write any programs that you could not write without them; you *could* create every part of a program from scratch, but reusing existing classes and interfaces makes your job easier.

You already have used many "as is" classes, such as `Console`, `Int32`, and `String`. Using these classes made programs easier to write than if you had to invent the classes yourself. Now that you have learned about inheritance, you can modify existing classes as well as just use them. When you create a useful, extendable superclass, you and other future programmers gain several advantages:

- Subclass creators save development time because much of the code that is needed for the class already has been written.

- Subclass creators save testing time because the superclass code already has been tested and probably used in a variety of situations. In other words, the superclass code is reliable.

- Programmers who create or use new subclasses already understand how the superclass works, so the time it takes to learn the new class features is reduced.

- When you create a subclass in C#, the superclass source code is not changed. Thus superclass maintains its integrity.

When you think about classes, you need to think about the commonalities between them, and then you can create superclasses from which to inherit. You might even be rewarded professionally when you see your own superclasses extended by others in the future.

CHAPTER SUMMARY

❐ Inheritance is the principle that you can apply your knowledge of a general category to more specific objects. The classes you create in object-oriented programming languages can inherit data and methods from existing classes. The ability to use inheritance makes programs easier to write, less error-prone, and easier to understand.

❐ A class that is used as a basis for inheritance is called a base class. When you create a class that inherits from a base class, it is called a derived class or extended class. A derived class always "is a" case or instance of the more general base class. You can use the terms *superclass* and *parent class* as synonyms for base class, and the terms *subclass* or *child class* as synonyms for derived class.

❐ When you create a class that is an extension or child of another class, you use a single colon between the derived class name and its base class name. The child class inherits all the methods and fields of its parent. Inheritance works only in one direction: A child inherits from a parent, and not the other way around.

❐ If you could use private data outside of its class, the principle of information hiding would be destroyed. On some occasions, however, you want to access parent class data from within a subclass. For those occasions, you declare parent class fields using the keyword **protected**, which provides you with an intermediate level of security between public and private access.

❐ You can declare a child class method with the same name and argument list as a method within its parent class. When you do so, you override the parent class method and allow your class objects to exhibit polymorphic behavior. You use the keyword **new** with the subclass method.

❐ When a subclass overrides a parent class method and you want to use the parent class version, you can use the keyword **base** to access the parent class method.

❐ Every subclass object "is a" specific instance of both the subclass and the superclass. Therefore, you can assign a subclass object to an object of any of its superclass types. When you do so, C# makes an implicit conversion from subclass to superclass.

❐ Every class you create in C# derives from a single class named **System.Object**. Because all classes inherit from the **Object** class, all classes inherit the **Object** class methods. The **Object** class contains four **public** instance methods: **Equals()**, **GetHashCode()**, **GetType()**, and **ToString()**.

❐ When you instantiate an object that is a member of a subclass, you actually call two constructors: the constructor for the base class and the constructor for the extended, derived class. When you create any subclass object, the base class constructor must execute first; only then does the subclass constructor execute.

❐ When you use a class as a superclass, and the class has a constructor that requires arguments, then within the header of the subclass constructor you must provide values for any arguments required by the base class constructor. Even if you have no other reason for creating a subclass constructor, you must write the subclass constructor so it can call its parent's constructor.

❐ An abstract class is one from which you cannot create any concrete objects, but from which you can inherit. Usually, abstract classes contain abstract methods; an abstract method has no method statements. Any class derived from a class containing an abstract method must override the abstract method by providing a body (that is, an implementation) for the method.

❐ C# provides an alternative to multiple inheritance, known as an interface. Much like an abstract class, an interface is a collection of methods (and perhaps other members) that can be used by any class as long as that class provides a definition to override the interface's abstract definitions. Within an abstract class, some methods

7

can be abstract, while others need not be. Within an interface, all methods are abstract. A class can inherit from only one abstract superclass, but it can implement any number of interfaces.

REVIEW QUESTIONS

1. The principle that you can apply your knowledge of a general category to more specific objects is _____.

   a. polymorphism

   b. encapsulation

   c. inheritance

   d. structure

2. Which is *not* a benefit of using inheritance when creating a new class?

   a. You save time, because you need not create fields and methods that already exist in a parent class.

   b. You reduce the chance of errors, because the parent class methods have already been used and tested.

   c. You make it easier for anyone who has used the parent class to understand the new class because the programmer can concentrate on the new features only.

   d. You save computer memory because when you create objects of the new class, storage is not required for parent class fields.

3. A child class is also called a(n) _____.

   a. extended class

   b. base class

   c. superclass

   d. delineated class

4. Assuming the following classes are well named, which is a parent class to `House`?

   a. `Apartment`

   b. `Building`

   c. `Victorian`

   d. `myHouse`

5. A subclass usually contains _____ than its parent.

   a. more fields and methods

   b. the same number of fields but fewer methods

   c. fewer fields but more methods

   d. fewer fields and methods

6. When you create a class that is an extension or child of another class, you use a(n) _____ between the derived class name and its base class name.

   a. ampersand

   b. colon

   c. dot

   d. hyphen

7. A superclass named `Garden` contains a `private` field `width` and a method `public int GetWidth()`. A child class named `VegetableGarden` does not contain a `GetWidth()` method. When you write a class in which you declare an object as `VegetableGarden myGarden = new VegetableGarden();`, which of the following can you use to access the `VegetableGarden`'s width?

   a. `myGarden.GetWidth()`

   b. `myGarden.base.GetWidth()`

   c. `base.GetWidth()`

   d. You cannot use `GetWidth()` with a `VegetableGarden` object.

8. When a parent class contains a `private` data field, the field is _____ the child class.

   a. hidden in

   b. not a member of

   c. directly accessible in

   d. stored in

9. When a base class and a derived class contain a method with the same name and argument list, and you call the method using a derived class object, _____.

   a. you receive an error message

   b. the base class version overrides the derived class version

   c. the derived class version overrides the base class version

   d. both method versions execute

10. Which of the following is an English-language form of polymorphism?

   a. seeing a therapist and seeing the point

   b. moving friends with a compelling story and moving friends to a new apartment

   c. both of these

   d. neither of these

7

11. When base and derived classes contain a method with the same name and argument list, you can use the base class method within the derived class by using the keyword _____ before the method name.

    a. new

    b. override

    c. base

    d. super

12. In a program that declares a subclass object, you _____ assign it to an object of its superclass type.

    a. can

    b. cannot

    c. must

    d. should not

13. The ultimate base class for all other types is _____.

    a. Base

    b. Super

    c. Parent

    d. Object

14. All of the following are Object class methods *except* _____.

    a. ToString()

    b. Equals()

    c. Print()

    d. GetHashCode()

15. When you create any subclass object, _____.

    a. the base class and subclass constructors execute simultaneously

    b. the base class constructor must execute first; then the subclass constructor executes

    c. the subclass constructor must execute first; then the base class constructor executes

    d. neither the base class nor the subclass constructor executes

16. When a superclass constructor requires arguments, then each subclass _____.

    a. must include a constructor

    b. must include a constructor that requires arguments

    c. must include two or more constructors

    d. must not include a constructor

17. When you create an abstract class, _____.

    a. you can inherit from it

    b. you can create concrete objects from it

    c. both of these are true

    d. neither of these is true

18. When you create an abstract method, you provide _____.

    a. the keyword **abstract**

    b. curly braces

    c. method statements

    d. all of these

19. Within an interface, _____.

    a. no methods can be abstract

    b. some methods might be abstract

    c. some, but not all, methods must be abstract

    d. all methods must be abstract

20. Abstract classes and interfaces are similar in that _____.

    a. you can instantiate concrete objects from both

    b. you cannot instantiate concrete objects from either one

    c. all methods in both must be abstract

    d. neither can contain nonabstract methods

7

EXERCISES

As you create the solution to each exercise, save the finished file in the Chapter.07 folder of your Student Disk.

1. a. Create a class named **Game** containing a string that holds the name of the **Game** and an integer that holds the maximum number of players. Include get and set methods for each field. Also include a **ToString()** method that overrides the **Object** class's **ToString()** method and returns a string containing the name of the **Game** along with the number of players. Save the file as **Game.cs**.

   b. Create a child class named **GameWithTimeLimit** that includes an integer time limit in minutes, and get and set methods for the field. Save the file as **GameWithTimeLimit.cs**.

   c. Write a program that instantiates an object of each class and demonstrates all the methods. Save the file as **GameDemo.cs**.

2. a. Create a class named `Tape` that includes fields for length and width, and get and set methods for each field. Also include a `ToString()` method that returns a string constructed from the return value of the object's `GetType()` method and the values of the length and width fields. Save the file as **Tape.cs**.

   b. Derive two subclasses—`VideoCassetteTape` and `AdhesiveTape`. The `VideoCassetteTape` class includes an integer field to hold playing time, and get and set methods for the field. The `AdhesiveTape` class includes an integer field that holds a stickiness factor—a number that must be a value from 1 to 10—and get and set methods for the field. Save the file as **VideoAndAdhesiveTape.cs**.

   c. Write a program that instantiates one object of each of the three classes, and demonstrate that all of each class's methods work correctly. Save the file as **TapeDemo.cs**.

3. a. Create a class named `Book` that includes fields for the title, author, and price. Include get and set metholds for each field. Save the file as **Book.cs**.

   b. Create a child class named `TextBook` that includes a grade level and a `CoffeeTableBook` child class that contains no additional fields. Create get and set methods for each class. In the child classes, override the method that sets a `Book`'s price so that `TextBooks` must be priced between $20.00 and $80.00, inclusive, and `CoffeeTableBooks` must be priced between $35.00 and $100.00, inclusive. Save the file as **TextAndCoffeeTableBooks.cs**.

   c. Write a program that creates a few objects of each type and demonstrate that all of the methods work correctly. Be sure to use invalid values when testing the child class set methods. Save the file as **BookDemo.cs**.

4. a. Create an abstract class named `Food` containing a string that holds the name of a food and an integer that holds a calorie count. Include methods to get and set the fields. Save the file as **Food.cs**.

   b. Create two derived classes named `Fruit` and `Candy`. `Fruit` contains a double that holds the percentage of a person's daily requirement of vitamin C, and get and set methods for this field. `Candy` contains a double that holds the percentage of sugar in the `Candy`, and get and set methods for this field. Save the file as **FruitAndCandy.cs**.

   c. Write a program that instantiates one `Fruit` object and one `Candy` object, and demonstrate all of the available methods with each object. Save the file as **FoodDemo.cs**.

5. a. Create an interface named `IRecovering`. It contains a single method named `Recover()`. Save the file as **IRecovering.cs**.

   b. Create classes named `Patient`, `Furniture`, and `Football`; each of these classes implements `IRecovering`. Create each class's `Recover()` method to display an appropriate message. For example, the `Patient`'s `Recover()` method might display "I am getting better." Save the file as **RecoveringObjects.cs**.

   c. Write a program that declares an object of each of the three types and uses its `Recover()` method. Save the file as **RecoveringDemo.cs**.

6. a. Create an interface named `ITurning`. It contains a single method named `Turn()`. Save the file as **ITurning.cs**.

   b. Create classes named `Page`, `Corner`, `Pancake`, and `Leaf`; each of these classes implements `ITurning`. Create each class's `Turn()` method to display an appropriate message. For example, the `Page`'s `Turn()` method might display "You turn a page in a book." Save the file as **TurningClasses.cs**.

   c. Write a program that declares an object of each of the four types and uses its `Turn()` method. Save the file as **TurningDemo.cs**.

7. a. Create an abstract class named `Salesperson`. Fields include first and last names; the `Salesperson` constructor requires both these values. Include a get method that returns a string that holds the `Salesperson`'s full name, which consists of the first and last names separated by a space. Save the file as **Salesperson.cs**.

   b. Create two child classes, `RealEstateSalesperson` and `GirlScout`. The `RealEstateSalesperson` class contains a total value sold in dollars field and a total commission earned field (both of which are initialized to 0), and a commission rate field required by the class constructor. The `GirlScout` class includes a field to hold the number of boxes of cookies sold, which is initialized to 0. Include set methods for every field. Save the file as **SalespersonSubclasses.cs**.

   c. Create an interface named `ISelling` that contains two methods: `SalesSpeech()` and `MakeSale()`. In each class, implement `SalesSpeech()` to display an appropriate one- or two-sentence sales speech that the objects of the class could use. In the `RealEstateSalesperson` class, implement the `MakeSale()` method to accept an integer dollar value for a house, add the value to the `RealEstateSalesperson`'s total value sold, and compute the total commission earned. In the `GirlScout` class, implement the `MakeSale()` method to accept an integer representing number of boxes of cookies sold and add it to the total field. Save the file as **ISelling.cs**.

   d. Write a program that instantiates a `RealEstateSalesperson` object and a `GirlScout` object. Demonstrate the `SalesSpeech()` method with each object, then use the `MakeSale()` method two or three times with each object. Display the final contents of each object's data fields. Save the file as **SalespersonDemo.cs**.

8. Each of the following files in the Chapter.07 folder on your Student Disk has syntax and/or logical errors. In each case, determine the problem and fix the program. After you correct the errors, save each file using the same filename preceded with *Fixed*. For example, DebugSeven01.cs will become FixedDebugSeven01.cs.

   a. DebugSeven01.cs

   b. DebugSeven02.cs

   c. DebugSeven03.cs

   d. DebugSeven04.cs

8

EXCEPTION HANDLING

In this chapter you will learn:

♦ About exceptions and the `Exception` class
♦ How to purposely generate a `SystemException`
♦ About traditional error-handling methods
♦ About object-oriented exception-handling methods
♦ How to use the `Exception` class's `ToString()` method and `Message` field
♦ How to `catch` multiple `Exceptions`
♦ How to use the `finally` block
♦ How to handle an `Exception` with a loop
♦ How to `throw` an `Exception`
♦ How to trace `Exceptions` through the call stack
♦ How to create your own `Exception` classes

While visiting Web sites, you have probably seen an unexpected and cryptic message that announces an error and then shuts down the program immediately. Perhaps something similar has happened to you while using a piece of application software. Certainly, if you have worked your way through all of the programming exercises in this book, you have encountered such errors while running your own programs. When a program just stops, it is aggravating, especially when you lose data you have typed and the program error message seems to indicate the program "knows" exactly what is wrong. You might grumble, "If it knows what is wrong, why doesn't it just fix it?" In this chapter you will learn how to handle these unexpected error conditions so your own programs can be more user-friendly than those that simply shut down in the face of errors.

UNDERSTANDING EXCEPTIONS

An **exception** is any error condition or unexpected behavior in an executing program. The programs you write can generate many types of potential exceptions, such as (but not limited to) when:

- Your program asks for user input, but the user enters invalid data.
- The program attempts to divide a value by zero.
- You attempt to access an array with a subscript that is too large or too small.
- You calculate a value that is too large for the answer's variable type.

These errors are called *exceptions* because presumably, they are not usual occurrences; they are "exceptional." The object-oriented techniques used to manage such errors make up the group of methods known as **exception handling**.

 Providing for exceptions involves an oxymoron; you must expect the unexpected.

 Errors you discover when compiling a program are not exceptions; only execution-time errors are called exceptions.

In C#, all exceptions are objects that are members of the `Exception` class or one of its derived classes. Like all other classes in the C# programming language, the `Exception` class is a descendant of the `Object` class. The `Exception` class has several descendant classes of its own, many with unusual names such as `CodeDomSerializerException`, `SUDSParserException`, and `SoapException`. Others have names that are more easily understood, such as `IOException` (for input and output errors), `InvalidPrinterException` (used when a user requests an invalid printer), and `PathTooLongException` (used when the path to a file contains more characters than a system allows).

Most exceptions you will use derive from two classes that in turn derive from the `Exception` class:

- The predefined Common Language Runtime exception classes derived from `SystemException`.
- The user-defined application exception classes you derive from `ApplicationException`.

PURPOSELY GENERATING A SystemException

You can deliberately generate a SystemException exception by forcing a program to contain an error. Of course, when you write professional programs, you would never create them to contain errors on purpose, but when learning about Exceptions, it's helpful to be able to intentionally cause errors. As an example, in every programming language it is illegal to divide a value by zero because the operation is mathematically undefined. In the next steps, you will purposely generate a SystemException by dividing by zero.

1. Open a new file in your text editor, and then type the following MathError class that attempts to divide by zero:

```
using System;
public class MathError
{
  public static void Main()
  {
    int num = 13, denom = 0, result;
    result = num / denom;
    Console.WriteLine("Result is {0}", result);
  }
}
```

You would never write a program that purposely divides a value by zero, but if the denom variable's value is the result of user input, the situation certainly could occur.

2. Save the file as **MathError.cs** in the Chapter.08 folder on your Student Disk, and then compile the program.

3. When the program compiles successfully, run the program. When the error is discovered, you will see a Just-In-Time debugging dialog box like the one shown in Figure 8-1. Near the top of the dialog box you can see that a System.DivideByZeroException has occurred in the MathError.exe program.

You first learned about the Just-In-Time compiler in Chapter 1; it converts intermediate language statements to native code appropriately for the machine on which your program runs.

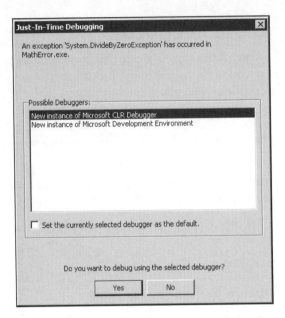

Figure 8-1   Just-In-Time debugging dialog box

4. Click the **No** button at the bottom of the dialog box. The screen looks like Figure 8-2. You can see that you have generated an "Unhandled Exception" and an explanation—the program attempted to divide by zero within the Main() method.

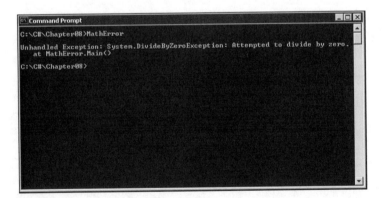

Figure 8-2   Error message generated by MathError.exe program

The DivideByZeroException object in the preceding example was generated automatically by C#. It is an instance of the DivideByZeroException class that has four ancestors. It is a child of the ArithmeticException class, which descends from the SystemException class. The SystemException class derives from the Exception class, which is a child of the Object class.

Just because an `Exception` occurs when an `Exception` object is created, you don't necessarily have to deal with it. In the `MathError` class, you simply let the offending program terminate; that's why the error message in Figure 8-2 indicates the `Exception` is "Unhandled." However, the termination of the program is abrupt and unforgiving. When a program divides two numbers, or even performs a more trivial task like playing a game, the user might be annoyed if the program ends abruptly. If the program is used for air-traffic control or to monitor a patient's vital statistics during surgery, an abrupt conclusion could be disastrous. Object-oriented error-handling techniques provide more elegant solutions.

UNDERSTANDING TRADITIONAL ERROR-HANDLING METHODS

Programmers had to deal with error conditions long before object-oriented methods were conceived. For example, dividing by zero is an avoidable error for which programmers always have had to plan. If you simply check a variable's value with an `if` statement before attempting to divide it into another number, you can prevent the creation of an `Exception` object. For example, the following code uses a traditional, non-object-oriented method to check a variable; it prevents division by zero by forcing the 0 `denom` variable to be 1.

```
if(denom != 0)
      result = num / denom;
else
      result = num / 1;
```

Next, you will modify the `MathError` program to make it interactive and to use an `if-else` to prevent division by zero.

1. Open a new file in your text editor. Enter the program shown in Figure 8-3. It declares integer variables that hold two values input by the user in the `DataEntry()` method. If the user's second value is zero, it is replaced with a 1 before division takes place.

2. Save the file as **MathErrorPreventedWithIf.cs** in the Chapter.08 folder of your Student Disk. Compile and execute the program a few times, sometimes using a nonzero value and sometimes using 0 as the second user-supplied value. Some typical executions are shown in Figure 8-4. Notice that when the user enters 0 in the second run of the program, the 0 is replaced with a 1.

```
using System;
public class MathErrorPreventedWithIf
{
      public static void Main()
      {
            int num, denom, result;
            DataEntry(out num, out denom);
            if(denom != 0)
                  result = num / denom;
            else
            {
                  Console.WriteLine
                    ("Attempt to divide by 0. Denominator replaced with 1");
                  result = num / 1;
            }
            Console.WriteLine("Result is {0}", result);
      }
      public static void DataEntry(out int num, out int denom)
      {
            string strNum;
            Console.Write("Enter a number ");
            strNum = Console.ReadLine();
            num = Convert.ToInt32(strNum);
            Console.Write("Enter a number to divide into the first ");
            strNum = Console.ReadLine();
            denom = Convert.ToInt32(strNum);
      }
}
```

Figure 8-3 MathErrorPreventedWithIf program

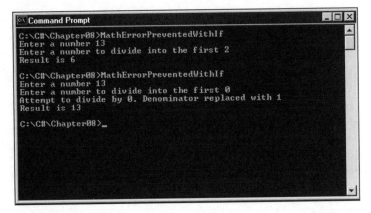

Figure 8-4 Two executions of MathErrorPreventedWithIf program

Figure 8-4 shows that the result of dividing 13 by 2 is 6, not 6.5. Recall that dividing an integer by an integer results in the loss of decimal places.

The code in Figure 8-3 successfully prevents division by zero, but it does not really "handle an exception" because no **Exception** class object is created. The example code illustrates a perfectly legal and reasonable method of preventing division by zero, and represents the most efficient method of handling the error if you think it will be a frequent problem. Because the **MathErrorPreventedWithIf** program does not have to instantiate an **Exception** object every time the user enters a 0 for the value of **denom**, much time and computer memory are saved. (Programmers say this program has little "overhead.") On the other hand, if you think dividing by zero will be infrequent—that is, the *exception* to the rule—then it is more efficient to eliminate the **if** test and instantiate an **Exception** object when needed.

The creators of C# define "infrequent" as an event that happens less than 30 percent of the time. That is, if you think an error will occur in less than 30 percent of all program executions, create an **Exception**; if you think the error will occur more often, use traditional error checking.

UNDERSTANDING OBJECT-ORIENTED EXCEPTION-HANDLING METHODS

In object-oriented terminology, you "try" a procedure that may not complete correctly. A method that detects an error condition or **Exception** "throws" an **Exception**, and the block of code that processes the error "catches" the **Exception**.

When you write a block of code in which something can go wrong, you can place the code in a **try** block. A **try block** consists of the following elements:

- The keyword **try**
- An opening curly brace
- Statements that might cause **Exceptions**
- A closing curly brace

You must code at least one **catch** block or **finally** block immediately following a **try** block. (You will learn about **finally** blocks later in this chapter.) Each **catch block** can "catch" one type of **Exception**. You create a **catch** block by typing the following elements:

- The keyword **catch**
- An opening parenthesis
- An **Exception** type

8

- A name for an instance of the `Exception` type

- A closing parenthesis

- An opening curly brace

- Statements that take the action you want to use to deal with the error condition

- A closing curly brace

Figure 8-5 shows the general format of a `try...catch` pair. The placeholder `XxxException` represents the `Exception` class or any of its more specific subclasses. If an `Exception` occurs during the execution of the `try` block, then the statements in the `catch` block will execute. If no `Exception` occurs within the `try` block, then the `catch` block will not execute. Either way, the statements following the `catch` block execute normally.

 As `XxxException` implies, `Exception` classes typically are created using `Exception` as the second half of the name, as in `SystemException` and `ApplicationException`. The compiler does not require this naming convention; it simply makes `Exception` descendants easier to identify.

```
try
{
    // Statements that might cause an Exception
}
catch(XxxException anExceptionInstance)
{
    // Do something about it
}
// Statements here execute even if there was no Exception
```

Figure 8-5   General form of a `try...catch` pair

 A `catch` block looks a lot like a method named *catch()* that takes an argument that is an instance of `XxxException`. However, it is not a method; it has no return type and you can't call it directly.

 Some programmers refer to a `catch` block as a `catch` *clause*.

Next, you will alter the `MathError` class so it catches the division-by-zero `Exception`.

1. Open the **MathErrorPreventedWithIf.cs** file in your text editor and immediately save it as **MathErrorPreventedWithException.cs**. Change the class name within the file to **MathErrorPreventedWithException**.

2. Remove the seven lines of code that make up the if-else statement, which computes the value of result differently depending on the value of denom. In their place, insert the following try...catch block.

```
try
{
  result = num / denom;
}
catch(Exception e)
{
  Console.WriteLine("Attempt to divide by 0.");
  Console.WriteLine("Denominator replaced with 1");
  result = num / 1;
}
```

Instead of coding result = num / 1;, you can achieve the same result by coding result = num;. The latter is more efficient; the former emphasizes that denom is being replaced with a 1.

8

3. Save the program and compile it. When you compile the program, you receive a warning message that "The variable 'e' is declared but never used." You declare e to be the Exception instance that is caught, but this program doesn't use e, so the message can safely be ignored.

4. Execute the program. When you run this program, the arithmetic expression result = num / denom; will be attempted. If you enter a nonzero value for the second number, division takes place normally. If you enter a 0 for the value of denom, an Exception object will be created and thrown to the catch block, where its name becomes e. If the catch block executes, the message you created is displayed and the num variable is divided by 1 instead of 0. The output looks identical to that shown in Figure 8-4. The method of handling the division-by-zero error is invisible to the user, whether it is through traditional means or by creating an Exception.

USING THE Exception CLASS'S ToString() METHOD AND Message FIELD

When the MathErrorPreventedWithException program prints the error message ("Attempt to divide by 0. Denominator replaced with 1"), and divides the user's first input value by 1, you actually cannot confirm that division by zero was the source of the error. In reality, *any* Exception generated from within the try block in the program would be caught by the catch block in the method because the argument in the catch block is an Exception.

Instead of writing your own message, you can use the ToString() method that every Exception inherits from the Object class and overrides to provide a descriptive error message. That way, the user receives more precise information about the nature of the

Exception that is thrown. In the next steps, you will modify the MathErrorPreventedWithException program to use the **ToString()** method with the **Exception** object thrown when division by zero is attempted.

You learned about using the **ToString()** method with **Objects** in Chapter 7.

1. Open the **MathErrorPreventedWithException.cs** file in your text editor and immediately save it as **UsingTheException.cs**. Change the class name to **UsingTheException**.

2. As the first line within the **catch** block, insert the following statement:

   Console.WriteLine(e.ToString());

   This statement uses the **ToString()** method that belongs to the **e** object, which is caught when division by zero is attempted.

3. Save the program and compile it. With this compilation, you do not receive a warning about not using the **e** object; that's because you do use this object with its **ToString()** method.

4. Execute the program. When you enter 0 as the second integer, you see the messages shown in Figure 8-6. In this case, both the **System** message and your own message are displayed.

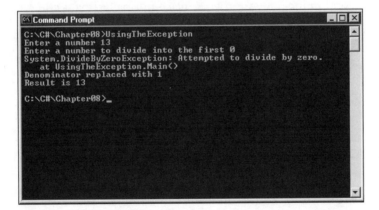

Figure 8-6 Output of **UsingTheException** program when user enters 0 for second number

The **Exception** class also contains a field named **Message** that contains useful information about an **Exception**. For example, the program in Figure 8-7 produces the output shown in Figure 8-8. The value of **error.Message** is a **string** that displays useful information about the **Exception** that was caught.

```
using System;
public class DemoMessage
{
        public static void Main()
        {
                int num = 13, denom = 0, result;
                try
                {
                        result = num / denom;
                }
                catch(Exception error)
                {
                        Console.WriteLine(error.Message); // using Message field
                }

        }
}
```

Figure 8-7   The DemoMessage class

8

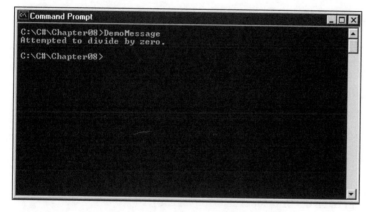

Figure 8-8   Output of DemoMessage program

CATCHING MULTIPLE EXCEPTIONS

You can place as many statements as you need within a **try** block, and you can **catch** as many different **Exceptions** as you want. If you **try** more than one statement, only the first error-generating statement throws an **Exception**. As soon as the **Exception** occurs, the logic transfers to the **catch** block, which leaves the rest of the statements in the **try** block unexecuted.

When multiple **catch** blocks are present, they are examined in sequence until a match is found for the **Exception** that occurred. The matching **catch** block then executes, and each remaining **catch** block is bypassed.

For example, consider the program in Figure 8-9. The **Main( )** method in the **TwoErrors** class throws two types of **Exceptions**—a **DivideByZeroException** and an **IndexOutOfRangeException**. (An **IndexOutOfRangeException** occurs when an array subscript is not within the allowed range. In the **TwoErrors** program, the array has only three elements but 13 is used as a subscript.)

The **TwoErrors** class declares three integers and an integer array with three elements. In the **Main( )** method, the **try** block executes, and at the first statement within the **try** block, an **Exception** occurs because the **denom** in the division problem is zero. The **try** block is abandoned, and the logic transfers to the first **catch** block. Division by zero causes a **DivideByZeroException**, and because the first **catch** block receives that type of **Exception**, the message "In first catch block" appears along with the **Message** value of the **Exception**. In this example the second **try** statement is never attempted, and the second **catch** block is skipped. Figure 8-10 shows the output.

```
using System;
public class TwoErrors
{
      public static void Main()
      {
            int num = 13, denom = 0, result;
            int[] array = {22,33,44};
            try
            {
                  result = num / denom; // First try
                  result = array[num]; // Second try
            }
            catch(DivideByZeroException error)
            {
                  Console.WriteLine("In first catch block: ");
                  Console.WriteLine(error.Message);
            }
            catch(IndexOutOfRangeException error)
            {
                  Console.WriteLine("In second catch block: ");
                  Console.WriteLine(error.Message);
            }
      }
}
```

Figure 8-9   TwoErrors class with two catch blocks

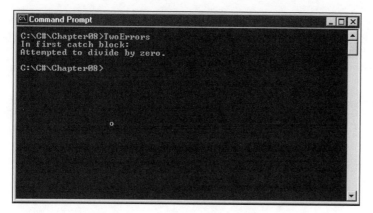

Figure 8-10   Output of `TwoErrors` program

If you reverse the two statements within the **try** block in the **TwoErrors** program, the process changes. If you use the following **try** block, the division by zero does not take place because the invalid array access throws an **Exception** first:

```
try
{
        result = array[num]; // New first try
        result = num / denom; // Old first try
}
```

The new first statement within the **try** block attempts to access element 13 of a three-element array, so it throws an **IndexOutOfRangeException**. The **try** block is abandoned, and the first **catch** block is examined and found unsuitable because the **Exception** is of the wrong type. The program logic proceeds to the second **catch** block, whose **IndexOutOfRangeException** argument type is a match for the thrown **Exception**. The message "In second catch block" and the **Exception**'s **Message** value are therefore displayed. Figure 8-11 shows the output.

Figure 8-11   Output of `TwoErrorsWithReversedTryBlock` program

Sometimes you want to execute the same code, no matter which `Exception` type occurs. For example, within the `TwoErrors` program in Figure 8-9, each of the two `catch` blocks prints a unique message. Instead, you might want both the `DivideByZeroException` catch block and the `IndexOutOfRangeException` catch block to simply use the thrown `Exception`'s `Message` field. Because both `DivideByZeroExceptions` and `IndexOutOfRangeExceptions` are subclasses of `Exception`, you can rewrite the `TwoErrors` class as shown in Figure 8-12 and include only one `Exception` catch block that catches any type of `Exception`.

```
using System;
public class TwoErrors2
{
    public static void Main()
    {
        int num = 13, denom = 0, result;
        int[] array = {22,33,44};
        try
        {
            result = num / denom; // First try
            result = array[num]; // Second try
        }
        catch(Exception error)
        {
            Console.WriteLine(error.Message);
        }
    }
}
```

Figure 8-12   `TwoErrors2` class with one `catch` block

The `catch` block in Figure 8-12 accepts a more generic `Exception` argument type than either of the potentially error-causing `try` statements throw, so the generic `catch` block can act as a "catch-all" block. That is, when either a division arithmetic error or an array error occurs, the thrown error is "promoted" to an `Exception` error in the `catch` block. Through inheritance, `DivideByZeroExceptions` and `IndexOutOf RangeExceptions` *are* `Exceptions`.

When you list multiple `catch` blocks following a `try`, you must be careful that some `catch` blocks don't become unreachable. For example, if successive `catch` blocks catch a `DivideByZeroException` and an "ordinary" `Exception`, then `DivideByZero Exception` errors will cause the first `catch` to execute and other `Exceptions` will "fall through" to the more general `Exception` catch. However, if you reverse the sequence of the `catch` blocks, then you indicate that even `DivideByZeroExceptions` should be caught by the `Exception` catch. The `DivideByZeroException` catch block is unreachable because the `Exception` catch block is in its way, and therefore, the class will not compile. Figure 8-13 shows a program in which the second `catch` block is not reachable, and Figure 8-14 shows the error message generated when you try to compile this program.

```
using System;
public class UnreachableCatch
{
        public static void Main()
        {
                int num = 13, denom = 0, result;
                try
                {
                        result = num / denom;
                }
                catch(Exception error)
                {
                        Console.WriteLine(error.Message);
                }
                catch(DivideByZeroException error)
                {
                        Console.WriteLine(error.Message);
                }
        }
}
```

Figure 8-13   Program with unreachable `catch` block

Figure 8-14   Error message generated by `UnreachableCatch` program

USING THE `finally` BLOCK

When you have actions to perform at the end of a `try...catch` sequence, you can use a `finally` block. The code within a `finally` block executes whether or not the `try` block identifies any `Exceptions`. Typically, you use the `finally` block to perform clean-up tasks that must occur, regardless of whether any errors occurred or were caught. Figure 8-15 shows the format of a `try...catch` sequence that uses a `finally` block.

```
try
{
        // Statements that might cause an Exception
}
catch(SomeException anExceptionInstance)
{
        // What to do about it
}
finally
{
        // Statements here execute
        // even if no Exception occurred
}
```

Figure 8-15   General form of a `try...catch` block with a `finally` block

At first, it seems as though the `finally` block serves no purpose. When a `try` block works without error, control passes to the statements that come after the `catch` block. Additionally, when the `try` code fails and throws an `Exception`, if the `Exception` is caught, then the `catch` block executes, and again, control passes to the statements after the `catch` block. At first glance, it seems as though the statements after the `catch` block always execute, so there is no need to place any statement within a special `finally` block. However, there are at least two reasons why the last set of statements after the `catch` might never execute:

- It is possible that an `Exception` for which you did not plan will occur.

- The `try` or `catch` block might contain a statement that quits the application.

You quit an application with the statement `Application.Exit();`. You will learn about the `Exit()` method when you learn about the `Application` class in Chapter 10.

The possibility exists that your `try` block might throw an `Exception` for which you did not provide a `catch`. After all, `Exceptions` occur all the time without your handling them, as one did in the first `MathError` program you created earlier in this chapter. In case of an unhandled `Exception`, program execution stops immediately, sending the error to the operating system for handling and abandoning the current method. Likewise, if the `try` block contains an `Exit()` statement, execution stops immediately.

When you include a `finally` block, you are assured that the `finally` statements will execute before the program is abandoned—even if the method concludes prematurely. The `finally` block is used most frequently with file input and output, to ensure that open files are closed.

You also might exit a catch block with a break statement. You encountered break statements when you learned about the switch statement in Chapter 4.

HANDLING AN Exception WITH A LOOP

Different programs require different ways of handling Exceptions. In some programs you write, you simply want to display an error message when an Exception occurs. In others, you want to remedy the situation the same way every time, such as replacing a dividing 0 with 1. In yet others, you want to keep trying the offending code until it is correct. In these cases, you can place a try...catch block within a loop that continues to execute until the code is successful.

As an example, consider the HandlingAFormatException program in Figure 8-16. This program asks a user to input an integer value that will be used as a sports team player's number. A Boolean variable named isGoodNumber is initialized to false; this variable controls the data entry loop that will continue to execute until the variable's value becomes true.

```
using System;

public class HandlingAFormatException
{
       public static void Main()
       {
         int playerNumber;
         string strNumber;
         bool isGoodNumber = false;
         while (!isGoodNumber)
         {
             try
             {
                     Console.Write("Enter player's number ");
                     strNumber = Console.ReadLine();
                     playerNumber = Convert.ToInt32(strNumber);
                     isGoodNumber = true;
             }
             catch(FormatException fe)
             {
                     Console.WriteLine
                           ("You must enter an integer for the player number");
             }
         }
       }
}
```

Figure 8-16   HandlingAFormatException program

Within the `try` block in Figure 8-16, a string value is read from the keyboard, then converted to an integer. However, when users enter values from the keyboard, they don't always enter the correct value types. For example, instead of an integer, a user might enter a floating-point number or a non-numeric character. Any keyboard data will successfully be accepted into a string, but only strings containing all digits (or a + or - sign) will successfully be converted to integers. If the user enters a non-integer, the `Convert.ToInt32()` method throws a `FormatException` and execution continues with the `catch` block at the bottom of the loop. The program "gets past" the `Convert.ToInt32()` method only when the user enters an integer and the `ToInt32()` method is successful. Only then will `isGoodNumber` change to `true`, ending the loop when the `while` statement executes. Figure 8-17 shows a typical execution of the program in which the user enters invalid data twice before "getting it right." Trying and catching the `Exception` in a loop ensures that the input data will be the correct type before the program proceeds.

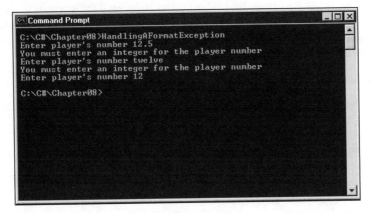

```
C:\C#\Chapter08>HandlingAFormatException
Enter player's number 12.5
You must enter an integer for the player number
Enter player's number twelve
You must enter an integer for the player number
Enter player's number 12

C:\C#\Chapter08>
```

Figure 8-17   Execution of `HandlingAFormatException` program

The `Convert.ToDouble()` method does not throw an `Exception` when you attempt to convert an integer, because an integer can be automatically promoted to a double.

THROWING Exceptions

An advantage of using object-oriented exception-handling techniques is the ability to deal with `Exceptions` appropriately as you make conscious decisions about how to handle them. When methods from other classes throw `Exceptions`, they don't have to catch them; instead, your calling program can catch them, and you can decide what you want to do. For example, in the `HandlingAFormatException` program in Figure 8-16, the `Convert.ToString()` method threw an `Exception` but did not `catch` it; instead, the HandlingAFormatException program caught it and handled it by placing the catch in a loop and forcing the user to reenter a value. A different program might choose to force the playerNumber to 0, or display an error message and quit the program. This flexibility is an advantage when you need to be able to make your reaction to thrown Exceptions specific for your current purposes.

When you design your own classes that might cause Exceptions, you should create them to throw the Exception but not to handle it. Handling an Exception should be left to the client—the program that uses your class—so the Exception can be handled in an appropriate way for the application.

You can throw any Object, whether it is an Exception or not. However, for clarity it is recommended that you throw only Exceptions.

In the next steps you will create a SoccerPlayer class containing a method that throws an Exception.

8

1. Open a new file in your text editor and create a SoccerPlayer class. The class contains a single integer that holds a player's number, and a single method that prompts the user for the number. The promptForNumber() method might cause an Exception if the user enters data in the wrong format, so the method tries the data entry statements and catches the error. However, instead of handling the thrown Exception, the catch block passes the Exception on by throwing it to the client that will use the SoccerPlayer class.

```
public class SoccerPlayer
{
    private int playerNumber;
    public void promptForNumber()
    {
        string strNumber;
        try
        {
            Console.Write("Enter player's number ");
            strNumber = Console.ReadLine();
            playerNumber = Convert.ToInt32(strNumber);
        }
        catch(FormatException fe)
        {
            throw(fe);
        }
    }
}
```

2. In the same file, above the `SoccerPlayer` class, insert a program that instantiates a `SoccerPlayer` object and then, within a `try` block, attempts the method that prompts for and gets a `playerNumber`. If the `SoccerPlayer promptForNumber()` method causes an `Exception`, this client program handles it by displaying an error message.

```
using System;
public class TrySoccerPlayer1
{
    public static void Main()
    {
        SoccerPlayer sp = new SoccerPlayer();
        try
        {
            sp.promptForNumber();
        }
        catch (Exception e)
        {
            Console.WriteLine(e.Message);
        }
    }
}
```

3. Save the file as **TrySoccerPlayer1.cs** in the Chapter.08 folder of your Student Disk.

4. Compile the program, and then execute it a few times, providing both valid data (an integer) and invalid data (data containing characters other than those that convert to an integer). Figure 8-18 shows two executions. When the user enters an integer, the program ends without an error message; when the user enters a floating-point number, an error message appears.

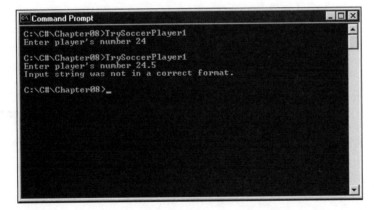

Figure 8-18   Two executions of `TrySoccerPlayer1` program

5. Create a second client program that handles the `SoccerPlayer` thrown `Exception` in a different way. Resave the program as **TrySoccerPlayer2.cs**. Change the class name from `TrySoccerPlayer1` to **TrySoccerPlayer2**.

6. Replace the `Main()` method of the program with the following `Main()` method, which tries the `promptForNumber()` method in a loop that continues until the user enters a number in the proper format.

```
public static void Main()
{
    SoccerPlayer sp = new SoccerPlayer();
    bool isNumberGood = false;
    while(!isNumberGood)
    {
        try
        {
            sp.promptForNumber();
            isNumberGood = true;
        }
        catch (Exception e)
        {
            Console.WriteLine(e.Message);
            Console.WriteLine
                ("You will have to reenter the number.");
        }
    }
}
```

8

7. Save the program, then compile and execute it. Figure 8-19 shows an execution of the program during which the user enters invalid data several times. The program loops until the `SoccerPlayer` class's `promptForNumber()` method is successful—that is, until it does not throw an `Exception`.

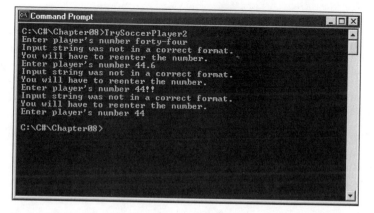

Figure 8-19 Execution of `TrySoccerPlayer2` program

You could write many applications using the `SoccerPlayer` class and allow each application to handle its thrown `Exceptions` in the best way for the application at hand. For the best software design, you should create your classes to `throw` any `Exceptions` and your application programs to `catch` them.

TRACING Exceptions THROUGH THE CALL STACK

When one method calls another, the computer's operating system must keep track of where the method call came from and program control must return to the calling method when the called method is complete. For example, if `MethodA()` calls `MethodB()`, the operating system has to "remember" to return to `MethodA()` when `MethodB()` ends. Similarly, if `MethodB()` calls `MethodC()`, then while `MethodC()` is executing, the computer needs to "remember" that it is going to return to `MethodB()`, and eventually to `MethodA()`. The memory location where the computer stores the list of locations to which the system must return is known as the **call stack**.

When a method throws an `Exception`, if the method does not catch it, then the `Exception` is thrown to the next method "up" the call stack or, in other words, to the method that called the offending method. If `MethodA()` calls `MethodB()`, and `MethodB()` calls `MethodC()`, and `MethodC()` throws an `Exception`, then C# looks first for a `catch` block in `MethodC()`. If none exists, then C# looks for the same thing in `MethodB()`. If `MethodB()` does not have a `catch` block, then C# looks to `MethodA()`. If `MethodA()` doesn't `catch` the `Exception`, then the program terminates and the operating system displays an error message.

This system of passing `Exceptions` through the chain of calling methods has great advantages because it allows your methods to handle `Exceptions` more appropriately. However, a program that uses several classes has the disadvantage of making it very difficult for the programmer to locate the original source of an `Exception`.

You already have used the `Message` field to obtain information about an `Exception`. Another useful `Exception` field is the `StackTrace` field. When you catch an `Exception`, you can print the value of the `StackTrace` field to display a list of methods in the call stack so you can determine the location of the `Exception`.

In the next steps you will display the `StackTrace` value to show how an `Exception` travels through methods.

1. Open the **TrySoccerPlayer1.cs** file in your text editor, and then immediately resave it as **TrySoccerPlayerUsingStackTrace.cs**. Within the file, change the class name from `TrySoccerPlayer1` to `TrySoccerPlayerUsingStackTrace`.

2. Position your cursor within the `catch` block after the line that prints the error message (`Console.WriteLine(e.Message);`) and press the **Enter** key to start a new line. Type the following statement to display the stack trace:

```
Console.WriteLine(e.StackTrace);
```

3. Save the file, and then compile and execute it. After the prompt appears, enter an invalid (non-integer) value. For example, if you enter "one", your screen looks like Figure 8-20. You see that the input string was not in the correct format in the `SoccerPlayer.promptForNumber()` method. That method was called by the `TrySoccerPlayerUsingStackTrace.Main()` method.

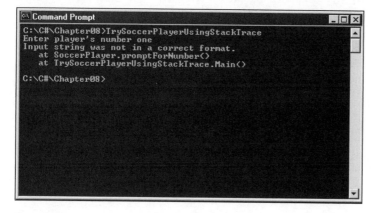

Figure 8-20   Execution of `TrySoccerPlayerUsingStackTrace` program

The `StackTrace` field can be a useful debugging tool. When your program stops abruptly, it is helpful to discover in which method the `Exception` occurred. Often, you do not want to display a `StackTrace` field in a finished program; the typical end user has no interest in the cryptic messages that would be printed. However, while you are developing a program, `StackTrace` can help you diagnose your program's problems.

> You might find it useful to locate `StackTrace` calls strategically throughout a program while testing it, then comment them out when the program is complete.

CREATING YOUR OWN EXCEPTION CLASSES

C# provides more than 100 categories of `Exceptions` that you can throw in your programs. However, C#'s creators could not predict every condition that might be an `Exception` in the programs you write. For example, you might want to declare an `Exception` when your bank balance is negative or when an outside party attempts to access your e-mail account. Most organizations have specific rules for exceptional data, such as "an employee number must not exceed three digits" or "an hourly salary must not be less than the legal minimum wage." Of course, you can handle these potential error situations with `if` statements, but you also can create your own `Exceptions`.

To create your own `Exception` that you can throw, you should extend the `ApplicationException` class, which is a subclass of `Exception`. Figure 8-21 shows a `NegativeBalanceException` class that extends `ApplicationException`. If you create an `ApplicationException` and display its `Message` field, you will see the message "Error in the application." When the `NegativeBalanceException` constructor passes the string "Bank balance is negative." to its parent's constructor, the `Message` field will hold this more descriptive message.

 The C# documentation recommends that you create all `Exception` messages to be grammatically correct, complete sentences ending in a period.

```
public class NegativeBalanceException : ApplicationException
{
        private static string msg = "Bank balance is negative.";
        public NegativeBalanceException() : base(msg)
        {
        }
}
```

Figure 8-21   The `NegativeBalanceException` class

When you create a `BankAccount` class like the one shown in Figure 8-22, you can create the `SetBalance()` method to throw a `NegativeBalanceException` when the balance parameter passed to the method is negative.

```
public class BankAccount
{
        private int accountNum;
        private double balance;
        public int GetAccountNum()
        {
                return accountNum;
        }
        public void SetAccountNum(int acctNumber)
        {
                accountNum = acctNumber;
        }
        public double GetBalance()
        {
                return balance;
        }
        public void SetBalance(double bal)
        {
                if(bal < 0)
                {
                        NegativeBalanceException nbe = new
                        NegativeBalanceException();
                        throw(nbe);
                }
                balance = bal;
        }
}
```

Figure 8-22   The BankAccount class

Figure 8-23 shows a program that attempts to set a `BankAccount` balance to a negative value. When the `BankAccount` class's `SetBalance()` method throws the `NegativeBalanceException`, the `catch` block in the `TryBankAccount` program executes, displaying both the `NegativeBalanceExceptionMessage` and the value of `StackTrace`. Figure 8-24 shows the output.

   Instead of creating the nbe object in the `SetBalance()` method in Figure 8-22, you could code `throw(new NegativeBalanceException());`, creating and throwing an unnamed `NegativeBalanceException` in a single step.

   The `StackTrace` begins at the point where an `Exception` is thrown, not where it is created. This consideration makes a difference when you create an `Exception` and throw it from two different methods.

```
using System;
public class TryBankAccount
{
    public static void Main()
    {
        BankAccount acct = new BankAccount();
        try
        {
            acct.SetAccountNum(1234);
            acct.SetBalance(-1000);
        }
        catch (Exception e)
        {
            Console.WriteLine(e.Message);
            Console.WriteLine(e.StackTrace);
        }
    }
}
```

Figure 8-23 The `TryBankAccount` program

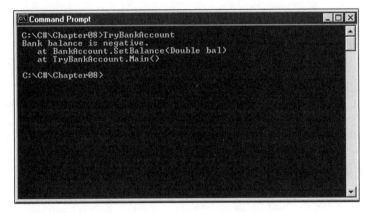

Figure 8-24 Output of `TryBankAccount` program

You can throw any type of **Exception** at any time, not just **Exceptions** of your own creation. For example, within any program you can code `throw(new ApplicationException());`. However, if the built-in **Exception** type suits your needs, you should use it. You should not create an excessive number of special **Exception** types for your classes, especially if the C# development environment already contains an **Exception** that accurately describes the error. Extra **Exception** types add a level of complexity for other programmers who will use your classes. Nevertheless, when appropriate, specialized **Exception** classes provide an elegant way for you to take care of error situations. They provide you with the capability of separating your error code from the usual, non-exceptional sequence of events. They also allow for errors to be passed up the stack and traced.

CHAPTER SUMMARY

- An exception is any error condition or unexpected behavior in an executing program; the object-oriented techniques used to manage such errors make up the group of methods known as exception handling. In C#, all exceptions are objects that are members of the **Exception** class or one of its derived classes. Most exceptions you will use are derived from two classes: **SystemException** and **ApplicationException**.

- You can purposely generate a **SystemException** exception by forcing a program to contain an error. Although you are not required to handle **Exceptions**, you can use object-oriented techniques to provide elegant error-handling solutions.

- When you think an error will occur frequently, it is most efficient to handle it in the traditional way, with **if** statements. If an error will occur infrequently, it is more efficient to instantiate an **Exception** object when needed.

- In object-oriented terminology, you "try" a procedure that may not complete correctly. A method that detects an error condition or **Exception** "throws" an **Exception**, and the block of code that processes the error "catches" the **Exception**.

- Every **Exception** object contains a **ToString()** method and a **Message** field.

- You can place as many statements as you need within a **try** block, and you can **catch** as many different **Exceptions** as you want. If you **try** more than one statement, only the first error-generating statement will throw an **Exception**. When multiple **catch** blocks are present, they are examined in sequence until a match is found for the **Exception** that occurred.

- When you have actions to perform at the end of a **try...catch** sequence, you can use a **finally** block.

- When you want to keep trying a block of code until some value or state within a program is correct, you can place a **try...catch** block within a loop.

- When methods throw **Exceptions**, they don't have to catch them; instead, the program that calls a method that throws an **Exception** can catch it and determine what to do. For the best software design, you should create your classes to **throw** any **Exceptions** and your application programs to **catch** them.

- When a method throws an **Exception**, if the method does not catch it, then the **Exception** is thrown to the method that called the offending method. When you catch an **Exception**, you can print the value of the **StackTrace** field to display a list of methods in the call stack, allowing you to determine the location of the **Exception**.

- To create your own **Exception** that you can throw, you should extend the **ApplicationException** class, which is a subclass of **Exception**.

8

Review Questions

1. Any error condition or unexpected behavior in an executing program is known as an _____.

   a. exception

   b. anomaly

   c. exclusion

   d. omission

2. Which of the following is *not* treated as a C# Exception?

   a. Your program asks the user to input a number, but the user enters a character.

   b. You attempt to execute a C# program, but the C# compiler has not been installed.

   c. You attempt to access an array with a subscript that is too large.

   d. You calculate a value that is too large for the answer's variable type.

3. Most exceptions you will use derive from two classes: _____.

   a. Object and ObjectException

   b. SystemException and ApplicationException

   c. ApplicationException and IOException

   d. IOException and FormatException

4. Exceptions can be _____.

   a. generated automatically by C#

   b. created by a program

   c. both of these

   d. neither of these

5. When a program creates an Exception, you _____.

   a. must handle it

   b. can handle it

   c. must not handle it

   d. Programs cannot create Exceptions.

6. Without using object-oriented techniques, _____.

   a. there are no error situations

   b. you cannot manage error situations

   c. you can manage error situations, but with great difficulty

   d. you can manage error situations

7. In object-oriented terminology, you _____ a procedure that may not complete correctly.

   a. circumvent

   b. attempt

   c. catch

   d. try

8. In object-oriented terminology, a method that detects an error condition _____ an **Exception**.

   a. throws

   b. catches

   c. tries

   d. unearths

9. When you write a block of code in which something can go wrong, you can place the code in a _____ block.

   a. `catch`

   b. `blind`

   c. `system`

   d. `try`

10. A `catch` block executes when its `try` block _____.

    a. completes

    b. throws any **Exception**

    c. throws an **Exception** of an acceptable type

    d. completes without throwing anything

11. Which of the following `catch` blocks will catch any **Exception**?

    a. `catch(Any e) {}`

    b. `catch(Exception e) {}`

    c. `catch(e)`

    d. All of the above will `catch` any **Exception**.

12. Which of the following is valid within a `catch` block with the header `catch(Exception error)`?

    a. `Console.WriteLine(error.ToString());`

    b. `Console.WriteLine(error.Message);`

    c. `return(error.ToString());`

    d. two of these

8

13. You can place _____ statement(s) within a **try** block.

    a. zero

    b. one

    c. two

    d. any number of

14. How many **catch** blocks can follow a **try** block?

    a. only one

    b. any number as long as it is greater than zero

    c. any number as long as it is greater than one

    d. any number, including zero or one

15. Consider the following **try** block. If **x** is greater than 10, what is the value of **a** when this code completes?

    ```
    try
    {
        a = 99;
        if(x > 10)
                throw(new Exception());
        a = 0;
        ++a;
    }
    ```

    a. 0

    b. 1

    c. 99

    d. undefined

16. Consider the following **catch** blocks. The variable **b** has been initialized to 0. If a **DivideByZeroException** occurs in a **try** block just before this **catch** block, what is the value of **b** when this code completes?

    ```
    catch(DivideByZeroException e)
    {
        ++b;
    }
    catch(DivideByZeroException e
    {
        ++b;
    }
    ```

    a. 0

    b. 1

    c. 2

    d. 3

17. Consider the following `catch` blocks. The variable `c` has been initialized to 0. If an `IndexOutOfRangeException` occurs in a `try` block just before this `catch` block, what is the value of `c` when this code completes?

```
catch(IndexOutOfRangeException e)
{
      ++c;
}
catch(Exception e)
{
      ++c;
}
finally
{
      ++c;
}
```

   a. 0

   b. 1

   c. 2

   d. 3

18. If your program throws an `IndexOutOfRangeException` and the only available `catch` block catches an `Exception`, _____.

   a. an `IndexOutOfRangeException` `catch` block is generated automatically

   b. the `Exception` `catch` block executes

   c. the `catch` block is bypassed

   d. an `Exception` is thrown to the operating system

19. When you design your own classes that might cause `Exceptions`, you should create them to _____.

   a. neither `throw` nor handle `Exceptions`

   b. `throw` `Exceptions` but not handle them

   c. handle `Exceptions` but not `throw` them

   d. both `throw` and handle `Exceptions`

20. When you create an `Exception` of your own, you should extend the _____ class.

   a. `SystemException`

   b. `PersonalException`

   c. `OverloadedException`

   d. `ApplicationException`

8

EXERCISES

Save the programs that you create for these exercises in the Chapter.08 folder on your Student Disk.

1. Write a program named `GoTooFar` in which you declare an array of five integers and store five values in the array. Initialize a subscript to 0. Write a `try` block in which you access each element of the array, subsequently increasing the subscript by 1. Create a `catch` block that catches the eventual `ArrayIndexOutOfRangeException`, and then print "Now you've gone too far." to the screen. Save the file as **GoTooFar.cs**.

2. The `Convert.ToInt32()` method requires a string argument that can be converted to an `int`. Write a program in which you prompt the user for a stock number and quantity ordered. Accept the strings the user enters and convert them to integers. Catch the `Exception` that is thrown when the user enters non-integer data for either field. Within the `catch` block, display an error message and set both the stock number and quantity values to 0. Save the file as **PlacingOrder.cs**.

3. `ArgumentException` is an existing class that derives from `Exception`; you use it when one or more of a method's arguments are invalid. Create a class named `CarInsurance` containing variables that can hold a driver's age and state of residence. Within the class, create a method that accepts the two input values and calculates a premium. The premium base price is $100 for residents of Illinois (IL) and $50 for residents of Wisconsin (WI). Additionally, each driver pays $3 times the value of 100 minus his or her age. If the driver is younger than 16, older than 80, or not a resident of IL or WI, throw an `ArgumentException` from the method. In the `Main()` method of the `CarInsurance` class, `try` code that prompts the user for each value. If the user does not enter a numeric value for age, `catch` a `FormatException` and display an error message. Call the method that calculates the premium and `catch` the potential `ArgumentException` object. Save the file as **CarInsurance.cs**.

4. The `Math` class contains a static method named `Sqrt()` that accepts a `double` and returns the parameter's square root. Write a program that declares two `doubles`: number and sqrt. Accept an input value for `number` from the user. Handle the `FormatException` that is thrown if the input value cannot be converted to a `double` by displaying the message "The input should be a number." and setting the `sqrt` variable to 0. If no `FormatException` is thrown, test the input number's value. If it is negative, `throw a new ApplicationException` to which you pass the message "Number can't be negative." and again set `sqrt` to 0. If the `number` is not negative, pass it to the `Math.Sqrt()` method returning the square root to the `sqrt` variable. As the last program statement, display the value of `sqrt`. Save the file as **FindSquareRoot.cs**.

5. a. Create an `EmployeeException` class whose constructor receives a string that consists of an employee's ID number and pay rate.

   b. Create an `Employee` class with two fields, `IDNum` and `hourlyWage`. The `Employee` constructor requires values for both fields. Upon construction, `throw` an `EmployeeException` if the `hourlyWage` is less than 6.00 or more than 50.00.

   c. Write a program that establishes, one at a time, at least three `Employee`s with `hourlyWage`s that are above, below, and within the allowed range. Immediately after each instantiation attempt, handle any thrown `Exception`s. Save the file as **EmployeeExceptionDemo.cs**.

6. a. Create an `IceCreamConeException` class whose constructor receives a string that consists of an ice cream flavor and number of scoops.

   b. Create an `IceCreamCone` class with two fields, `iceCreamFlavor` and `scoops`. The `IceCreamCone` constructor calls two data-entry methods, `GetFlavor()` and `GetScoops()`. The `GetFlavor()` method throws an `IceCreamConeException` if the flavor is not one of the following: vanilla, chocolate, strawberry, peach, or banana. The `GetScoops()` method throws an `IceCreamConeException` when the scoop quantity exceeds 3.

   c. Write a program that establishes several `iceCreamCone` objects and handles any thrown `IceCreamConeExceptions`. Save the file as **IceCreamConeExceptionDemo.cs**.

7. a. Create a `BookException` class whose `Message` field contains the string "This Book is invalid."

   b. Create a `Book` class containing fields for title, author, price, and number of pages. Include get and set methods for each field. Throw a `BookException` if the pages exceed 800 or the price exceeds $120.

   c. Create a program that creates at least four `Book` objects—one with too many pages, one with a price that is too high, one where both fields are invalid, and one where both fields are valid. Catch any thrown exceptions and display the `BookException` `Message` field. Save the file as **BookExceptionDemo.cs**.

8. Each of the following files in the Chapter.08 folder on your Student Disk has syntax and/or logical errors. In each case, determine the problem and fix the program. After you correct the errors, save each file using the same filename preceded with *Fixed*. For example, DebugEight1.cs will become FixedDebugEight1.cs.

   a. DebugEight1.cs

   b. DebugEight2.cs

   c. DebugEight3.cs

   d. DebugEight4.cs

9

USING GUI OBJECTS AND THE VISUAL STUDIO IDE

In this chapter you will learn:

♦ How to create a `MessageBox`
♦ How to add functionality to `MessageBox` buttons
♦ How to create a `Form`
♦ How to create a `Form` that is a program's main window
♦ How to place a `Button` on a window
♦ How to use the Visual Studio IDE to design a `Form`
♦ About the code created by the IDE
♦ How to add functionality to a `Button` on a `Form`
♦ How to use the Visual Studio Help Search function

Using the knowledge you have gained so far in this book, you can write many useful C# applications that can accept input, produce output, perform arithmetic, make decisions, handle exceptions, and so on. You also can create classes and instantiate objects from those classes using the fundamental object-oriented principles of encapsulation, polymorphism, and inheritance. You can create a virtually infinite number of applications that will solve users' problems. Unfortunately, your applications look dull. When you execute the programs you have written so far, input is accepted from a lackluster command prompt and output is displayed in the same way. Most modern applications, and certainly most programs you have used on the Internet, use more visually pleasing graphic objects when they interact with users. These **graphical user interface (GUI)**, objects include the buttons, check boxes, and toolbars you are used to controlling with a mouse when you interact with Windows-type programs. You can apply everything you have learned about C# classes and methods to the GUI objects that are built into the Visual Studio .NET environment so you can create your own interactive GUI applications.

The programs you have written have also been relatively small. When you start to use graphical objects in your programs, the program size quickly can become daunting. So far, you may have been using a simple text editor, such as Notepad, to write your C# programs. If so, it is time to explore the tools available to you in the Visual Studio integrated development environment (IDE). These tools automatically create much of the code you need to develop appealing and attention-grabbing GUI programs. Of course, if you do not understand the C# code that the tools create, you cannot say you have mastered the C# programming language. In this chapter, you will build some graphical objects "by hand." Then, after you understand the details, you will create the same objects using the IDE.

CREATING A **MessageBox**

A **MessageBox** is a GUI object that can contain text, buttons, and symbols that inform and instruct a user. You cannot create a new instance of the **MessageBox** class because its constructor is not public. Instead, you use the static class method **Show( )** to display a **MessageBox**. The **MessageBox** class contains 12 overloaded versions of the **Show( )** method; the simplest version accepts a string argument that is displayed within the **MessageBox**. Figure 9-1 shows a program that uses the **MessageBox.Show( )** method with the string argument "Hello!". The program must contain the statement **using System.Windows.Forms;** to include the **MessageBox** class. Figure 9-2 shows the output.

 You could remove the statement using System.Windows.Forms; from the program in Figure 9-1 and change the Show( ) statement to System. Windows.Forms.MessageBox.Show("Hello!");.

 Including the statement to use the System.Windows.Forms namespace provides you with access to many Form features in addition to the MessageBox. You will use many of these features as you work through the exercises in the next few chapters.

```
using System;
using System.Windows.Forms;
public class MessageBox1
{
      public static void Main()
      {
             MessageBox.Show("Hello!");
      }
}
```

Figure 9-1 Program that displays a MessageBox

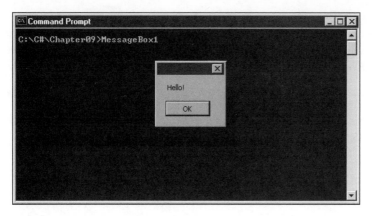

Figure 9-2 Output of `MessageBox1` program

The `MessageBox` in Figure 9-2 is similar to ones you have seen when using many Windows programs. It contains a title bar at the top, a Close button in the upper-right corner, the message "Hello!", and an OK button. When the user clicks either the close button or the OK button, the `MessageBox` disappears. Because Visual Studio .NET contains the `MessageBox` class, you do not have to design these standard `MessageBox` features and capabilities yourself when you write a program. Instead, you can simply use the `MessageBox` class and concentrate on the message you want to convey within the `MessageBox`.

Besides a simple string, you can pass additional arguments to the `MessageBox.Show()` method when you want to display a caption in a `MessageBox`'s title bar, or add buttons and an icon. Table 9-1 summarizes the features of six of the 12 versions of the `MessageBox.Show()` method. (The other six versions correspond to the table entries, with the addition of naming a component in front of which you want the `MessageBox` to display.) When you use a version of the `Show()` method, you must provide a value in the correct order for each argument listed in the table.

Table 9-1 Arguments used with the MessageBox.Show() method

Argument to MessageBox.Show()	Explanation
String	Displays a message box with the specified text
String, string	Displays a message box with the specified text and caption
String, string, MessageBoxButtons	Displays a message box with specified text, caption, and buttons
String, string, MessageBoxButtons, MessageBoxIcon	Displays a message box with specified text, caption, buttons, and icon
String, string, MessageBoxButtons, MessageBoxIcon, MessageBoxDefaultButton	Displays a message box with the specified text, caption, buttons, icon, and default button
String, string, MessageBoxButtons, MessageBoxIcon, MessageBoxDefaultButton, MessageBoxOptions	Displays a message box with the specified text, caption, buttons, icon, default button, and options

9

For example, the program in Figure 9-3 uses two string arguments with the
`MessageBox.Show()` method. Figure 9-4 shows the execution; notice that the second
string argument passed to the `Show()` method in the program appears in the title bar
of the `MessageBox`.

```
using System;
using System.Windows.Forms;
public class MessageBox2
{

    public static void Main()
    {
            MessageBox.Show("Hello!","MessageBox2 program");
    }

}
```

Figure 9-3   Using two string parameters with `MessageBox.Show()`

Figure 9-4   Output of program using two string arguments to `MessageBox.Show()`

Besides strings, the `MessageBox.Show()` method can also accept `MessageBoxButtons`,
`MessageBoxIcon`, `MessageBoxDefaultButton`, and `MessageBoxOptions` arguments. Tables 9-2 through 9-5 describe all of the possible values for each of these arguments.
Using all of these `MessageBox.Show()` arguments provides you with a wide variety of
appearances for your `MessageBox` objects.

The `MessageBoxOptions` values are not used frequently. They are listed in
Table 9-5 but won't be used in this chapter.

Table 9-2 `MessageBoxButtons` values

Member Name	Description
AbortRetryIgnore	The message box contains Abort, Retry, and Ignore buttons
OK	The message box contains an OK button
OKCancel	The message box contains OK and Cancel buttons
RetryCancel	The message box contains Retry and Cancel buttons
YesNo	The message box contains Yes and No buttons
YesNoCancel	The message box contains Yes, No, and Cancel buttons

Table 9-3 `MessageBoxIcon` values

Member Name	Description
Asterisk	The message box contains a symbol consisting of a lowercase letter *i* in a circle. (Notice the result is the same as Information)
Error	The message box contains a symbol consisting of a white *X* in a circle with a red background
Exclamation	The message box contains a symbol consisting of an exclamation point in a triangle with a yellow background. (Notice the result is the same as Warning)
Hand	The message box contains a symbol consisting of a white *X* in a circle with a red background. (Notice the result is the same as Stop)
Information	The message box contains a symbol consisting of a lowercase letter *i* in a circle
None	The message box contains no symbols
Question	The message box contains a symbol consisting of a question mark in a circle
Stop	The message box contains a symbol consisting of a white *X* in a circle with a red background
Warning	The message box contains a symbol consisting of an exclamation point in a triangle with a yellow background

 The description of each `MessageBoxIcon` value contains a typical representation of the symbol. The actual graphic displayed is a function of the operating system in which the program is running.

Table 9-4 `MessageBox` default `Button` values

Member Name	Description
Button1	The first button on the message box is the default button
Button2	The second button on the message box is the default button
Button3	The third button on the message box is the default button

Table 9-5 `MessageBoxOptions` values

Member Name	Description
DefaultDesktopOnly	The message box appears on the active desktop
RightAlign	The message box text is right-aligned
RtlReading	The message box text is displayed with right-to-left reading order
ServiceNotification	The message box appears on the active desktop

You can combine `MessageBoxOptions` values by placing an ampersand (&)
between them. The ampersand is the bitwise AND operator; it allows you to
combine bits within a single byte that controls which options are active.

In the next steps you will experiment with `MessageBox.Show()` method arguments.

1. Open a new file in your text editor. Enter the first few lines of a program that
will instantiate several `MessageBox` objects.

```
using System;
using System.Windows.Forms;
public class MessageBoxExperiment
{
```

2. Add a `Main()` method that declares two strings to serve as the `MessageBox`
messages and captions, as well as an integer count to keep track of the number of `MessageBox` objects displayed.

```
public static void Main()
    {
        string message = "This is message ";
        string caption = "Message box experiment";
        int count = 1;
```

3. Create a `MessageBox` with a single string argument containing the
`count` value.

```
MessageBox.Show(message + count);
```

4. Add 1 to the `count`, and then display a `MessageBox` containing the message
with the new `count` value and a caption for the title bar.

```
++count;
MessageBox.Show(message + count, caption);
```

5. Add 1 more to the `count`, and display a `MessageBox` containing three
defined features: a message, a caption, and some buttons. Add 1 more to the
`count`, and display a `MessageBox` containing four features: a message, a caption, some buttons, and an icon.

```
++count;
MessageBox.Show(message + count, caption,
  MessageBoxButtons.OKCancel);
```

```
++count;
MessageBox.Show(message + count, caption,
   MessageBoxButtons.RetryCancel, MessageBoxIcon.Warning);
```

6. For the last `MessageBox`, add 1 to the `count` and create a `Message Box` that employs five options, including naming `Button3` as the default button.

```
++count;
MessageBox.Show(message + count, caption,
   MessageBoxButtons.YesNoCancel,
   MessageBoxIcon.Information,
   MessageBoxDefaultButton.Button3);
```

7. Add two closing curly braces—one for the `Main()` method and one for the class.

8. Save the file as **MessageBoxExperiment.cs** in the Chapter.09 folder on your Student Disk. Compile and execute the program. The first `MessageBox` appears as shown in Figure 9-5. Notice that the string "This is message" and the `count` value 1 have been combined to create the `MessageBox` message. No caption appears in the `MessageBox` title bar, but a Close button is available in the upper-right corner of the `MessageBox`. A `MessageBox` is a **modal dialog box**, meaning that the program can progress no further until you dismiss the box. Whether you click OK or Close, the second `MessageBox` appears, including the caption and updated `count` value, as shown in Figure 9-6. Notice that this `MessageBox` is slightly wider than the first one to accommodate the title bar caption.

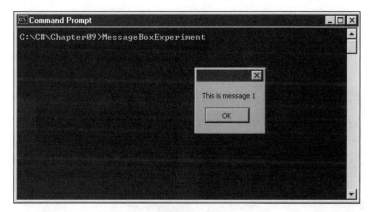

Figure 9-5   First `MessageBox` of `MessageBoxExperiment` program

Figure 9-6 Second `MessageBox` of `MessageBoxExperiment` program

9. Whether you click OK or Close in the second `MessageBox`, the third `MessageBox` appears, containing OK and Cancel buttons (see Figure 9-7). The OK button has a darker outline than the Cancel button, which means that the former button has focus. When a button has focus, not only is the user's attention drawn to it, but if the user presses the Enter key, the action associated with the button executes. If you press the Tab key or use the right and left arrow keys on your keyboard, you can change the focus from one button to the other. Whether you dismiss this `MessageBox` by pressing the Enter key, closing the box, or clicking one of the two buttons, the fourth `MessageBox` appears as shown in Figure 9-8.

 If your computer has speakers, you might hear a different sound when the Warning icon appears. Because you normally would use the Warning icon in a "dangerous" situation, this sound is intended to get the user's attention.

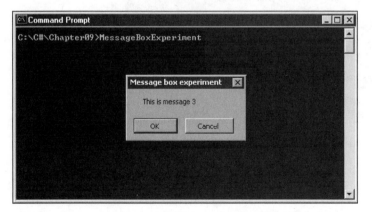

Figure 9-7 Third `MessageBox` of `MessageBoxExperiment` program

Figure 9-8   Fourth `MessageBox` of `MessageBoxExperiment` program

10. The fourth **MessageBox** contains Retry and Cancel buttons and the Warning icon. Again, you can change the focus of the buttons, and proceed to the next **MessageBox** using either of the option buttons, the Enter key, or the Close button. Figure 9-9 shows the last **MessageBox**. When this box appears, the focus is on the rightmost of the three buttons because you selected **MessageBoxDefaultButton.Button3** when creating the **MessageBox**. Dismiss this last **MessageBox**.

9

Figure 9-9   Fifth `MessageBox` of `MessageBoxExperiment` program

11. Run the program several times and experiment by clicking the different buttons.

12. Resave the program as **MessageBoxExperiment2.cs**, then experiment by using different values for the message, caption, **MessageBoxButtons**, **MessageBoxIcon**, **MessageBoxDefaultButton**, and **MessageBoxOptions** for the individual **MessageBox**es.

ADDING FUNCTIONALITY TO MessageBox BUTTONS

MessageBox objects provide an easy way to display information to a user in a GUI format. When you use a MessageBox to display some text you want the user to read, it makes sense to include only an OK button that the user can click after reading the text. However, including multiple MessageBoxButtons, all of which dismiss the MessageBox, doesn't make sense. Usually you want to determine users' interactions with a MessageBox's buttons and take appropriate action based on the users' choices. DialogResult is an **enumeration**, or list of values that correspond to a user's potential MessageBox button selections. Table 9-6 contains DialogResult values you can compare to a MessageBox. The DialogResult member names correspond to the button labels available within a MessageBox.

Table 9-6   DialogResult values

Member Name	Description
Abort	The dialog box return value is Abort
Cancel	The dialog box return value is Cancel
Ignore	The dialog box return value is Ignore
No	The dialog box return value is No
None	Nothing is returned from the dialog box; which means that the modal dialog box stays open
OK	The dialog box return value is OK
Retry	The dialog box return value is Retry
Yes	The dialog box return value is Yes

Figure 9-10 shows a program written for a fast-food restaurant. Its MessageBox asks the user to click Yes or No in response to a standard fast-food question. If the user clicks the Yes button, the price increases by 0.75; otherwise, the price remains at $3.00. Whichever button the user chooses, a new MessageBox displays the final meal price. Figures 9-11 and 9-12 show the MessageBox that contains the question and the result when the user clicks Yes.

```
using System;
using System.Windows.Forms;
public class HamburgerAddition
{

        public static void Main()
```

Figure 9-10   HamburgerAddition program

```
        {
                string question = "Do you want fries with that?";
                string caption = "Hamburger addition";
                double price = 3.00;
                if(MessageBox.Show(question, caption,
                        MessageBoxButtons.YesNo, MessageBoxIcon.Question)
                        == DialogResult.Yes)
                        price += 0.75;
                MessageBox.Show("Total is " + price.ToString("C"));
        }

}
```

Figure 9-10   `HamburgerAddition` program (continued)

Figure 9-11   First `MessageBox` of `HamburgerAddition` program

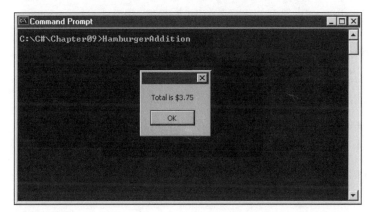

Figure 9-12   Second `MessageBox` of `HamburgerAddition` program

Instead of the single if statement

```
if(MessageBox.Show(question, caption,
    MessageBoxButtons.YesNo, MessageBox
Icon.Question)
    == DialogResult.Yes)
```

you can create a `DialogResult` object and assign the result of the `MessageBox.Show()` method to it, as in the following code:

```
DialogResult dr = MessageBox.Show(question, caption,
    MessageBoxButtons.YesNo, MessageBox
Icon.Question);
```

Then the if statement becomes simpler:

```
if( dr = DialogResult.Yes)
```

Also, when you use this technique, you can compare `dr` to different values one at a time.

Creating a Form

`MessageBox`es offer a large, but not infinite, number of ways to interact with users. They provide information and can allow a user to select one of two or three button options. However, some applications require more components than a few buttons; for example, they might require additional buttons, lists of available options from which to select, or text fields in which to type. **Forms** provide an interface for collecting, displaying, and delivering such information; they are key components of GUI programs. You can use a **Form** to represent any window you want to display within your application. Although they are not required, **Forms** often contain controls such as text fields, buttons, and check boxes that users can manipulate to interact with a program.

The **Form** class descends from the **Object** class like all other C# classes, but not directly. It is six generations removed from the **Object** class in the following line of descent:

- `Object`
- `MarshalByRefObject`
- `Component`
- `Control`
- `ScrollableControl`
- `ContainerControl`
- `Form`

Unlike with the `MessageBox` class, you can create an instance of the `Form` class. Figure 9-13 shows a program that creates the simplest `Form` possible, and Figure 9-14 shows the output. The object `form1` is an instance of the `Form` class. The `ShowDialog()` method displays the form as a modal dialog box, so the user must dismiss the box before the program proceeds. The `Form` contains neither a caption nor components, but it does possess a title bar with an icon. You can use your mouse to minimize, restore, resize (by dragging on the `Frame` borders), and close the `Form`, just as you can with most of the `Frame`s you have encountered when using programs written by others.

```
using System;
using System.Windows.Forms;
using System.Drawing;
public class CreateForm1
{
        public static void Main()
        {
                Form form1 = new Form();
                form1.ShowDialog();
        }
}
```

Figure 9-13 `CreateForm1` program

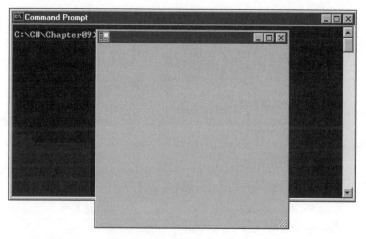

Figure 9-14 Output of `CreateForm1`

You can change the appearance, size, color, and window management features of a `Form` by setting its instance fields or properties. The `Form` class contains approximately 100 properties (many of which it inherits from the `Control` class); Table 9-7 lists just some of them. For example, setting the `Text` property allows you to specify the caption of the `Frame` in the title bar. The `Size` and `DesktopLocation` properties allow you to define the size and position of the window when it is displayed.

If you use the Visual Studio .NET Search option, you can find descriptions for all the Form class properties. Additionally, if you highlight a property and press F1 or click a property name, you will see a description of the property at the bottom of the Property list.

 Every property available to use with a Form does not appear in the Properties list within the Visual Studio IDE—only those most frequently used are listed.

Table 9-7   Properties of Forms

Member Name	Description
AcceptButton	Gets or sets the button on the form that is clicked when the user presses the Enter key
AllowDrop	Gets or sets a value indicating whether the control can accept data that the user drags and drops into it
BackColor	Gets or sets the background color for this control
BackgroundImage	Gets or sets the background image displayed in the control
Bottom	Gets the distance between the bottom edge of the control and the top edge of its container's client area
CancelButton	Gets or sets the button control that is clicked when the user presses the Esc key
CanFocus	Gets a value indicating whether the control can receive focus
CanSelect	Gets a value indicating whether the control can be selected
ContainsFocus	Gets a value indicating whether the control, or one of its child controls, currently has the input focus
ControlBox	Gets or sets a value indicating whether a control box is displayed in the caption bar of the form
Cursor	Gets or sets the cursor that is displayed when the user moves the mouse pointer over this control
DesktopBounds	Gets or sets the size and location of the form on the Windows desktop
DesktopLocation	Gets or sets the location of the form on the Windows desktop
DialogResult	Gets or sets the dialog result for the form
Focused	Gets a value indicating whether the control has input focus
Font	Gets or sets the current font for the control
ForeColor	Gets or sets the foreground color of the control
FormBorderStyle	Gets or sets the border style of the form
Height	Gets or sets the height of the control
HelpButton	Gets or sets a value indicating whether a Help button should be displayed in the caption box of the form
Icon	Gets or sets the icon for the form
Left	Gets or sets the x-coordinate of a control's left edge in pixels

Table 9-7   Properties of `Forms` (continued)

Member Name	Description
Location	Gets or sets the coordinates of the upper-left corner of the control relative to the upper-left corner of its container
MaximizeBox	Gets or sets a value indicating whether the Maximize button is displayed in the caption bar of the form
MaximumSize	Gets the maximum size to which the form can be resized
Menu	Gets or sets the main menu that is displayed in the form
MinimizeBox	Gets or sets a value indicating whether the Minimize button is displayed in the caption bar of the form
MinimumSize	Gets the minimum size to which the form can be resized
Modal	Gets a value indicating whether this form is displayed modally
Name	Gets or sets the name of the control
Opacity	Gets or sets the opacity level of the form
Right	Gets the distance between the right edge of the control and the left edge of its container
RightToLeft	Gets or sets whether the alignment of the control's elements is reversed to support locales using right-to-left fonts
ShowInTaskbar	Gets or sets a value indicating whether the form is displayed in the Windows taskbar
Size	Gets or sets the size of the form
StartPosition	Gets or sets the starting position of the form at run time
TabStop	Gets or sets a value indicating whether the user can give the focus to this control using the Tab key
Text	Gets or sets the text associated with this control
Top	Gets or sets the top coordinate of the control
Visible	Gets or sets a value indicating whether the control is visible
Width	Gets or sets the width of the control

9

Figure 9-15 shows a `CreateForm2` class that instantiates a `Form` object and sets several of its properties: in the title bar a caption is set, a Help button (displaying a question mark) appears, and the Minimize and Maximize buttons that usually appear on a `Form` are removed. Figure 9-16 shows the output.

```
using System;
using System.Windows.Forms;
using System.Drawing;
public class CreateForm2
{
        public static void Main()
        {
                Form form2 = new Form();
                form2.Text = "This is a Form2 Form";
                form2.HelpButton = true;
                form2.MaximizeBox = false;
                form2.MinimizeBox = false;
                form2.ShowDialog();
        }
}
```

Figure 9-15   CreateForm2 class

Figure 9-16   Output of CreateForm2 class

CREATING A Form THAT IS A PROGRAM'S MAIN WINDOW

You can instantiate a Form within an application and use the ShowDialog() method to display it, as in the program in Figure 9-15. Alternatively, you can create a child class from Form that becomes the main window of an application. When you create a new main window, you must complete two steps:

- You must derive a new custom class from the base class System.Windows.Forms.Form.

- You must write a Main() method that calls the Application.Run() method, and you must pass an instance of your newly created Form class as an argument. This activity starts the program and makes the form visible.

Figure 9-17 shows the simplest program you can write that creates a new main window for a program. You must include the using System.Windows.Forms; statement at the top of the program. In Figure 9-17, the class name is Window1; it extends the Form class.

```
using System;
using System.Windows.Forms;
public class Window1 : Form
{
        public static void Main()
        {
                Application.Run(new Window1());
        }
}
```

Figure 9-17   Window1 class

The statement Application.Run(new Window1()); creates an unnamed instance of the Window1 class. Alternately, you could instantiate a named Window object using Window1 aWindow = new Window(); and then call Application.Run(aWindow);. However, because you never use the name aWindow, there is no need to provide the new Window1 object with a unique identifier.

The Window1 class in Figure 9-17 contains a single method: a Main() method that calls the Application.Run() method, passing a new instance of the Window1 object. Figure 9-18 shows the output. The Form created has no title and contains no components, but possesses a title bar that displays an icon.

Figure 9-18   The Window1 object

The Application.Run() method processes messages from the operating system to the application. Without the call to Application.Run(), the program would compile and execute, but the program would end without displaying the window.

When you want to add property settings to a program's main window, you can do so within the class constructor. Figure 9-19 shows a Window2 class in which the Size and Text attributes of a Window are set. The keyword this in the constructor method refers to "this Form being constructed"; you could eliminate this and the constructor would work in the same way. The Size field uses the System.Drawing.Size() method, which takes two parameters. The first indicates the horizontal size, or width, of a component; the second indicates the vertical size (or height) of a component. Setting the Size to System.Drawing.Size(500,100) creates a window that is five times wider than it is tall. The Text field supplies the caption that appears in the window's title bar. Figure 9-20 shows the created Window2 object.

```
using System;
using System.Windows.Forms;
public class Window2 : Form
{
        public Window2()
        {
                this.Size = new System.Drawing.Size(500,100);
                this.Text = "This is a Window2 Object";
        }
        public static void Main()
        {
                Application.Run(new Window2());
        }
}
```

Figure 9-19   Window2 class

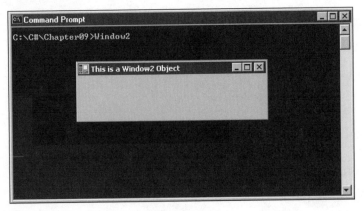

Figure 9-20   The Window2 object

PLACING A Button ON A WINDOW

Although it has interesting dimensions, the window in Figure 9-20 is not yet as useful as a MessageBox. However, a window is more flexible than a MessageBox because you can place manipulatable Window components wherever you like on the surface of the window. You identify these components as a Form's Controls.

One type of object the user can manipulate is a Button. A **Button** is a GUI object you can click to cause some action. (Alternatively, you can press the Enter key if the Button has focus.) You can create your own Button objects by using the Button class. This class contains 68 properties; two of the most useful are its Text and Location properties. You use the Text property to set a Button's label. You can use the Location property to position a Button relative to the upper-left corner of the Form (or any other ContainerControl object) containing it.

 When you use the Location property, you must supply two integer arguments to the System.Drawing.Point() method. The first argument represents a number of horizontal pixels to the right of the upper-left corner of a Form (or other container). The second argument represents the vertical position down from the top. You will use the System.Drawing.Point() method in the next set of steps you complete in this chapter.

For a Button to be clickable, you need to use the System.Windows.Forms.Control class, which implements very basic functionality required by any classes that display GUI objects to the user. This class handles user input through the keyboard and pointing device. To use the System.Windows.Forms.Control class, you can create an array of GUI components (such as Buttons) and add them to a Form's Controls property with the AddRange() method. The statement that adds components to the list of a Form's controls takes the following form:

```
this.Controls.AddRange(new System.Windows.Forms.Control[]
{this.button1});
```

It takes a fair amount of code to make a Form's Button clickable; it is easiest to show an example of such a Form. In the next steps, you will create a Form containing a Button.

1. Open a new file in your text editor, and start a WindowWithButton class that descends from the Form class as follows:

```
using System;
using System.Windows.Forms;
public class WindowWithButton : Form
{
```

2. Create a Button object named button1.

```
Button button1 = new Button();
```

3. Add a `WindowWithButton` constructor that sets the `Size` and `Text` fields for the `Form` as well as the `Text` field for the `Button`. Then use a `Controls.AddRange()` method to indicate that the `Button` you created will become one of the `Form`'s usable controls. Finally, locate the `Button` at position 100, 50 on the `Form`.

```
public WindowWithButton()
{
    this.Size = new System.Drawing.Size(300,300);
    this.Text = "Window Object With Button";
    button1.Text = "Press";
    this.Controls.AddRange(new
      System.Windows.Forms.Control[]
          {this.button1});
    this.button1.Location = new
      System.Drawing.Point(100, 50);
}
```

4. Add the following `Main()` method to execute the application.

```
public static void Main()
{
    Application.Run(new WindowWithButton());
}
```

5. Add a closing curly brace for the class. Save the file as **WindowWithButton.cs** in the Chapter.09 folder on your Student Disk. For reference, Figure 9-21 shows the entire program.

```
using System;
using System.Windows.Forms;
public class WindowWithButton : Form
{
        Button button1 = new Button();
        public WindowWithButton()
        {
                this.Size = new System.Drawing.Size(300,300);
                this.Text = "Window Object With Button";
                button1.Text = "Press";
                this.Controls.AddRange(new System.Windows.Forms.Control[]
                        {this.button1});
                this.button1.Location = new System.Drawing.Point(100, 50);
        }
        public static void Main()
        {
                Application.Run(new WindowWithButton());
        }
}
```

Figure 9-21   WindowWithButton program

6. Compile and execute the program. Figure 9-22 shows the output. Notice that the upper-left corner of the `Button` you placed in location 100, 50 is about one-third of the distance from the left edge of the 300-by-300 form, and about one-sixth of the distance vertically from the top.

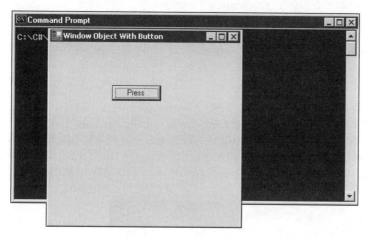

Figure 9-22   Output of `WindowWithButton` program

7. Click the `Button`. Nothing happens because you have not yet added the code necessary for the `Button` to cause some action.

8. Change the horizontal and vertical coordinates in the statement `this.button1.Location = new System.Drawing.Point(100, 50);`. Save, compile, and execute the program several times until you can accurately predict where the `Button` will appear on the `Form`.

Using the Visual Studio IDE to Design a Form

The window in Figure 9-22 consists of only a `Form` and a `Button`, and even though the `Button` doesn't do anything yet, scores of additional options are available to you. The program in Figure 9-21 sets only two attributes for the `Form` (`Size` and `Text`), yet Table 9-7 shows dozens of additional properties you can set—and that table lists only half the available properties. Likewise, the program in Figure 9-22 sets only two `Button` properties (`Text` and `Location`); by the time you create a full-blown Windows application, you might want to set several more properties for the existing `Button`, add more `Buttons`, and set all their properties. You might want to add other components to the window, supplying locations and appropriate actions for each of them as well. Just determining an attractive and useful layout in which to position all the components on your `Form` would take many lines of code and a lot of trial and error. Even a simple but fully functional GUI program might require several hundred statements. Therefore, coding such a program can be tedious.

The Visual Studio IDE provides a wealth of tools to help make the `Form` design process easier. Rather than having to write multiple assignment statements and guess at appropriate component locations, it allows you to use a visual environment for designing your `Forms`. You can most easily understand the Visual Studio environment by using it. In the next steps, you will use the IDE to create a `Form` with a `Button`.

Designing aesthetically pleasing, functional, and user-friendly `Forms` is an art; entire books are devoted to the topic.

1. Open Microsoft Visual Studio .NET. You might have a desktop shortcut you can double-click, or you might click **Start** on the taskbar, click **Programs**, point to **Microsoft Visual Studio.NET**, and then click **Microsoft Visual Studio.NET**, as shown in Figure 9-23. If you are using a school network, you might be able to select Visual Studio from the school's computing menu.

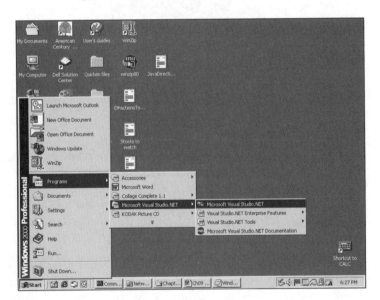

Figure 9-23   Opening Visual Studio .NET

2. Click **File** on the menu bar, point to **New**, and then click **Project**, as shown in Figure 9-24.

3. A New Project dialog box like the one shown in Figure 9-25 appears on your screen. In the window under Project Types, click **Visual C# Projects**. Under Templates, click **Windows Application**. Near the bottom of the New Project dialog box, click in the Name text box and type **WindowCreatedWithIDE** as the name for your application. Make sure the Location text box contains the name of the **Chapter.09** folder on your Student Disk.

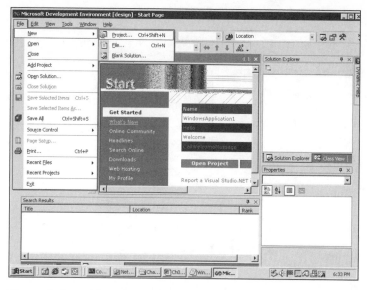

Figure 9-24   Choosing a new project

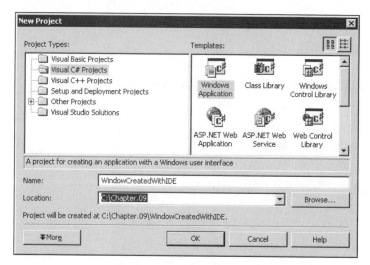

Figure 9-25   New Project dialog box

4. Click **OK** at the bottom of the dialog box. Figure 9-26 shows the design screen that appears. The blank **Form** in the center of the screen has an empty title bar. The bottom-right corner of the screen contains a Properties window that holds a list of the **Form**'s properties. In Figure 9-26, you can see that the **Text** property is set to Form 1. ("Form 1" is listed in the Settings box just to the right of "Text" in the Properties list.) Take a moment to scroll through the Properties list, examining the values of other properties of the **Form**. For example, the value of the **Size** property is 300, 300.

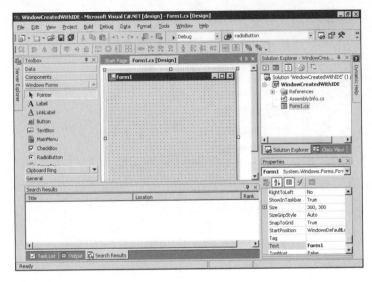

Figure 9-26   Design screen

5. In the Properties list, click on the description **Form 1** in the Settings box for the **Text** property. Delete **Form 1** and type **My IDE Form**. Press **Enter**; the title of the **Form** in the center of the screen changes to "My IDE Form". See Figure 9-27.

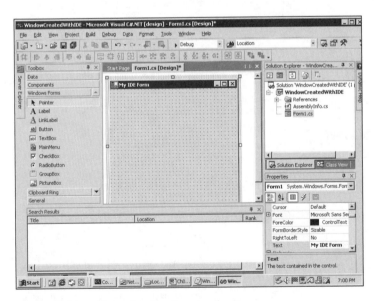

Figure 9-27   Changing the **Text** of a **Form**

6. At the left side of the design screen, you see a list of components that can be added to a `Form`, including `Pointer`, `Label`, `LinkLabel`, and `Button`. Click **Button** and drag a `Button` onto the `Form`, as shown in Figure 9-28. When you release your mouse button, the `Button` appears on the `Form` and contains the text "button1".

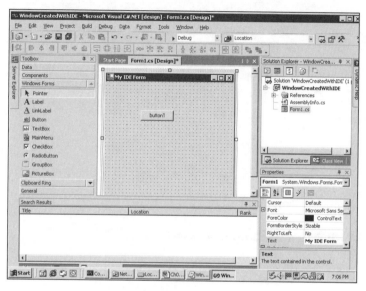

Figure 9-28   A `Button` placed on the `Form`

7. At the right side of the screen, under Properties, the list box shows that you are viewing the properties for `Form1`. If necessary, click the list arrow at the right of the list box to change the Properties list to show the properties of `button1`. Change the `Text` property of `button1` to **Press**, then press **Enter**. The text of the `Button` on the `Form` changes to "Press". See Figure 9-29.

8. Scroll through the other `button1` properties. In Figure 9-30, notice that the value in the Settings box for the `Location` property is 80, 64. Your `Location` property might be different, depending on where you released the `Button` when you dragged it onto the `Form`. Drag the button across the `Form` to a new position. Each time you release your mouse button, the value of the button's `Location` property is updated to reflect the new location. Try to drag the `Button` to `Location` 80, 64. Alternatively, delete the contents of the `Location` property field and type **80, 64**. The `Button` moves to the requested location on the `Form`.

9. Save the form you have created by clicking **File** on the menu bar, then clicking **Save All**. Alternatively, you can click the **Save All** button on the toolbar; its icon is a stack of diskettes.

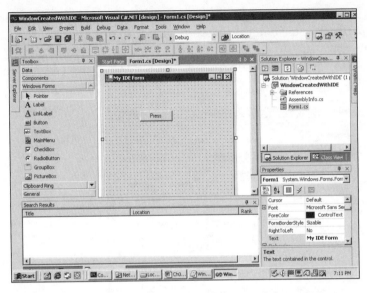

Figure 9-29   Changing the Text property of the Button

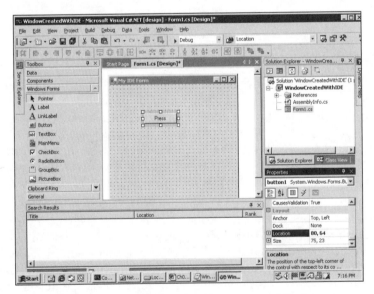

Figure 9-30   Examining the Location property of button1

10. Although the Form you have designed doesn't do much yet, you can execute the program anyway. Click **Debug** on the menu bar and then click **Start Without Debugging**, or press **Ctrl+F5**. The Output window at the bottom of the screen shows 0 errors, and the Form appears. (See Figure 9-31.) You can drag, minimize, and restore it and click its button just as you could with the Forms you developed earlier in this chapter by writing all of the code.

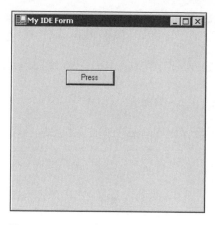

Figure 9-31   The `Form1` Form created with the IDE

11. Click **View** on the menu bar, then click **Code**. Figure 9-32 shows the menu from which you can select the Code view.

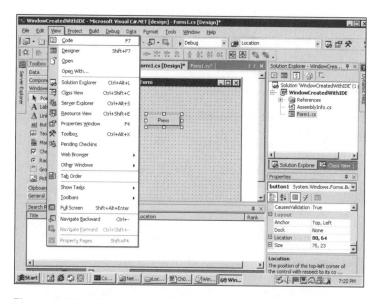

Figure 9-32   Viewing the code used to create the form

12. Figure 9-33 shows the code used to create the `Form`. It includes more than 80 lines of code, much of which looks confusing. However, if you examine it closely, you will find many familiar statements. For example, locate the class header for the `Form1` class at about the twelfth line of code: `public class Form1 : System.Windows.Forms.Form`. This header shows that the `Form1` class descends or inherits from `System.Windows.Forms.Form`. You could shorten the header to `public class Form1 : Form` because the

using statement `using System.Windows.Forms;` appears at the top of the file; however, the C# IDE uses the fully qualified version in the code for clarity.

You learned about inheritance in Chapter 7.

A discussion of the other statements in this code follows the completion of these steps.

```
using System;
using System.Drawing;
using System.Collections;
using System.ComponentModel;
using System.Windows.Forms;
using System.Data;

namespace WindowCreatedWithIDE
{
    /// <summary>
    /// Summary description for Form1.
    /// </summary>
    public class Form1 : System.Windows.Forms.Form
    {
        private System.Windows.Forms.Button button1;
        /// <summary>
        /// Required designer variable.
        /// </summary>
        private System.ComponentModel.Container
components = null;
        public Form1()
        {
            //
            // Required for Windows Form Designer support
            //
            InitializeComponent();

            //
            // TODO: Add any constructor code after
            // InitializeComponent call
            //
        }
        /// <summary>
        /// Clean up any resources being used.
        /// </summary>
        protected override void Dispose( bool disposing )
```

Figure 9-33   The code for the `WindowCreatedWithIDE` program

```
        {
            if( disposing )
            {
                if (components != null)
                {
                    components.Dispose();
                }
            }
            base.Dispose( disposing );
        }

        #region Windows Form Designer generated code
        /// <summary>
        /// Required method for Designer support - do not modify
        /// the contents of this method with the code editor.
        /// </summary>
        private void InitializeComponent()
        {
            this.button1 = new System.Windows.Forms.Button();
            this.SuspendLayout();
            //
            // button1
            //
            this.button1.Location = new
              System.Drawing.Point(80, 64);
            this.button1.Name = "button1";
            this.button1.TabIndex = 0;
            this.button1.Text = "Press";
            //
            // Form1
            //
            this.AutoScaleBaseSize = new
              System.Drawing.Size(5, 13);
            this.ClientSize = new System.Drawing.Size(292, 273);
            this.Controls.AddRange
              (new System.Windows.Forms.Control[] {
                        this.button1});
            this.Name = "Form1";
            this.Text = "My IDE Form";
            this.ResumeLayout(false);
        }
        #endregion
        /// <summary>
        /// The main entry point for the application.
        /// </summary>
        [STAThread]
        static void Main()
        {
            Application.Run(new Form1());
        }
    }
}
```

Figure 9-33   The code for the `WindowCreatedWithIDE` program (continued)

13. The code in Figure 9-33 was created for you when you used the IDE. Still, it is simply code. You can change it just as you might with code that you typed yourself. Take a while to experiment with this code. For example, locate the `InitializeComponent()` method and find the statement that sets the location of the button:

```
this.button1.Location = new System.Drawing.Point(80, 64);
```

Change the `Location` coordinates to **200, 150**, then execute the program again. The button will appear in a new location, farther to the right and down from its first location. Find the statement that sets the button's text:

```
this.button1.Text = "Press";
```

Change the text from "Press" to "Press Me". When you run the program, this change takes effect.

When you use the IDE, you can work visually or with the code text, whichever you find easier or more appropriate to the task at hand. Click **View** on the menu bar, then click **Designer** if you want to switch back to the Designer view. When you want to work with the code, click **View** on the menu bar, then click **Code**. The **F7** and **Shift+F7** keys also switch you from Designer view to Code view, and back again.

14. Exit Visual Studio by clicking the **Close** button in the upper-right corner of the screen, or by clicking **File** on the menu bar and then clicking **Exit**. If you have made changes since the last time you saved in Step 9, you will be asked if you want to save your changes. Choose **No** and the program exits.

UNDERSTANDING THE CODE CREATED BY THE IDE

Using the Visual Studio IDE, it is easy to create elaborate forms with a few keystrokes. However, if you don't understand the code behind the forms you create, you cannot say you have truly mastered the C# language. Everything you have learned to this point has prepared you to understand the code that underlies a visually designed form. The generated code is simply a collection of C# statements and method calls similar to ones you have been using throughout this book. When you use the Designer in the IDE to design your forms, you save a lot of typing, which reduces the errors you create. As shown in Figure 9-33, it takes quite a bit of code to create even a simple form with a single button. Examine the code piece by piece.

Because the IDE generates so much code automatically, it is often more difficult to find and correct errors in programs created using the IDE than in programs you code by hand.

The first section of the code in Figure 9-33 contains a list of using statements as follows:

```
using System;
using System.Drawing;
using System.Collections;
using System.ComponentModel;
using System.Windows.Forms;
using System.Data;
```

You have placed many statements like these within your earlier programs. These statements simply list the classes that the program will use.

The next code segment creates a namespace using the name you supplied when you began to create the C# Windows project. You have been using the System namespace since Chapter 1, and you created your own namespaces in Chapter 3 when you created multifile assemblies. Here, C# creates a namespace for you. The namespace declaration is followed by an opening curly brace and three comments that describe the next section of code.

```
namespace WindowCreatedWithIDE
{
    /// <summary>
    /// Summary description for Form1.
    /// </summary>
```

 C# uses three slashes (///) to begin an XML comment. When C# inserts the tag pairs <summary> and </summary> within the code, it allows the IntelliSense feature within Visual Studio to display additional information about the members contained between the tags. The IntelliSense feature automatically completes statements for you within the Visual Studio IDE. You first learned about XML comments when you learned about block and line comments in Chapter 1. Recall that XML stands for eXtensible Markup Language. To obtain more information, search for XML in the Visual Studio Help facility; it will direct you to several articles that discuss XML.

The next code segment taken from Figure 9-33 declares the Form1 class. The name Form1 was supplied by default; you can change this name using the form's Name property if you want. The Form1 class header shows that the class descends from the Form class. The class header is followed by an opening curly brace.

```
public class Form1 : System.Windows.Forms.Form
{
```

The next statement defines a Button object named button1:

```
private System.Windows.Forms.Button button1;
```

This object declaration was added to the code when you dragged the Button onto the Form's surface. You can change the Button's access from private to public if you like, but it is defined as `private`, because it will be used only within this class. You also can eliminate the fully qualified `System.Windows.Forms.Button` class name and replace it with `Button` because the `using` statement at the top of the file includes `System.Windows.Forms`. You also can change the name of `button1` to any other legal identifier you choose. However, if you delete `button1` in the declaration and replace it with a new name, then you must be sure to change every instance of `button1` in the program. The safer alternative is to change `button1`'s `Name` property in the IDE, either in the code or in the Settings box for the `Name` field in the Properties list of the Designer view. Either way, every instance of `button1` will be replaced with its new identifier.

> If you change `button1`'s `Name` property within the code, switch to Designer view and then double-click the button to switch back to Code view. You will find every instance of `button1` has been changed to the new name you assigned.

After the `button1` `Button` is declared, three comments appear, followed by a declaration of a `Container` object named `components`, set to `null`, or nothing.

```
/// <summary>
/// Required designer variable.
/// <summary>
private System.ComponentModel.Container components = null;
```

The code in Figure 9-33 continues with the definition for the `Form1` constructor. The `Form1` constructor looks similar to many constructor methods you have created:

```
public Form1()
{
    //
    // Required for Windows Form Designer support
    //
    InitializeComponent();

    //
    // TODO: Add any constructor code after
    // InitializeComponent call
    //
}
```

The `Form1` constructor contains several comments and a single method call to a method named `InitializeComponent()`. The tasks performed by `InitializeComponent()` could be performed directly within the constructor; `InitializeComponent()` is simply used as a helper method, to organize all of the component initialization tasks in one location. The comments following `InitializeComponent()` begin with "TODO." These are not XML comments, but rather plain C# line comments. C# uses comments beginning with "TODO" to remind you of tasks you might need to do. If your application requires any additional constructor statements for `Form1`, you can place them here.

The IDE provides the form with a `Dispose()` method as follows:

```
/// <summary>
/// Clean up any resources being used.
/// </summary>
protected override void Dispose( bool disposing )
{
    if( disposing )
    {
        if (components != null)
        {
            components.Dispose();
        }
    }
    base.Dispose( disposing );
}
```

This method contains any cleanup activities you need when a `Form` is dismissed. When you write an application that leaves open files or other unfinished business, you might want to add statements to this method. For now, you can let C# take care of the cleanup tasks that are invisible to you.

The next statement in the code, `#region`, is a preprocessor directive. Any code placed between `#region` and `#endregion` statements forms a group that can be used by some of the IDE's automated tools. The `#region` and `#endregion` statements do not affect the way the code operates; for now, you can ignore them.

```
#region Windows Form Designer generated code
/// <summary>
/// Required method for Designer support - do not modify
/// the contents of this method with the code editor.
/// </summary>
private void InitializeComponent()
{
    this.button1 = new System.Windows.Forms.Button();
    this.SuspendLayout();
    //
    // button1
    //
    this.button1.Location = new
      System.Drawing.Point(80, 64);
    this.button1.Name = "button1";
    this.button1.TabIndex = 0;
    this.button1.Text = "Press";
    //
```

9

```
// Form1
//
this.AutoScaleBaseSize = new
   System.Drawing.Size(5, 13);
this.ClientSize = new System.Drawing.Size(292, 273);
this.Controls.AddRange
   (new System.Windows.Forms.Control[] {
               this.button1});
this.Name = "Form1";
this.Text = "My IDE Form";
this.ResumeLayout(false);

}
#endregion
```

You might need to click a + to the left of #region so you can read the generated code.

The statements within the **InitializeComponent()** method should look familiar to you. These statements reflect the code generated by the properties you have selected for the **Form**. For example, the **button1.Text** and **Form this.Text** fields contain values you typed into the Settings boxes in the Properties list.

The last section of the program contains a **Main()** method that runs the application. Two curly braces follow—one ends the **Form1** class and the other ends the **WindowCreatedWithIDE** namespace.

```
/// <summary>
/// The main entry point for the application.
/// </summary>
[STAThread]
static void Main()
{
        Application.Run(new Form1());
}
    }
}
```

Just above **Main()**, [STAThread] indicates that this program uses the Single Threaded Apartment Thread model. You will learn more about threads as you continue to study C#.

ADDING FUNCTIONALITY TO A Button ON A Form

In most cases, it is easier to design a Form using the IDE than it is to write by hand all the code a Form requires. Adding functionality to a Button is particularly easy using the IDE. In the next steps, you will make the Button on the WindowCreatedWithIDE form functional; it will display a MessageBox when the user clicks it.

1. Start Visual Studio. Click **File** on the menu bar, point to **Open**, and then click **Project**, as shown in Figure 9-34. Make sure the **Look in**: box at the top of the screen indicates that you are looking in the Chapter.09 folder on your Student Disk.

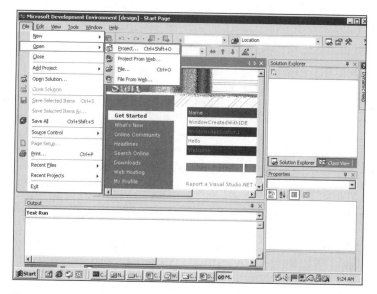

Figure 9-34   Opening an existing project

2. Double-click the **WindowCreatedWithIDE** folder. Double-click the **WindowCreatedWithIDE** C# source code file. See Figure 9-35.

3. The Form you created should appear. If you see the code behind the Form instead of the Form itself, click **View** on the menu bar and then click **Designer**, or press **Shift+F7**. Double-click the **Press** button on the Form. The program code appears, revealing a newly created method:

```
private void button1_Click(object sender,
System.EventArgs e)
{

}
```

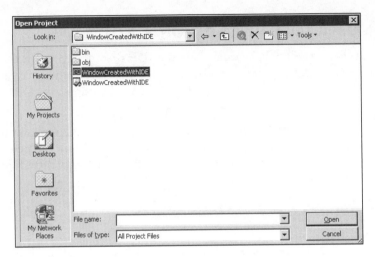

Figure 9-35   Selecting the source file

4. The method named `button1_Click()` will contain the code that identifies the actions you want to perform when a user clicks `button1`. The method receives two arguments—an object named `sender` and an `EventArgs` object named `e`. You will examine these objects more thoroughly in Chapter 10. For now, you will add some code that will display a `MessageBox` when the user clicks `button1`. Place your insertion point between the curly braces of the `button1_Click()` method, if necessary, and add the following:

```
MessageBox.Show("Thank you");
```

5. Save the file, then run the program by clicking **Debug** on the menu bar and clicking **Start Without Debugging**, or press **Ctrl+F5**. When `My IDE Form` appears, click the **Press** button. The `MessageBox` containing "Thank you" appears, as shown in Figure 9-36.

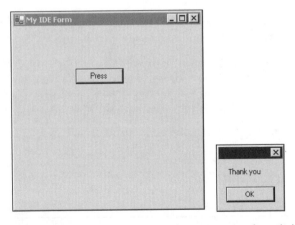

Figure 9-36   `MessageBox` that appears after clicking Press

6. Dismiss the `MessageBox`, then close the `Form`.

7. Examine the code for the `Form`. In the `InitializeComponent()` method, a new statement has been added:

```
this.button1.Click += new System.EventHandler(this.
button1_Click);
```

This statement associates the `button1_Click()` method with the `button1.Click` event that is generated when a user clicks the `button1` Button. In Chapter 10, you will learn more about events. Fortunately, with the IDE you can use an event without being required to understand all the details of how one operates.

ADDING A SECOND BUTTON TO A FORM

`Forms` often contain multiple `Button` objects; a `Form` can contain as many `Buttons` as you need. Because each `Button` has a unique identifier, you can provide unique methods that execute when a user clicks each `Button`.

In the next steps, you will create a form that allows a pizzeria customer to select one of two buttons identifying two types of pizza—Cheese or Sausage. The form will then display one of two pizza prices—$10 or $12, depending on the user's selection.

1. Open Visual Studio .NET, if necessary. Click **File** on the menu bar, point to **New**, click **Project**, and then click **Visual C# Projects** and **Windows Application**. Change the name of the project to **WindowWithTwoButtons** and make sure the Chapter.09 folder on your Student Disk is designated as the storage location, as shown in Figure 9-37. Click **OK**.

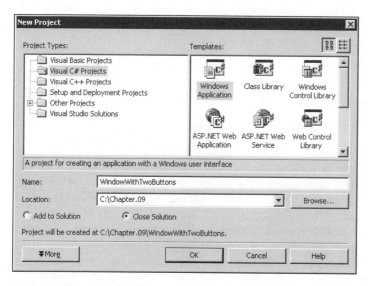

Figure 9-37   Starting the `WindowWithTwoButtons` project

9

2. Click the title bar of the form designer that appears. In the Form's properties list, change the text of the form to "Make a Choice". When you press **Enter**, "Make a Choice" appears in the Form's title bar. Drag a Button onto the Form. Release your mouse button to place the Button on the surface of the Form, then drag a second Button onto the Form. The Buttons automatically will contain text labels button1 and button2, as shown in Figure 9-38.

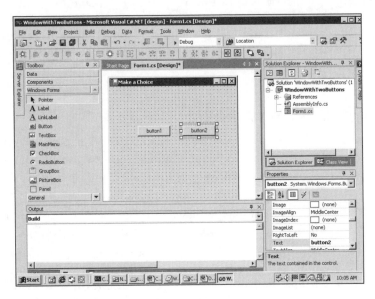

Figure 9-38 Two Buttons on a Form

3. In the Properties window, click the list box and click **button1**. Change its `Text` property setting to **Cheese**. In the Properties list box, click **button2**. Change its `Text` property to **Sausage**. See Figure 9-39.

4. Double-click the **Cheese** button to view the code for the `button1_Click()` method. Between the curly braces, type the following:

```
MessageBox.Show("Price is $10");
```

5. Return to Designer view. Double-click the **Sausage** button. Between the curly braces of the method, add **MessageBox.Show("Price is $12");**.

6. Save the file, and then run the program by pressing **Ctrl+F5** or by clicking **Debug** on the menu bar and clicking **Start Without Debugging**. When the Form appears, notice that the Cheese button has a darker outline than the Sausage button; this means the Cheese button has focus. When a Button has **focus**, it appears darker than other Buttons, and you can activate it by clicking it or pressing the Enter key. By default, the first Button you place on a Form has focus. The user can press the Tab key to change the focus from one Button to the next. Experiment with the **Tab** key, then click either Button and confirm that the correct price message is displayed.

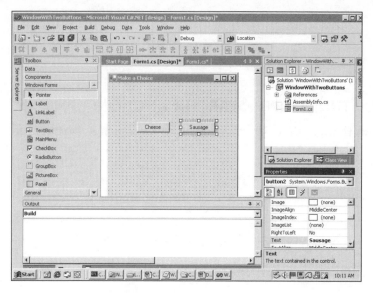

Figure 9-39   Two `Buttons` containing `Text` properties "Cheese" and "Sausage"

7. Dismiss the `MessageBox` and click the other button. Again, the correct price is displayed. Figure 9-40 shows the result when the user clicks Sausage.

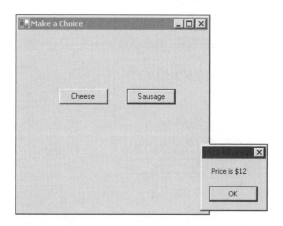

Figure 9-40   Make a Choice `Form` after user clicks Sausage button

8. Dismiss the `MessageBox` and close the `Form`. In the IDE, switch to Code view. Within the `InitializeComponent()` method, locate the statements that set the `button1.TabIndex` property: `this.button1.TabIndex = 0;` and `this.button2.TabIndex = 1;`. The `TabIndex` property specifies the order (0, 1, 2, and so on) in which `Button` objects receive focus when the user presses the Tab key. (If you set both `Buttons` to the same `TabIndex`, the last one set will receive focus.)

You will learn to manipulate the `TabIndex` property in Chapter 11.

USING THE VISUAL STUDIO HELP SEARCH FUNCTION

When you are working with a class that is new to you, such as `Button` or `Form`, no book can answer all of your questions. The ultimate authority on the classes available in C# is the Visual Studio Search facility. You will want to use this tool often as you continue to learn about C# in particular and the Visual Studio products in general. In the next steps, you will search for information on the `Button` class.

1. In the Visual Studio IDE, click **Help** on the menu bar, then click **Search**. (Alternatively, you can press **Ctrl+Alt+F3**.) See Figure 9-41.

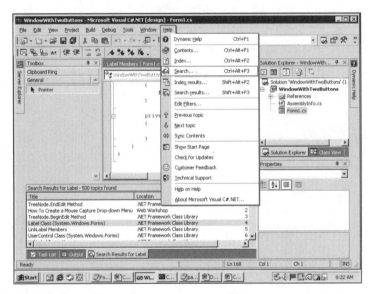

Figure 9-41   Using Search

2. In the Search dialog box near the upper-right corner of the screen, type a term for which you want to search. (You can choose Visual C# and Related in the Filtered by list box to narrow the search from the superset of all Visual Studio topics.) For example, you can type **Button**. Press **Enter** and a list of topics appears at the bottom of the screen. See Figure 9-42.

3. Double-click the topic you want to pursue (for example, Button Class). Documentation appears in the Visual Studio main window. See Figure 9-43.

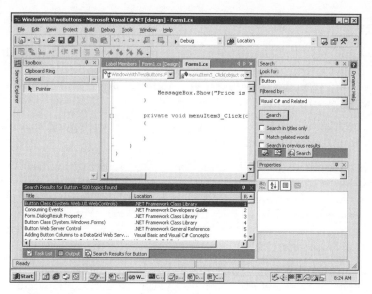

Figure 9-42   Topics found after searching for `Button`

9

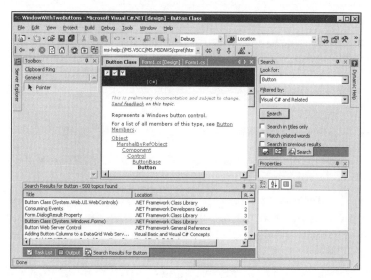

Figure 9-43   Button Class documentation

4. Scroll through the documentation. You can read a definition of `Button`, examine its inheritance hierarchy, see how its constructor is configured, and so on. At the bottom of the `Button` information, the See Also section provides you with links to appropriate related topics, such as all the `Button` members—that is, the properties and methods associated with `Button`s.

5. Experiment by searching for other topics you have studied. When you are done, close the Visual Studio IDE.

CHAPTER SUMMARY

❑ A `MessageBox` is a GUI object that can contain text, buttons, and symbols that inform and instruct a user. You use the static class method `Show()` to display a `MessageBox`. You can pass a string message, caption, buttons, and an icon to the `MessageBox.Show()` method.

❑ `DialogResult` is an enumeration, or list of values that correspond to a user's potential `MessageBox` button selections.

❑ `Forms` provide an interface for collecting, displaying, and delivering user information. You use a `Form` to represent any window you want to display within your application. `Forms` often contain controls such as text fields, buttons, and check boxes that users can manipulate to interact with a program. You can change the appearance, size, color, and window management features of a `Form` by setting its instance fields or properties.

❑ You can create a child class from `Form` that becomes the main window of an application. When you create a new main window, you must derive a new custom class from the base class `System.Windows.Forms.Form`, you must write a `Main()` method that calls the `Application.Run()` method, and you must pass an instance of your newly created `Form` class as an argument.

❑ A window is more flexible than a `MessageBox` because you can place manipulatable `Window` components wherever you like on the surface of the window. One type of object the user can manipulate is a `Button`, a GUI object you can click to cause some action. The `Button` class contains many properties, including `Text` and `Location` properties.

❑ The Visual Studio integrated development environment (IDE) provides a wealth of tools to help make the `Form` design process easier. The IDE generates code for you as you drag components onto a `Form`. Alternatively, you can change the code just as you might with code you typed yourself.

❑ Using the Visual Studio IDE, it is easy to create elaborate forms with a few keystrokes. When you use the Designer in the IDE to design your forms, you save a lot of typing, which reduces errors. However, you should attempt to understand each line of code generated.

❑ In most cases, it is easier to design a `Form` using the IDE than it is to write by hand all the code a `Form` requires. Adding functionality to a `Button` is particularly easy using the IDE.

❑ `Forms` often contain multiple `Button` objects; a `Form` can contain as many `Buttons` as you need. Because each `Button` has a unique identifier, you can provide unique methods that execute when a user clicks each `Button`.

REVIEW QUESTIONS

1. Which is true of the `MessageBox` class?
   a. You cannot create a new instance of this class.
   b. Its constructor is `public`.
   c. Its methods cannot be overloaded.
   d. A single version of its `Show()` method exists.

2. A programmer who uses a `MessageBox` must _____.
   a. determine the message that will appear on the OK button
   b. write the message that will appear in the `MessageBox`
   c. write an overloaded version of the `Show()` method
   d. select an icon to be displayed within the `MessageBox`

3. Optionally, a programmer can select all of the following for a `MessageBox` except _____.
   a. a message within the `MessageBox`
   b. a caption in the title bar of the `MessageBox`
   c. a default button for the `MessageBox`
   d. the modality of the `MessageBox`

4. A `MessageBox` is modal, meaning _____.
   a. it can appear in several different styles
   b. the program will not progress until a user dismisses the `MessageBox`
   c. it is always rectangular with a title bar
   d. it appears in the Windows style so that all components have the same look and feel

5. An enumeration is a _____ in a program.
   a. list of values you can use
   b. sum or total of values used
   c. count of the number of values used
   d. list of values that cannot be used

6. Which of the following is not a possible `DialogResult`?
   a. `Cancel`
   b. `OK`
   c. `End`
   d. `Retry`

7. The `Form` class descends from the _____ class.
   a. `Object`
   b. `Component`
   c. `Control`
   d. all of these

8. The `Form` class differs from the `MessageBox` class in that _____.

    a. you can create an instance of the `Form` class, but not `MessageBox`

    b. you can create an instance of the `MessageBox` class, but not the `Form` class

    c. `Form`s can contain buttons, but not `MessageBox`es

    d. `MessageBox`es can contain buttons, but not `Form`s

9. The `Form` class contains _____ properties.

    a. 5

    b. 13

    c. 101

    d. more than 4000

10. Which of the following is not a `Form` property?

    a. `BackColor`

    b. `DesktopLocation`

    c. `Invisible`

    d. `Size`

11. When you create a new main window, you must _____.

    a. derive a new custom class from the base class `System.Windows.Forms.Form`

    b. write a `Main()` method that calls the `Application.Run()` method

    c. either a or b, but not both

    d. both a and b

12. When used with a component, the `System.Drawing.Size()` method takes two parameters representing _____.

    a. width and height

    b. line thickness and horizontal position

    c. height and degrees of rotation

    d. horizontal position and width

13. A `Form`'s `Controls` are its _____.

    a. static methods

    b. nonstatic methods

    c. manipulatable components

    d. parents

14. For a `Button` to be clickable, you _____.

    a. need only to add the `Button` to a `Form`

    b. use the `System.Windows.Forms.Control` class

    c. include a `GUIImplement()` method within your program

    d. write a method named `ClickButton()`

15. The main reason to use the Visual Studio integrated development environment is to _____.

    a. use methods that are not available when you write code by hand

    b. have access to the Studio's private data types

    c. make the program design process easier

    d. all of these

16. When you begin to create a `Form` using the Visual Studio IDE, the default `Form` name is _____.

    a. `MyForm`

    b. `IDEForm`

    c. `Form1`

    d. `null`

17. When you design a `Form` using the IDE, _____.

    a. much less code is generated than when you design a `Form` by hand

    b. the generated code is written in machine language so you cannot read it

    c. you cannot alter the generated code

    d. none of these

18. If you do not like the default name the IDE gives to a `Button`, you can _____.

    a. change the `Name` property in the code

    b. change the `Name` field in the Properties list in the IDE

    c. either of these

    d. none of these

19. C# uses comments beginning with "TODO" to _____.

    a. flag errors

    b. remind you of tasks you might need to do

    c. indicate places where the compiler will generate code when the program executes

    d. pay tribute to Bill Gates' boyhood dog, Todo

20. If a `Form` contains a `Button` named `agreeButton`, then you code the actions to be performed when the user clicks the `Button` in a method named _____.

    a. `ButtonClick()`

    b. `Button_Click()`

    c. `agreeButtonClick()`

    d. `agreeButton_Click()`

9

EXERCISES

Save the programs that you create in these Exercises in the Chapter.09 folder on your Student Disk.

1. Write a program that displays a MessageBox containing contact information for your company. Save the program as **Contact.cs**.

2. Write a program for an Internet provider that displays a MessageBox asking users to choose whether they want unlimited access. Display a second MessageBox showing the price: $10.95 per month for limited access or $19.95 per month for unlimited access. Save the program as **InternetAccess.cs**.

3. Write a program for an Internet provider that displays a MessageBox asking users whether they want to read the company's usage policy. If the user chooses Yes, display a short usage policy. If the user chooses No, remind the user to read the policy later. If the user chooses Cancel, end the program. Save the program as **Policy.cs**.

4. Write a program that simulates an Internet connection error. Display a MessageBox that notifies the user of the error and provide three buttons: Abort, Retry, and Ignore. If the user chooses Retry, display a message indicating that the connection succeeded. If the user chooses Ignore, display a message indicating that the user will work offline. If the user chooses Abort, end the program. Save the program as **Connection.cs**.

5. Using the Visual Studio IDE, create a Form that contains a button labeled "About". When a user clicks the button, display a MessageBox containing your personal copyright statement for the program. Save the program as **About.cs**.

6. Create a Form containing two buttons for a book publisher. If a user clicks the Paperback button, display a MessageBox that contains a book price of $6.99. If the user clicks the Hardback button, display $24.99. Save the program as **Book.cs**.

7. Create a game Form containing six buttons. Display different prizes depending on the button the user selects. Save the program as **Game.cs**.

8. Each of the following files in the Chapter.09 folder on your Student Disk has syntax and/or logical errors. In each case, determine the problem and fix the program. After you correct the errors, save each file using the same filename preceded with *Fixed*. For example, DebugNine1.cs will become FixedDebugNine1.cs.

   a. DebugNine1.cs

   b. DebugNine2.cs

   c. DebugNine3.cs

   d. DebugNine4.cs

CHAPTER

10

USING CONTROLS

In this chapter you will learn:

♦ About `Controls`

♦ How to create a `Form` containing `Labels`

♦ How to set a `Label`'s `Font`

♦ How to add `Color` to a `Form`

♦ How to add `CheckBox` and `RadioButton` objects to a `Form`

♦ How to add a `PictureBox` to a `Form`

♦ How to add `ListBox`, `ComboBox`, and `CheckedListBox` items to a `Form`

♦ How to add functionality to a `ListBox` with one `SelectedItem`

♦ How to add functionality to a `ListBox` with multiple `SelectedItems`

♦ How to supply a default selection for a `ListBox`

In the last chapter you learned to create `Form`s both by hand using an ordinary text editor and by using the Visual Studio IDE. Both approaches yielded the same results, but the IDE provides you with an easy-to-use design environment. Additionally, by examining the IDE-generated program code, you can learn more about code you want to write by hand.

The objects you used in Chapter 9, `Form`s and `Button`s, represent only a tiny fraction of the objects available to you in C#. When using programs or visiting Internet sites, you have encountered and used many other interactive **widgets**—short for "windows gadgets"—such as labels, scroll bars, check boxes, and radio buttons. C# has many classes that represent these GUI objects, and the Visual Studio IDE makes it easy to add them to your programs. In this chapter you will learn to incorporate some of the most common and useful widgets into your programs. Additionally, you will see how these components work in general so you can use other widgets that are not covered in this book or that become available to C# programmers in future releases of Visual Studio.

UNDERSTANDING Controls

When you design a Form, you can place Buttons and other controls on the Form surface. The Control class provides the definitions for these GUI objects. Control objects such as Forms and Buttons, like all other objects in C#, ultimately derive from the Object class. Figure 10-1 shows where the Control class fits into the inheritance hierarchy.

```
Object
      MarshalByRefObject
            Component
                  Control
                        ByteViewer
                        AxHost
                        ButtonBase
                              Button, CheckBox, and RadioButton
                        DataGrid
                        DateTimePicker
                        GroupBox
                        Label
                        ListControl
                              ListBox, ComboBox
                                    CheckedListBox
                        ListView
                        MonthCalendar
                        PictureBox
                        PrintPreviewControl
                        ProgressBar
                        ScrollableControl
                        ContainerControl
                              Form
                        ScrollBar
                        Splitter
                        StatusBar
                        TabControl
                        TextBoxBase
                        ToolBar
                        TrackBar
                        TreeView
```

Figure 10-1   Control's inheritance hierarchy

Figure 10-1 shows all 23 direct descendants of Control, but does not show all of the descendants of those classes; rather, it shows only those descendants covered in this chapter. When you learn to use some Controls you will find that others work in much the same way; additionally, you can read more about them in the Visual Studio Help documentation.

Table 10-1 Some Control Properties

Property	Function
AllowDrop	Gets or sets a value indicating whether the control can accept data that the user drags and drops into it
Anchor	Gets or sets which edges of the control are anchored to the edges of its container
BackColor	Gets or sets the background color for the control
BackgroundImage	Gets or sets the background image displayed in the control
BorderStyle	Gets or sets the border style for the control
Bottom	Gets the distance between the bottom edge of the control and the top edge of its container's client area
Bounds	Gets or sets the bounding rectangle for the control
CanFocus	Gets a value indicating whether the control can receive focus
CanSelect	Gets a value indicating whether the control can be selected
Container	Returns the container that contains the component
ContainsFocus	Gets a value indicating whether the control, or one of its child controls, currently has the input focus
ContextMenu	Gets or sets the shortcut menu associated with the control
Controls	Gets or sets the collection of controls contained within the control
Created	Gets a value indicating whether the control has been created
Cursor	Gets or sets the cursor that is displayed when the user moves the mouse pointer over the control
Dock	Gets or sets the edge of the parent container to which a control is docked
Enabled	Gets or sets a value indicating whether the control is enabled
Focused	Gets a value indicating whether the control has input focus
Font	Gets or sets the current font for the control
ForeColor	Gets or sets the foreground color of the control
HasChildren	Gets a value indicating whether the control contains one or more child controls
Height	Gets or sets the height of the control
IsAccessible	Gets or sets a value indicating whether the control is visible to accessibility applications
Left	Gets or sets the x-coordinate of a control's left edge in pixels
Location	Gets or sets the coordinates of the upper-left corner of the control relative to the upper-left corner of its container
Name	Gets or sets the name of the control
Right	Gets the distance between the right edge of the control and the left edge of its container
Size	Gets or sets the height and width of the control
TabIndex	Gets or sets the tab order of this control within its container
Text	Gets or sets the text associated with this control
Top	Gets or sets the top coordinate of the control
TopLevelControl	Gets the top-level control that contains the current control
Visible	Gets or sets a value indicating whether the control is visible
Width	Gets or sets the width of the control

10

The figure shows that all Controls are Objects, of course. They are also all MarshalByRefObjects. (A **MarshalByRefObject** is one you can instantiate on a remote computer; then you can manipulate a reference to the object rather than a local copy of the object.) Controls also descend from Component. (The **Component** class provides containment and cleanup for other objects. The Control class adds visual representation to Components.) The Control class implements very basic functionality required by classes that appear to the user—in other words, the GUI objects the user sees on the screen. This class handles user input through the keyboard and pointing devices as well as message routing and security. It defines the bounds of a Control by determining its position and size.

You have already used a child class of ButtonBase—the Button. In this chapter you will use two other ButtonBase children—CheckBox and RadioButton. You also have used a ScrollableControl grandchild—the Form, which descends from ContainerControl. Other useful Controls covered in this chapter include PictureBox, ListBox, CheckedListBox, and ComboBox.

Table 10-1 shows just some of the properties associated with Controls in general.

CREATING A Form WITH Labels

A Label is one of the simplest GUI Control objects you can place on a Form. The Label class descends directly from Control. Typically, you use a **Label** control to provide descriptive text for another Control object (for example, to tell the user what pressing a Button will accomplish) or to display other text information on a Form.

You can create a Label in a manner very similar to the way in which you create a Button. You use the class name and an identifier and then call the class constructor—for example, Label label1 = new Label();. Figure 10-2 shows a program that creates two Labels and places them on a Form. The Form's constructor assigns Text values to each Label and positions those values on the Form surface. Figure 10-3 shows the output.

Just as with Buttons, it is easier to create Forms containing Labels using the Visual Studio Integrated Development Environment. In the next steps you will begin to create an application for Bailey's Bed and Breakfast. The main Form will allow the user to select one of two suites and discover the amenities and price associated with each choice. You will start by placing two Labels on a Form.

```
using System;
using System.Windows.Forms;
public class FormWithLabels : Form
{
        Label label1 = new Label();
        Label label2 = new Label();
        public FormWithLabels()
        {
                this.Size = new System.Drawing.Size(300,300);
                this.Text = "Two Labels";
                label1.Text = "This is one label";
                label2.Text = "This is another";
                this.Controls.AddRange(new System.Windows.Forms.Control[]
                        {this.label1, label2});
                this.label1.Location = new System.Drawing.Point(30,50);
                this.label2.Location = new System.Drawing.Point(30,100);
        }
        public static void Main()
        {
                Application.Run(new FormWithLabels());
        }
}
```

Figure 10-2   `FormWithLabels` program

10

Figure 10-3   Output of `FormWithLabels` program

The screen images you see in the next steps represent a typical Visual Studio environment. Based on options selected in your installation, your screen might differ from the figures.

1. Open Microsoft Visual Studio .NET. You might be able to use a desktop shortcut, or you might click **Start** on the taskbar, point to **Programs**, click **Microsoft Visual Studio.NET**, and then click **Microsoft Visual Studio.NET** again.

2. Click **File** on the menu bar, point to **New**, and then click **Project**.

3. A New Project dialog box appears. In the window under Project Types, click **Visual C# Projects**. Under Templates, click **Windows Application**. Near the bottom of the New Project dialog box, click in the Name text box and type **BedAndBreakfast** as the Name for your application. Make sure the Location text box contains the name of the **Chapter.10** folder on your Student Disk. See Figure 10-4.

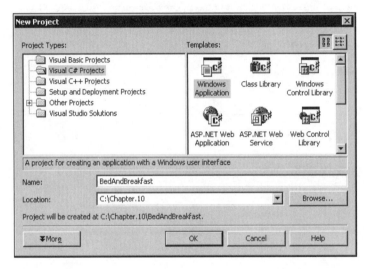

Figure 10-4   Opening a new BedAndBreakfast project

4. Click **OK**. Figure 10-5 shows the design screen that appears. The blank Form in the center of the screen has an empty title bar. Click the Form. The lower-right corner of the screen contains a Properties window that lists the Form's properties. In Figure 10-5 you can see that the Text property is set to **Form 1**.

5. In the Properties list, click the description **Form 1** in the Settings box for the Text property. Delete **Form 1** and type **Bailey's Bed and Breakfast**. Press **Enter**, and the title of the Form in the center of the screen changes to "Bailey's Bed and Breakfast."

6. On the left side of the design screen, note the list of components that can be added to a Form, including, Label, LinkLabel, Button, and so on. Click **Label** and drag a Label onto the Form. When you release your mouse button, the Label appears on the Form and contains the text "label1." On the right of the screen, under Properties, make sure the list box shows that you are viewing the properties for label1.

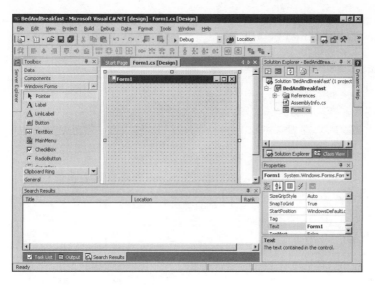

Figure 10-5   Design screen

7. Change the `Text` property of `label1` to **Welcome to Bailey's**, then press **Enter**. The text of the `Label` on the `Form` changes. Drag and resize the `Label` so it is close to the position and size of the `Label` in Figure 10-6. (If you prefer to set the `Label`'s attributes manually in the Properties list, the `Location` should be **64,40** and the `Size` should be **144,23**.)

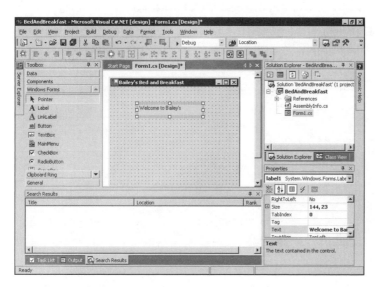

Figure 10-6   "Welcome to Bailey's" `Label`

8. Drag a second `Label` onto the `Form` as shown in Figure 10-7, and then set its `Text` property to **Check our rates**. (If you prefer to set the `Label`'s

attributes manually in the Properties list, the `Location` should be **64,80** and the `Size` should be **100,23**.)

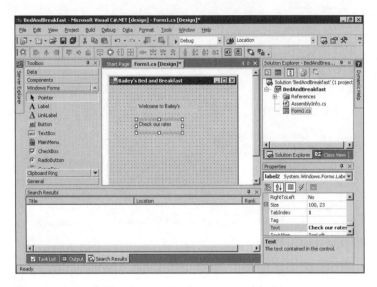

Figure 10-7 "Check our rates" `Label` added to `Form`

9. Save the project using one of the following methods: Click **File** on the menu bar and then click **Save All**, click the **Save All** button (the one that resembles a stack of diskettes), or press **Ctrl+Shift+S**.

10. Click **Debug** on the menu bar and then click **Start Without Debugging**, or press **Ctrl+F5**. The `Form` appears as shown in Figure 10-8.

Figure 10-8 Bailey's `Form` with two `Labels`

11. Dismiss the `Form` by clicking the **Close** button in the upper-right corner of the `Form`.

SETTING A Label's Font

You use the Font class to change the appearance of printed text on your Forms. The Font class includes a number of overloaded constructors. For example, you can create a Font using two arguments (a type and a size) as follows:

```
Font myFavoriteFont = new Font("Times Roman", 12.5F);
```

You also can type the fully qualified Font class name, as in the following example:

```
System.Drawing.Font myFavoriteFont =
        new System.Drawing.Font("Times Roman", 12.5F);
```

If you include using System.Drawing; at the top of your file, you can use the shortened version of the class name.

The Font name you pass to the Font constructor is a string. The second value is a float that represents the font size. Notice that you must use an *F* (or an *f*) following the Font size value constant when it contains a decimal point to ensure that the constant will be recognized as a float and not a double. The Font constructor argument list contains a float variable for size; using a double will generate a compiler error indicating that the double cannot be converted to a float.

Alternatively, you can create a Font using three arguments, adding a FontStyle, as in the following example:

```
Font aFancyFont = new Font("Arial", 24, FontStyle.Italic);
```

Table 10-2 lists the available FontStyles. You can combine multiple styles using the pipe (|) (which is also called the bitwise operator). For example, the following code creates a Font that is bold and underlined:

```
Font boldAndUnderlined = new
Font("Helvetica",10, FontStyle.Bold | FontStyle.Underline);
```

Table 10-2   FontStyle Enumeration

Member Name	Description
Bold	Bold text
Italic	Italic text
Regular	Normal text
Strikeout	Text with a line through the middle
Underline	Underlined text

Once you have defined a `Font`, you can set a `Label`'s `Font` with a statement like the following:

```
label1.Font = myFavoriteFont;
```

Alternatively, you can create and assign a `Font` in one step without providing an identifier for the `Font`, as in this example:

```
label1.Font = new System.DrawingFont("Times Roman", 12.5F);
```

If you don't provide an identifier for a `Font`, you can't reuse it and will have to create it again if you want to use it with additional `Controls`.

Of course, you can also create a `Font` from within the Visual Studio IDE. In the next steps, you will change the `Font` of the `Labels` you have already placed on the Bailey's Bed and Breakfast `Form`.

1. Within the Bed And Breakfast project, select the **Welcome to Bailey's** `Label` by clicking it on the `Form`. (Alternatively, choose `label1` from the list box under Properties in the lower-right corner of the screen.)

2. Locate the `Font` property in the Properties list. Currently, it lists the default `Font`, Microsoft Sans Serif, 8.25 pt. Notice the ellipsis (three dots) at the right of the `Font` property name. (You might have to click in the Property to see the button.) Click the ellipsis to display the Font dialog box, as shown in Figure 10-9. It shows 8-point, Regular, Microsoft Sans Serif as the selected `Font`.

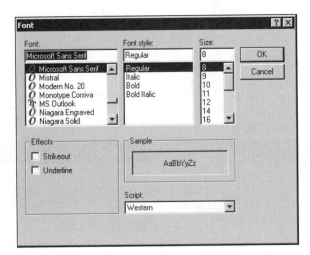

Figure 10-9   Font dialog box

3. Scroll through the Font choices and select **Lucida Calligraphy**, **Bold**, and **16** as the `Font`, `FontStyle`, and `Size`, respectively. Click **OK**. (If Lucida Calligraphy is not available on your system, choose any other font you like.)

4. The "Welcome to Bailey's" `Label` text no longer fits in the display area allotted on the `Form`. Click the `Label` and use your mouse to drag the left, right, top, and bottom arrows until the entire welcome message appears. Figure 10-10 shows the `Label` at `Location` 16, 32 and `Size` 256, 32.

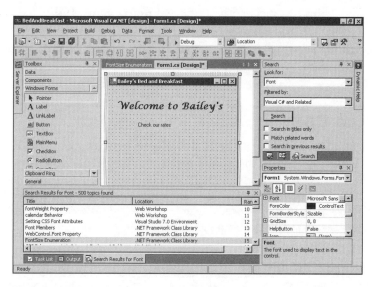

Figure 10-10 "Welcome to Bailey's" `Label` with new `Font`, `FontStyle`, and `Size`

5. Click **View** on the menu bar, and then click **Code** (or press **F7**) to view the code. Click the plus (+) sign as necessary to expand lines of code, and then locate the line of code in which `label1`'s `Font` is set:

```
this.label1.Font = new System.Drawing.Font
    ("Lucida Calligraphy", 15.75F,
    System.Drawing.FontStyle.Bold,
    System.Drawing.GraphicsUnit.Point,
    ((System.Byte)(0)));
```

You can easily locate a line of code in a long listing by clicking Edit on the main menu in the IDE. Then click Find and Replace, Find, type in a key phrase to search for, and click the Find Next button.

The IDE creates an unnamed instance of the `Font` you selected. It uses the fully qualified `Font` class name (`System.Drawing.Font`) and a string representing the `Font` name. Notice that the point value is 15.75F instead of 16; the IDE selects an appropriate size close to your choice. If you want the point size to be exactly 16, you can click the + to the left of the Font property in the Properties list. The list will then expand allowing you to change the Size property to any size you like. For now, leave it at 15.75.

The IDE also uses a more thorough version of the constructor, which includes arguments representing a GraphicsUnit and a byte value representing a character set. These default values can be eliminated without any change in the resulting program.

6. Change the label2 object so its Font is **Lucida Sans**, **Italic**, **8**. (Adjust the size of the label, if necessary, to prevent its text from wrapping.)

7. If necessary, click **View** on the menu bar, and then click **Designer** to return to the Designer view. Save the project.

ADDING Color TO A Form

The Color class contains a wide variety of predefined Colors that you can use with your Controls. Table 10-3 shows the predefined Color properties you can use.

 Visual Studio also allows you to create custom colors. If none of the colors listed in Table 10-3 suits your needs, search for *Custom Color* in the Visual Studio Help Search facility to obtain more information.

Table 10-3   Color Properties

AliceBlue	DeepPink	Lime	RosyBrown
AntiqueWhite	DeepSkyBlue	LimeGreen	RoyalBlue
Aqua	DimGray	Linen	SaddleBrown
Aquamarine	DodgerBlue	Magenta	Salmon
Azure	Firebrick	Maroon	SandyBrown
Beige	FloralWhite	MediumAquamarine	SeaGreen
Bisque	ForestGreen	MediumBlue	SeaShell
Black	Fuchsia	MediumOrchid	Sienna
BlanchedAlmond	Gainsboro	MediumPurple	Silver
Blue	GhostWhite	MediumSeaGreen	SkyBlue
BlueViolet	Gold	MediumSlateBlue	SlateBlue
Brown	Goldenrod	MediumSpringGreen	SlateGray
BurlyWood	Gray	MediumTurquoise	Snow
CadetBlue	Green	MediumVioletRed	SpringGreen
Chartreuse	GreenYellow	MidnightBlue	SteelBlue
Chocolate	Honeydew	MintCream	Tan
Coral	HotPink	MistyRose	Teal

Table 10-3 Color Properties (continued)

CornflowerBlue	IndianRed	Moccasin	Thistle
Cornsilk	Indigo	NavajoWhite	Tomato
Crimson	Ivory	Navy	Transparent
Cyan	Khaki	OldLace	Turquoise
DarkBlue	Lavender	Olive	Violet
DarkCyan	LavenderBlush	OliveDrab	Wheat
DarkGoldenrod	LawnGreen	Orange	White
DarkGray	LemonChiffon	OrangeRed	WhiteSmoke
DarkGreen	LightBlue	Orchid	Yellow
DarkKhaki	LightCoral	PaleGoldenrod	YellowGreen
DarkMagenta	LightCyan	PaleGreen	
DarkOliveGreen	LightGoldenrodYellow	PaleTurquoise	
DarkOrange	LightGray	PaleVioletRed	
DarkOrchid	LightGreen	PapayaWhip	
DarkRed	LightPink	PeachPuff	
DarkSalmon	LightSalmon	Peru	
DarkSeaGreen	LightSeaGreen	Pink	
DarkSlateBlue	LightSkyBlue	Plum	
DarkSlateGray	LightSlateGray	PowderBlue	
DarkTurquoise	LightSteelBlue	Purple	
DarkViolet	LightYellow	Red	

10

As examples of how to use `Colors`, you can declare a `Label`'s `BackColor` and `ForeColor` properties with statements like the following:

```
label1.BackColor = System.Drawing.Color.Blue;
label1.ForeColor = System.Drawing.Color.Gold;
```

 If you include the statement using `System.Drawing;` at the top of your file, then instead of `label1.BackColor = System.Drawing.Color.Blue;` you can use a shorter statement like `label1.BackColor = Color.Blue;`.

Next, you will change the `BackColor` property of the Bailey's Bed and Breakfast `Form`.

1. In the Designer view for the Bed And Breakfast project within the Visual Studio IDE, make sure **Form1** is selected in the Properties list.

2. Change the `BackColor` option to `Yellow` by clicking the **BackColor** property field, typing **Yellow**, and then pressing **Enter**, or by clicking the list arrow, clicking the **Web** tab, and clicking **Yellow** from the list of available colors.

3. View the code and confirm that the Form's BackColor property is set to **Yellow**.

4. Save the project.

USING CheckBox AND RadioButton OBJECTS

You have already placed Button objects on a Form. The Button class derives from the ButtonBase class. The ButtonBase class has two other descendants: CheckBox and RadioButton.

CheckBox objects are GUI widgets the user can click to select or deselect an option. When a Form contains multiple CheckBoxes, any number of them can be checked or unchecked at the same time. RadioButtons are similar to CheckBoxes, except that when they are placed on a Form, only one RadioButton can be selected at a time—selecting any RadioButton automatically deselects the others. You can place multiple groups of RadioButtons on a Form by using a GroupBox. If you place several GroupBox Controls on a Form and you place several RadioButtons in each GroupBox, then, at any point in time, one RadioButton can be selected from each GroupBox; in other words. each GroupBox operates independently from all others.

Both CheckBox and RadioButton objects have a Checked property whose value is true or false. For example, if you create a CheckBox named extraToppings and you want to add $1.00 to a pizzaPrice value when the user checks the box, you can write the following:

```
if (extraToppings.Checked)
        pizzaPrice = pizzaPrice + 1.00;
```

Both CheckBox and RadioButton objects also have a CheckedChanged() method that is called when a user clicks any CheckBox or RadioButton.

In the next steps, you will add two RadioButtons to the BedAndBreakfast Form allowing the user to select a specific available room and view information about the room.

1. In the Designer view of the Bed And Breakfast project in the Visual Studio IDE, drag a RadioButton onto the Form below the "Check our rates" Label. (See Figure 10-11 for its approximate placement.) Change the Text property of the RadioButton to **BelleAire Suite**.

2. Drag a second RadioButton onto the Form beneath the first one. Change its Text property to **Lincoln Room**. See Figure 10-11.

3. Next, you will create two new Forms: one that will appear when the user selects the BelleAire RadioButton and one that will appear when the user selects the Lincoln RadioButton. Click **File** on the menu bar, then click **Add New Item**. In the Templates window, double-click **Windows Form**. A new Form named Form2 appears, as shown in Figure 10-12.

Figure 10-11   Bailey's Bed and Breakfast Form containing two RadioButtons

10

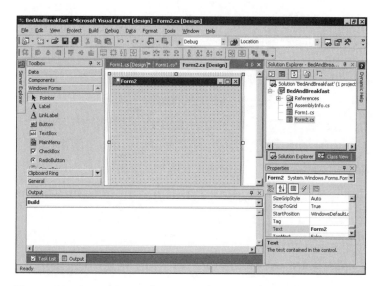

Figure 10-12   Form2

4. Change the **Text** property of the second **Form** to **BelleAire Suite**.

5. Drag a **Label** onto the **Form** (use Figure 10-14 as a guide to approximate its placement). Change the **Text** property of the **Label** to contain the following: **The BelleAire Suite has two bedrooms, two baths and a private balcony.** Adjust the size of the **Label** until all of the text is visible.

6. Drag a second `Label` onto the `Form` and type the price as the `Text` property: **$199.95 per night**.

7. Change the `BackColor` property of `Form2` to **Yellow**.

8. In the Solution Explorer at the right of the screen, double-click `Form1`. Double-click the BelleAire Suite `RadioButton`. The program code appears in the IDE main window. Within the `radioButton1_CheckedChanged()` method, add an `if` statement that determines whether `radioButton1` is checked. If the `RadioButton` is checked, create a new instance of `Form2` and display it.

```
private void radioButton1_CheckedChanged
    (object sender, System.EventArgs e)
{
    if(radioButton1.Checked)
    {
        Form2 belleAireForm = new Form2();
        belleAireForm.ShowDialog();
    }
}
```

9. Save and then execute the program. When the Bed and Breakfast `Form` appears, it looks like Figure 10-13.

Figure 10-13   Bailey's Bed and Breakfast with `RadioButtons`

10. Click the **BelleAire Suite** `RadioButton`. The BelleAire Suite `Form` appears as shown in Figure 10-14.

11. Close the BelleAire Suite `Form`. On the Bed and Breakfast `Form`, click the **Lincoln Room** `RadioButton`. Nothing happens because you have not created any action to occur when the user clicks here. Close the Bed and Breakfast form.

Figure 10-14   BelleAire Suite `Form`

12. Click **File** on the menu bar, and then click **Add New Item**. Double-click **Windows Form**. When `Form3` appears, change its `Text` property to **Lincoln Room**. Then add two `Labels` to the `Form`. The first should say: **Return to the 1850s in this lovely room with private bath**. The second should say: **$110.00 per night**. Change the `Form's` `BackColor` property to **White**. See Figure 10-15.

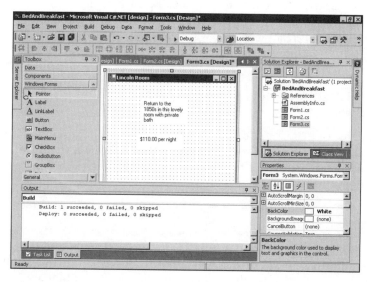

Figure 10-15   Lincoln Room `Form`

13. In the Solution Explorer, choose Form1, double-click **radioButton2** (the Lincoln Room button), and add the following if statement to the radioButton2_CheckedChanged( ) method:

```
private void radioButton2_CheckedChanged
    (object sender, System.EventArgs e)
{
    if(radioButton2.Checked)
    {
        Form3 lincolnForm = new Form3();
        lincolnForm.ShowDialog();
    }
}
```

14. Save the project, and then execute it. When the Bed and Breakfast Form appears, click either RadioButton—the appropriate informational Form appears. Close it, and then click the other RadioButton. Again, the appropriate Form appears.

15. Close all forms.

ADDING A PictureBox TO A Form

A PictureBox is a Control in which you can display graphics from a bitmap, icon, JPEG, GIF, or other image file type. Just as with a Button or a Label, you can easily add a PictureBox to a Form by dragging a Control onto the Form in the Visual Studio IDE. In the next steps, you will add a PictureBox to the Bed and Breakfast application.

1. In the Bed And Breakfast project in the IDE, select the **Lincoln** Form object (Form3).

2. From the list of Controls on the left side of the screen, select a PictureBox Control. (You might have to scroll down the list of controls using your down arrow key to locate PictureBox.) Drag a PictureBox Control onto the Form.

3. Arrange the components as shown in Figure 10-16, so the picture box is to the left and the two labels sit to the right.

4. In the Properties list for pictureBox1, select the **Image** property. Click the ellipsis and browse for an image. The Chapter.10 folder on your Student Disk contains a file named **Lincoln_4** that you can select. The Lincoln_4 file was obtained at *www.free-graphics.com*. You can visit that site and download other images to use in your own applications, if you like.

5. Adjust the size of the PictureBox until you can see the entire image, and then save the project.

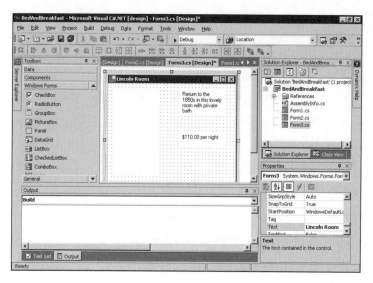

Figure 10-16   Lincoln Room Form containing an empty PictureBox

6. Execute the project. At the Bed and Breakfast Frame, click the RadioButton for the **Lincoln** room. Figure 10-17 shows the result.

10

Figure 10-17   Lincoln Room Form with Image

7. Close the Lincoln Room Form. Close the Bed and Breakfast Form.

8. Exit Visual Studio.

9. Figure 10-18 shows the entire program for the application you just created. Examine the code until you are comfortable with each section. (Some single code lines are divided into multiple lines here to accommodate the book's page size.)

```
// **********Form1 begins here
using System;
using System.Drawing;
using System.Collections;
using System.ComponentModel;
using System.Windows.Forms;
using System.Data;
namespace BedAndBreakfast
{
    /// <summary>
    /// Summary description for Form1.
    /// </summary>
    public class Form1 : System.Windows.Forms.Form
    {
        private System.Windows.Forms.Label label1;
        private System.Windows.Forms.Label label2;
        private System.Windows.Forms.RadioButton
            radioButton1;
        private System.Windows.Forms.RadioButton
            radioButton2;
        /// <summary>
        /// Required designer variable.
        /// </summary>
        private System.ComponentModel.Container
            components = null;
        public Form1()
        {
            //
            // Required for Windows Form
            // Designer support
            //
            InitializeComponent();
            //
            // TODO: Add any constructor code
            // after InitializeComponent call
            //
        }
        /// <summary>
        /// Clean up any resources being used.
        /// </summary>
        protected override void Dispose
            ( bool disposing )
        {
            if( disposing )
            {
                if (components != null)
                {
                    components.Dispose();
                }
            }
            base.Dispose( disposing );
        }
```

Figure 10-18 BedAndBreakfast code

```
#region Windows Form Designer generated code
/// <summary>
/// Required method for Designer
/// support - do not modify
/// the contents of this method
/// with the code editor.
/// </summary>
private void InitializeComponent()
{
    this.label1 = new
     System.Windows.Forms.Label();
    this.label2 = new
     System.Windows.Forms.Label();
    this.radioButton1 = new
     System.Windows.Forms.RadioButton();
    this.radioButton2 = new
     System.Windows.Forms.RadioButton();
    this.SuspendLayout();
    //
    // label1
    //
    this.label1.Font =
     new System.Drawing.Font
         ("Lucida Calligraphy", 15.75F,
         System.Drawing.FontStyle.Bold,
         System.Drawing.GraphicsUnit.Point,
         (System.Byte)(0)));
    this.label1.Location =
         new System.Drawing.Point(16, 32);
    this.label1.Name = "label1";
    this.label1.Size =
         new System.Drawing.Size(256, 32);
    this.label1.TabIndex = 0;
    this.label1.Text =
         "Welcome to Bailey\'s";
    //
    // label2
    //
    this.label2.Font =
     new System.Drawing.Font
     ("Lucida Sans", 8.25F,
     System.Drawing.FontStyle.Italic,
     System.Drawing.GraphicsUnit.Point,
     ((System.Byte)(0)));
    this.label2.Location = new
         System.Drawing.Point(64, 80);
    this.label2.Name = "label2";
    this.label2.Size =
     new System.Drawing.Size(96, 24);
    this.label2.TabIndex = 1;
    this.label2.Text = "Check our rates";
    //
```

Figure 10-18 BedAndBreakfast code (continued)

```
                    // radioButton1
                    //
                    this.radioButton1.Location = new
                         System.Drawing.Point(80, 120);
                    this.radioButton1.Name =
                         "radioButton1";
                    this.radioButton1.TabIndex = 2;
                    this.radioButton1.Text =
                         "BelleAire Suite";
                    this.radioButton1.CheckedChanged +=
                         new System.EventHandler
                      (this.radioButton1_CheckedChanged);
                    //
                    // radioButton2
                    //
                    this.radioButton2.Location =
                     new System.Drawing.Point(80, 160);
                    this.radioButton2.Name =
                         "radioButton2";
                    this.radioButton2.TabIndex = 3;
                    this.radioButton2.Text =
                      "Lincoln Room";
                    this.radioButton2.CheckedChanged +=
                     new System.EventHandler
                    (this.radioButton2_CheckedChanged);
                    //
                    // Form1
                    //
                    this.AutoScaleBaseSize =
                     new System.Drawing.Size(5, 13);
                    this.BackColor =
                         System.Drawing.Color.Yellow;
                    this.ClientSize =
                         new System.Drawing.Size(292, 273);
                    this.Controls.AddRange
                         (new System.Windows.Forms.Control[]
                          {   this.radioButton2,
                              this.radioButton1,
                              this.label2,
                              this.label1});
                    this.Name = "Form1";
                    this.Text =
                         "Bailey\'s Bed and Breakfast";
                    this.Load += new System.EventHandler
                         (this.Form1_Load);
                    this.ResumeLayout(false);
                }
              #endregion
              /// <summary>
              /// The main entry point for the
              /// application.
              /// </summary>
```

Figure 10-18   BedAndBreakfast code (continued)

```
                    [STAThread]
                    static void Main()
                    {
                          Application.Run(new Form1());
                    }

                    private void radioButton1_CheckedChanged
                          (object sender, System.EventArgs e)
                          {
                                if(radioButton1.Checked)
                                {
                                      Form2 belleAireForm =
                                            new Form2();
                                      belleAireForm.ShowDialog();
                                }
                          }
                    private void Form1_Load
                          (object sender, System.EventArgs e)
                    {
                    }
                    private void radioButton2_CheckedChanged
                          (object sender, System.EventArgs e)
                    {
                          if(radioButton2.Checked)
                          {
                                Form3 lincolnForm = new Form3();
                                lincolnForm.ShowDialog();
                          }
                    }

             }
}
// **********Form2 begins
using System;
using System.Drawing;
using System.Collections;
using System.ComponentModel;
using System.Windows.Forms;

namespace BedAndBreakfast
{
      /// <summary>
      /// Summary description for Form2.
      /// </summary>
      public class Form2 :
             System.Windows.Forms.Form
      {
             private System.Windows.Forms.Label label1;
             private System.Windows.Forms.Label label2;
             /// <summary>
             /// Required designer variable.
             /// </summary>
```

Figure 10-18   BedAndBreakfast code (continued)

```
        private System.ComponentModel.Container
         components = null;
        public Form2()
        {
            //
            // Required for Windows Form
            // Designer support
            //
            InitializeComponent();

            //
            // TODO: Add any constructor code
            // after InitializeComponent call
            //
        }
        /// <summary>
        /// Clean up any resources being used.
        /// </summary>
        protected override void
            Dispose( bool disposing )
        {
            if( disposing )
            {
                if(components != null)
                {
                    components.Dispose();
                }
            }
            base.Dispose( disposing );
        }
        #region Windows Form Designer generated code
        /// <summary>
        /// Required method for Designer
        /// support - do not modify
        /// the contents of this method with
        /// the code editor.
        /// </summary>
        private void InitializeComponent()
        {
            this.label1 = new
             System.Windows.Forms.Label();
            this.label2 = new
             System.Windows.Forms.Label();
            this.SuspendLayout();
            //
            // label1
            //
            this.label1.Location = new
             System.Drawing.Point(80, 40);
            this.label1.Name = "label1";
            this.label1.Size = new
             System.Drawing.Size(100, 72);
```

Figure 10-18   `BedAndBreakfast` code (continued)

```
                    this.label1.TabIndex = 0;
                    this.label1.Text = "The BelleAire " +
                        "Suite has two bedrooms, two" +
                        " baths and a private balcony";
                    //
                    // label2
                    //
                    this.label2.BackColor =
                     System.Drawing.Color.Yellow;
                    this.label2.Location = new
                     System.Drawing.Point(72, 152);
                    this.label2.Name = "label2";
                    this.label2.Size = new
                     System.Drawing.Size(104, 24);
                    this.label2.TabIndex = 1;
                    this.label2.Text =
                        "$199.95 per night";
                    //
                    // Form2
                    //
                    this.AutoScaleBaseSize =
                     new System.Drawing.Size(5, 13);
                    this.BackColor =
                        System.Drawing.Color.Yellow;
                    this.ClientSize = new
                     System.Drawing.Size(292, 273);
                    this.Controls.AddRange(new
                     System.Windows.Forms.Control[] {
                            this.label2,
                            this.label1});
                    this.Name = "Form2";
                    this.Text = "BelleAire Suite";
                    this.ResumeLayout(false);
                }
            #endregion
        }
}
// *********Form 3 begins here
using System;
using System.Drawing;
using System.Collections;
using System.ComponentModel;
using System.Windows.Forms;
namespace BedAndBreakfast
{
    /// <summary>
    /// Summary description for Form3.
    /// </summary>
    public class Form3 : System.Windows.Forms.Form
    {
        private System.Windows.Forms.Label label1;
        private System.Windows.Forms.Label label2;
```

Figure 10-18 BedAndBreakfast code (continued)

```
            private System.Windows.Forms.PictureBox
                pictureBox1;
/// <summary>
/// Required designer variable.
/// </summary>
private System.ComponentModel.Container
      components = null;
public Form3()
{
    //
    // Required for Windows Form
    // Designer support
    //
    InitializeComponent();

    //
    // TODO: Add any constructor code
    // after InitializeComponent call
    //
}

/// <summary>
/// Clean up any resources being used.
/// </summary>
protected override void
      Dispose( bool disposing )
{
    if( disposing )
    {
        if(components != null)
        {
            components.Dispose();
        }
    }
    base.Dispose( disposing );
}

#region Windows Form Designer generated code
/// <summary>
/// Required method for Designer support -
    /// do not modify
/// the contents of this method
///  with the code editor.
/// </summary>
private void InitializeComponent()
{
    System.Resources.ResourceManager
          resources= new
          System.Resources.ResourceManager
          type of(Form3));
      this.label1 = new
       System.Windows.Forms.Label();
```

Figure 10-18   BedAndBreakfast code (continued)

```
        this.label2 = new
         System.Windows.Forms.Label();
        this.pictureBox1 = new
            System.Windows.Forms.PictureBox();
        this.SuspendLayout();
        //
        // label1
        //
        this.label1.Location =
            new System.Drawing.Point(168, 16);
        this.label1.Name = "label1";
        this.label1.Size =
            new System.Drawing.Size(100, 56);
        this.label1.TabIndex = 0;
        this.label1.Text =
            "Return to the 1850s in this" +
            "lovely room with private bath";
        //
        // label2
        //
        this.label2.Location = new
            System.Drawing.Point(168, 112);
        this.label2.Name = "label2";
        this.label2.Size = new
            System.Drawing.Size(104, 32);
        this.label2.TabIndex = 1;
        this.label2.Text =
            "$110.00 per night";
        //
        // pictureBox1
        //
        this.pictureBox1.Image =
            ((System.Drawing.Bitmap)
            resources.GetObject
                ("pictureBox1.Image")));
        this.pictureBox1.Location =
            new System.Drawing.Point(0, 8);
        this.pictureBox1.Name = "pictureBox1";
        this.pictureBox1.Size = new
            System.Drawing.Size(152, 192);
        this.pictureBox1.TabIndex = 2;
        this.pictureBox1.TabStop = false;
        //
        // Form3
        //
        this.AutoScaleBaseSize = new
            System.Drawing.Size(5, 13);
        this.BackColor =
            System.Drawing.Color.White;
        this.ClientSize = new
            System.Drawing.Size(292, 273);
```

Figure 10-18   BedAndBreakfast code (continued)

10

```
            this.Controls.AddRange
                (new
                System.Windows.Forms.Control[]
                {  this.pictureBox1,
                        this.label2,
                        this.label1});
        this.Name = "Form3";
        this.Text = "Lincoln Room";
        this.ResumeLayout(false);
    }
    #endregion
}
}
```

Figure 10-18   BedAndBreakfast code (continued)

ADDING ListBox, CheckedListBox, AND ComboBox Controls TO A Form

Buttons, RadioButtons, and CheckBoxes represent a GUI family because they all descend from the ButtonBase class and they all share certain characteristics. Similarly, ListBox, ComboBox, and CheckedListBox objects descend from the same family—they all are list-type widgets that descend from ListControl. Of course, they are also Controls and so inherit properties such as Text and BackColor from the Control class. Other properties are more specific to list-type objects. Table 10-4 describes some commonly used ListBox properties.

Table 10-4   Frequently Used ListBox Properties

ListBox Property	Description
ScrollAlwaysVisible	Gets or sets a value indicating whether the vertical scroll bar is shown at all times
SelectedIndex	Gets or sets the zero-based index of the currently selected item in a ListBox
SelectedIndices	Gets a collection that contains the zero-based indices of all currently selected items in the ListBox
SelectedItem	Gets or sets the currently selected item in the ListBox
SelectedItems	Gets a collection containing the currently selected items in the ListBox
SelectionMode	Gets or sets the method in which items are selected in the ListBox
Sorted	Gets or sets a value indicating whether the items in the ListBox are sorted alphabetically
TopIndex	Gets or sets the index of the first visible item in the ListBox

The **ListBox** Control enables you to display a list of items that the user can select by clicking. With a **ListBox**, you can allow the user to make a single selection only or multiple selections by setting the **SelectionMode** property appropriately. For example, when the **SelectionMode** property is set to **One**, the user can make only a single selection from the **ListBox**. When the **SelectionMode** is set to **MultiExtended**, pressing Shift and clicking the mouse or pressing Shift and one of the arrow keys (up arrow, down arrow, left arrow, or right arrow) extends the selection to span from the previously selected item to the current item. Pressing Ctrl and clicking the mouse selects or deselects an item in the list. Table 10-5 lists the possible **SelectionMode** values.

Table 10-5   SelectionMode Enumeration List

Member Name	Description
MultiExtended	Multiple items can be selected, and the user can press the Shift, Ctrl, and arrow keys to make selections
MultiSimple	Multiple items can be selected
None	No items can be selected
One	Only one item can be selected

In the next steps, you will create an application for a doctor's office appointment manager. You will create three **ListBox** items by hand to demonstrate how the **SelectionMode**s operate. Later in the chapter, you will use the IDE to create another application containing a **ListBox**.

1. Open a new file in your text editor. Type the beginning of a program that will contain a main **Form** with three **ListBox** controls and a **Label**.

```
using System;
using System.Windows.Forms;
public class FormWithListBoxes : Form
{
    ListBox listBox1 = new ListBox();
    ListBox listBox2 = new ListBox();
    ListBox listBox3 = new ListBox();
    Label label1 = new Label();
```

2. Add the beginning of the FormWithListBoxes constructor by setting the Size and Text properties of the Form and adding instructions to the Label.

```
public FormWithListBoxes()
{
    this.Size = new System.Drawing.Size(600,300);
    this.Text = "Appointment Manager";
    label1.Text = "Select the doctor you want to see" +
        "\nand all dates and times you are available.";
```

3. Set the Label's Size property and its Location value. Next, add all four Control objects—the Label and the three ListBox items—to the Form.

```
this.label1.Size = new System.Drawing.Size(250,24);
this.label1.Location = new System.Drawing.Point(30,20);
this.Controls.AddRange
    (new System.Windows.Forms.Control[]
    {this.label1, this.listBox1, this.listBox2,
    this.listBox3});
```

4. Locate the three ListBox objects as follows:

```
this.listBox1.Location = new System.Drawing.Point(30,70);
this.listBox2.Location = new System.Drawing.Point(160,70);
this.listBox3.Location = new System.Drawing.Point(290,70);
```

5. To demonstrate SelectionMode.One, assume the user can select only one doctor to see. To demonstrate SelectionMode.MultiExtended, assume the user can select multiple dates and times.

```
this.listBox1.SelectionMode =
    System.Windows.Forms.SelectionMode.One;
this.listBox2.SelectionMode =
    System.Windows.Forms.SelectionMode.MultiExtended;
this.listBox3.SelectionMode =
    System.Windows.Forms.SelectionMode.MultiExtended;
```

6. One way to add items to a ListBox is by using the Add() method to include one string at a time. Use this method to populate listBox1 as follows:

```
this.listBox1.Items.Add("Harris");
this.listBox1.Items.Add("Scaffoldi");
this.listBox1.Items.Add("Patel");
```

7. Another way to add items to a ListBox is by using a loop. Use this approach to add each of the 31 dates in the month of March for listBox2:

```
for(int date = 1; date < 32; ++date)
    this.listBox2.Items.Add("March " + date.ToString());
```

8. Another possibility is to use the AddRange() method to add an array of objects to a ListBox. You can use this approach to include a list of available appointment times within listBox3.

```
this.listBox3.Items.AddRange(new object[]
    {"9am","10am","noon", "2pm"});
```

9. Add the closing curly brace for the FormWithListBoxes constructor method.

10. Add the Main() method that runs the application to the class.

```
public static void Main()
{
    Application.Run(new FormWithListBoxes());
}
```

11. As the last line in the file, add a closing curly brace for the class.

12. Save the file as **FormWithListBoxes.cs** in the Chapter.10 folder on your Student Disk. Then compile and execute the program. For reference, Figure 10-19 shows the complete program. Figure 10-20 shows the output.

```
using System;
using System.Windows.Forms;
public class FormWithListBoxes : Form
{
        ListBox listBox1 = new ListBox();
        ListBox listBox2 = new ListBox();
        ListBox listBox3 = new ListBox();
        Label label1 = new Label();
        public FormWithListBoxes()
        {
                this.Size = new System.Drawing.Size(600,300);
                this.Text = "Appointment Manager";
                label1.Text = "Select the doctor you want to see" +
                        "\nand all dates and times you are available.";
                this.label1.Size = new System.Drawing.Size(250,24);
                this.label1.Location = new System.Drawing.Point(30,20);
                this.Controls.AddRange(new System.Windows.Forms.Control[]
                        {this.label1, this.listBox1, this.listBox2, this.listBox3});
                this.listBox1.Location = new System.Drawing.Point(30,70);
                this.listBox2.Location = new System.Drawing.Point(160,70);
                this.listBox3.Location = new System.Drawing.Point(290,70);
                this.listBox1.SelectionMode =
                        System.Windows.Forms.SelectionMode.One;
                this.listBox2.SelectionMode =
                        System.Windows.Forms.SelectionMode.MultiExtended;
                this.listBox3.SelectionMode =
                        System.Windows.Forms.SelectionMode.MultiExtended;
                this.listBox1.Items.Add("Harris");
                this.listBox1.Items.Add("Scaffoldi");
                this.listBox1.Items.Add("Patel");
                for(int date = 1; date < 32; ++date)
                        this.listBox2.Items.Add("March " + date.ToString());
                this.listBox3.Items.AddRange(new object[]
                        {"9am","10am","noon", "2pm"});
        }
        public static void Main()
        {
                Application.Run(new FormWithListBoxes());
        }
}
```

Figure 10-19   FormWithListBoxes class

10

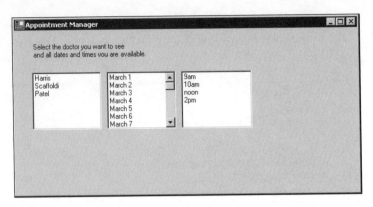

Figure 10-20   Output of `FormWithListBoxes`

13. Experiment by making selections from the `ListBox` objects. For example, select a doctor, then hold down the **Ctrl** key and select a different doctor. Because this `ListBox`'s `SelectionMode` is `One`, only the last option remains selected. Next, select a date, then hold down the **Ctrl** key and select another date. Because this `ListBox`'s `SelectionMode` is `MultiExtended`, multiple selections can be made. Similarly, if you select a date or time, and then hold down the **Shift** key and select another item from the same `ListBox`, every item between the two endpoints will also be selected.

14. You have not written any code to take action when the user makes selections from these `ListBox` items, so close the `Form`.

The `ListBox` also provides the Boolean `MultiColumn` property, which you can set to display items in columns instead of a straight vertical list. This approach allows the control to display more visible items and avoids the need for the user to scroll down to an item.

A **ComboBox** is similar to a `ListBox`, except that it displays an additional editing field allowing the user to select from the list or to enter new text. The default `ComboBox` displays an editing field with a hidden list box. A **CheckedListBox** is also similar to a `ListBox`, with check boxes appearing to the left of each desired item.

ADDING FUNCTIONALITY TO A `ListBox` WITH ONE `SelectedItem`

The `SelectedItem` property of a `ListBox` contains the value of the item a user has selected. As with the other `Controls`, it is easiest to write a complete application that uses a `ListBox` or its close relatives through the Visual Studio IDE. In fact, an excellent way to learn how to hand-code applications is to create them visually within the

IDE and then examine the generated code. In the next steps, you will create an application for Hemingway Homes, a home-building company that offers several options in new homes.

1. Open Visual Studio .NET, and then open a new Windows Application in the Chapter.10 folder on your Student Disk. Name the project **HemingwayHomes**.

2. When the main Form appears, change the Text property to **Hemingway Homes**. See Figure 10-21.

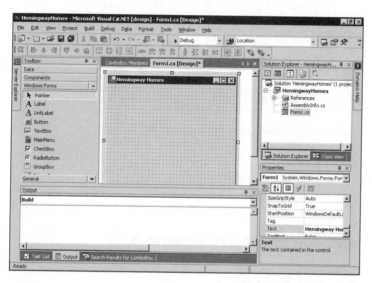

Figure 10-21   Main Form for HemingwayHomes application

3. From the list of available Controls shown at the left side of the IDE, drag a Label onto the Form's surface and position it approximately as shown in Figure 10-22. (In Figure 10-22 the precise values for Location are 32, 16 and for Size are 216, 24.) Change the Text value to **Select your new home's options**.

4. Drag a second Label onto the Form and set its Text to an empty string by deleting the default text in the Properties box. (The exact Location of label2 in Figure 10-22 is 192, 176; the exact Size is 80, 96.)

5. Drag a ListBox onto the Form as shown in Figure 10-23.

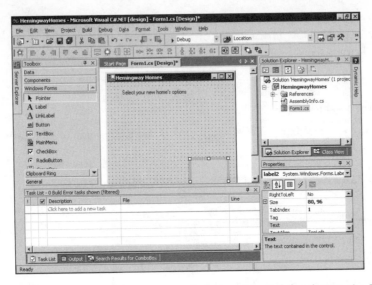

Figure 10-22 HemingwayHomes Form containing two Labels

6. In the ListBox Properties list, locate Items and click the ellipsis following Collection. A String Collection Editor appears. The String Collection Editor makes it easy for you to add options to a ListBox—you can type options, one string per line, into the editor as shown in Figure 10-24.

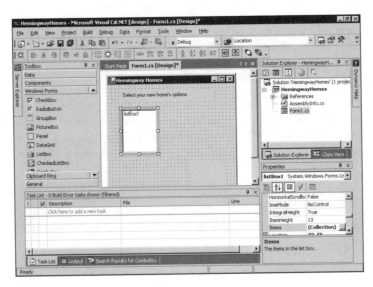

Figure 10-23 ListBox on HemingwayHomes Form

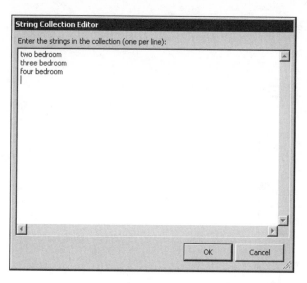

Figure 10-24   Using the String Collection Editor to type **ListBox** options

7. When you have finished typing the list of strings in the editor, click **OK**. Next, click **View** on the IDE menu bar and then click **Code**. The code for the listBox1.AddRange() method appears as follows. It is the same list of strings you could have created by hand. (You might need to expand the code.)

```
this.listBox1.Items.AddRange(new object[] {

    "two bedroom",

    "three bedroom",

    "four bedroom"});
```

8. Choose the **Designer** view, and adjust the size of the **ListBox** until it shows all the options you entered.

9. Double-click the **ListBox** to view the code for the listBox1_Selected IndexChanged() method. This method will execute each time the user changes the selection in the **ListBox**. The empty method appears as follows:

```
private void listBox1_SelectedIndexChanged
    (object sender, System.EventArgs e)
        {

        }
```

A **ListBox**'s **SelectedItem** property contains the value of the currently selected item. When the user changes a selection, you can display this information by adding the following statement between the curly braces of the listBox1_SelectedIndexChanged() method:

```
label2.Text = "You selected a " +
    listBox1.SelectedItem + " home";
```

10. Click the **Save All** button, and then execute the application. Select an option from the `ListBox`, and the `Label` shows the appropriate result. See Figure 10-25.

Figure 10-25   Selecting a `ListBox` option to change a `Label`

11. Dismiss the `Form`.

ADDING FUNCTIONALITY TO A `ListBox` WITH MULTIPLE `SelectedItems`

When you create a `ListBox`, by default its `SelectionMode` is `One`. For example, the Hemingway Homes `ListBox` allows you to select a number of bedrooms; if you make one choice and then make a second choice, the last choice replaces the previous choice. Only one `SelectedItem` can exist at a time, and you can access that item's value by using the `SelectedItem` property. When a `ListBox` mode allows for more than one selection, the procedure for handling the selections becomes slightly more complex. Instead of a `SelectedItem` field, you use a **`SelectedItems`** array that contains a list of all currently selected item names. You access each `SelectedItems` element in the same way you access any other array element—with square brackets and a subscript. For example, the first selected item in a `ListBox` named `listBox1` is `listBox1.SelectedItems[0]`. You can determine how many items are selected by using the **`SelectedItems.Count`** field, which will always hold a value ranging from 0 to the total number of items in the list.

In the next steps, you will add a `ListBox` with `MultiExtendedMode` to the Hemingway Homes `Form`.

1. In the Visual Studio IDE, return to the **Designer** view for the Hemingway Homes `Form`.

2. Drag a new `ListBox` just to the right of the `ListBox` containing the bedroom options. (The `ListBox` shown in Figure 10-27 is in `Location` 168, 56 and its `Size` is 96, 69. Your `Location` and `Size` values do not have to match exactly. If your `ListBox` obscures your `Label`, move one or both.)

3. Select the second `ListBox` and click `Items (Collection)` from its Properties list. Using the String Collection Editor, add the options shown in Figure 10-26; and then click **OK**.

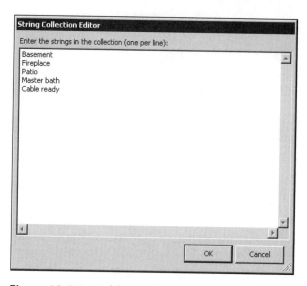

Figure 10-26   Adding options to the String Collection Editor for the second `ListBox`

4. Users will be allowed to select as many options as they want from this second `ListBox`. In the `ListBox`'s Properties list, change the `SelectionMode` to **`MultiExtended`**.

5. When the user chooses a bedroom option from the `ListBox` on the left, each new selection replaces the previous one. Because the user can continuously select and deselect multiple items from the `ListBox` on the right, you can choose to not make the group of selections "final" until the user clicks a button to signal acceptance of the completed option list. Drag a `Button` onto the `Form` (see Figure 10-27 for its approximate placement), change the `Text` property of the `Button` to **Press when ready**, and adjust the size of the `Button` if necessary until you can read all of the `Button`'s `Text`. (The `Button` in Figure 10-27 has `Location` 24, 184 and its `Size` is 104, 24.)

6. Double-click the `Button` to view the code for the `button1_Click()` method that will execute when the user clicks the `Button`. Its shell appears as follows:

```
private void button1_Click
    (object sender, System.EventArgs e)
{
}
```

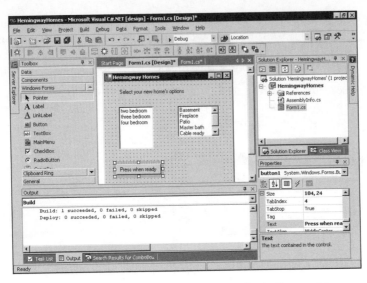

Figure 10-27   Hemingway Homes Form including Button

Within the method, you can add a loop that accesses each item in the ListBox's SelectedItems array. When you vary a subscript from 0 to the Count of SelectedItems, you access each in turn. In this example, you add a new line and each selected string to the Label that currently displays the bedroom selection.

```
for(int x = 0;
    x < listBox2.SelectedItems.Count; ++x)
    label2.Text += "\n" +
        listBox2.SelectedItems[x].ToString();
```

Because the SelectedItems are strings, when creating the Label you can omit the ToString() method call associated with each SelectedItems array element. It is included here for clarity and completeness.

By convention, C# method names begin with an uppercase letter. The button1_Click() method that the IDE automatically creates begins with a lowercase letter to match the style used in the name of the button1 object.

7. Click the **Save All** button and execute the program. Select a bedroom option and observe the change in the Label, then select multiple additional features and click the Button when you are done. For example, Figure 10-28 shows the result when Basement, Patio, and Master bath are selected—each is added to the Label.

8. Close the Form.

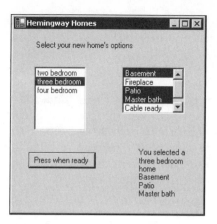

Figure 10-28   Selecting multiple options and observing the changes in the Label

SUPPLYING A DEFAULT SELECTION FOR A ListBox

When you execute a program containing a ListBox, at first no items are selected; high-lighting appears within a ListBox only after you click an option. Instead of waiting for a user to click a control, you can force an item to be the default, or currently selected, item by using the SetSelected() method. The SetSelected() method requires two arguments—the position of the item to select, and one of the two Boolean values true and false. The position of the item to select is the array index of the item; there-fore, positions that can be legally selected are 0 through one less than the Count of items selected. For example, you can select the first item in a ListBox named listBox1 with the statement listBox1.SetSelected(0, true);.

When you execute the Hemingway Homes program as it stands now, you can select only one bedroom option but any number of other options. However, when the Button is clicked, the user has not necessarily selected any options at all. Suppose you want to dis-play the price of a Hemingway Home when the user clicks the Button. In that case, a base price should be provided even when the user has not selected anything. Additionally, even if the user has selected home options such as a fireplace or patio, you might want to assume that the home will contain some number of bedrooms.

In the next steps, you will add a price variable to the Hemingway Homes application and display the price when the user clicks the Button. You will assume that a two-bedroom home's base price is $90,000. A third bedroom adds $15,000 to the base price, and a fourth bedroom adds $22,000 to the base price. If the user has not selected a bed-room option, the program will assume the home contains two bedrooms.

1. Within the Visual Studio IDE, view the code for the Hemingway Homes application.

10

2. The base price for a Hemingway Home is $90,000. Near the beginning of the code, immediately after the declaration for **button1**, add a variable for the price as follows:

```
int price = 90000;
```

3. As the first statement within the **button1_Click()** method, add an **if** statement that determines whether any bedroom options have been selected. If not, inform the user that the two-bedroom option has become the default selection. You also can use the **SetSelected()** method to highlight the first item in **listBox1**. When no items are selected in the bedroom option **ListBox**, the home price will be the initial value of $90,000.

```
if(listBox1.SelectedItems.Count == 0)
{
   label2.Text =
       "Two bedroom option selected by default";
   listBox1.SetSelected(0,true);
}
```

4. Add an **else** clause that executes when the user has selected a bedroom option. If the user has selected two bedrooms, there still is no need to alter the original price. If the user has selected the second or third option in the bedrooms **ListBox** (position 1 or 2), however, then 15,000 or 22,000 is added to the base price, respectively.

```
else
    if(listBox1.SelectedItem.Equals(listBox1.Items[1]))
            price += 15000;
    else
            price += 22000;
```

5. As the last statement in the **button1_Click()** method, add the price to the display contained within **label2**. Include formatting so the price appears as currency with no decimals.

```
label2.Text += "\n" + price.ToString("C0");
```

6. Click the **Save All** button, and then execute the program. Make any selections you like and confirm that the program operates correctly when you click the **Button**. Figure 10-29 shows a typical execution. Execute the program at least once without selecting a bedroom option and confirm that it assumes the default two-bedroom option when no choices are selected from the bedroom option **ListBox**. For reference, Figure 10-30 shows the complete Hemingway Homes application.

7. Close the **Form** and close Visual Studio.

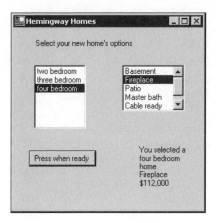

Figure 10-29   Typical execution of Hemingway Homes application

```
using System;
using System.Drawing;
using System.Collections;
using System.ComponentModel;
using System.Windows.Forms;
using System.Data;
namespace HemingwayHomes
{
    /// <summary>
    /// Summary description for Form1.
    /// </summary>
    public class Form1 : System.Windows.Forms.Form
    {
        private System.Windows.Forms.Label
            label1;
        private System.Windows.Forms.Label
            label2;
        private System.Windows.Forms.ListBox
            listBox1;
        private System.Windows.Forms.ListBox
            listBox2;
        private System.Windows.Forms.Button
            button1;
        int price = 90000;
        /// <summary>
        /// Required designer variable.
        /// </summary>
        private System.ComponentModel.Container
            components = null;
        public Form1()
        {
            //
            // Required for Windows Form
```

Figure 10-30   HemingwayHomes application code

```
        // Designer support
        //
        InitializeComponent();
        //
        // TODO: Add any constructor code
        // after InitializeComponent call
        //
    }
    /// <summary>
    /// Clean up any resources being used.
    /// </summary>
    protected override void
        Dispose( bool disposing )
    {
        if( disposing )
        {
            if (components != null)
            {
                components.Dispose();
            }
        }
         base.Dispose( disposing );
    }

    #region Windows Form Designer generated code
    /// <summary>
    /// Required method for Designer support
    /// - do not modify
    /// the contents of this method with
    /// the code editor.
    /// </summary>
    private void InitializeComponent()
    {
        this.label1 = new
            System.Windows.Forms.Label();
        this.label2 = new
            System.Windows.Forms.Label();
        this.listBox1 = new
            System.Windows.Forms.ListBox();
        this.listBox2 = new
            System.Windows.Forms.ListBox();
        this.button1 = new
            System.Windows.Forms.Button();
        this.SuspendLayout();
        //
        // label1
        //
        this.label1.Location = new
            System.Drawing.Point(32, 16);
        this.label1.Name = "label1";
```

Figure 10-30   HemingwayHomes application code (continued)

```
                    this.label1.Size = new
                        System.Drawing.Size(216, 24);
                    this.label1.TabIndex = 0;
                    this.label1.Text =
                      "Select your new home\'s options";
                    //
                    // label2
                    //
                    this.label2.Location = new
                        System.Drawing.Point(192, 176);
                    this.label2.Name = "label2";
                    this.label2.Size = new
                        System.Drawing.Size(80, 96);
                    this.label2.TabIndex = 1;
                    //
                    // listBox1
                    //
                    this.listBox1.Items.AddRange
                        (new object[] {
                        "two bedroom",
                        "three bedroom",
                        "four bedroom"});
                    this.listBox1.Location = new
                        System.Drawing.Point(32, 56);
                    this.listBox1.Name = "listBox1";
                    this.listBox1.Size = new
                        System.Drawing.Size(80, 95);
                    this.listBox1.TabIndex = 2;
                    this.listBox1.SelectedIndexChanged +=
                        new System.EventHandler
                    (this.listBox1_SelectedIndexChanged);
                    //
                    // listBox2
                    //
                    this.listBox2.Items.AddRange
                    (new object[] {
                        "Basement",
                        "Fireplace",
                        "Patio",
                        "Master bath",
                        "Cable ready",""});
                    this.listBox2.Location = new
                        System.Drawing.Point(168, 56);
                    this.listBox2.Name = "listBox2";
                    this.listBox2.SelectionMode =
                    System.Windows.Forms.SelectionMode.MultiExtended;
                    this.listBox2.Size = new
                        System.Drawing.Size(96, 69);
                    this.listBox2.TabIndex = 3;
                    //
                    // button1
                    //
```

10

Figure 10-30   HemingwayHomes application code (continued)

```
            this.button1.Location = new
                System.Drawing.Point(24, 184);
            this.button1.Name = "button1";
            this.button1.Size = new
                System.Drawing.Size(104, 24);
            this.button1.TabIndex = 4;
            this.button1.Text =
                "Press when ready";
            this.button1.Click += new
                System.EventHandler
                    (this.button1_Click);
            //
            // Form1
            //
            this.AutoScaleBaseSize = new
                System.Drawing.Size(5, 13);
            this.ClientSize = new
                System.Drawing.Size(292, 273);
            this.Controls.AddRange
            (new System.Windows.Forms.Control[]
                    {
                    this.button1,
                    this.listBox2,
                    this.listBox1,
                    this.label2,
                    this.label1});
            this.Name = "Form1";
            this.Text = "Hemingway Homes";
            this.ResumeLayout(false);
        }
        #endregion
        /// <summary>
        /// The main entry point
        /// for the application.
        /// </summary>
        [STAThread]
        static void Main()
        {
            Application.Run(new Form1());
        }
        private void listBox1_SelectedIndexChanged
            (object sender, System.EventArgs e)
        {
            label2.Text =
                "You selected a " +
                listBox1.SelectedItem + " home";
        }
        private void button1_Click
            (object sender, System.EventArgs e)
        {
            if(listBox1.SelectedItems.Count == 0)
```

Figure 10-30   HemingwayHomes application code (continued)

```
                    {
                        label2.Text = "Two bedroom " +
                        "option selected by default";
                        listBox1.SetSelected(0,true);
                    }
                    else
                    if(listBox1.SelectedItem.Equals
                        (listBox1.Items[1]))
                        price += 15000;
                    else price += 22000;
                    for(int x = 0;
                        x < listBox2.SelectedItems.Count;
                        ++x)
                        label2.Text += "\n" +
                    listBox2.SelectedItems[x].ToString();
                    label2.Text += "\n" +
                        price.ToString("C0");
                }
            }
        }
```

Figure 10-30   `HemingwayHomes` application code (continued)

10

CHAPTER SUMMARY

- ❑ The `Control` class provides the definitions for GUI objects. All `Control`s are `Objects`, `MarshalByRefObjects`, and `Containers`. Some `Control` properties include `BackColor`, `Size`, and `Location`.

- ❑ Typically, you use a `Label` control to provide descriptive text for another `Control` object.

- ❑ You use the `Font` class to change the appearance of printed text on `Forms`. The `Font` class has a number of overloaded constructors, including one that accepts a font type and size and another that accepts a font, size, and style.

- ❑ The `Color` class contains a wide variety of predefined `Colors` that you can use with your `Controls`.

- ❑ The `Button`, `CheckBox`, and `RadioButton` classes all descend from `ButtonBase`. `CheckBox` objects are GUI widgets that the user can click to select or deselect an option. `RadioButtons` are similar to `CheckBoxes`, except that when they are placed on a `Form`, only one `RadioButton` can be selected at a time—that is, selecting any `RadioButton` automatically deselects the others. You can place multiple groups of `RadioButtons` on a `Form` by using a `GroupBox`.

- ❑ A `PictureBox` is a `Control` in which you can display graphics from a bitmap, icon, JPEG, GIF, or other image file type.

❏ `ListBox`, `ComboBox`, and `CheckedListBox` objects descend from the same family—these list-type widgets all descend from `ListControl`. The `ListBox Control` enables you to display a list of items that the user can select by clicking. With a `ListBox`, you can allow the user to make a single selection only or multiple selections by setting the `SelectionMode` property appropriately. A `ComboBox` is similar to a `ListBox`, except that it displays an additional editing field allowing the user to select from the list or to enter new text. A `CheckedListBox` is also similar to a `ListBox`, with check boxes appearing to the left of each desired item.

❏ The `SelectedItem` property of a `ListBox` contains the value of the item a user has selected.

❏ When a `ListBox` mode allows for more than one selection, instead of a `SelectedItem` field, you use a `SelectedItems` array that contains a list of all currently selected item names. You can determine how many items are selected by using the `SelectedItems.Count` field.

❏ Instead of waiting for a user to click a control, you can force a `ListBox` item to be the default, or currently selected, item by using the `SetSelected()` method.

REVIEW QUESTIONS

1. `Labels`, `Buttons`, and `CheckBoxes` are all _____.

   a. GUI objects

   b. `Controls`

   c. widgets

   d. all of these

2. All `Control` objects descend from _____.

   a. `Form`

   b. `Component`

   c. `ButtonBase`

   d. all of these

3. Of the following, which is the closest relative to a `RadioButton`?

   a. `ListControl`

   b. `CheckedListBox`

   c. `PictureBox`

   d. `Button`

4. Which is not a commonly used `Control` property?

   a. `BackColor`

   b. `Language`

   c. `Location`

   d. `Size`

5. The `Control` you use to provide descriptive text for another `Control` object is a _____.

   a. `Form`

   b. `Label`

   c. `CheckBox`

   d. `MessageBox`

6. Which of the following creates a `Label` named `firstLabel`?

   a. `firstLabel = new firstLabel();`

   b. `Label = new firstLabel();`

   c. `Label firstLabel = new Label();`

   d. `Label firstLabel = Label();`

7. The property that determines what the user reads on a `Label` is the _____ property.

   a. `Text`

   b. `Label`

   c. `Phrase`

   d. `Setting`

8. Which of the following correctly creates a `Font`?

   a. `Font myFont = new Font("Arial", 14F, FontStyle.Bold);`

   b. `Font myFont = new Font("Courier", 13.6);`

   c. `myFont = Font new Font("TimesRoman", FontStyle.Italic);`

   d. `Font myFont = Font(20, "Helvetica", Underlined);`

9. Which of the following is not a predefined `Color` property in Visual Studio?

   a. `Black`

   b. `Rembrandt`

   c. `Gainsboro`

   d. `Bisque`

10. Assume you have created a `Label` named `myLabel`. Which of the following sets `myLabel`'s background color to green?

    a. `myLabel = BackColor.System.Drawing.Color.Green;`

    b. `myLabel.BackColor = System.Drawing.Color.Green;`

    c. `myLabel.Green = System.DrawingColor;`

    d. `myLabel.Background = new Color.Green;`

10

11. A difference between CheckBox and RadioButton objects is _____.

    a. RadioButtons descend from ButtonBase; CheckBoxes do not

    b. only one RadioButton can be selected at a time

    c. only one CheckBox can appear on a Form at a time

    d. RadioButtons cannot be placed in a GroupBox; CheckBoxes can

12. The Checked property of a RadioButton can hold the values _____.

    a. true and false

    b. Checked and Unchecked

    c. 0 and 1

    d. Yes, No, and Undetermined

13. The Control in which you can display a bitmap or JPEG image is a(n) _____.

    a. DisplayModule

    b. ImageHolder

    c. BitmapControl

    d. PictureBox

14. ListBox, ComboBox, and CheckedListBox objects descend from the same family: _____.

    a. ListControl

    b. List

    c. ButtonBase

    d. ListBase

15. Which of the following properties is associated with a ListBox but not a Button?

    a. BackColor

    b. SelectedItem

    c. Location

    d. IsSelected

16. With a ListBox you can allow the user to choose _____.

    a. only a single option

    b. multiple selections

    c. either of these

    d. none of these

17. You can add items to a `ListBox` by using the _____ method.

    a. `Add( )`

    b. `Append( )`

    c. `List( )`

    d. `AddRange( )`

18. A `ListBox`'s `SelectedItem` property contains _____.

    a. the position of the currently selected item

    b. the value of the currently selected item

    c. a Boolean value indicating whether an item is currently selected

    d. a count of the number of currently selected items

19. When you create a `ListBox`, by default its `SelectionMode` is _____.

    a. `Simple`

    b. `MultiExtended`

    c. `One`

    d. `false`

20. A `ListBox`'s `SelectedItems` field is a(n) _____.

    a. integer

    b. `Boolean` value

    c. array of integers

    d. array of `strings`

10

EXERCISES

Save the programs that you create in these Exercises in the Chapter.10 folder on your Student Disk.

1. Create a `Form` containing two `Button`s, one labeled Stop and one labeled Go. Add a `Label` telling the user to click a button. When the user clicks Stop, change the `BackColor` of the `Form` to Red; when the user clicks Go, change the `BackColor` of the `Form` to Green. Save the program as **StopGo.cs**.

2. Create a `Form` containing at least five `RadioButton` objects, each labeled with a color. When the user clicks a `RadioButton`, change the `BackColor` of the `Form` appropriately. Save the program as **FiveColors.cs**.

3. Create a `Form` for a video store containing a `ListBox` that lists the titles of at least eight videos available to rent. Allow users to select as many videos as they want. When the user clicks a `Button` indicating the choices are final, display the total rental price, which is $2.50 per video. Save the file as **Video.cs**.

4. Create a `Form` with two `ListBox`es—one contains at least four `Font` names and the other contains at least four `Font` sizes. Let the first item in each list be the default selection if the user fails to make a selection. After the user clicks a `Button`, display "Hello" in the selected `Font` and size. Save the program as **FontSelector.cs**.

5. Create a `Form` for a car rental company. Allow the user to choose a car model (compact, standard, or luxury) and a number of days (1 through 7). After the user makes the desired selections, display the total rental charge, which is $19.95 per day for a compact car, $24.95 per day for a standard car, and $39.00 per day for a luxury car. Save the file as **CarRental.cs**.

6. Create a `Form` for a restaurant. Allow the user to choose from at least three options in each of the following categories—appetizer, entrée, vegetable, dessert. Assign a different price to each selection and display the total when the user clicks a `Button`. Save the file as **Restaurant.cs**.

7. Create a `Form` for an automobile dealer. Include options for at least three car models. After users make a selection, proceed to a new `Form` containing information about the selected model. Save the program as **CarDealer.cs**.

8. Each of the following files in the Chapter.10 folder on your Student Disk has syntax and/or logical errors. In each case, determine the problem and fix the program. After you correct the errors, save each file using the same filename preceded with *Fixed*. For example, DebugTen1.cs will become FixedDebugTen1.cs.

   a. DebugTen1.cs

   b. DebugTen2.cs

   c. DebugTen3.cs

   d. DebugTen4.cs

CHAPTER 11

HANDLING EVENTS

In this chapter you will learn:

♦ About delegates

♦ How to create composed delegates

♦ How to handle events

♦ How to use the built-in `EventHandler`

♦ How to handle `Control` component events

♦ How to add more events to an application

♦ How to use the Visual Studio IDE to generate event-handling code

♦ How to set `Controls'` tab order

♦ How to use the `sender` object in an event

♦ How to add a main menu to a `Form`

♦ How to continue your exploration of C#

Throughout this book, you have learned how to create C# programs that perform a variety of tasks. In the last few chapters, you expanded your repertoire from creating functional but dull-looking command-line applications to creating attractive and interactive GUI windows.

The aspect of Windows widgets that makes them useful is their ability to cause events when a user interacts with them. An event is a message sent by an object to signal the occurrence of an action—for example, a mouse click. The object that triggers the event (for example, a button) is called the event sender. The object that captures the event and responds to it (for example, a specific method) is called the event receiver. In the .NET framework, a delegate is an object that acts as an intermediary in transferring the message from the source to the receiver. In this chapter you will learn how to create delegates and manage interactive events.

UNDERSTANDING DELEGATES

A **delegate** is an object that contains a reference to a method; object-oriented programmers would say that a delegate encapsulates a method. In government, a delegate is a representative that you authorize to make choices for you—for example, you select a delegate to a presidential nominating convention. When human delegates arrive at a convention, they are free to make choices based on current conditions. Similarly, C# delegates provide a way for a program to take alternative courses when running. When you write a method you don't always know which actions will occur, so you give your delegates authority to run the correct methods.

In Chapter 1, you learned that encapsulation is one of the basic features of object-oriented programming. Recall that encapsulation is the technique of packaging an object's attributes and methods into a cohesive unit that can then be used as an undivided entity.

After you have declared a C# delegate, you can pass this object to a method, which then can call the method referenced within the delegate. In other words, a delegate provides a way to pass a reference to a method as an argument to another method. For example, if d is a delegate containing a reference to the method m1(), then you can pass d to a new method named MyMethod(). Alternatively, you could create a delegate named d containing a reference to a method named m2() and then pass this version to MyMethod(). When you write MyMethod(), you don't have to know whether it will call m1() or m2(); you need know only that it will call whichever method is referenced within d.

A C# delegate is similar to a function pointer in C++. A function pointer is a variable that holds a method's memory address. In the C++ programming language, you pass a method's address to another method using a pointer variable. The Java programming language does not allow function pointers because they are dangerous—if the program alters the address, you might inadvertently execute the wrong method. C# provides a compromise between the dangers of C++ pointers and the Java ban on passing functions. Delegates allow flexible method calls but remain secure because you cannot alter the method addresses.

You declare a delegate using the keyword **delegate**, followed by an ordinary method declaration including a return type, method name, and argument list. For example, you can declare a delegate named **GreetingDelegate()** that accepts a **string** argument and returns nothing with the following statement:

```
delegate void GreetingDelegate(string s);
```

The **GreetingDelegate** can encapsulate any method as long as it has a **void** return type and a single **string** argument. After declaring the delegate, when you write a method with the same return type and argument list, you can assign it to the delegate. For example, the following `Hello()` method is a `void` method that takes a `string` argument:

```
public static void Hello(string s)
{
        Console.WriteLine("Hello, {0}!", s);
}
```

Because the `Hello()` method matches the `GreetingDelegate` definition, you can assign a reference to the `Hello()` method to a new instance of `GreetingDelegate` as follows:

```
GreetingDelegate myDel = new GreetingDelegate(Hello);
```

Once the `Hello()` method is assigned to `myDel`, then each of the following statements will result in the same output: `Hello, Kim!`.

```
Hello("Kim");
myDel("Kim");
```

To demonstrate how delegates work, in the next steps you will create two delegate instances and assign different method references to them.

1. Open a new file in your text editor. Type the necessary `using` statement, then create a delegate that encapsulates a `void` method that accepts a `string` argument:

```
using System;
delegate void GreetingDelegate(string s);
```

2. Begin creating a `GreetingClass` containing a `void Hello()` method that accepts a `string` parameter and uses it in a greeting.

```
class GreetingClass
{
    public static void Hello(string s)
    {
            Console.WriteLine("Hello, {0}!", s);
}
```

3. Add a `void Goodbye()` method that also accepts a `string` parameter and uses it in a greeting.

```
public static void Goodbye(string s)
{
   Console.WriteLine("Goodbye, {0}!", s);
}
```

4. Write a `Main()` method that declares two `GreetingDelegate` objects named `firstDel` and `secondDel`. Assign a reference to the `Hello()` method to one object and a reference to the `Goodbye()` method to the other object. Then call each delegate using a different string.

11

```
public static void Main()
{
    GreetingDelegate firstDel, secondDel;
    firstDel = new GreetingDelegate(Hello);
    secondDel = new GreetingDelegate(Goodbye);
    firstDel("Angela");
    secondDel("Brian");
}
```

5. Add a closing curly brace for the class. Save the file as **Delegate1.cs**, and then compile and execute it. Figure 11-1 shows the results.

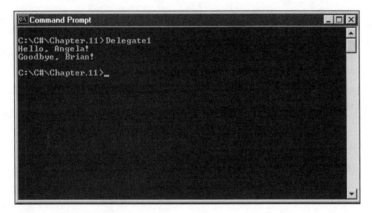

Figure 11-1   Output of Delegate1 program

The ability to use the delegates firstDel and secondDel in the Delegate1 program does not seem to provide any benefits over using regular method calls to Hello() and Goodbye(). If you have a program in which you pass the delegate to a method, however, the method becomes more flexible; you gain the ability to send a reference to an appropriate method you want to execute at the time. In the next steps, you will alter the Delegate1 program so that you can observe how to pass different delegates to the same method.

1. Open the **Delegate1** file in your text editor. Immediately save it as **Delegate2.cs**.

2. Within the Main() method, delete the two statements that use the delegates:

```
firstDel("Angela");
secondDel("Brian");
```

Replace these statements with two separate calls to a method named GreetMethod(). The GreetMethod() will accept two parameters—a reference to a GreetingDelegate and a string—and use the string in a call to the method represented by the delegate.

```
GreetMethod(firstDel, "Cathy");
GreetMethod(secondDel, "Bob");
```

3. Position your cursor after the closing curly brace for the `Main()` method but before the closing curly brace for the `GreetingClass`. Insert the following `GreetMethod()` that accepts a `delegate` and a `string`, then calls the appropriate method using the `string`.

```
public static void GreetMethod
   (GreetingDelegate gd, string name)
{
  Console.WriteLine("The greeting is:");
  gd(name);
}
```

4. Save the program; and then compile and execute it. For reference, Figure 11-2 shows the complete program. Figure 11-3 shows the output. `GreetMethod()` can receive a reference to any method that has the proper return type and argument list. When you write a method that calls `GreetMethod()`, you can pass it any appropriate delegate to use.

```
using System;
delegate void GreetingDelegate(string s);
class GreetingClass
{
      public static void Hello(string s)
      {
            Console.WriteLine("Hello, {0}!", s);
      }
      public static void Goodbye(string s)
      {
            Console.WriteLine("Goodbye, {0}!", s);
      }
      public static void Main()
      {
            GreetingDelegate firstDel, secondDel;
            firstDel = new GreetingDelegate(Hello);
            secondDel = new GreetingDelegate(Goodbye);
            GreetMethod(firstDel, "Cathy");
            GreetMethod(secondDel, "Bob");
      }
      public static void GreetMethod
        (GreetingDelegate gd, string name)
      {
            Console.WriteLine("The greeting is:");
            gd(name);
      }
}
```

Figure 11-2   `Delegate2 program`

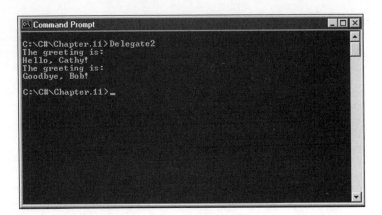

Figure 11-3   Output of `Delegate2` program

CREATING COMPOSED DELEGATES

You can assign one delegate to another using the = operator. You also can use the + and += operators to combine delegates into a **composed delegate** that calls the delegates from which it is built. As an example, assume that you declare three delegates (with the same argument lists) named `del1`, `del2`, and `del3`, and that you assign a reference to the method `m1( )` to `del1` and a reference to method `m2( )` to `del2`. When the statement `del3 = del1 + del2` executes, `del3` becomes a delegate that executes both `m1( )` and `m2( )`, in that order. Only delegates with the same argument list can be composed, and the delegates used must have a `void` return value. Additionally, you can use the — and -= operators to remove a delegate from a composed delegate.

In the next steps, you will create a composed delegate to demonstrate how composition works.

1. Open the **Delegate1.cs** file (not Delegate2.cs) in your text editor. Immediately save it as **Delegate3.cs**.

2. The program uses two delegates: `firstDel` with the `string` "Angela" and `secondDel` with the `string` "Brian". As the last line in the `Main( )` method, type a statement that adds `secondDel` to `firstDel`, changing `firstDel` into a composed delegate.

```
firstDel += secondDel;
```

3. Use the composed `firstDel` delegate with a different `string`:

```
firstDel("Yolanda");
```

4. Save the file, and then compile and execute the program. Figure 11-4 shows the program, and Figure 11-5 shows the output. When you use `firstDel` with "Angela", the output is "Hello, Angela!". When you use `secondDel`

with "Brian", the output is "Goodbye, Brian!". After **firstDel** becomes a composed delegate, using it with "Yolanda" makes both the **Hello()** and **Goodbye()** methods execute.

```
using System;
delegate void GreetingDelegate(string s);
class GreetingClass
{
    public static void Hello(string s)
    {
        Console.WriteLine("Hello, {0}!", s);
    }
    public static void Goodbye(string s)
    {
        Console.WriteLine("Goodbye, {0}!", s);
    }
    public static void Main()
    {
        GreetingDelegate firstDel, secondDel;
        firstDel = new GreetingDelegate(Hello);
        secondDel = new GreetingDelegate(Goodbye);
        firstDel("Angela");
        secondDel("Brian");
        firstDel += secondDel;
        firstDel("Yolanda");
    }
}
```

11

Figure 11-4   **Delegate3** program

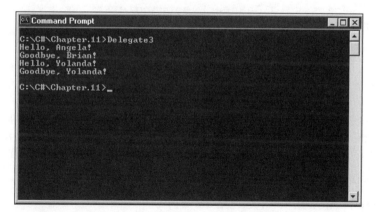

Figure 11-5   Output of **Delegate3** program

 For static methods, like those you just created, a **delegate** object encapsulates the method to be called. When creating a class containing instance methods, you create **delegate** objects that encapsulate both an instance of the class and a method on the instance. You will create this type of delegate in the next section.

HANDLING EVENTS

In C#, an **event** occurs when something interesting happens to an object. When you create a class, you decide exactly what is considered "interesting." For example, when you create a `Form`, you might decide to respond to a user clicking a `Button` but ignore a user who clicks a `Label`—clicking the `Label` is just not "interesting" to the `Form`.

You use an event to notify a client program when something happens to a class object the program is using. Events are used frequently in GUI programs—for example, you notify a program when the user clicks a `Button` or chooses an option from a `ListBox`. In addition, you can use events with ordinary classes that do not represent GUI controls. Events enable any object to signal any changes that occur about which the object's client might want to know.

To declare an event, you use a delegate. An event provides a way for a class to allow clients to provide delegates to methods that should execute when the event occurs. When an event occurs, any delegate that a client has given or passed to the event is invoked. An event handler `delegate` requires two arguments—the object where the event was initiated (the **sender**) and an `EventArgs` argument. Because all objects descend from the `Object` class, you can use a generic `object` as the event handler's first parameter. For the second parameter, you can use an `EventArgs` object. `EventArgs` is a C# class designed for holding event information. You can create an `EventArgs` object containing event information, or you can use the `EventArgs` class static field named `Empty`, which represents an event containing no event data. In other words, using the `Empty` field simply lets the client know that an event has occurred without specifying any details. For example, you can declare a `delegate` event handler named `ChangedEventHandler` with the following statement:

```
public delegate void ChangedEventHandler
    (object sender, EventArgs e);
```

In the next set of steps, you will create a simple `Student` class that is similar to many classes you already have created. The `Student` class will contain just two data fields and will generate an event when the data contained in either field changes.

1. Open a new file in your text editor. Type the `using System;` statement, then create a delegate named `ChangedEventHandler` that you will use whenever a field value for a `Student` changes. The delegate defines the set of arguments that will be passed to the method that handles the event.

   ```
   using System;
   public delegate void ChangedEventHandler
       (object sender, EventArgs e);
   ```

2. Begin a `Student` class containing two data fields that hold an ID number and a grade-point average.

   ```
   public class Student
   {
       private int idNum;
       private double gpa;
   ```

3. Provide a third `Student` class attribute—an event named `Changed`. The declaration for an event looks like a field, but instead of being an `int` or a `double`, it is a `ChangedEventHandler`. You defined this `delegate` type in the second line of the file.

 Events usually are declared as `public`, but you can use any accessibility modifier.

```
public event ChangedEventHandler Changed;
```

4. Add two `public` get methods that return the `private` field values.

```
public int GetId()
{
   return idNum;
}
public double GetGpa()
{
   return gpa;
}
```

5. Create two set methods, which are similar to set methods you have created earlier in this book. Each takes an argument and assigns its value to the appropriate class instance field. However, in the `Student` class, when either the `idNum` or the `gpa` changes, you will also call a method named `OnChanged()`. You can use `EventArgs.Empty` as the argument to `OnChanged()`.

```
public void SetId(int num)
{
   idNum = num;
   OnChanged(EventArgs.Empty);
}
public void SetGpa(double avg)
{
   gpa = avg;
   OnChanged(EventArgs.Empty);
}
```

6. Write the `OnChanged()` method, which calls `Changed()` using two arguments—a reference to the `Student` object that was changed and the empty `EventArgs` object. Calling `Changed()` is also known as **invoking the event**.

```
public void OnChanged(EventArgs e)
{
   Changed(this, e);
}
```

> If no client has hooked up a delegate to the event, the `Changed` field will be `null`, rather than referring to the delegate that should be called when the event is invoked. Therefore, programmers often check for `null` before invoking the event, as in the following example:
>
> ```
> if (Changed != null)
>         Changed(this, e);
> ```
>
> For simplicity, this set of steps does not bother checking for null.

7. Add a closing curly brace for the `Student` class. Save the file as **StudentWithEvent.cs**.

The `Student` class event (`Changed`) looks and acts like an ordinary field. However, you cannot assign values to the event field as easily as you can to ordinary data fields. You can take only two actions on an event field: you can compose a new delegate onto the field using the `+=` operator, and you can remove a delegate from the field using the `-=` operator. For example, to add `StudentChanged` to the `Changed` field of a `Student` object named `stu`, you would write the following:

```
stu.Changed += new ChangedEventHandler(StudentChanged);
```

To allow a client program to listen for `Student` events, you will create an `EventListener` class.

1. Add an `EventListener` class at the end of the `StudentWithEvent` file. After the closing curly brace of the `Student` class, type the following `EventListener` class containing a `Student` object that is initialized at its construction. Using the `+=` operator, add the `StudentChanged()` method to the event `delegate`. Next, write the `StudentChanged()` method to display a message and information about the `Student`.

```
class EventListener
{
  private Student stu;
  public EventListener(Student student)
  {
    stu = student;
    stu.Changed += new ChangedEventHandler
      (StudentChanged);
  }
  private void StudentChanged
    (object sender, EventArgs e)
  {
    Console.WriteLine("The student has changed.");
    Console.WriteLine
      ("   ID# {0}   GPA {1}", stu.GetId(), stu.GetGpa());
  }
}
```

2. Create a class to test the `Student` and `EventListener` classes. Below the closing curly brace for the `EventListener` class, create a `DemoStudentEvent` class that contains a single `Main()` method. This method declares one `Student` and registers the program to listen for events from the `Student` class.

```
class DemoStudentEvent
{
  public static void Main()
  {
    Student oneStu = new Student();
    EventListener listener = new EventListener(oneStu);
```

3. Use the `SetId()` and `SetGpa()` methods several times. Because this program is registered to listen for events from the `Student`, each change in a data field causes an event. That is, each data change will not only change the data field, but also execute the `StudentChanged()` method that displays two lines of explanation.

```
oneStu.SetId(2345);
oneStu.SetId(4567);
oneStu.SetGpa(3.2);
```

4. Add two closing curly braces—one for the `Main()` method and another for the `DemoStudentEvent` class.

5. Save the file, and then compile and execute it. For reference, Figure 11-6 shows the entire file listing. Figure 11-7 shows the program output. The output shows that an event occurs three times—once when the ID becomes 2345 (and the grade-point average is still 0), a second time when the ID becomes 4567 (and the grade-point average still has not changed), and a third time when the GPA becomes 3.2.

11

```
using System;
public delegate void ChangedEventHandler
  (object sender, EventArgs e);
public class Student
{
    private int idNum;
    private double gpa;
    public event ChangedEventHandler Changed;
    public int GetId()
    {
        return idNum;
    }
    public double GetGpa()
    {
        return gpa;
    }
```

Figure 11-6 `StudentWithEvent` program

```
          public void SetId(int num)
          {
                idNum = num;
                OnChanged(EventArgs.Empty);
          }
          public void SetGpa(double avg)
          {
                gpa = avg;
                OnChanged(EventArgs.Empty);
          }
          public void OnChanged(EventArgs e)
          {
                Changed(this, e);
          }
   }
   class EventListener
   {
          private Student stu;
          public EventListener(Student student)
          {
                stu = student;
                stu.Changed += new ChangedEventHandler
                  (StudentChanged);
          }
          private void StudentChanged(object sender, EventArgs e)
          {
                Console.WriteLine("The student has changed.");
                Console.WriteLine("   ID# {0}  GPA {1}",
                  stu.GetId(), stu.GetGpa());
          }
   }
   class DemoStudentEvent
   {
          public static void Main()
          {
                Student oneStu = new Student();
                EventListener listener = new EventListener
                  (oneStu);
                oneStu.SetId(2345);
                oneStu.SetId(4567);
                oneStu.SetGpa(3.2);
          }
   }
```

Figure 11-6 `StudentWithEvent` program (continued)

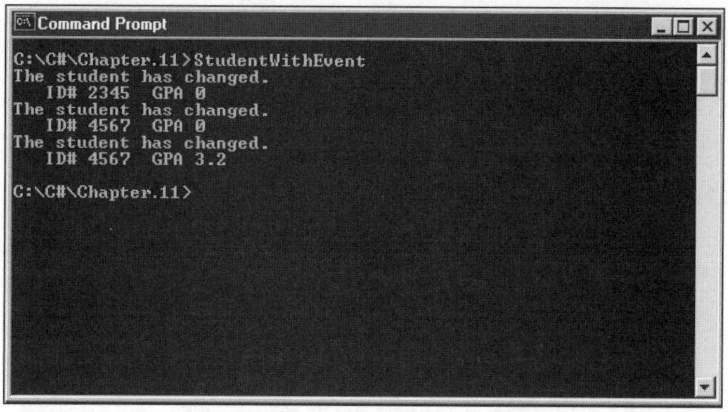

Figure 11-7   Output of `StudentWithEvent` program

USING THE BUILT-IN `EventHandler`

The C# language allows you to create events using any delegate type. However, the .NET Framework provides guidelines you should follow if you are developing a class that will be used by others. These guidelines indicate that the delegate type used for an event should take exactly two parameters: a parameter indicating the source of the event, and an `EventArgs` parameter that encapsulates any additional information about the event. For events that do not use any additional information, the .NET Framework has already defined an appropriate type named **`EventHandler`**.

Next, you will modify the `StudentWithEvent` file to use the `EventHandler` delegate type.

1. Open the **StudentWithEvent** file in your text editor and immediately save it as **StudentWithEvent2.cs**.

2. Because you will use the already-created `EventHandler` type, you do not need to declare your own delegate named `ChangedEventHandler`. Delete the second line in the file, which is shown in the following code:

   ```
   public delegate void ChangedEventHandler
     (object sender, EventArgs e);
   ```

3. Within the `Student` class, alter the definition of the event so it becomes an `EventHandler` instead of a `ChangedEventHandler`.

   ```
   public event EventHandler Changed;
   ```

4. Within the constructor for the `EventHandler` class, change the statement that composes `stu.Changed` so it uses an `EventHandler` instead of a `ChangedEventHandler`.

   ```
   stu.Changed += new EventHandler(StudentChanged);
   ```

11

5. Save the file, and then compile and execute it. The output is the same as in Figure 11-7. You have substituted the built-in `EventHandler` for the one named `ChangedEventHandler` you created yourself.

HANDLING Control COMPONENT EVENTS

You use the same techniques to handle events generated or **raised** by GUI `Control`s as you do to handle events raised by non–`Control`-generated events. The major difference is that when you create your own classes, like `Student`, you must define both the data fields and events you want to generate, but when you use already-created `Control` components like `Button`s and `ListBox`es, they already contain fields (or properties) like `Text` as well as events with names like `Click`. Table 11-1 lists just some of the more commonly used `Control` events.

 You can consult the Visual Studio Help feature to discover additional `Control` events as well as more specific events assigned to individual `Control` child classes.

Table 11-1 Some `Control` Class Public Instance `Events`

Event	Description
BackColorChanged	Occurs when the value of the BackColor property has changed
Click	Occurs when a control is clicked
ControlAdded	Occurs when a new control is added
ControlRemoved	Occurs when a control is removed
CursorChanged	Occurs when the Cursor property value has changed
DragDrop	Occurs when a drag-and-drop operation is completed
DragEnter	Occurs when an object is dragged into a control's bounds
DragLeave	Occurs when an object has been dragged into and out of control's bounds
DragOver	Occurs when an object has been dragged over a control's bounds
EnabledChanged	Occurs when the Enabled property value has changed
Enter	Occurs when a control is entered
FontChanged	Occurs when the Font property value has changed
ForeColorChanged	Occurs when the ForeColor property value has changed
GotFocus	Occurs when a control receives focus
HelpRequested	Occurs when a user requests help for a control
KeyDown	Occurs when a key is pressed down while a control has focus
KeyPress	Occurs when a key is pressed while a control has focus
KeyUp	Occurs when a key is released while a control has focus
Leave	Occurs when a control is left

Table 11-1   Some Control Class Public Instance Events (continued)

Event	Description
LocationChanged	Occurs when the Location property value has changed
LostFocus	Occurs when a control loses focus
MouseDown	Occurs when the mouse pointer hovers over a control and a mouse button is pressed
MouseEnter	Occurs when the mouse pointer enters a control
MouseHover	Occurs when the mouse pointer hovers over a control
MouseLeave	Occurs when the mouse pointer leaves a control
MouseMove	Occurs when the mouse pointer moves over a control
MouseUp	Occurs when the mouse pointer hovers over a control and a mouse button is released
MouseWheel	Occurs when the mouse wheel moves while a control has focus
Move	Occurs when a control is moved
Resize	Occurs when a control is resized
SizeChanged	Occurs when the Size property value has changed
TextChanged	Occurs when the Text property value has changed
VisibleChanged	Occurs when the Visible property value has changed

11

As an example, in the next steps you will create a Form containing a Button, then add an event that is generated when the user clicks the Button—specifically, the background color of the Form will change.

1. Open a new file in your text editor. Type the using statements that you will need for this application:

```
using System;
using System.Drawing;
using System.Windows.Forms;
```

2. Begin to create a Form named Form1 that contains a Button named button1.

```
public class Form1 : Form
{
   private Button button1;
```

3. Begin to create a constructor for the Form1 class. Set the Text property for the Form, then create a Button instance, locate it on the Form, and set its Text property.

```
public Form1()
{
   this.Text = "Form turns pink";
   this.button1 = new Button();
```

```
this.button1.Location = new
   System.Drawing.Point(56, 64);
this.button1.Text = "Pink";
```

4. Using the += operator, compose the Click delegate event that is automatically included in Button objects so it uses the EventHandler delegate type and a method named button1_Click().

```
this.button1.Click += new EventHandler
   (this.button1_Click);
```

5. Include the Controls.AddRange() method that adds the Button to the list of the Form's controls.

```
this.Controls.AddRange(new System.Windows.Forms.Control[]
           {this.button1});
```

6. Type a closing curly brace for the Form1 constructor method.

7. Add the Main() method for the Form1 class to run the application.

```
static void Main()
{
    Application.Run(new Form1());
}
```

8. Add the button1_Click() method that you specified as the EventHandler. When the user clicks the Button, the Form's background will change color.

```
private void button1_Click(object sender, EventArgs e)
{
   this.BackColor = Color.Pink;
}
```

9. Add the closing curly brace for the Form1 class. Save the file as **ButtonEvent.cs**, then compile and execute the program. For reference, Figure 11-8 shows the entire program listing. Figure 11-9 shows the generated Form. When you click the Pink button, the Form's background color changes to pink.

```
using System;
using System.Drawing;
using System.Windows.Forms;
public class Form1 : Form
{
     private Button button1;
     public Form1()
     {
          this.Text = "Form turns pink";
          this.button1 = new Button();
          this.button1.Location = new System.Drawing.Point
             (56, 64);
```

Figure 11-8 ButtonEvent program

```
            this.button1.Text = "Pink";
            this.button1.Click += new EventHandler
              (this.button1_Click);
            this.Controls.AddRange
              (new System.Windows.Forms.Control[]
              {this.button1});
      }
      static void Main()
      {
            Application.Run(new Form1());
      }
      private void button1_Click(object sender, EventArgs e)
      {
            this.BackColor = Color.Pink;
      }
}
```

Figure 11-8   ButtonEvent program (continued)

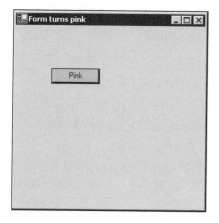

Figure 11-9   Output of ButtonEvent program

11

ADDING MORE EVENTS TO AN APPLICATION

A Form can contain any number of Controls that might have events associated with them. Additionally, a single control might be able to raise any number of events. Table 11-1 lists only a sample of the many events available with Controls, and any Control could conceivably raise many of those events. In the next steps, you will add a MouseEnter event to the Button on the ButtonEvent program's Form.

1. Open the **ButtonEvent.cs** file in your text editor. Immediately save it as **ButtonEvent2.cs**.

2. Within the `Form1` constructor, just after the composition of the `button1.Click` event, add a composition for the `MouseEnter` event—the event raised when the user passes a mouse over a `Control`.

```
this.button1.MouseEnter +=
    new EventHandler(this.button1_MouseEnter);
```

3. After the closing curly brace for the `button1_Click()` method, but before the closing curly brace for the class, add the `button1_MouseEnter()` method that will turn the `Button` yellow when the user passes the mouse over it (whether or not the user clicks).

```
private void button1_MouseEnter(object sender,
    EventArgs e)
{
    button1.BackColor = Color.Yellow;
}
```

4. Save the program, and then compile and execute it. When the `Form` appears, move your mouse over the `Button`. As soon as the mouse enters the `Button` `Control`, the `Button`'s background color changes. When you click the `Button`, the `Form`'s background color changes as before.

Using the IDE to Generate Event-Handling Code

In Chapters 9 and 10, you used the Visual Studio IDE to add events to a program. Now you will create the `ButtonEvent` project again in Visual Studio and compare the process to writing the code by hand.

1. Open the Visual Studio IDE. Click **File** on the menu bar, point to **New**, and then click **Project**. In the New Project dialog box, click **Visual C# Projects** and **Windows Application**. Type the name of your new project as **ButtonEventIDE**, and make sure the Location is set to the **Chapter.11** folder on your Student Disk.

2. Change the `Text` property of `form1` to **Form turns pink**.

3. Drag a `Button` onto the `Form` to approximately **Location 56, 64** and set its `Text` property to **Pink**. Your screen looks like Figure 11-10.

4. Double-click the `Button` to view the code for the `button1_Click` method. Between the curly braces for the method, insert the following statement that changes the background color of the `Form`:

```
this.BackColor = Color.Pink;
```

Compare this method to the method you wrote by hand when creating the ButtonEvent program earlier in this chapter. The methods are identical.

5. Scroll through the ButtonEventIDE code until you find the statement that assigns the `button1_Click()` method to the event. (If the `private void InitializeComponents()` method is not expanded, click the + to the left of the method header to view its code.)

```
this.button1.Click +=
   new System.EventHandler(this.button1_Click);
```

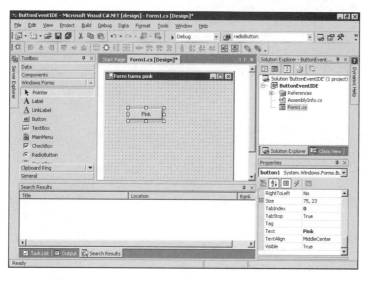

Figure 11-10   ButtonEvent Project Design view with `Form` and `Button`

Except for the fact that the IDE uses the fully qualified name for `EventHandler` (including the otherwise implied `System` namespace), the statement is identical to its counterpart in the `ButtonEvent` program. You have saved a lot of tedious typing (and potential typographical errors) by using the Integrated Development Environment. (If necessary, expand any collapsed code sections by clicking the plus sign (+) to the left of the code.

6. Click **View** on the IDE menu bar, and then click **Designer** to return to the Designer view. Select the `Button` object on the `Form`. In the Properties list at the right of the screen, click the **Events** button, which resembles a lightning bolt. A list of available `Button` events appears.

7. Scroll through the list to find the **MouseEnter** event. When you click the `MouseEnter` event, a list box appears and suggests methods you might want to associate with this event. The only available selection is the `button1_click()` method, as shown in Figure 11-11. If you choose the `button1_Click()` method, then the same method will execute whether the user clicks `button1` or simply places the mouse over `button1`. In this case, you want to execute a different method that turns the `Button`'s background yellow, so do not select the `button1_Click()` method. Instead type a new method name: **button1_MouseEnter**. Press **Enter**.

11

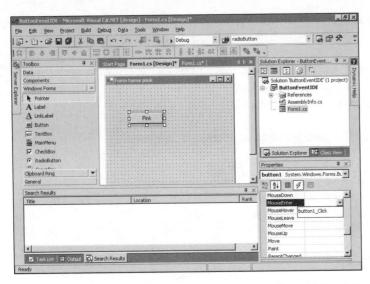

Figure 11-11   Associating a method with an event in Visual Studio

8. The IDE returns you to the program's code view, where the shell for the `button1_MouseEnter()` method has already been created for you. Between the method's curly braces, type the statement that will change the `Button`'s background color to yellow when the mouse is placed over it:

```
button1.BackColor = Color.Yellow;
```

9. Examine the rest of the code and locate the statement in which the `button1_MouseEnter()` method is associated with the `button1.MouseEnter` event.

10. Click the **Save All** button, and then run the program. It operates in the same way as the original `ButtonEvent` program you created by hand earlier. When you place the mouse over the `Button`, the `Button` changes color; when you click the `Button`, the `Form` itself changes color. Figure 11-12 shows the complete code for the ButtonEventIDE program.

11. Dismiss the `Form`. Close Visual Studio.

```
using System;
using System.Drawing;
using System.Collections;
using System.ComponentModel;
using System.Windows.Forms;
using System.Data;
namespace ButtonEventIDE
```

Figure 11-12   `ButtonEventIDE` program

```
{
    /// <summary>
    /// Summary description for Form1.
    /// </summary>
    public class Form1 : System.Windows.Forms.Form
    {
        private System.Windows.Forms.Button button1;
        /// <summary>
        /// Required designer variable.
        /// </summary>
        private System.ComponentModel.Container
              components = null;
        public Form1()
        {
            //
            // Required for Windows Form Designer support
            //
            InitializeComponent();
            //
            // TODO: Add any constructor code after
            // InitializeComponent call
            //
        }
        /// <summary>
        /// Clean up any resources being used.
        /// </summary>
        protected override void Dispose( bool disposing )
        {
            if( disposing )
            {
                if (components != null)
                {
                    components.Dispose();
                }
            }
            base.Dispose( disposing );
        }
        #region Windows Form Designer generated code
        /// <summary>
        /// Required method for Designer support
        /// do not modify
        /// the contents of this method with the code editor.
        /// </summary>
        private void InitializeComponent()
        {
            this.button1 = new System.Windows.Forms.Button();
            this.SuspendLayout();
            //
            // button1
            //
```

Figure 11-12   ButtonEventIDE program (continued)

```
              this.button1.Location = new
                System.Drawing.Point(56, 64);
              this.button1.Name = "button1";
              this.button1.Size = new System.Drawing.Size(64, 24);
              this.button1.TabIndex = 0;
              this.button1.Text = "Pink";
              this.button1.Click += new System.EventHandler
                (this.button1_Click);
              this.button1.MouseEnter +=
                    new System.EventHandler(this.button1_MouseEnter);
              //
              // Form1
              //
              this.AutoScaleBaseSize = new
                    System.Drawing.Size(5, 13);
              this.ClientSize = new
                    System.Drawing.Size(292, 273);
              this.Controls.AddRange
                    (new System.Windows.Forms.Control[] {
                    this.button1});
              this.Name = "Form1";
              this.Text = "Form turns pink";
              this.ResumeLayout(false);
        }
        #endregion
        /// <summary>
        /// The main entry point for the application.
        /// </summary>
        [STAThread]
        static void Main()
        {
              Application.Run(new Form1());
        }
        private void button1_Click
          (object sender, System.EventArgs e)
        {
              this.BackColor = Color.Pink;
        }
        private void button1_MouseEnter
          (object sender, System.EventArgs e)
        {
              button1.BackColor = Color.Yellow;
        }
    }
}
```

Figure 11-12   `ButtonEventIDE` program (continued)

The only difference between the ButtonEvent program you created by hand and the one you created using the IDE is that the IDE automatically created a lot of code for you, including some that you don't need in order to make the program work, but that you might use as you continue to make additions and improvements to the program.

The advantage to using the IDE is the time you save typing and correcting typing errors. However, the advantage to knowing how to create a GUI program containing events by hand is greater—you understand what each statement accomplishes and are able to customize methods to perform exactly the tasks you want.

SETTING Controls' TAB ORDER

When users encounter multiple GUI `Controls` on a `Form`, usually one `Control` has **focus**. That is, if the user presses the Enter key, the `Control` will raise an event.

`TabStop` is a Boolean property of a `Control` that identifies whether the `Control` will serve as a stopping place in a sequence of Tab key presses. `TabIndex` is a numeric property that indicates the order in which the `Control` will receive focus when the user presses the Tab key. Programmers typically use small numbers for `TabIndex` values, beginning with 0. When a `Control` has a `TabIndex` of 0, it receives focus when the `Form` is initialized.

 Setting two or more `Controls`' `TabIndex` values to 0 does not cause an error. Only one `Control` will receive focus, however.

In the next steps, you will create a `Form` containing three `Buttons` so you can demonstrate how to manipulate the `TabStop` and `TabIndex` properties.

1. Open the Visual Studio IDE. Start a new Project. Define it to be a **Visual C# Project**, **Windows Application** named **ManyButtons** stored in the Chapter.11 folder on your Student Disk.

2. Change the `Text` property of the main `Form` to **Many Buttons**.

3. Drag three `Buttons` onto the `Form` and place them approximately where they are shown in Figure 11-13. Change the `Text` on the three `Buttons` to **Red**, **White**, and **Blue**, respectively.

4. Examine the Properties list for the Red button. The `TabStop` property has been set to `True` and the `TabIndex` is 0. Examine the Properties for the White and Blue buttons. The IDE has set their `TabIndex` values to 1 and 2, respectively.

5. Click the **Save All** button, and then run the program. When the `Form` appears, the Red button has focus. Press the **Tab** key, and notice that focus changes to the White button. Press the **Tab** key a second time, and focus changes to the Blue button. Press the **Tab** key several more times and observe that the focus rotates among the `Buttons`.

6. Close the `Form`.

11

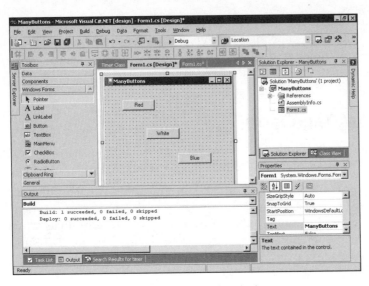

Figure 11-13 ManyButtons Form with three Buttons

7. Change the TabIndex property of the Blue button to **0**, and change the TabIndex of the Red button to **2**. (The TabIndex of the White button remains 1.) Save the program again, and then run it. This time, the Blue button begins with focus. When you press the Tab key, the order in which the Buttons receive focus is Blue, then White, then Red. (Clicking the Buttons or pressing Enter raises no event because you have not assigned events to the Buttons.)

8. Select the White button and change its TabStop property to **False**. Save the program, and then execute it. This time, when the Form appears, the Blue button has focus. When you press the **Tab** key, focus alternates between the Blue and Red buttons, bypassing the White button, which is no longer part of the tabbing sequence.

9. Change the White button's TabStop value back to **True**. Change the TabIndex property for the Red button back to **0** and the TabIndex property for the Blue button back to **2**. Click the **Save All** button.

USING THE sender OBJECT IN AN EVENT

When a Form contains multiple widgets that you can manipulate, you can write event-handling methods for each one. Alternatively, you can write a single event-handling method that can take appropriate action based on which Control generated the event. The Control that causes an event is represented as a generic object in the object sender argument to an event method.

In the next steps, you will add a single method to the ManyButtons Form and cause this method to execute no matter which Button the user clicks.

1. Open the **Many Buttons** project in the Visual Studio IDE. Drag a `Label` onto the `Form`, placing it at the approximate location of the one shown in Figure 11-14. Change the `Label`'s `Text` property to **Click a button**. Set the `Size` property of the `Label` to **100, 48**. (Relocate any `Buttons` necessary so that the `Label` and `Buttons` do not obscure each other on the `Form`.)

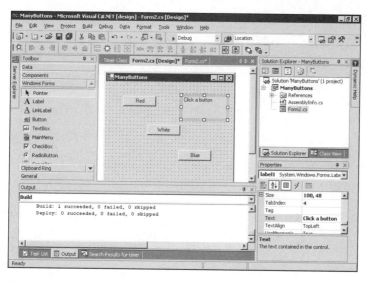

Figure 11-14   ManyButtons Form including `Label`

2. Double-click the **Red** button on the `Form` to view the code for the shell of a `button1_Click()` method. Between the method's curly braces, insert a statement that will display the `ToString()` value of the object that generates the `button1_Click()` method:

```
label1.Text = sender.ToString();
```

3. Click the **Save All** button, and then execute the program. When the `Form` appears, the `Label` displays "Click a button." If you click the White or Blue button, nothing happens (because you have not yet assigned an event to those `Buttons`). When you click the Red button, however, the `Label` changes to show the `ToString()` representation of the sender object within the `button1_Click()` method. See Figure 11-15. The `ToString()` method for the object contains the object type (`System.Windows.Forms.Button`), a comma, and the object's `Text` property (`Text: Red`).

4. Dismiss the `Form`. Within the IDE, return to Designer view.

5. Select the **White** button. In its Properties list, click the **Events** button (the lightning bolt). Select the `Click` event. From the list box next to the `Click` event, select **button1_Click()** as the method to associate with a click on **button2**.

11

6. On the Form, select the **Blue** button. In its **Events** list, select its `Click` event and associate it with the **button1_Click( )** method.

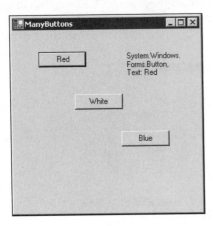

Figure 11-15 ManyButtons Form after clicking the Red button

7. Click the **Save All** button, and then execute the program. No matter which `Button` you choose, an appropriate string appears within the `Label`, proving that a different object becomes the `sender` each time the method executes.

Besides `ToString( )`, every object has an `Equals( )` method that returns a Boolean value indicating whether two objects are the same object at the same memory location—that is, whether one object name is an alias for the other. Within the `button1_Click` method, you can use the `sender`'s `Equals( )` method to determine which object (`button1`, `button2`, or `button3`) raised the event.

1. With the **ManyButtons** program still open in the Visual Studio IDE, view the code for the `Form` and locate the `button1_Click( )` method. After the statement that changes the `Label`'s `Text` property, but before the closing curly brace of the method, add a nested `if` statement that compares the `sender` object first to `button1` (in which case you set the `Form`'s `BackColor` to red), then to `button2` (setting the `Form`'s `BackColor` to white), and by default assumes the sender is `button3` (setting the `Form`'s color to blue).

```
if (sender.Equals(button1))
    this.BackColor = Color.Red;
else
    if(sender.Equals(button2))
        this.BackColor = Color.White;
else
        this.BackColor = Color.Blue;
```

2. Click the **Save All** button, and then execute the program. As you select `Buttons`, both the `Label` message and the `Form`'s background color change appropriately.

ADDING A MAIN MENU TO A Form

Most programs you use in a Windows environment contain a **main menu**, which is a horizontal list of general options that appears under the title bar of a Form and which you can click to see list boxes containing more specific options. For example, the Visual Studio IDE contains a main menu that begins with the options File, Edit, and View. Undoubtedly you have used word processing, spreadsheet, and even game programs with similar menus. You can add a MainMenu Control object to any Form you create, either by hand or by using the Visual Studio IDE. In the next steps, you will add a MainMenu to ManyButtons' main Form.

Users expect menu options to appear in conventional order. For example, when looking to exit an application, users expect the leftmost main menu option to be File, with the Exit option appearing under File. Similarly, if an application contains a Help option, users expect to find it at the right side of the main menu. You should follow these conventions when designing your own main menus.

If you create each main menu item so it starts with a unique letter, then, besides clicking menu items with the mouse, the user can press Alt and the initial letter to activate the menu choice.

If possible, your main menu selections should be single words. That way, a user will not mistake a single menu item as representing multiple items.

1. From the Windows Forms Controls toolbox on the left side of the IDE screen, drag a **MainMenu** object onto the Form.

2. When you release the mouse, the MainMenu docks at the top of the Form, where you expect a menu to be located. The prompt "Type Here" appears, as shown in Figure 11-16.

3. When you click **Type Here**, new potential menu items appear both below and to the right of the currently selected item. You can navigate to these potential menu item locations using the arrow keys on the keyboard. In the top-left option, type **File**. Press the down arrow, and in the option below File, type **Exit**. See Figure 11-17.

11

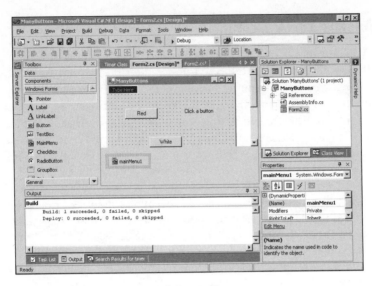

Figure 11-16   Form containing `MainMenu`

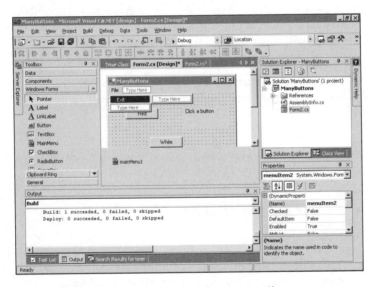

Figure 11-17   `MainMenu` containing two options

4. Press the up arrow, and then press the right arrow to start a second main menu selection. Type **Color**, press the down arrow, and then type **Green**. Notice that new options become available both below and to the right of each entry you make. Below Green, add **Yellow** and **Pink**. See Figure 11-18.

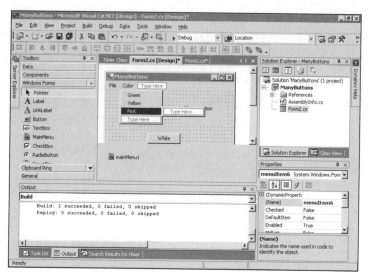

Figure 11-18   MainMenu containing several options

5. In the MainMenu, choose the **File** option. Notice its default name in the properties box—menuItem1. Click **Exit**; its default name is menuItem2. You can change the names of these items if you want (using the Name property field). For now, allow them to retain their default names.

6. In the MainMenu, choose **File**, then double-click **Exit**. You see the code for a newly created menuItem2_Click() method. When the user chooses this option, you want the Form to close. Between the curly braces of the menuItem2_Click() method, add the statement that closes the Form:

```
this.Close();
```

7. Click the **Save All** button, and then run the program. When the Many Buttons Form appears, click **File**, then **Exit**. The Form closes just as if the user had clicked the Close button in the upper-right corner of the Form.

8. Return to the **Designer** view for Form1 in the Visual Studio IDE. Select the MainMenu option **Color**, then double-click **Green**. You see code for the menuItem4_Click() method, including an argument named object sender. Between the method's curly braces, add the following code that compares the sender to each Button and takes appropriate action. Later, you will associate this method with all three of the Color menu options.

```
if(sender.Equals(menuItem4))
      this.BackColor = Color.Green;
else
      if(sender.Equals(menuItem5))
            this.BackColor = Color.Yellow;
else
            this.BackColor = Color.Pink;
```

9. Return to **Designer** view. Now you will associate the remaining Color menu options with the `menuItem4_Click()` method. Select the **Yellow** option (menuItem5). Under Properties, choose its associated `Click` event to be **menuItem4_Click**. Select the **Pink** option from the Color menu. Choose its associated `Click` event to be **menuItem4_Click** as well.

10. Click the **Save All** button, and then run the program. Whether you select a menu item color from the list box or select a color by using a `Button`, the `Form`'s `BackColor` changes appropriately. You can dismiss the `Form` using either the Exit option in the File menu or the Close button. Figure 11-19 shows the complete code for the `ManyButtons` program.

11. Exit Visual Studio.

```
using System;
using System.Drawing;
using System.Collections;
using System.ComponentModel;
using System.Windows.Forms;
using System.Data;
namespace ManyButtons
{
    /// <summary>
    /// Summary description for Form1.
    /// </summary>
    public class Form1 : System.Windows.Forms.Form
    {
        private System.Windows.Forms.Button button1;
        private System.Windows.Forms.Button button2;
        private System.Windows.Forms.Button button3;
        private System.Windows.Forms.Label label1;
        private System.Windows.Forms.MainMenu mainMenu1;
        private System.Windows.Forms.MenuItem menuItem1;
        private System.Windows.Forms.MenuItem menuItem2;
        private System.Windows.Forms.MenuItem menuItem3;
        private System.Windows.Forms.MenuItem menuItem4;
        private System.Windows.Forms.MenuItem menuItem5;
        private System.Windows.Forms.MenuItem menuItem6;
        /// <summary>
        /// Required designer variable.
        /// </summary>
        private System.ComponentModel.Container
            components = null;
        public Form1()
        {
            //
            // Required for Windows Form Designer support
            //
            InitializeComponent();
```

Figure 11-19 `ManyButtons` program

```
            //
            // TODO: Add any constructor code after
            // InitializeComponent call
            //
    }
    /// <summary>
    /// Clean up any resources being used.
    /// </summary>
    protected override void Dispose( bool disposing )
    {
        if( disposing )
        {
            if (components != null)
            {
                components.Dispose();
            }
        }
        base.Dispose( disposing );
    }
    #region Windows Form Designer generated code
    /// <summary>
    /// Required method for Designer support - do not modify
    /// the contents of this method with the code editor.
    /// </summary>
    private void InitializeComponent()
    {
        this.button1 = new System.Windows.Forms.Button();
        this.button2 = new System.Windows.Forms.Button();
        this.button3 = new System.Windows.Forms.Button();
        this.label1 = new System.Windows.Forms.Label();
        this.mainMenu1 = new
            System.Windows.Forms.MainMenu();
        this.menuItem1 = new
            System.Windows.Forms.MenuItem();
        this.menuItem2 = new
            System.Windows.Forms.MenuItem();
        this.menuItem3 = new
            System.Windows.Forms.MenuItem();
        this.menuItem4 = new
            System.Windows.Forms.MenuItem();
        this.menuItem5 = new
            System.Windows.Forms.MenuItem();
        this.menuItem6 = new
            System.Windows.Forms.MenuItem();
        this.SuspendLayout();
        //
        // button1
        //
        this.button1.Location = new
            System.Drawing.Point(40, 32);
        this.button1.Name = "button1";
```

11

Figure 11-19   ManyButtons program (continued)

```
        this.button1.TabIndex = 3;
        this.button1.Text = "Red";
        this.button1.Click += new
            System.EventHandler(this.button1_Click);
        //
        // button2
        //
        this.button2.Location = new
            System.Drawing.Point(96, 96);
        this.button2.Name = "button2";
        this.button2.TabIndex = 1;
        this.button2.Text = "White";
        this.button2.Click += new
            System.EventHandler(this.button1_Click);
        //
        // button3
        //
        this.button3.Location = new
            System.Drawing.Point(168, 152);
        this.button3.Name = "button3";
        this.button3.TabIndex = 0;
        this.button3.Text = "Blue";
        this.button3.Click += new
            System.EventHandler(this.button1_Click);
        //
        // label1
        //
        this.label1.Location = new
            System.Drawing.Point(176, 32);
        this.label1.Name = "label1";
        this.label1.Size = new
            System.Drawing.Size(100, 48);
        this.label1.TabIndex = 4;
        this.label1.Text = "Click a button";
        //
        // mainMenu1
        //
        this.mainMenu1.MenuItems.AddRange(new
            System.Windows.Forms.MenuItem[] {
        this.menuItem1,
        this.menuItem3});
        //
        // menuItem1
        //
        this.menuItem1.Index = 0;
        this.menuItem1.MenuItems.AddRange(new
            System.Windows.Forms.MenuItem[] {
                this.menuItem2});
        this.menuItem1.Text = "File";
        //
        // menuItem2
```

Figure 11-19 ManyButtons program (continued)

```
//
this.menuItem2.Index = 0;
this.menuItem2.Text = "Exit";
this.menuItem2.Click += new
    System.EventHandler(this.menuItem2_Click);
//
// menuItem3
//
this.menuItem3.Index = 1;
this.menuItem3.MenuItems.AddRange
    (new System.Windows.Forms.MenuItem[] {
        this.menuItem4,
        this.menuItem5,
        this.menuItem6});
this.menuItem3.Text = "Color";
//
// menuItem4
//
this.menuItem4.Index = 0;
this.menuItem4.Text = "Green";
this.menuItem4.Click += new
    System.EventHandler(this.menuItem4_Click);
//
// menuItem5
//
this.menuItem5.Index = 1;
this.menuItem5.Text = "Yellow";
this.menuItem5.Click += new
    System.EventHandler(this.menuItem4_Click);
//
// menuItem6
//
this.menuItem6.Index = 2;
this.menuItem6.Text = "Pink";
this.menuItem6.Click += new
    System.EventHandler(this.menuItem4_Click);
//
// Form1
//
this.AutoScaleBaseSize = new
    System.Drawing.Size(5, 13);
this.ClientSize = new
    System.Drawing.Size(292, 273);
this.Controls.AddRange
    (new System.Windows.Forms.Control[] {
        this.label1,
        this.button3,
        this.button2,
        this.button1});
this.Menu = this.mainMenu1;
this.Name = "Form1";
```

Figure 11-19 ManyButtons program (continued)

11

```
            this.Text = "ManyButtons";
            this.ResumeLayout(false);


        }
        #endregion
        /// <summary>
        /// The main entry point for the application.
        /// </summary>
        [STAThread]
        static void Main()
        {
            Application.Run(new Form1());
        }
        private void button1_Click
            (object sender, System.EventArgs e)
        {
            label1.Text = sender.ToString();
            if(sender.Equals(button1))
                this.BackColor = Color.Red;
            else
                if(sender.Equals(button2))
                    this.BackColor = Color.White;
                else
                    this.BackColor = Color.Blue;
        }
        private void menuItem2_Click
            (object sender, System.EventArgs e)
        {
            this.Close();
        }

        private void menuItem4_Click
            (object sender, System.EventArgs e)
        {
            if(sender.Equals(menuItem4))
                this.BackColor = Color.Green;
            else
                if(sender.Equals(menuItem5))
                    this.BackColor = Color.Yellow;
                else
                    this.BackColor = Color.Pink;
        }
    }
}
```

Figure 11-19   ManyButtons program (continued)

CONTINUING TO EXPLORE C#

If you examine the Visual Studio IDE, you will discover many additional `Controls` containing hundreds of properties and events. No single book or programming course can demonstrate all of them for you. However, if you understand good programming principles and, more specifically, the syntax and structure of C# programs, you will find learning about each new C# feature easier than learning about the last one. Continue to explore the Help facility in the Visual Studio IDE. Particularly, read the Tutorials, or brief lessons, found there. Also, you should search the Internet for C# discussion groups. C# is a new, dynamic language, and programmers will have many questions that they pose to one another online. Reading these discussions can provide you with valuable information and suggest new approaches to resolving problems.

CHAPTER SUMMARY

- ❑ A delegate is an object that contains a reference to, or encapsulates, a method. It provides a way to pass a reference to a method as an argument to another method. You declare such an object using the keyword `delegate` followed by an ordinary method declaration including a return type, method name, and argument list.

- ❑ You can assign one delegate to another using the = operator. You also can use the + and += operators to combine delegates into a composed delegate that calls the delegates from which it is built.

- ❑ In C#, an event occurs when something considered "interesting" happens to an object. You declare an event by using a delegate. When an event occurs, any delegate that a client has given to the event is invoked. An event handler `delegate` requires two arguments—the object where the event was initiated (the sender) and an `EventArgs` argument. The only actions you can take on an event field are to compose a new `delegate` object onto the field using the += operator, or to remove a `delegate` object from the field using the -= operator.

- ❑ For events that do not use any additional information, the .NET Framework has defined an appropriate delegate type named `EventHandler`.

- ❑ When you use `Controls` like `Button`s and `ListBox`es, they already contain events with names like `Click`, `DragOver`, `MouseEnter`, and `MouseLeave`.

- ❑ A `Form` can contain any number of `Controls` that might have events associated with them. Additionally, a single `Control` might be able to raise any number of events.

- ❑ When designing a `Form` with events, you can use the Visual Studio IDE to automatically create a lot of code for you. The advantage to using the IDE is the time you save typing and correcting typing errors. However, the advantage to knowing how to create a GUI program containing events by hand is greater—you understand what each statement accomplishes and can customize methods to perform exactly the tasks you want.

11

❑ When users encounter multiple GUI Controls on a Form, usually one Control has focus. TabStop is a Boolean property of a Control that identifies whether the Control will serve as a stopping place in a sequence of Tab key presses. TabIndex is a numeric property that indicates the order in which the Control will receive focus when the user presses the Tab key.

❑ When a Form contains multiple widgets that you can manipulate, you can write event-handling methods for each one. Alternatively, you can write a single event-handling method that can take appropriate action based on the object sender that caused the event.

❑ Most programs you use in a Windows environment contain a main menu, which is a horizontal list of general options that appears under the title bar of a Form and which you can click to see list boxes containing more specific options. You can add a MainMenu Control object to any Form you create, either by hand or by using the Visual Studio IDE.

❑ If you understand good programming principles and, more specifically, the syntax and structure of C# programs, you will find learning about each new C# feature easier than learning about the last one. Continue to explore the Help facility in the Visual Studio IDE. Particularly, read the Tutorials found there.

REVIEW QUESTIONS

1. A delegate is an object that contains a reference to a(n) —————————.

   a. object

   b. class

   c. method

   d. Control

2. C# delegates provide a way for a program to —————————.

   a. take alternative courses when running

   b. include multiple methods

   c. include methods from other classes

   d. include multiple Controls that use the same method

3. Which of the following correctly declares a delegate type?

   a. void aDelegate(int num);

   b. delegate void aDelegate(num);

   c. delegate void aDelegate(int num);

   d. delegate aDelegate(int num);

4. If you have declared a **delegate** instance, you can assign a reference to a method to it as long as the method has the same _____ as the **delegate**.

   a. return type

   b. identifier

   c. both of these

   d. neither of these is required

5. You can combine two delegates to create a(n) _____ delegate.

   a. assembled

   b. classified

   c. artificial

   d. composed

6. To combine two delegates using the + operator, the **delegate** objects must _____.

   a. have the same argument list

   b. have the same return type

   c. both of these

   d. neither of these

7. In C#, a(n) _____ occurs when something interesting happens to an object.

   a. delegate

   b. event

   c. notification

   d. instantiation

8. In C#, an event provides a way for a class to allow clients to provide

   _____.

   a. GUI objects that other classes can use

   b. delegates to methods

   c. arguments to other classes

   d. widgets to **Forms**

9. An event handler **delegate** requires _____ arguments.

   a. zero

   b. one

   c. two

   d. any number greater than zero

11

10. Using an event handler, the sender is the _____.

    a. delegate associated with the event

    b. method called by the event

    c. object where the event was initiated

    d. class containing the method that the event invokes

11. The `EventArgs` class contains a static field named _____.

    a. `Empty`

    b. `Text`

    c. `Location`

    d. `Source`

12. When creating events, you can use a predefined delegate type that is automatically provided by the .NET Framework named _____.

    a. `EventArgs`

    b. `EventHandler`

    c. `EventType`

    d. `Event`

13. Which of the following is not a predefined `Control` event?

    a. `MouseEnter`

    b. `Click`

    c. `Destroy`

    d. `TextChanged`

14. A single `Control` can raise _____ events.

    a. one

    b. two

    c. five

    d. any number of

15. When you create `Forms` containing `Controls` that raise events, an advantage to creating the code by hand over using the Visual Studio IDE is _____.

    a. you are less likely to make typing errors

    b. you save a lot of repetitious typing

    c. you are less likely to forget to set a property

    d. you gain a clearer understanding of the C# language

16. When a `Form` contains three `Control`s and one has focus, you can raise an event by _____.

   a. clicking any `Control`

   b. pressing the Enter key

   c. either of these

   d. none of these

17. The `TabStop` property of a `Control` is a(n) _____.

   a. integer value indicating the tab order

   b. Boolean value indicating whether the `Control` has a position in the tab sequence

   c. string value indicating the name of the method executed when the `Control` raises an event

   d. `delegate` name indicating the event raised when the user tabs to the `Control`

18. The `TabIndex` property of a `Control` is a(n) _____.

   a. integer value indicating the tab order

   b. Boolean value indicating whether the `Control` has a position in the tab sequence

   c. string value indicating the name of the method executed when the `Control` raises an event

   d. `delegate` name indicating the event raised when the user tabs to the `Control`

19. The `Control` that causes an event is the _____ argument to an event method.

   a. first

   b. second

   c. third

   d. fourth

20. The `Control` that provides a horizontal grouping of list box items in a `Form`, and typically contains options such as File and Edit, is the _____.

   a. `ListBox`

   b. `HorizontalGrid`

   c. `MainMenu`

   d. `MenuBar`

11

EXERCISES

Save the programs that you create in these exercises in the Chapter.11 folder on your Student Disk.

1. Create a `Form` that allows the user to select a preferred music style, then suggests an appropriate musical recording to purchase. Your `Form` should look similar to Figure 11-20. Save the program as **MusicFinder.cs**.

Figure 11-20   MusicFinder form

2. Create a `Form` containing two `ListBox`es. One should contain a list of baseball teams; the other should contain a list of seat types. Box seats cost $25, Grandstand seats cost $18.50, and Bleacher seats cost $10. After the user selects a team and a seat type and clicks a `Button`, the program should display a `Label` that informs the user of the selected team and the ticket price. Figure 11-21 shows the results of a typical execution. Save the file as **BaseballTickets.cs**.

Figure 11-21   BaseballTickets form

3. Create a **Form** that contains three **Label**s that hold famous quotes of your choice. When the program starts, the background color of the **Form** and each **Label** should be black. When the user passes a mouse over a **Label**, change its **BackColor** to white, revealing the text of the quote. Save the file as **DisplayQuotes.cs**.

4. The Sunshine Subdivision allows users to select siding for their new homes, but only specific trim colors are available to combine with each siding color. Create a **Form** for Sunshine Subdivision that allows a user to choose one of four siding colors from a **ListBox**—white, gray, blue, or yellow. When the user selects a siding color, the program should display a second **ListBox** that contains only the following choices:

   ❑ White siding—black, red, or green trim

   ❑ Gray siding—black or white trim

   ❑ Blue siding—white or dark blue trim

   After the user selects a trim color, the program should display a congratulatory message on a **Label** indicating the choice is a good one. *Hint:* You can remove the entire contents of a **ListBox** using the **Items.Clear()** method, as in **this.listBox2.Items.Clear();**. Save the file as **SunshineSubdivision.cs**.

5. Create a **Form** for use by customers of Airbourne Airlines. Include a **ListBox** containing at least five destination cities, each with a different ticket price. Also include radio buttons that allow the user to select either a vegetarian, kosher, or regular meal. When the user clicks a button indicating the choices are complete, the program should display the details of the trip along with the ticket price. Save the file as **AirbourneAirlines.cs**.

6. Create a **Form** containing a main menu that provides a user with three options—File, Topic, and About. Under the File option, the user should be able to select Exit to quit the program. Under the Topic option, allow the user to select one of at least three choices, such as Art, History, Television, and so on. If the user selects the About option, show a **MessageBox** that identifies the program's author and copyright date.

   The **Form** should contain two buttons and two labels. When the user clicks the first button, you should display a question in the category previously selected from the main menu. When the user clicks the second button, display the correct answer to the question.

   When the user selects a new option from the Topic main menu category, make the contents of the two labels invisible until the user selects the button to get the question or the answer.

   Save the file as **QuizMaster.cs**.

11

7. C# contains a namespace named `System.Security.Cryptography;` that contains a class named `RNGCryptoServiceProvider`, which can generate an array of random nonzero bytes. (Recall that a byte can contain any value from 0 through 255.) For example, the following three statements fill the array named `random` with five random numbers.

```
Byte[] random = new Byte[5];
RNGCryptoServiceProvider rng = new
    RNGCryptoServiceProvider();
rng.GetNonZeroBytes(random);
```

Create a **Form** containing two randomly generated arrays each containing 100 numbers, and set a position variable to 0. Ask the user to guess which array (the first or the second) contains the higher number in the position and to click one of two buttons indicating his or her guess. After each button click, the program should display a message indicating the values of the numbers as well as a running total of how many the user has guessed correctly and incorrectly so far. Then increase the position variable so that the user can make another guess using two new randomly selected numbers. If the user makes more than 100 selections, the program should reset the position indicator to 0, but continue to keep a running score. Save the file as **ButtonPick.cs**.

8. Each of the following files in the Chapter.11 folder on your Student Disk has syntax and/or logical errors. In each case, determine the problem and fix the program. After you correct the errors, save each file using the same filename preceded with *Fixed*. For example, DebugEleven1.cs will become FixedDebugEleven1.cs.

   a. DebugEleven1.cs

   b. DebugEleven2.cs

   c. DebugEleven3.cs

   d. DebugEleven4.cs

A

OPERATOR PRECEDENCE AND ASSOCIATIVITY

When an expression contains multiple operators, the **precedence** of the operators controls the order in which the individual operators are evaluated. For example, multiplication has a higher precedence than addition, so the expression 2 + 3 * 4 evaluates as 14 because the value of 3 * 4 is calculated before adding 2. Table A-1 summarizes all operators in order of precedence from highest to lowest.

Category	Operators	Associativity
Primary	`x.y  f(x)  a[x]  x++  x--  new` `typeof  checked  unchecked`	`left`
Unary	`+  -  !  ~  ++x  --x  (T)x`	`right`
Multiplicative	`*  /  %`	`left`
Additive	`+  -`	`left`
Shift	`<<  >>`	`right`
Relational and type testing	`<  >  <=  >=  is  as`	`left`
Equality	`==  !=`	`left`
Logical AND	`&`	`left`
Logical XOR	`^`	`left`
Logical OR	`|`	`left`
Conditional AND	`&&`	`left`
Conditional OR	`||`	`left`
Conditional	`?:`	`right`
Assignment	`=  *=  /=  %=  +=  =  <<=  >>=  &=` `^=  |=`	`right`

Table A-1: Operator Precedence

When you use two operators with the same precedence, the **associativity** of the operators controls the order in which the operations are performed:

- Except for the assignment and conditional operators, all binary operators, those that take two arguments, are **left-associative**, meaning that operations are performed from left to right. For example, 5 + 6 + 7 is evaluated as 5 + 6, or 11, first; then 7 is added, bringing the value to 18.

- The assignment operators and the conditional operator (? :) are **right-associative**, meaning that operations are performed from right to left. For example, x = y = z is evaluated as y = z first, then x is set to the result.

- All unary operators, those that take one argument, are right-associative. If b is 5, the value of - ++b is determined by evaluating ++b first (6) then taking its negative value (-6).

You can control precedence and associativity by using parentheses. For example, a + b * c first multiplies b by c and then adds the result to a. The expression (a + b) * c forces the sum of a and b to be calculated first; then the result is multiplied by c.

Index